Library of
Davidson College

VOID

Behrman

Cases in International Business

Cases in International Business

MANECK S. WADIA

Professor of Anthropology and Administration
United States International University
California Western University Campus

INTERNATIONAL TEXTBOOK COMPANY
An Intext Publisher

Scranton, Pennsylvania 18515

658.02
W122c

ISBN 0-7002-2256-1

COPYRIGHT © 1970 BY INTERNATIONAL TEXTBOOK COMPANY

80-606

All rights reserved. No part of the material protected by this copyright notice may be reproduced or utilized in any form or by any means, electronic or mechanical, including photocopying, recording, or by any informational storage and retrieval system, without written permission from the copyright owner. Printed in the United States of America by The Haddon Craftsmen, Inc., Scranton, Pennsylvania. Library of Congress Catalog Card Number: 73-117424.

To my children

Sara Jean and Mark

Preface

During the past decade, schools of business in the United States have increasingly moved away from organizing around the major business functions, such as marketing, finance, industrial relations and production, towards a wider classification centering around the behavioral, the quantitative, and the international approaches to business education. This has not only come about from the increasing eclectic approach to the study of business administration, but has also led to a greater utilization of the eclectic approach in the various fields encompassed by the business school.

The eclectic approach is one of the most significant features of business education, and its importance is perhaps best evidenced in the field of international business. The present book exemplifies this approach by covering all of the major functions of international business, using both the behavioral and the quantitative approaches whenever appropriate.

In order to write and compile a book of cases covering such a vast area, the author needed the help and cooperation of many individuals and institutions. I am especially grateful to the assistance provided by Dr. Edward J. Mock. Dr. Mock also prepared the Introductor's Manual for each of these cases.

I am also fortunate in working with administrators who provided me with both the time and encouragement to complete this project. I am grateful to Provost R. Carroll Cannon of California Western University and to Dean Ernest C. Arbuckle of Stanford University, for providing an environment suitable to scholarly pursuits.

All cases were class tested at either Stanford University, California Western University, Pennsylvania State University, or the University of Southern California. I would like to thank the students for their many helpful suggestions. I am especially grateful to the many professors from abroad who attended the International Center for the Advancement of Management Education at Stanford University. They not only were helpful in the initial development of some of the cases but were very cooperative and hospitable during my three round-the-world trips to collect research data.

Many of these cases were written by scholars from various parts of the globe. Wherever possible they have been given due credit in the footnotes. I am grateful to them, as well as to the anonymous authors, for their kind and willing cooperation. Copyrights on some of these cases are held by institutions around the world as shown in the footnotes. I appreciate their generosity in permitting me to use their case studies. To the many businessmen who gave of their valuable time and knowledge, the author owes a special debt of gratitude.

Colleagues at various universities, but especially those at the Pennsylvania State University, Stanford University, the University of Southern California, and California Western University, provided valuable leads and suggestions. To them, and all the others who helped, go my sincere thanks for any merits that this book may possess; but for any of the book's shortcomings, the responsibility rests with the author.

M.S.W.

San Diego, California
March, 1970

Contents

General Introduction xi

ENGLAND . . . 1
   1. Ford Motor Company Ltd. (A–D) 3
   2. Broadhurst Industrial Chemical Company Limited 24
   3. Scripto Pens, Ltd. 28

ITALY . . . 41
   4. The Moderno Oil Company (A–D) 43
   5. G. Ottolini & C., S. p. A. 67
   6. Frassati Company (A–E) 75

INDIA . . . 89
   7. The Universal Parts Company 91
   8. S. G. H. Products Company 103
   9. Bharat Company (A–B) 109
  10. Korewala Kwality Kore Mills 112
  11. Entrepreneurship in Village Culture 123

EGYPT . . . 131
  12. Standard Refrigeration Company 133
  13. Gomhouria Tobacco Company 148
  14. Standard Trading 164
  15. The Egyptian Motors Company 173
  16. The Nasr Bicycle Manufacturing Company 187

JAPAN . . . 201
  17. Carnation Company Ltd. 203
  18. Sumiyoshi Corporation 235
  19. Toyakawa Ltd. 257

THE PHILIPPINES . . . 283
  20. Interview with Earl Carroll 285
  21. Eduardo Mendoza, Inc. 294
  22. Peter Paul, Inc. 310
  23. Coproducts Corporation 319

BRAZIL . . . 333
  24. Credibook S.A. 335
  25. Liomar Printing Co. Ltd. 338
  26. Peter Werner S.A. 348
  27. Arco Industrial S.A. 358
  28. Caldaco S.A. I 365

General Introduction

In the past decade, there has been an increasing trend in schools of business toward offering courses in the international sphere. This trend has come about because of the increasing interest of United States' businessmen in starting operations abroad, or going into partnership with foreign firms, rather than just exporting home-made products. Another reason for this trend is the growing tendency of our government to help other nations help themselves through the development of their own industrial potential. Moreover, the student today has a greater interest in the world around him and realizes that his oyster of challenges and rewards lies in every corner of the world. Finally, scholars have long known that one of the best ways of learning about certain aspects of one's own culture is through comparison of similar aspects in other cultures.

Most courses in international business have the objective of fulfilling the needs implied in these trends. The present book shares this objective. It hopes to provide the scholar, student, and practitioner with pertinent data on various countries; the cases reflect the problems that arise, due not only to the nature of the business, but also to the nature of the cultural backgrounds in which the business functions.

The most important aspect of the field of international business, as well as of this book, is the cross-cultural insights it brings to the subculture of business. The concept of culture,[1] and the related concept of subculture, play a major role in our understanding of the field of international business.

The concept of culture is the major theme of cultural anthropology,[2] and is also "central to the behavioral sciences."[3] This concept is a very comprehensive one, and is not restricted to any one group. Anthropologists do not talk of cultured ladies sipping tea at a PTA meeting. Such people are properly styled "cultivated," i.e., persons who have proper manners and are well versed in music, art, and literature. Historians, when they speak of culture, think in terms of special developments in artistic and intellectual fields, such as "Greek Culture," referring specifically to some learned Greeks of the Golden Age in Greece's

---

[1] For a more detailed exploration of this concept see Maneck S. Wadia, "The Concept of Culture," *Journal of Retailing*. (Summer, 1965), pp. 21-30. Reprinted in part, by permission of the publishers.

[2] The term social anthropology is sometimes used instead of cultural anthropology, mainly under British influence.

[3] Bernard Berelson and Gary A. Steiner, *Human Behavior: An Inventory of Scientific Findings* (New York: Harcourt, Brace & World, Inc., 1964), p. 644.

history. Others confuse culture with civilization. The two are not synonymous. Civilization is a particular type of culture.[4]

What is culture? Some anthropologists conceive of culture as that which separates humans from nonhumans. Others think of culture as communicable knowledge. There are some anthropologists who speak of culture as the sum of historical achievements produced by man's social life. These differences in conceiving culture are differences of emphasis rather than of total content, and are not mutually exclusive. Yet, these differences have led to the formulation of many definitions of culture, some of which were analyzed by Kroeber and Kluckhohn.[5] It was found that practically every definition had something in common with the others. Kluckhohn himself defined culture as "the historically created designs for living, explicit and implicit, rational, irrational and non-rational, which exist at any given time as potential guides for the behavior of men."[6] The father of cultural anthropology, E. B. Tylor, defined culture as "that complex whole which includes knowledge, belief, art, morals, law, customs, and any other capabilities and habits acquired by man as a member of society."[7]

As can be seen from the foregoing discussion, the concept of culture is an all-encompassing one. It would be practically impossible to investigate in detail the total culture of each country represented in this book. However, our main concern is with the business aspects of the cultures represented by the cases and with the business problems unique to these countries. Hence, concentrating on the subculture of business.

In a society, group or nation, sharing many common culture traits or elements, there may be some characteristic traits that distinguish one group from another, These distinguishing characteristics may be shared by an age group, class group, sex group, race group, occupation group, or some other entity, which is then called a subculture. Thus, for example, teenagers share certain characteristic traits and we can refer to a teenage subculture. Similarly, Negroes share certain cultural traits, as do the middle class, which form separate subcultures. Subcultures may also be narrowed to refer to a combination of certain common traits in a specific group such as Negro teenage girls from middle-class families. The concept of subculture refers to the special characteristics of a segment of a culture. Such distinctions are especially important in large and complex cultures.

---

[4]Ralph L. Beals and Harry Hoijer, *An Introduction to Anthropology* (2nd ed., New York: The Macmillan Co., 1959), pp. 226-227.

[5]A. L. Kroeber and Clyde Kluckhohn, *Culture: A Critical Review of Concepts and Definitions* ("Papers of the Peabody Museum of Archaeology and Ethnology," Vol. XLVII, No. 1a, Cambridge, Mass.: Harvard University Press, 1952).

[6]Clyde Kluckhohn and William Kelby, "The Concept of Culture," *The Science of Man in World Crisis*, ed. Ralph Linton (New York: Columbia University Press, 1945), p. 97.

[7]Edward B. Tylor, Primitive Culture: *Researches into the Development of Mythology, Philosophy, Religion, Language, Art and Custom* (3rd ed., 2 vols., London: John Murray, 1891), p. 1.

General Information

Another aspect of the concept of subculture is the sharing of certain characteristic cultural traits by groups which otherwise differ in many ways. Thus, a number of nations which greatly vary from each other in culture and language could still share certain common characteristics. Nations could, for example, share a subculture of Catholicism or Communism, or the subculture characteristics of poverty, or class distinctions, or the subculture of large cities, etc. Here the concept of subculture refers to certain cultural traits shared by societies which otherwise differ from each other.

Usually these traits appear in clusters. A number of related traits are shared by the subcultures. Thus, the poor people of India will share with the poor of China, a number of related traits such as lack of housing, hunger, high birth and death rates, illiteracy, etc. Similarly, the communists of Russia will share a cluster of traits with the communists of France and certain related large city characteristics appear in clusters in all large cities.

Hence, a subculture refers to a distinguishable entity within a larger culture or to the clustered cultural traits shared by certain entities in differing cultures. Certain cultural traits may belong within a larger culture as well as be shared by differing cultures. Thus, Beatlemania in the United Kingdom was a part of the teenage subculture within that nation and the cluster of traits (screaming, wigs, jelly beans, etc.) associated with Beatlemania were also shared with the teenage subculture of the United States.

It is important to understand that even subcultures, though they may share certain cultural traits in common, also have certain unique traits, and that both the common traits and the unique traits are strongly affected by the total cultures in which they function. Hence, the subculture of business has certain common traits as well as certain unique traits in each country represented in this book, and all these traits are affected in varying degrees by the cultures in which these businesses function.[8] Thus, for example, businessmen in all countries have the common trait of dealing with government regulations; however, these regulations differ considerably from one country to another. Some countries have unique traits of paternalism, the paternalism taking on particular characteristics, depending upon the culture in which it functions.

The challenge of international business lies in bringing to the world of business the new dimension of cross-cultural perspective. This perspective not only helps us to better understand and apply our knowledge to businesses in other countries, but through comparison, also provides further insights into business operations in our own culture.

[8] For further exploration of this interrelationship, see Maneck S. Wadia, *Management and the Behavioral Sciences* (Boston: Allyn and Bacon, 1968).

Cases in International Business

England

1

Ford Motor Company Ltd.*

Ford Motor Company Ltd. (A)†

In March 1953, senior executives of the Ford Motor Company Ltd. were considering the problems and difficulties that they faced in connection with Ford's recent acquisition of the Briggs Motor Body Company. Amongst the general problems of production integration, expansion and increasing efficiency there were a variety of difficulties in the area of personnel and labour relations. These problems arose from the different histories of the two companies, different personnel policies, different management philosophies and different management-union relationships. In particular, Ford management was debating whether conditions of work in the two companies should be standardised, what type of negotiation and grievance procedure should be adopted with the unions, and to what extent something of the Ford philosophy of management could be injected into Briggs.

LABOUR RELATIONS IN THE FORD MOTOR COMPANY

The British manufacturing subsidiary of the American Ford Motor Company had started operations in Manchester in 1911 as the Ford Motor Company Ltd. The company was largely responsible for introducing into Great Britain the methods of manufacturing and mass production which Henry Ford had applied with such success in the United States. Originally, assembly operations only were carried on in Manchester but over the years, in line with the American company, the British subsidiary developed its own manufacturing facilities for the majority of its parts.

In the United States Henry Ford had consistently refused to recognise trade unions in his plants, and it was not until 1941 after scenes of considerable violence, appeals to the governor of the state and a decision against the company and in favour of the union by the Supreme Court of the United States, that Ford U.S. finally gave recognition to the United Automobile Workers' Union. A similar reluctance to recognise trade unions characterised the English company. The

*Copyright 1961 by l'Institut pour l'Etude des Méthodes de Direction de l'Entreprise (IMEDE), Lausanne, Switzerland.
†This case was prepared by Basil W. Denning under the guidance of Professor Stephen H. Fuller as a basis for class discussion.

trade unions were not recognised and Ford did not join the National Federation of Engineering and Allied Employers. The company paid little attention to the established systems of craft prerogatives since the arrangements for mass production were so different from established manufacturing practices. Not unlike others in the automobile industry in the inter-war period, the company acquired a reputation for being tough employers, operating on a "hire and fire" basis with "no nonsense about workers' representation." Ford paid high wages, about double the prevailing local rates, and worked a 40 hour week, which at that time was almost unheard of in England.

The company prospered and expanded, and in 1931 moved its principal manufacturing operation to Dagenham, Essex, an outer suburb of London. Despite the increase in power and status of the trade unions during this period, the company maintained its traditional policy of non-recognition of any trade unions, high wages and complete management freedom.

When war broke out in 1939, the trade unions were called upon by the government and given wide consultative and advisory powers on national manpower problems. Even so, Ford refused to recognise the unions for negotiating purposes and it was not until 1944 when the chairman of the board, Lord Perry, was approached by the general secretary of the Trades Union Congress, Sir Walter Citrine, that Ford was persuaded to recognise unions at all. Lord Perry commented at the time, "I recognise the unions in the sense that I cannot refuse to recognise the existence of St. Paul's Cathedral."

Subsequently in the same year, 1944, an agreement was reached between Ford and a number of unions who had members in Ford plants. This agreement gave no recognition to union representation inside the plants, and laid down that all negotiations should be handled at a national level between the top management of the company and the national executive officers of the unions concerned. While this agreement represented an advance from the union point of view, there was consistent trouble on the shop floor from workers who seemed to resent major decisions which affected their welfare being taken at such a remote level. Furthermore, despite the newly signed agreement with the unions, no special steps were taken to train line managers to handle their relationship differently from the past.

In 1946, a new agreement was signed between Ford and the National Executives of those trade unions who had members working at Ford. This agreement created a Joint Negotiating Committee on which both Ford and appropriate National Union Officers were represented. This committee was to negotiate wages and major conditions of employment. The agreement also laid down a clear procedure for channeling a grievance arising on the shop floor through various stages until it was brought to the Joint Negotiating Committee. (See Exhibit 1 for steps in the grievance procedure.) In the event of disagreement at this level, provision was made for voluntary arbitration. In another important section of the agreement Ford gave limited recognition for the first time to shop stewards. Management accepted one shop steward to represent *all* men in a

Ford Motor Company Ltd. (A)

EXHIBIT 1
FORD MOTOR COMPANY LTD. (A)
Grievance and Negotiating Procedure Applicable to Ford Motor Company 1953

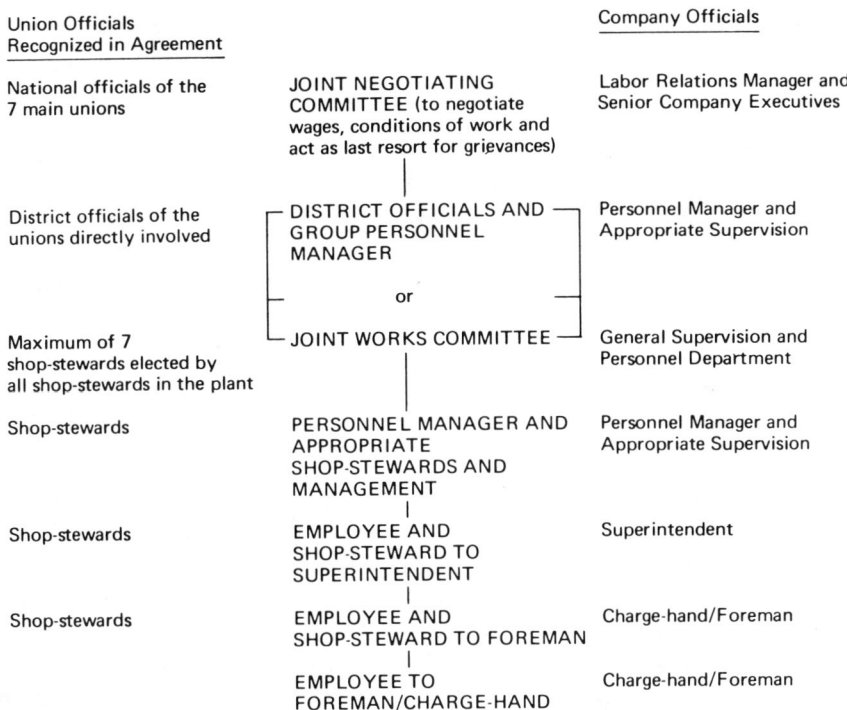

department, even though it was recognised that under this system men of one union might be represented by a shop steward who was himself a member of another union. No sooner had official recognition to shop stewards been given, than these stewards formed a shop steward's committee, 75 strong. This committee set up its own offices outside the plant and by various means such as lotteries, raffles, subscriptions, etc. arranged its own independent financing to pay for the expenses of shop stewards when on union business, pamphlets, etc. The committee also appointed an editorial board to issue its own paper called "The Voice of Ford's workers." Management did not officially recognise this shop stewards' committee except as an electoral body to choose representatives to the Joint Works Committee.

Also in 1946 for the first time, Ford introduced a new staff department solely concerned with labour relations and personnel administration. To head this department they appointed as labour relations manager a man of some 20 years experience of labour and personnel administration in other companies. Under his leadership, more consistent policies were introduced, agreements with the unions were extended, a joint works committee was started, and management organisation to implement the grievance procedure was improved. In addition, a number of training programmes were started to encourage line management to handle their personnel in a method appropriate to the new climate resulting from the company's recognition of trade unions and the agreements made with them. A senior official of the company commenting on this aspect of the personnel department's work said that he did not feel that success had been completely achieved and that many line managers had continued to operate in their traditional ways.

In the section of the 1946 agreement which laid down the procedure for grievances rising from the shop floor it was stipulated that there should be no strike until the proper procedure had been exhausted. (See Exhibit 1.) In the event of failure to settle the grievance at the Joint Negotiating Committee and refusal by either side to proceed to arbitration, the unions were free to strike. Despite this clear provision, Ford suffered a large number of stoppages of work from 1946 to 1952. Most of these were minor stoppages; some were major. The majority of the stoppages were called by one or more shop stewards over matters which might have formed legitimate grievances but which could probably have been settled through the grievance procedure if sufficient time had been allowed, rather than through resort to an unofficial strike.[1] Management found these stoppages particularly annoying since during this period wages were steadily increased, a sickness benefit scheme was started, and other labour policies of a more "enlightened" nature were gradually being introduced. Management normally reacted to these unofficial strikes by threatening to take disciplinary action against the individuals or groups of men primarily responsible for the stoppage. Under sufficient provocation, the threats were carried out.

Matters came to a head in June 1952 with an all out stoppage of work in contravention of the 1946 agreement. The trouble started at Briggs Motor Bodies Ltd., the sole supplier of bodies to Ford at Dagenham. A general strike was called at Briggs in support of a wage claim. This strike completely stopped the flow of motor bodies to Ford who were forced to shut down their entire assembly operation and lay off all assembly workers. In protest against this action all 12,000 production workers at Ford walked off their jobs at two hours notice. At the very moment that this impressive array of workers marched out of the plant, the present labour relations manager, Mr. L. T. Blakeman,[2] drove up to his office to take over his new post of personnel manager responsible to the labour relations manager.

The strike lasted 14 days. When work was resumed management called a meeting of the Joint Negotiating Committee. At this meeting management accused the unions of having no control over the rank and file and insisted that the unions must take disciplinary action against their unruly members. As one example of a flagrant lack of union discipline, in addition to the many unofficial

---

[1] An unofficial strike is a strike which is not authorised by the district or national officers of a trade union and for which no strike pay is paid by the union.
[2] Mr. Blakeman took over as Labour Relations Manager in 1954.

Ford Motor Company Ltd. (A)

stoppages, management pointed out that although the trade union secretary of the Joint Negotiating Committee had issued a notice saying that men should not go on strike without official union authorisation, the principal shop steward had refused to display this notice. The unions retaliated to this attack by laying the blame for the trouble on Ford's previous insistence that there should only be one shop steward per department, so that a shop steward from one union was representing men from four or five different unions. Under such circumstances, they said, the unions could not impose the necessary degree of discipline and they demanded that Ford should allow each union to have a shop steward to represent its own members' interests in each department.

After some discussion Ford reluctantly agreed. However, the unions' proposal was bitterly resisted by the existing shop stewards who expressed themselves fully satisfied with the present organisation of a shop stewards' committee and departmental representation. Faced with this new opposition, Ford management decided that it must attempt to negotiate a totally new agreement with the unions to replace the 1946 agreement. Negotiations with the trade unions were started, but despite preliminary agreement on a draft, which was later rejected, no agreement had been reached by March 1953, nor was there much prospect of any agreement in the near future.

The difficulties in reaching agreement appeared again to lie with the shop stewards' committee. The first draft which had been accepted by the national union officers was not acceptable to the shop stewards' committee and without their cooperation, the national union officers refused to sign. The principal point that the shop stewards objected to was a new method of electing representatives to the Joint Works Committee. In the past, the shop stewards' committee had elected the workers' representatives. Under the draft agreement, the representatives were to be elected directly by vote from the shop floor.

Meanwhile unofficial stoppages continued and Mr. Blakeman, commenting on this phase of the company's history stated that "In Ford at this time there were very bad labour-management relationships." Into this complex state of affairs on March 30, 1953 came the announcement that Ford had taken over Briggs Motor Bodies Ltd. by an acquisition of shares.

LABOUR RELATIONS AT BRIGGS MOTOR BODIES LTD.

Briggs Motor Bodies Ltd. was a subsidiary of W. O. Briggs & Co. who supplied motor bodies to Ford U.S. in Detroit. The Dagenham plant was opened in 1931 as a wholly owned subsidiary, but subsequently 49% of the share capital was sold to private British shareholders. Shortly after the death of W. O. Briggs, in March 1953, the family sold their holding in the British company to Ford (England). The Company's principal business was to supply motor bodies to Ford. Two of their main plants were sited at Dagenham just across the road from the main Ford plant and their production was integrated with Ford so that no large inventory accumulation was necessary. Completed bodies flowed out of Briggs straight into the assembly plant of Ford. In March 1953 there were 14,872 hourly paid workers at Briggs of whom about 11,000 worked in the two plants at Dagenham.

Labour-management relations at Briggs had followed a rather different pattern from that which had developed at Ford. In May 1941 the Minister of Labour set up a court of inquiry under the late Sir Charles Doughty Q.C. to investigate a dispute at Briggs over the dismissal of a shop steward. As one result of the Court's findings, known as the Doughty award, Briggs agreed to permit its employees in the engineering division to elect representatives to negotiate with management. This was essentially a company agreement between the management and the men concerned, with no intervention of the national trade union officials specified. A procedure to settle disputes was also established, but, in the event of "failure to agree," no further method of negotiating a peaceful solution beyond a management meeting with shop stewards was allowed for. The only further possibility was a reconsideration by the management with the trade unions at the level of the local district committee of the Confederation of Shipbuilding and Engineering Unions.

Originally, these arrangements applied only to the engineering division, but, after a period of agitation and strikes, and under pressure of a threat to strike, an agreement was entered into in October 1944 covering the entire company. This wider agreement was in virtually the same terms as the 1941 agreement. As a result of this agreement there were rather less stoppages of work. (See Exhibit 2 for details of procedure agreement.)

The resultant structure of bargaining relationships at Briggs was as follows: Briggs was not a member of the National Federation of Engineering and Allied Employers. It was therefore responsible for its own negotiations with the group of unions associated in the local district committee of the Confederation of Shipbuilding and Engineering Unions.[3] All questions were negotiated between Briggs and those unions associated with the district committee of the confederation which the company recognised. In general agreements followed the terms separately negotiated by the Federation of Employers and the Confederation of Unions. There was no reference beyond district official level. Outside the plant, therefore, the district committee of the Confederation of Unions represented the key point of contace between Briggs and the national unions.

Now it happened that at this time the dominant union in the district committee of the confederation was the Amalgamated Engineering Union (AEU). This union had a reputation for being left wing in its policies and militant about pursuing them. A man of particular importance was the secretary of the district committee, Mr. Berridge, divisional organiser of the AEU division in which Briggs and Ford lay. Mr. Berridge had been a member of the Communist Party

[3] Ford had never recognised the Confederation of Shipbuilding and Engineering Unions.

Ford Motor Company Ltd. (A)

EXHIBIT 2
FORD MOTOR COMPANY LTD. (A)
Grievance and Negotiating Procedure at Briggs Motor Bodies 1953

Union Officials Involved	Stages in Grievance Procedure	Company Officials
District Officials[1] & Senior Shop-stewards (Conveners & Deputies)	"WORKS CONFERENCE" (negotiation of rates of pay and working conditions)	Works Manager Industrial Relations Manager Personnel Manager Other Senior Officials
Committee of Shop-stewards	WORKS COMMITTEE	Works Manager Industrial Relations Manager Personnel Manager Other Senior Supervisors
Shop-stewards	EMPLOYEE AND SHOP-STEWARD TO SUPERINTENDENT	Superintendent (and Personnel Manager if appropriate)
Shop-stewards	EMPLOYEE AND SHOP-STEWARD TO CHARGE-HAND/FOREMAN	Charge-hand/Foreman
	EMPLOYEE TO CHARGE-HAND/FOREMAN	Charge-hand/Foreman

[1] These district officials were members of the London District Committee of the Confederation of Shipbuilding and Engineering Unions.

for many years. It was also suspected that a number of other members of the district committee and several of the Briggs shop stewards were Communist Party members although the company did not concern itself with the political affiliations of employees. Furthermore, several of the Briggs shop stewards were members of the divisional committee of the AEU, under Mr. Berridge as chairman. Hence, with the dominance of the AEU under Mr. Berridge in the district committee of the Confederation and the militant left wing policies which it advocated, management had a difficult task to maintain working relationships with the unions.

Management also found that the shop stewards at Briggs were difficult to deal with, particularly those from the AEU. As at Ford, the shop stewards had formed a committee which raised its own quite substantial funds, published its own paper and had its own office. This office was in the same building as the office of the Ford shop stewards' committee. However, the record of unofficial stoppages at Briggs was much better than it had been at Ford. The principal reason for this appeared to be in the approach which Briggs top management had taken to threats of stoppages of work made by their shop stewards.

Ford was Briggs' only customer at Dagenham and their production was closely integrated with Ford. Hence there was an imperative necessity to keep production going. If Briggs failed to supply bodies, Ford would come to a stop and after a few occurrences of this type, Ford might build its own plant to make its own bodies. The existence of Briggs, therefore, depended on fulfilling Ford's requirements accurately and efficiently. Under these circumstances top management believed that a stoppage was the most disastrous event that could take place. The way in which they acted on this belief prevented any of the lower and middle management, foremen and supervisors, from taking a firm stand or insisting on proper discipline. If a shop steward threatened a stoppage for however trivial and unjustified a reason, top management would step in, grant the shop steward's demands and keep production going.

A foreman at Briggs commenting on his feeling at that time stated:

> Whenever there was a grievance or a request from the shop floor through the foreman there was always a terrible delay from top management in getting an answer. So the men lost faith in the supervisor and turned to the shop stewards. But if a shop steward threatened a stoppage (I remember one complaining about a dirty lampshade) then top management gave in right away ..... A stoppage was always the supervisor's fault ...... Charge hands used to say to me "What's the good of asking higher management to do anything" ..... There was a great feeling of distrust of management on the part of workers and supervisors ..... We (the foremen) never knew what was going on.

An open letter to the management from the shop stewards in 1947 complaining about the way in which layoffs had been carried out ended with these words:

> The purpose of this letter is to bring to the notice of the Managing Director of Briggs Motor Bodies these facts and to urge you to remove this daily fear of redundancy from the minds of the workers, giving workers some news of the prospects of the Company. Take the workers into your confidence, make them feel a part of the Company and not just a number.

In July 1952, as mentioned earlier, negotiations over a wage claim at Briggs broke down and a strike was called. This strike spread to Ford and lasted 14 days. Once the strike had been settled, in view of the unsatisfactory relations which Briggs had had with the district officials, Briggs management decided to seek negotiating arrangements with the national union officers. By March 1953, the time of the takeover, no new arrangements had been made and the national officers of the unions had questioned whether it would be possible to change from negotiating at a local and district level to negotiating at a national level.

FURTHER CONSIDERATIONS

In addition to the factors already mentioned, there were a number of other points which top management at Ford had to consider. The most important of these were as follows:

1. With Briggs and Ford now combined, the combined unit would be by far the dominant employer in the area. There was little other industry

Ford Motor Company Ltd. (A)

nearby where a man declared redundant or discharged could find work of a similar nature without travelling a considerable distance. However, the whole of the London area was experiencing full employment and finding alternative work was not difficult even though it might have been less lucrative.

2. In the opinion of Ford managers there was considerable scope for making the Briggs plant more efficient by capital investment and rearrangement of existing plant. While they anticipated that the measures that they would have to take would improve physical working conditions, they realized that there would be considerable dislocation of present working arrangements, a good deal of technical change and a need for retraining of labour. These improvements would take place as part of a major five year expansion and re-equipment programme which had been already planned for Ford and some expansion would also be required at Briggs.

3. It was realised that with the increased mechanisation and integration of the whole manufacturing operation, the plant would become increasingly vulnerable to unofficial stoppages.

4. Both companies paid time rates of pay to all workers. Ford, however, had only four grades of workers—skilled, semi-skilled, unskilled and female. All workers were in one of these four categories and were paid the appropriate basic rate. The rates of pay for these four categories were negotiated at the Joint Negotiating Committee. In addition, merit increases were paid on a personal basis.

   Briggs, on the other hand, had a large number of different grades with the rate for each grade negotiated separately as the occasion arose. All rates, however, were subject to general negotiated increases. Payments for merit were also granted on a more general and less personal basis than at Ford.

5. In general Ford paid slightly higher wages than Briggs. In addition, Ford had a contributory sickness benefit scheme, a non-contributory pension scheme and an annual holiday bonus, none of which benefits were enjoyed by Briggs employees. However, Briggs had made certain concessions to the shop stewards such as longer tea-breaks, five minutes washing time at the end of the day, allowing meetings on company premises etc.

6. Ford had a clear policy of attempting to avoid redundancy in times of low demand by varying the amount of overtime worked. In fact, a certain amount of overtime was normal. Brigg's policy on this matter was to work less overtime and as a consequence employees were occasionally laid off.

Ford Motor Company Ltd. (B)*†‡

Shortly after the acquisition of Briggs Motor Bodies Ltd. by the Ford Motor Company Ltd. Dagenham, some important decisions were taken about personnel and labour relations policies to be pursued in both companies. These decisions were as follows:

1. The present negotiations with the unions in the Joint Negotiating Committee to revise the procedures agreement of 1946 would be continued.
2. Whatever agreement was eventually reached would be applied to Briggs and Ford.
3. The present procedure agreement between Briggs and the unions would be cancelled.
4. Conditions of work, wages, grading of occupations and all other personnel policies at Briggs would be modified so as to conform with the conditions at Ford. No worker at Briggs should suffer a loss of pay and previous service with Briggs would count as Ford Service.
5. All Briggs employees would be required to sign that they were prepared to work reasonable overtime as a normal condition of employment and that they were prepared to work alternately on day and night shifts as required. Both these practices were normal procedure at Ford but they were new to Briggs.
6. The introduction of policies 4 and 5 would be carried out by negotiation with the unions through the Ford negotiating machinery.
7. In view of the large numbers of unofficial stoppages at Ford penalties would be applied to shop stewards or other men who failed to observe the procedures agreement. This policy of applying stronger disciplinary measures would be extended to Briggs if it became necessary.
8. In view of the retirement of the production manager at Ford, a younger man with greater experience of dealing with trade unions, Mr. H. H. Jeffreys, would be appointed in his place. As production manager, Mr. Jeffreys would be chairman of the company side of the Joint Negotiating Committee.
9. Mr. Barke, a man with many years of experience at Ford, would be appointed as the new general manager of Briggs.

*For background to this case see Ford Motor Company Ltd. (A).
†Copyright 1961 by l'Institut pour l'Etude des Méthodes de Direction de l'Entreprise, (IMEDE), Lausanne, Switzerland.
‡This case was prepared by Basil W. Denning under the guidance of Professor Stephen H. Fuller as a basis for class discussion.

Ford Motor Company Ltd. (B)

REACHING A COMBINED NEGOTIATION AND PROCEDURE AGREEMENT

Ford management felt that they would have to move slowly in implementing all these policies. The new production manager at Ford, Mr. Jeffreys, took over in the summer of 1953, and Mr. Barke was moved in as general manager of Briggs as soon as possible. Negotiations with the unions about the Ford agreement were continued. No further moves were made until December 1953 when Ford offered all Briggs workers a general increase of pay of 2d. an hour, an offer which was accepted by the unions. At the same time Mr. Barke informed the unions and the workers that he was giving three months' notice of termination of the Briggs procedure agreement of 1944. Mr. Barke stated that discussions would be held with union officials to devise a satisfactory procedure for the processing of grievances and that he hoped to establish good working relationships with the unions. Shop stewards would be informed of the measures that management proposed for the processing of grievances until an overall agreement with national union officers was reached.

On the expiry of the three months' on 4th March, 1954, Mr. Barke addressed a letter to the national officers of the unions concerned, in which he stated that the agreement of 1944 was now terminated and added, "You will appreciate that matters of major importance which are national in character can from now on only be discussed at National Executive level." Mr. Barke then attempted to institute the Ford procedure.

On the 9th March, 1954, Mr. Barke received the following letter:

Dear Sir,
   We have your letter of the 4th March which, quite frankly, amazes us.
   We question very much your right to unilaterally enter into agreements of the character set out in your letter. We must make it perfectly clear to you that between now and the time in which an effective signed agreement exists between your company and our union, the union will reserve itself the right, at all times, to negotiate for and on behalf of its members in accordance with the constitution of this union.

Yours faithfully,
B. Gardner
General Secretary
Amalgamated Engineering Union

As a result, the national Ford procedure did not become effective at Briggs and to all intents and purposes the Briggs grievance procedure continued to be practised internally. However, there were no arrangements for the negotiation of wages and conditions of work between Briggs and the unions as a whole.

In June 1954, the trade unions submitted a claim to Ford at the Joint Negotiating Committee for an increase of wages for Ford workers. Management felt that they could not give an increase to Ford workers without applying it to Briggs, but they did not wish to apply such a wage increase unilaterally. Accordingly, they requested the unions to form a national body to negotiate for Briggs workers. Since nothing happened in reply to this request, on the 20th September, 1954, management stated that they would unilaterally apply the wage increase to Briggs unless the unions did something. Hastily, the unions formed an ad hoc committee of national executive officials to accept the company's offer.

At this same meeting on the 20th September, management put forward its firm proposals for the standardisation of Ford's and Briggs' negotiating procedures, wages and conditions of employment. On the question of a procedures agreement four further meetings between management and the unions took place in October and November. A comprehensive agreement was drafted, agreed to by the national union officers and recommended by them to the workers. It was rejected out of hand by the shop stewards of both Ford and Briggs. Their objections to it were based primarily on the proposed method of election of representatives to the Joint Works Committee. In the past these representatives were shop stewards elected by the shop stewards' committee. The draft agreement proposed that representatives should be elected directly by the work people.

By this time, October, 1954, the separate unofficial shop stewards' committees of Ford and Briggs had taken to having regular joint meetings. While they preserved their separate identities, over major questions of concern to both companies they would meet and formulate a joint policy. Also, the two independent publications, "Voice of Ford's Workers" and "Voice of Briggs' Workers," had been combined into one paper, the "Voice of Ford's Workers," which advanced the shop stewards' ideas on joint problems yet had separate sections for Ford news and Briggs news. The first issue of the new journal in January, 1955, contained this statement signed by the chief shop stewards of Ford and Briggs:

> The workers at Ford and Briggs wish to make it quite clear to all concerned that in rejecting once again a Procedure Document which deprives us of the single essential principles of trade union democracy, we cannot allow this wrangling to delay progress on outstanding matters and all things relating to wages and conditions in our establishments. We must sharpen our attitude on these matters to make both our employers and our unions thoroughly aware of where we stand.

Finally, on 23rd August, 1955, agreement was reached between the company and the unions over a new procedures agreement. Various points about this agreement are worth noting. (See Exhibit 1 for details of stages in grievance and negotiating machinery.)

1. There were now 22 unions represented in the company. It was agreed that the new National Joint Negotiating Committee (N.J.N.C.) would have 22 union members, one from each union, and that up to 22 management representatives could attend. The Joint Negotiating Committee

Ford Motor Company Ltd. (B)

EXHIBIT 1
FORD MOTOR COMPANY LTD. (B)
Grievance and Negotiating Procedure Applicable to Ford Motor Company 1956

under the previous agreement had consisted of seven people on either side.
2. The new agreement would apply to both Ford and Briggs.
3. There would be a Joint Works Committee at each major plant for which the workpeople's representatives would be elected by and from the shop stewards.

THE RECORD OF UNOFFICIAL STOPPAGES

During the period between the acquisition of Briggs and the signing of the new agreement a curious phenomenon had been taking place. The serious incidence of unofficial stoppages in the Ford plant prior to 1953 had sharply declined. The influence of the new production manager had made itself felt, the work of the personnel department was clearly taking effect, and the firm support, accompanied by disciplinary measures if necessary, given to lower supervisors in their dealings with the shop stewards and workers also appeared to be producing better results. In Briggs, exactly the opposite trend was apparent. Having had up to March 1953 comparatively few unofficial stoppages, the rate suddenly started to increase and in the period 1st February 1954 to 13th May 1955 there were 289 unofficial stoppages or almost one each working day. Typical of the type of stoppage was the following incident. During a night shift in one department a foreman's desk was moved from one position to another. The employees resented this saying that it was a new form of policing, and stopped work. The two shop stewards went to the personnel officer who called in the senior night shift shop steward. He went down to the department where he found the men were already putting on their coats and going home. In spite of the senior shop steward's appeals to stay and discuss the matter, the men walked off and there was a stoppage of 6¼ hours.

With the new procedure agreement signed in August 1955, management was hopeful that the number of stoppages would sharply decrease at Briggs. They were sadly disappointed. Between August 1955 and December 1956 there were 234 stoppages of work, all unofficial. Again most of them were of short duration and confined to one or more departments, but with the highly integrated plant that was evolving as a result of the major capital investment and expansion programme, the stoppages were becoming increasingly expensive and the costs were running into millions of pounds. During this period management made repeated appeals to the union representatives of the N.J.N.C. asking them to take effective action to control their shop stewards. For example, a letter sent out by the union chairman of the N.J.N.C., Mr. Beard, to the workers at Briggs on 13th February, 1956, read in part as follows:

> In view of the fact that every union is now represented at national level, this state of affairs (i.e., the large number of stoppages) is not only disturbing but brings discredit upon our movement, for just as we would insist on employers observing an agreement, so we must be prepared to do the same ourselves.
>
> Failure to do this must result in anarchy.[1]

Management found that it was extraordinarily difficult to pin down responsibility for a particular stoppage on one man or a group of men. Furthermore, at Briggs they were at first reluctant to take severe disciplinary measures, preferring to believe that the unions could put their own house in order. However, by March of 1956 they had decided that action must be taken. Accordingly, after a

---

[1] The calling of a stoppage of work without the authority of the national or district officials of a union was a contravention of union rules as well as a contravention of the procedures agreement.

Ford Motor Company Ltd. (B)

particularly blatant violation of the procedure agreement resulting in a stoppage, they informed the unions and the shop stewards at various meetings that in future disciplinary action would be taken against men involved in unofficial stoppages. They also posted a notice to the workers at Briggs which read in part:

> The company has already informed the national trade union officials and now informs all employees that these deliberate and flagrant breaches of the procedure agreement will lead to disciplinary action being taken against the employees concerned.

On the 17th May, 26 paint sprayers walked off the job. They were discharged. However, the men were also informed that if they would undertake in future to observe the agreement they would be rehired. The 26 men gave this undertaking and were re-employed.

Further stoppages took place in other departments. On the 4th September the following notice was posted in the Briggs plant:

> Employees responsible for these unofficial stoppages of work are reminded that they render themselves liable to disciplinary measures.

Management decided also at this time to start documenting very carefully each incident as it occurred. An exact diary of events from the start of the stoppage to the final settlement was maintained and all relevant details were included.

THE STANDARDISATION OF WAGES AND WORKING CONDITIONS

The other major proposal which had been raised at the J.N.C. on the 20th September 1954 concerned the standardisation of wages, grading of occupations, conditions of work, and fringe benefits. Ford had only four grades of workers with a nationally negotiated basic rate for each grade. Briggs, on the other hand, had a large number of grades of workers and each grade's rate was negotiated locally. For administrative purposes, Ford felt that it was imperative that conditions be standardised between the two companies. The question was of increasing importance at this time since the rapid rate of technical change during the expansion and the movement of men between jobs which this involved was raising multitudinous difficulties over rates of pay. Ford offered to guarantee that no worker would suffer a drop in pay or other cash benefits and in fact the vast majority of Briggs workers would receive an increase of just over 4d. an hour. All service at Briggs would be counted as service for Ford for pension and seniority purposes. Even though the additional cost to Ford was of the order of £3,000,000, Ford felt that in the long run this expenditure would be justified if standardisation could be achieved.

Negotiations were started at the N.J.N.C. without any great success. The union representatives on this committee were prepared to accept for Briggs the conditions which they had already negotiated for Ford, but they met with the

determined opposition of the Briggs shop stewards, centered round the following points.
1. It was a custom at Briggs to have an organised tea-break of 10 minutes in the afternoon. Ford practice in the afternoon was to have a mobile canteen which took tea round to the workers at their jobs and there was no break in production.
2. At Briggs the hooter marking the end of work was sounded five minutes before the end of the shift, so that the men had five minutes "washing time." At Ford the hooter sounded at the end of the shift and men were expected to work until this time.
3. The agreed use of systematic overtime at Ford was new practice at Briggs. The reasons for it were not properly understood and as a practice it was resented.
4. The Ford custom of working men alternately week by week on day and night shifts was new to Briggs. It was not welcomed because it was claimed that Briggs had always been a daywork factory.
5. The procedures agreement of 1955 laid down that no meetings should be held on company premises without management permission. This conflicted with the practice of Briggs employees holding regular meetings in their departments during the lunch break.

The shop stewards' resistance to standardisation was sustained and bitter. Symptomatic of their thinking was the following extract from the "Voice of Ford's Workers" of August 1955.

> The Briggs workers especially deserve our congratulations in face of the advantages that a Ford procedure could bring them. Ford rates of pay, holiday bonus, pension and sick benefit schemes, in exchange for overtime being a condition of employment, no meetings to be held on company premises without permission, shiftwork and nightwork to be a condition of employment and the loss of many other conditions won by the Briggs lads over the years. They certainly did not fall for the 30 pieces of silver, but used their trade unions to pursue their claims for the advantageous points with a definite NO to any worsening of their working conditions and hard won rights.

As a result of this opposition, no agreement on standardisation had been reached by December 1956.

THE McLOUGHLIN INCIDENT, JANUARY 1957

Matters were in this state then in November 1956. The procedures agreement for Ford and Briggs was in operation, but there had been a serious record of unofficial stoppages at Briggs which continued unabated after the agreement was signed. Management had issued notices informing the employees at Briggs that further unofficial stoppages would be met with disciplinary measures. The union leaders had appealed in vain to their members to observe their agreements. Negotiations on the standardisation of conditions had been in progress for two

Ford Motor Company Ltd. (B)

years but the shop stewards at Briggs were firmly resisting the management's proposals. And finally, over the three years 1953-56 as a result of the expansion programme the labour force at both Ford and Briggs had increased. At Ford, Dagenham, about 1,500 men had been added to the payroll, and at Briggs' Dagenham plants about 1,000 additional workers had been taken on.

In November 1956 as a result of the Suez crisis, Britain suffered a serious fuel shortage and a consequent reduction in the demand for vehicles. This forced upon the company first of all a four and then a three day week. Management found this three day working most uneconomic and on January 4th, management informed the unions at the National Joint Negotiating Committee and the Joint Works Committee that they would revert to four day working and lay off 1,750 men.

To select the actual men to be laid off, Mr. Blakeman appointed a special committee from the personnel department to review impartially the record of every man proposed for discharge by his line supervisor. In Mr. Blakeman's words, "I believe in being firm and fair, but you have to be fair first." All the men selected for discharge were given one week's pay in lieu of notice and were informed on the afternoon of Friday, 16th January, 1957, by notice that their employment had been terminated. In the engineering division at Briggs some craftsmen over 65 years old, the normal retiring age, and a small number of labourers were discharged. Among other effects, this action led to a resolution being passed in the jigs and fixtures department of the engineering division of the River Plant that if anyone was dismissed, suspended, or ordered on night shift,[2] an immediate shop meeting was to be called by the shop steward, Mr. J. McLoughlin.

A meeting of the Ford N.J.N.C. was arranged for the 24th January, 1957, to discuss redundancy policy. Mr. Berridge, divisional organiser of the AEU, recently appointed to the AEU national executive council and the N.J.N.C., asked the company on his own authority to grant leave of absence to Mr. Moore (chief shop steward at the Briggs River Plant and president of the AEU South Essex district committee) and to Mr. Friedman, another Briggs shop steward. This represented a departure from the usual practice since, at the trade union's request, shop stewards had been stopped from attending N.J.N.C. meetings. The company therefore telephoned the trade union secretary of the N.J.N.C. and, on being told by him that the attendance of Messrs. Moore and Friedman was not required, refused leave of absence. The two shop stewards nevertheless took time off to attend the meeting and for this they were summoned to their superintendent's office on the afternoon of Friday, January 25th. Mr. Moore invited Mr. McLoughlin to accompany him to the appointment as an observer.

Mr. McLoughlin, a member of the AEU, had been employed as a tool maker in the jigs and fixtures department of the Briggs River plant since 1951. That department was one in which, by Briggs' standards, little industrial trouble had

---

[2] In order to achieve efficiency the company was anxious to obtain balanced day and night shift working.

occurred. Mr. McLoughlin was also a member of the AEU South Essex district committee. He had been elected as a shop steward at Briggs to replace a man who had fallen ill at the end of 1956.

Thus, at 4:30 p.m. on Friday, January 25th, Messrs. Moore, Friedman and McLoughlin reported to the superintendent's office. Mr. Moore and Mr. Friedman were notified that they were suspended for three days. Mr. McLoughlin was apparently thunderstruck at this unexpected news and on return to his department at about 4:45 went immediately over to a handbell which he started ringing. This was the customary method of calling a meeting of all men in the shop. As he was about to start ringing the bell, Mr. Martin, the foreman, and Mr. Smith, the general foreman, came up to him and in shop floor language told him not to ring the bell. Mr. McLoughlin replied "Leave it alone, Ted. Give yourself a rest," and rang it harder. All the men in the department stopped work and gathered round. Mr. McLoughlin addressed them shortly and the men urged him to carry out their recent resolution about action to be taken in the event of a layoff. The meeting lasted about 10 minutes. At 4:55 the men returned to their benches to tidy up before stopping work at the normal time of 5:00 p.m. Mr. Martin and Mr. Smith then approached Mr. McLoughlin and on getting his admission that he had called the meeting, suspended him indefinitely pending a decision by higher management. On Monday morning, the 28th, Mr. Barke, the general manager of Briggs, consulted his colleagues and decided to discharge Mr. McLoughlin.

On Saturday, 26th January, Mr. Wyman, the acting AEU divisional organiser, had asked the company for a conference to discuss the suspensions and this was arranged for the afternoon of Monday 28th. It did not, however, take place because on the morning of that day there was a walk-out in the engineering divisions at both Briggs plants and a mass meeting was held which, in the presence of local officials of the AEU, decided on strike action. This unofficial stoppage continued and on Wednesday, 30th January, a further mass meeting was held at which Mr. McLoughlin's discharge became the focus of attention since the suspensions of Mr. Moore and Mr. Friedman were due to expire that night.

The company meantime had appealed by letter to the trade union side of the N.J.N.C. to use their utmost influence to enable the dispute to be handled in accordance with the procedure agreement. On Thursday, 31st January, on the initiative of the president of the AEU, there was an informal meeting between the company and the AEU executive council at which, in response to an appeal from the AEU for a gesture which would assist the unions to achieve results in the Briggs environment, the company agreed to consider McLoughlin suspended until the final outcome of negotiations under the procedure agreement. It was agreed that negotiations could not start without a full resumption of work.

On Friday, 1st February, the Briggs shop stewards called a mass meeting of their own and castigated the executive council's action. At a further mass meeting on 4th February they resolved to give their officials 48 hours in which to achieve Mr. McLoughlin's reinstatement. This ultimatum was ignored by the AEU national officers. The men returned to work on 5th February. The company met the AEU executive council a second time on a formal basis on the 6th February and failure to agree was registered on the issue of Mr. McLoughlin's reinstatement. The matter was referred to the Ford N.J.N.C. which met on 11th February.

At this meeting the unions made an appeal for reinstatement, partly on the merits of the case and partly in an endeavour to clear the way for the unions to improve discipline amongst their members at Briggs. The unions maintained that McLoughlin had been made the scape-goat for a whole series of incidents for which he was in no way responsible. They argued that in the general setting of unchecked stoppages of work, aggravated to a large extent by the supervisory staff, it was unjust suddenly to single out Mr. McLoughlin for so severe a punishment, particularly when the part of the works in which he had been employed had given comparatively little trouble in the past.

The company, on the other hand, argued that their policy of disciplinary action for flagrant breaches of the procedure agreement had been well and repeatedly advertised to all concerned since March 1956, and that in any way to concone Mr. McLoughlin's blatant defiance of the agreement on this occasion would make the vital functions of the supervisory staff impossible to perform. They felt also that the promises of the union about getting better cooperation if McLoughlin were reinstated could hardly be effective since the N.J.N.C. had so frequently in the past promised action but nothing had happened. The company offered to submit the case to arbitration but this offer was refused by the unions.

At the meeting the following points were made:

> Mr. Carron (President of AEU) stated that the blame should not fall on one individual. His action arose from doing things that had the sanctity of custom and practice. The discharge of McLoughlin was not the right foundation for a new body of industrial relations.
>
> Mr. Beard (United Patternmakers Association. Union chairman of N.J.N.C.) pointed out that he had taken a considerable number of steps to get the men back to work and that his union was now insisting on the honouring of agreements.
>
> Mr. Brotherton (Sheetmetal Workers and Braziers Union) said that the company had made its point and that to continue would be a vendetta. It behoved the company to be generous.
>
> Mr. Kealey (Transport and General Workers' Union) said that his union stood firmly with the AEU. He believed that the company was not blameless and that local supervision was responsible for many of the troubles.

These and other appeals left Mr. Jeffreys, Mr. Blakeman and their colleagues in no doubt that there was considerable solidarity on the union side. Towards the end of the meeting references were made by some of the union leaders to official strike action.

Ford Motor Company Ltd. (C)*

Failure to agree was recorded at the N.J.N.C. meeting on the 11th February.

Considerable public interest had been aroused by the whole incident and developments were followed closely by the national press. On Tuesday the 12th February, the following headline appeared in the *Daily Mail*,

"FORDS CRUSH NEW STRIKE"
"COMMANDOS KEEP PLANT RUNNING"

On Tuesday, 12th February at 12:20 p.m. Mr. Blakeman received a telephone call from Sir Wilfred Neden, chief conciliation officer at the Ministry of Labour. He stated that a question would be raised in the House of Commons that afternoon and that the Minister intended to reply by saying that an inquiry by the Minister might be called for but that meanwhile the services of his department were available to either side.

At 2:15 p.m. the executive committee of the AEU decided to hold a strike ballot amongst its members at Briggs to decide whether or not official strike action should be taken.

At 2:30 p.m. Sir Vincent Tewson, Secretary-General of the T.U.C., tried unsuccessfully to telephone Mr. Thacker, the Managing Director. At 3:00 p.m. Mr. Beard spoke to Mr. Blakeman and asked him to attend talks at Transport House with Sir Vincent Tewson in an effort to avoid all unions being involved in an official strike, the possibility of which could not be ruled out.

At 3:15 p.m. Mr. Blakeman and Mr. Jeffreys, after discussing the forthcoming talks with Mr. Thacker, left to attend the talks.

*Copyright 1961 by l'Institut pour l'Etude des Méthodes de Direction de l'Entreprise, (IMEDE), Lausanne, Switzerland.

Ford Motor Company Ltd. (D)*

No agreement was reached at the talks at Transport House.

At 5:30 p.m. on Tuesday, 12th February, a meeting of all the Ford shop stewards passed a resolution to take any action necessary to support their union officials in securing the reinstatement of McLoughlin.

On Thursday, 14th February, Sir Wilfred Neden called Mr. Blakeman and said that the position of the company would not necessarily be compromised if they approached the Ministry with a view to using the conciliation machinery.

On Friday, 15th February, Mr. Blakeman received a letter from Sir Wilfred Neden saying that he had written to the secretary of the trade union side of the N.J.N.C. suggesting that before any decision was taken which might result in a strike, the situation should be discussed with him. He would also want to hear the company's side of the case. Mr. Blakeman informed Sir Wilfred that he would attend an informal meeting at the Ministry of Labour at 11:00 a.m. the next day.

The same afternoon, Mr. Blakeman heard the results of the AEU strike ballots. Of an estimated membership of 2,000 men, 1,118 were for striking, 429 were against striking and there were seven spoilt papers. Management was put on formal notice that an official strike would be called by the AEU on Wednesday, 27th February unless McLoughlin was reinstated. Even if the other unions did not support this strike with official strikes of their own, management realised that the AEU alone could cause a complete stoppage of work in the entire plant. They also realised that the AEU was a wealthy union which would have no difficulty in maintaining the strike for an indefinite period of time.

*Copyright 1961 by l'Institut pour l'Etude des Méthodes de Direction de l'Entreprise (IMEDE), Lausanne, Switzerland.

2

Broadhurst Industrial Chemical Company Limited*†

In the summer of 1965, Mr. R. C. Dixon, the Chief Accountant of the Broadhurst Industrial Chemical Company, was examining the Company's policy for the control of receivables. The existing policy had been developed over the years, but it was Mr. Dixon's practice, from time to time, to review the methods and procedures of control.

BACKGROUND: THE SITUATION PRIOR TO 1964

Founded in the period immediately after World War I, the Broadhurst Industrial Chemical Company had grown rapidly to become one of the three largest producers in its own particular section of the chemical industry: the manufacture of inorganic chemicals used in the production of plastics, paint and dyestuffs. This growth had been achieved very largely through mergers and by the acquisition of less efficient producers. By 1965 the company had a total of 9 individual plants widely dispersed over the industrial areas of Great Britain.

Broadhurst had for many years maintained a central sales organisation, coupled with a regional organisation providing coverage of the entire country in six territories, each with a regional sales manager. All orders taken were passed to the Production Planning Department which controlled effectively the onward transmission of the order to whichever plant could most economically supply the required product, having in mind the various production and transport costs of the company's plants. Until 1964, the plants (which consisted mostly of large autonomous subsidiary companies) had retained full responsibility for invoicing the customer for products supplied, for maintaining a record of the extent of each customer's indebtedness for items supplied by that plant and, in theory at

---

*Case material of the Management Case Research Programme, Cranfield, Bedford, England, and prepared as a basis for class discussion. This case was made possible through the co-operation of a Company which remains anonymous. Cases are not designed to illustrate correct or incorrect handling of business situations.

†Copyright by Department of Education and Science, December, 1965.

least, for providing follow-up to ensure that no excessive credit was being allowed.

The Broadhurst Chemical Company's customers comprised more than 1,000 accounts although the greatest part of the turnover was attributable to less than 100 large industrial users, the majority of whom regularly purchased chemicals from more than one of the Company's plants. Thus, the accounts receivable from any one customer were maintained by the accounting staffs of a number of plants and nowhere in the Broadhurst organisation was there any record of the total indebtedness to Broadhurst of any customer except for the very small minority of customers who purchased chemicals from only one Broadhurst plant.

THE CREATION OF A CENTRAL SALES LEDGER

In 1964 Mr. Dixon decided that a central sales ledger should be set up at the London headquarters. In September of that year Mr. G. Jarvis, who had previously been employed as section head in the sales ledger section of a large firm supplying components to the motor industry, joined Broadhurst with full responsibility for setting up this centralised activity. By spring 1965, the new system was considered to be fully effective.

Speaking to the casewriter in July 1965, Mr. Dixon said: 'until we set up a central sales ledger we had never given any real thought to credit control because no effective control was possible. In theory the salesmen working from regional sales offices were responsible for the collection of overdue accounts, but in order to learn the up-to-date position of any customer before visiting him the salesmen would have to telephone a varying number of Broadhurst plants. This was not unsatisfactory. Only now that the central ledger is working and can we see at a glance the state of a customer's account, and can we begin to develop a policy for the control of our receivables.'

CREDIT CONTROL AS OF JULY 1965

The Company's terms were, in theory, net monthly, by which was meant that all deliveries made during April, for instance, and included in the end of the month statement sent to each customer on the last day of April, should be paid for by the end of May. This system, if strictly enforced, would have given an average collection period of six weeks. In practice, however, no action would be taken unless the account remained unpaid at the end of June, and no formal request for settlement made until a further month had elapsed.

Under the new system, customer invoices were still raised by the supplier plant but a copy of the invoice known as the 'Posting Copy' was sent to the central sales ledger activity who debited each customers' account accordingly. Invoices were identified by a Code Number with the supplier plant. Each customer now had only one account with the Broadhurst Company. When the monthly statements of accounts were prepared for each customer at the end of every month, two 'overdue' lists were compiled. The first showing all customers whose accounts were more than one month overdue, was sent to regional sales offices, where sales representatives had been instructed to call upon the overdue accounts to try to arrange settlement. The second, listing all accounts now more than two months overdue, was sent to the directors of the company and in particular to Mr. Dixon, whose responsibility it was, to decide what measures should be used to collect the accounts on this second list.

Under the existing system, therefore, the only form of credit control was a review procedure based upon the length of receivables, coupled with the following up of overdue accounts by means of personal letters and telephone conversations between Mr. Dixon and individual executives in the debtor organisations. No limit in terms of the maximum credit to be allowed to individual customers at any one point in time had been developed.

Referring to the accounts receivable position in July, 1965, Mr. Dixon said: 'We do not consider the control of receivables to be a particular problem in this company. Indeed we think we have done rather well, despite our lack of formal controls. Many of our competitors have considerably greater problems in this area than we do. The control of credit through our regional sales organisations acting on the 1 month overdue list is now beginning to work very effectively.'

On July 1st, 1965, the total accounts receivable was £1,449,692, consisting of the following accounts.

Due by end of current month	£608,871	42%
Due by end of June (i.e. becoming overdue in July)	£521,892	36%
Now one month overdue	£231,952	16%
Now two months overdue	£ 72,485	5%
Now more than two months overdue	£ 14,492	1%

In 1964, the Broadhurst Company's total sales had been £10,000,000.

NEW THOUGHTS ON CREDIT CONTROL

In a subsequent conversation Mr. Dixon told the casewriter: 'Although we do not consider the collection of accounts receivable to have been one of our major problems, we are now beginning to think in terms of a much more sophisticated system of credit control. Basically, credit control is common-sense. I keep trying to drum this into our sales people. But there are a number of factors to be borne in mind.

I realise now that we must control both the length of credit and the top limit we allow to each customer, and we have made some bad mistakes in the past by not taking both into account. We can, in the last resort, stop supplies to any customer whose account is continually in arrears and can place the matter in the hands of our legal department to enforce collection. This we have sometimes done, usually with our smaller customers, although we are currently considering similar action in respect of two of our larger ones.

Some of our largest customers are particularly bad offenders, because they were allowed extended credit by Broadhurst at a time when business was bad and it was important to us to have their business on almost any terms. In effect, we had developed special unwritten agreements with these customers.

You must remember also that all our products are available from our competitors and that there is usually little to choose between us in either price or quality. We compete largely in terms of the Broadhurst reputation and of the service we are able to provide.

Finally, the order book for some of our products is short and some items which remain in production sell only to two or three customers. If one of these few customers fails to settle his account within our normal terms, we must think twice before stopping supplies, for we may have no other outlet for the product.'

Mr. Jarvis, who had been asked by Mr. Dixon to develop proposals for a more effective credit control system, said he had already discussed this problem with executives of the central sales office and had agreed with them that credit limits should be established for every customer. In the discussion on the ways in which such limits be established, he said: 'As a first step we are compiling a personal history for each of our customers, providing us with a summary of all our dealings with that customer over the last six months.

We are also subscribing to Dunn and Bradstreet, a list of the majority (certainly the better known) public and private companies giving selected information about each, including a suggested credit limit.[1] We have been interested to find that so far our own experience with companies has agreed fairly closely with Dunn and Bradstreet.'

FINAL THOUGHTS

Summarising the problem as it appeared to him, Mr. Dixon said: "Our next step will be to evaluate our progress so far. I would like to know just how useful the measures we have taken prove to be. The credit worthiness of any customer must depend on his indebtedness to *all* his creditors. Moreover a customer who is trying to use his overdue accounts with his suppliers as a source of short-term credit, is a very different proposition from one who has already exhausted his bank borrowing capacity."

[1] This was a fairly coarse system by which each company was given a key letter A to E and the key provided inside the cover gave the information
    A: up to £1,000
    B: up to £5,000 etc.

Scripto Pens, Ltd.*

In September of 1959, Mr. Paul J. Brown, Managing Director of Scripto Pens, Ltd., of London, England, was evaluating his company's current competitive situation in the British ball-point pen industry. He was particularly concerned about a recent pricing move by the Biro-Swan company, Scripto's largest competitor, and was wondering what, if anything, Scripto should do in response to the move.

BACKGROUND

In 1956, the Scripto Pen Corporation of Atlanta, Ga., U.S.A., purchased the Scroll Pen Company of London and renamed the new company Scripto Pens, Ltd. Prior to its acquisition by Scripto, Scroll had traditionally concentrated on the manufacture and sale of ball-point pens in the "medium" price range. Ball-point pens in this range usually sold at retail for a price somewhere between 2/6d and 6/6d.[1] These pens were designed so that the original ink cartridge, when empty, could be replaced by a refill cartridge, which Scroll also manufactured.

After the 1956 acquisition, Scripto Pens, Ltd., continued to manufacture a medium-priced line of ball-point pens and ink refill cartridges under the SCROLL brand name. At the same time, however, the company brought out a line of ball-point pens which it marketed under its own brand name of SCRIPTO. Most of the models in this line were also in the medium price range, although the line did include a few higher priced models. As time went on the company began to place major emphasis on the Scripto brand and gradually to phase out the Scroll brand. As of late 1959, the old line of Scroll pens was still being manufactured, but only on a limited scale.

Scripto manufactured the ball-point pens which it supplied to the domestic British market in a plant adjacent to its offices in London. The manufacturing process was one of mass production utilizing much specialized machinery. In

*Copyright 1959 by l'Institut pour l'Etude des Méthodes de Direction de l'Entreprise (IMEDE), Lausanne, Switzerland.
[1] Approximate conversion rates:

    1 £   = 12.28 Swiss Francs
    1 shilling = 61 Swiss Centimes
    1 pence   = 5 Swiss Centimes

Example: 2/6d = 2 shillings; 6 pence = 1.52 Swiss Francs

Scripto Pens, Ltd.

1956 the plant had an annual production capacity of 12.5 million ball-point pens and ink refill cartridges and employed over 450 workers.

To sell its products Scripto maintained a force of 24 full-time salesmen. These salesmen sold about two-thirds of the company's total volume to 1,000 wholesalers. Wholesalers, in turn, sold SCRIPTO and SCROLL pens to many thousand retail dealers located throughout the British Isles. These retail dealers included stationers, department stores, drug stores, news agents, tobacconists, and other miscellaneous outlets. The remaining one-third of the company's sales volume was generated by Scripto salesmen selling directly to 15,000 retailers and to five or six large chain organizations. Generally speaking, both the wholesalers and retailers through whom Scripto sold its pens also carried the pens of competing manufacturers.

Scripto allowed all wholesalers a 25% markup on the price at which they sold to retailers. Retailers, in turn, were granted an average markup of 30% to 35% (depending on the model), regardless of whether they purchased from wholesalers or from Scripto's direct salesmen. Neither wholesalers nor retailers were granted additional discounts for volume purchases.

Despite the fact that Scripto sold direct to a number of retail outlets, the company made an effort to protect its wholesalers as much as possible so as to insure that these wholesalers would devote maximum effort to the sale of Scripto's products. Thus, Scripto made it a practice never to sell directly to retailers at a price below that being charged by the wholesalers. Moreover, direct salesmen tried not to visit retailers who were already being adequately serviced by wholesalers. In most cases wholesalers did not seem to mind the fact that Scripto salesmen were selling direct to some retailers. Mr. Brown, Scripto's Managing Director, felt this was due to the fact that even when a Scripto salesman did visit a retailer directly, he did so only about once every six weeks; consequently his efforts very often resulted in repeat orders for pens or refills for the wholesalers who visited these retailers in the interim: On the whole, Mr. Brown felt Scripto's wholesaler relationships were quite satisfactory.

The retailers whom Scripto salesmen visited, in turn, generally welcomed the opportunity to deal directly with the company, the main advantages being that company salesmen offered on-the-spot delivery, in-store display service, and immediate attention to retailer or customer complaints.

To back up the sales plan, Scripto annually budgeted an amount equal to approximately 15% of total factory sales for advertising and promotion. Of this amount, about 12½% was allocated to newspaper and television advertising, the remainder was set aside for promotion of Scripto's products to wholesalers and retailers. Prior to 1959 the company had never used up the total amount of its annual advertising and promotion budget. Approximate actual expenditure since 1957 were as follows:

     1957: £55,000
     1958: £65,000
     1959: £75,000 (estimated)

TRENDS IN THE SALES OF BALL-POINT PENS

The English ball-point pen industry had been expanding at an extremely rapid rate for several years prior to 1959. From sales of approximately

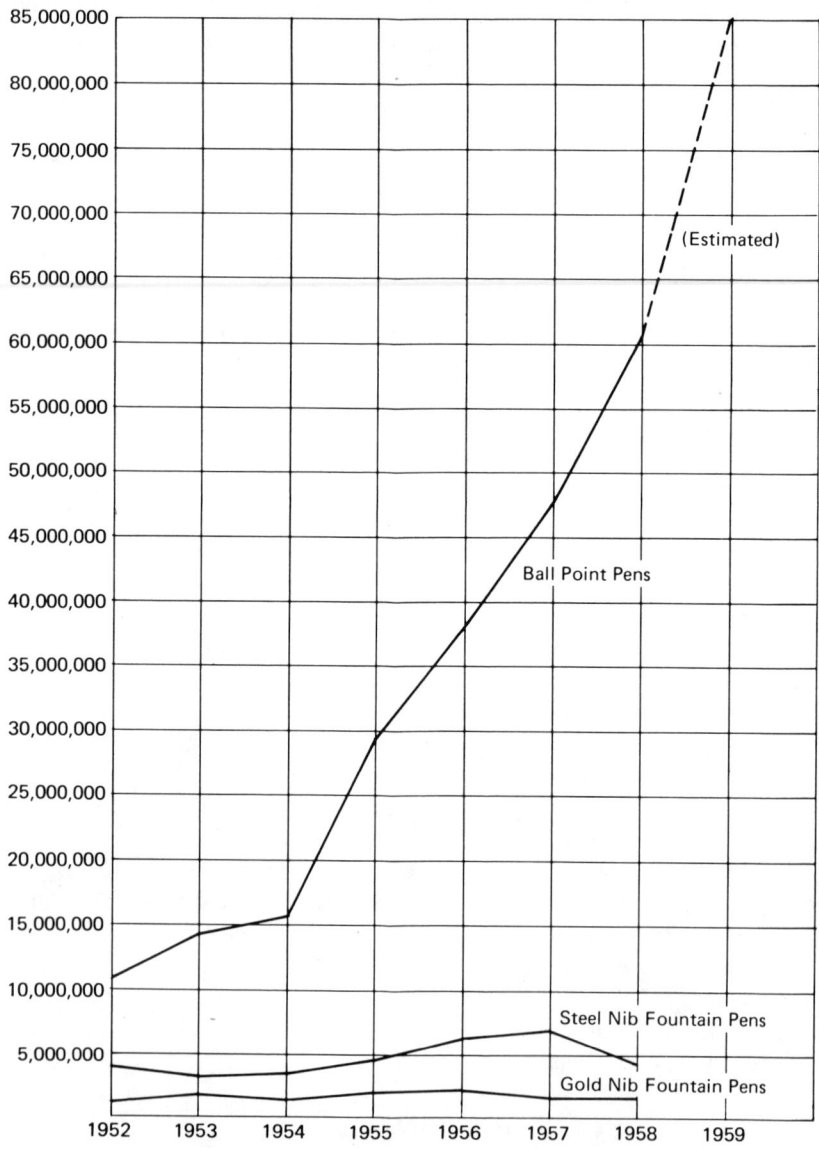

EXHIBIT 1
SCRIPTO PENS, LTD.
Trends In The Unit Sales Of Pens—United Kingdom

Source: The Board of Trade, London.

Scripto Pens, Ltd.

11 million ball-point pens in 1952, the industry had grown to the point where, in 1959, sales were estimated at 86 million units, a seven year increase of almost 800%. Meanwhile, sales of fountain pens and mechanical pencils had remained fairly constant. Exhibit 1 presents the trends in unit sales of writing instruments in the British Isles.

In pounds sterling, industry-wide sales of ball-point pens and ink refill cartridges had risen from about £930,000 in 1952 to an estimated £3,500,000 in 1959, an increase of about 375%. Exhibit 2 shows the magnitude of sterling sales of writing instruments between 1952 and 1959.

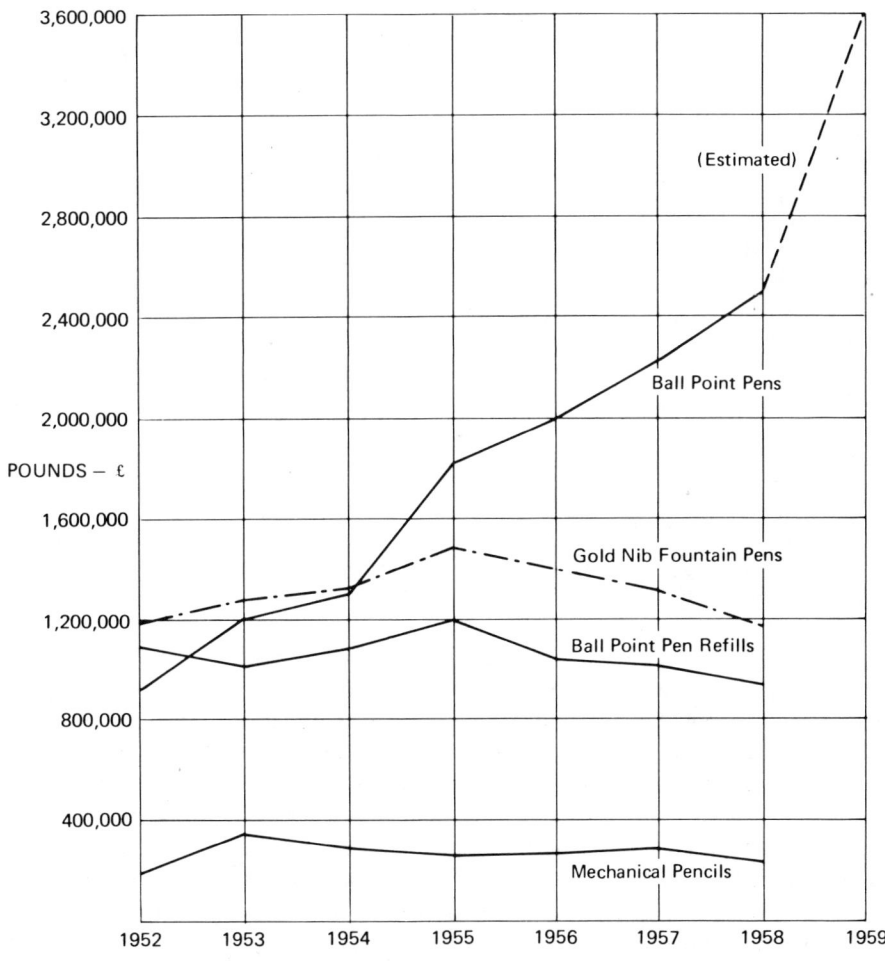

EXHIBIT 2
SCRIPTO PENS, LTD.
Trends in the Sale of Ball Point Pens
in Pounds Sterling—United Kingdom

Source: The Board of Trade, London

During this same period, the average price of an individual ball-point pen dropped measurably. An indication of the magnitude of this drop is given in Exhibit 3.

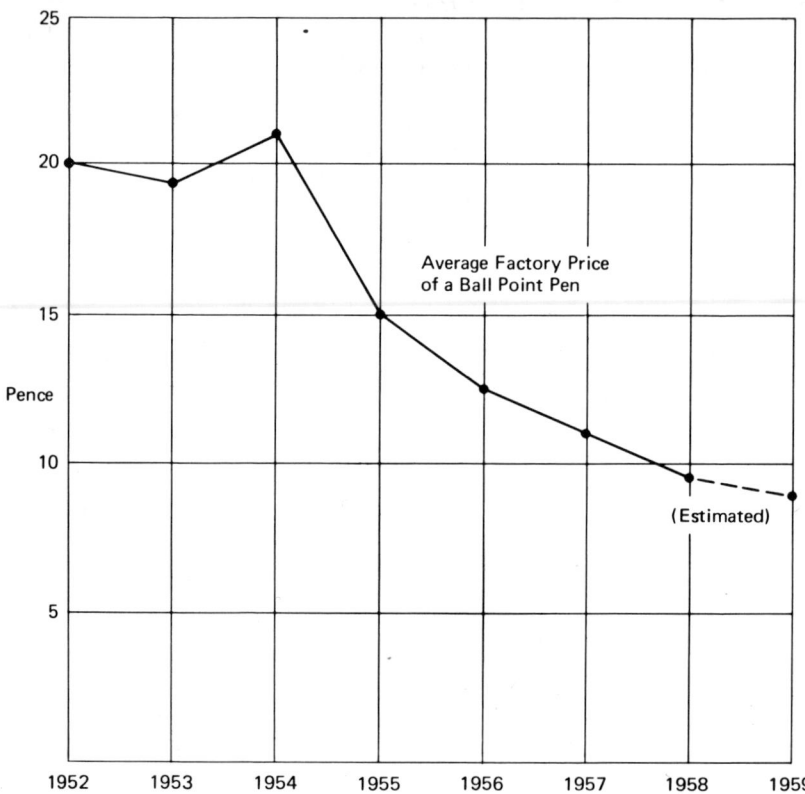

Mr. Brown had conducted some informal market research into the public's pen buying habits and had reached some tentative conclusions concerning the reasons why people bought pens. He felt that the primary reason for the tremendous increase in the popularity of ball-point pens was that people felt that they represented an ideal compromise between the permanance and attractiveness of an ink writing instrument and the convenience, cleanliness and inexpensiveness of a lead pencil. Generally speaking, Mr. Brown felt that a ball-point pen was an impulse purchase. To most people a ball-point was neither a large enough nor an important enough purchase to demand much forethought. Finally, Mr. Brown believed, on the basis of his experience, that the following factors, in order of

Scripto Pens, Ltd.

importance, most influenced the sales of a particular brand of ball-point pens:
1. Quality of pen
2. Availability of brand in a large number of retail outlets
3. Price
4. Appearance and attractiveness of pens and retail display material
5. Media advertising

COMPOSITION OF THE INDUSTRY

As of 1956, when Scripto bought out the Scroll Pen Company, there was one other major manufacturer of ball-point pens in the United Kingdom. This company, Biro Swan Limited, was the largest in the industry. Biro Swan had about 45% of the 1956 sterling sales volume of ball-point pens and ink refill cartridges,[2] Scroll had about 22% and a number of other small manufacturers together accounted for the remaining 33% of the market.

At the time of Scroll's acquisition by Scripto, all of the above companies concentrated their major efforts on the manufacture of ball-point pens which sold at retail in the medium (2/6d to 6/6d) or high (6/6d and up) price ranges. They also, of course, manufactured refill cartridges for these pens.

In September of 1957, a controlling interest in Biro Swan Ltd., was acquired by the BIC Pen Company of France.[3] Following this transaction it was rumored within the trade that an overall internal management re-organization occurred within the ranks of the Biro Swan Company. At the same time it was also rumored that Biro Swan began a program to expand significantly its production capacity for ball-point pens. This management re-organization and expansion of production capacity supposedly continued for about a year.

INTRODUCTION OF A LOW-PRICED LINE OF BALL-POINT PENS BY BIRO SWAN

Following this year of preparation, Biro Swan made a move which marked the industry's first large scale departure from its traditional emphasis on marketing pens in the medium price range. Thus, in August of 1958, Biro Swan introduced the first low-priced line of ball-point pens to be seen in England. This new line of pens, which was initially launched in the Midlands and then quickly expanded to the rest of England, was sold under the "BIC" brand name. Three pen models made up the line: the non-refillable[4] "BIC Crystal" retailing at 1/-;

---

[2] Refill cartridges manufactured by one company, generally speaking, could not be used in the ball-point pens made by other manufacturers.

[3] BIC was the largest French manufacturer of ball-point pens and had almost 80% of France's annual 100,000,000 unit market.

[4] "Non-refillable" meant that once the original ink cartridge went dry, it was not possible to replace it with a refill cartridge. Non-refillable ball-point pens were sometimes also known as "throw-away" pens.

the non-refillable "BIC Clic" retailing at 1/6d; and the refillable "BIC Coronet" retailing at 2/-.

To announce the introduction of its new low price line of ball-point pens, Biro Swan made heavy expenditures on consumer advertising. Throughout England extensive use was made of both spot television commercials and advertisements in local newspapers. In this widespread advertising campaign, the company placed major emphasis on trying to create heavy public demand for the one shilling "BIC Crystal." To achieve this goal, the company's advertising strongly stressed the price appeal of the new one shilling pen.

Biro Swan had little difficulty getting retailers all over England to carry the new low-priced line. In attempting to achieve intensive distribution for the new line, Biro Swan followed its traditional policy of selling both through wholesalers and direct to the retail trade. For its selling activities the company employed a force of "van salesmen" who operated more in the capacity of "order takers" than as "salesmen." Thus, they visited wholesalers and retailers, took orders, and immediately filled these orders from the supply of merchandise which they carried in their vehicles.

One fundamental difference existed in the pricing policies of Biro Swan and Scripto. Whereas Scripto's direct salesmen made it a point never to undersell the company's wholesalers when visiting a retail account, Biro Swan salesmen would grant an additional "wholesale" discount to any retailer who ordered in sufficient quantity.

Biro Swan's venture with the one shilling, throw-away pen proved to be extremely successful. As of August 1959, one year after its introduction to the public, production of the "BIC Crystal" had grown to the annual rate of 53 million units. This figure compared with the annual production rate for the "BIRO" medium priced, ball-point pen line of seven million units.

SCRIPTO'S REACTION TO THE INTRODUCTION OF THE ONE SHILLING "BIC CRYSTAL"

Biro Swan launched its one shilling BIC pen shortly after Mr. Brown arrived in England from the United States to take over as Managing Director of Scripto Pens, Limited. By coincidence, Mr. Brown happened to be traveling in the Midlands at the time that the "BIC Crystal" was introduced to the public there in August, 1958. Upon noticing the apparent initial success of this low price competitive pen, Mr. Brown hurried back to London to assess the overall situation and decide what, if anything, Scripto should do in response to Biro-Swan's move.

As soon as it became evident that one shilling ball-point pens were going to become tremendously popular in the eyes of the English buying public, Mr. Brown decided that Scripto must also introduce a comparable low-price line in order to protect its overall interest in the ball-point pen industry. At the same

Scripto Pens, Ltd.

time, however, Mr. Brown felt that the introduction of a one shilling Scripto pen should be viewed primarily as a defensive move. In other words, although he felt it essential that Scripto eventually market a pen in the low-priced field, he thought that the company should continue to place primary emphasis on its medium priced line of pens. Mr. Brown felt that there would continue to be a strong market for medium-priced ball-point pens; consequently he thought that the medium-priced line could continue to be the most profitable segment of Scripto's business. He therefore decided that Scripto's strategy should be to "knock the pins out from under the BIC Crystal" by introducing a one shilling Scripto pen, while at the same time attempting to keep sales of Scripto's regular line of medium-priced pens at a normal level.

Before Scripto could come out with a one shilling ball-point pen, Mr. Brown felt it would be necessary to increase the company's production capacity. If demand for a one shilling Scripto were high, it might easily surpass the factory's 1958 capacity of 12.5 million pens annually. Therefore, in September, 1958, Mr. Brown initiated steps to increase plant capacity by designing and installing a number of new high-speed, special purpose machine that automated various stages of the production process which were previously performed by hand. By early 1959, this program of expansion through automation had enabled Scripto to cut its factory force from 450 to 400 employees while, at the same time, increasing production capacity from 12.5 million units to 40 million units.

Simultaneously with his program to increase production capacity, Mr. Brown made an effort to "add more value" to Scripto's medium-priced pens. The quality of these pens was improved by increasing the ink supply in each cartridge 50%, installing a new metal tip on one end of the pens, and by introducing more stringent quality control. This program of increased quality was in line with Mr. Brown's desire to continue to place major emphasis on medium-priced pens. By making the above improvements, he felt that Scripto's competitive position in that field would be strengthened.

Finally, Mr. Brown embarked on a project to design a new one shilling pen. In undertaking this project, Mr. Brown felt that, if possible, Scripto should come out with a one shilling pen which would be superior in quality to the one shilling "BIC Crystal" and yet which still could be sold at a satisfactory profit to Scripto. The quality of the first pen that was designed seemed to be equal, but not superior, to the "BIC Crystal." Like the BIC, it was non-refillable and did not have a retractable point. In spite of the fact that this pen had no substantial quality advantages, Mr. Brown decided to introduce it to the trade as an interim competitive measure to help arrest the gains being made daily by the "BIC Crystal." Consequently, in April of 1959, Scripto's wholesalers and dealers were offered the opportunity to stock the new one shilling pen and sell it as the "SCROLL Longline." Despite the fact that the introduction of the "Longline" was not backed up by any consumer advertising, total sales of the new pen reached the 5 million mark by the beginning of September.

Meanwhile, Mr. Brown succeeded in developing a second ball-point pen model which Scripto could profitably sell at retail for one shilling and which had the added advantage of a retractable point. Because of this added feature, Mr. Brown felt that the new model was just what was needed to compete successfully against the "BIC Crystal."

Accordingly, Mr. Brown named the new model the "SCRIPTO BOBBY" and made plans to introduce it to the public. During the beginning of August, Scripto salesmen made a concerted effort to sell advance supplies of the "SCRIPTO BOBBY" to wholesalers and retailers all over England. In selling the new pen, the salesmen emphasized the fact that Scripto had plans to promote its introduction to the public by means of a widespread television and newspaper advertising campaign. Beginning the first of September, Scripto had lined up a five week schedule of frequent spot T.V. commercials devoted solely to the "BOBBY." Following this period of intensive T.V. advertising, Mr. Brown planned to promote the new pen through a series of advertisements in local newspapers all over England during the remaining months of 1959.

EXHIBIT 4
SCRIPTO PENS, LTD.
Price List As of 15 August 1959

	Price to Wholesalers (dozen)	Price to Retailers (dozen)	Purchase Tax (dozen)	Retailer's Margin (dozen)	Retail Price (each)
SCRIPTO LINE					
Low Price Pens					
"Bobby"	5/–	6/8	1/8	3/8	1/–
Medium Price Pens					
"250"	12/6	16/8	4/2	9/2	2/6
"490"	23/7	31/6	7/10	16/8	4/8
"T200"	32/6	43/4	10/10	21/10	6/4
High Price Pens					
"T650"	38/6	51/4	12/10	25/10	7/6
"Satellite"	87/6	116/8	29/2	58/2	17/–
Refills	8/9	11/8	2/11	6/5	1/9
SCROLL LINE					
Low Price Pens					
"Longline"	5/–	6/8	1/8	3/8	1/–
Medium Price Pens					
"320"	17/6	23/4	5/10	11/10	3/5
"420"	20/–	26/8	6/8	13/8	3/11
"520"	28/9	38/4	9/7	20/1	5/8
Refills	8/9	11/8	2/11	6/5	1/9

Scripto Pens, Ltd.

In anticipation of this year-end advertising campaign to introduce the "BOBBY," Mr. Brown had conserved on advertising expenditures early in the year. Up until the beginning of September he had spent only about £17,000 of his £75,000 advertising budget. Consequently, he planned to spend about £60,000 on the introductory advertising campaign for the "BOBBY."

Mr. Brown had designed the format of this campaign with the idea in mind of directing it almost as much toward wholesalers and retailers as toward the general public. This strategy was in line with Scripto's policy of maintaining strong wholesale and retail relationships. Thus, it was with the feeling that wholesalers and retailers would be favorably impressed by the prestige of T.V., that Mr. Brown had decided to make such heavy use of this medium.

As a result of the August selling efforts of Scripto's salesmen about 1,750,000 "BOBBY" pens had been distributed to the trade by the beginning of September. Although Mr. Brown did not, as yet, have any specific figures, he thought that these "BOBBY" pens had already begun to move off the retailers

EXHIBIT 5
BIRO SWAN LIMITED
Price List of 15 August, 1959

	Price to Wholesalers (dozen)	Price to Retailers (dozen)	Purchase Tax (dozen)	Retailer's Margin (dozen)	Retail Price (each)
BIC LINE					
Low Priced Pens					
Crystal	5/–	6/8	1/7½	3/8½	1/–
Clic	7/6	10/–	2/5½	5/6½	1/6
Coronet	9/9	13/–	3/2½	7/9½	2/–
Refills (Clic and Coronet only)	3/9	5/–	1/3	2/6	9d
BIRO LINE					
Medium and High Priced Pens					
Minor	14/7	19/6	4/10	11/8	3/–
Citizen	19/–	25/4	6/2	13/6	3/9
Retractable	22/2	29/6	7/4	17/2	4/6
Stylist	28/9	38/4	9/4	21/4	5/9
Deluxe	52/6	70/–	17/–	39/–	10/6
Squire	7/3 ea	9/8 ea	2/5 ea	5/5 ea	17/6 ea
Magnum	7/10 ea	10/7 ea	2/7 ea	5/10 ea	19/– ea
Refills					
Recharge	7/6	10/–	2/5½	5/6½	1/6
Magnum	8/9	11/8	3/–	6/5	1/9
Insert	9/9	13/–	3/2½	7/9½	2/–

shelves at a fairly brisk rate in spite of the fact that the consumer advertising program had not yet commenced. Meanwhile sales of Scripto's medium priced ball-point pen lines had continued at what Mr. Brown considered to be a "normal" level.

THE SITUATION OF AUGUST, 1959

As of August, 1959, Scripto was marketing a full line of ball-point pens with models in every price range. Sales of the one shilling line, both in units and in pounds sterling, were still minimal when compared to sales of the company's medium priced line. However, the company was poised to launch its £60,000 introductory advertising campaign for the "BOBBY" in September.

A list of the company's most important ball-point pen models, along with the price schedule at which each pen was sold, is shown in Exhibit 4.

Biro Swan, meanwhile, was also marketing a full line of ball-point pens; its

EXHIBIT 6
BIRO SWAN, LIMITED
Price List as of 1 September, 1959

	Price to Wholesalers (dozen)	Price to Retailers (dozen)	Purchase Tax (dozen)	Retailer's Margin (dozen)	Retail Price (each)
BIC LINE					
Low Priced Pens					
Crystal	5/–	6/8	1/7½	3/8½	1/–
Clic	7/6	10/–	2/5½	5/6½	1/6
Coronet	9/9	13/–	3/2½	7/9½	2/–
Refills (Clic and Coronet only)	3/9	5/–	1/3	2/6	9d
BIRO LINE					
Medium and High Priced Pens					
Minor	9/9	13/–	3/2½	7/9½	2/–
Citizen	13/10	18/6	4/6½	9/11½	2/9
Retractable	17/3	23/–	5/7½	13/4½	3/6
Stylist	23/8	31/6	7/8½	17/9½	4/9
Deluxe	37/6	50/–	12/2½	27/9½	7/6
Squire	6/3 ea	8/4 ea	2/0½ ea	4/7½ ea	15/–
Magnum	7/3 ea	9/8 ea	2/5 ea	5/5 ea	17/6
Refills					
Recharge	3/9	5/–	1/3	2/9	9d
Magnum	5/–	6/8	1/7½	3/8½	1/–
Insert	5/–	6/8	1/7½	3/8½	1/–

Scripto Pens, Ltd.

low price line being sold under the "BIC" brand name and its medium and high priced lines under the "BIRO" brand name. Biro Swan was currently producing BIC's at the rate of 53 million units per year and BIRO's at the rate of about 7 million units per year. Biro Swan's August, 1959 price list is shown in Exhibit 5.

ANNOUNCEMENT OF BIRO SWAN'S PRICE CHANGE

On August 26th, the management of Biro Swan suddenly announced to the trade that, effective September 1st, big price cuts would be made on all pens and

EXHIBIT 7
Excerpts of Letter from Biro-Swan Management
to Biro-Swan Wholesalers and Retailers

26th August, 1959

Dear Sirs:

On September 14th, we are announcing to the public the most-important-ever news concerning the genuine Biro range.

All Biro prices will be substantially reduced from 1st September; all pen prices will be down by at least 1/–, most refill prices will be slashed by half.

....Advanced techniques backed by new, ultra-modern machinery have enabled us to make significant reductions in our production costs, at the same time as increasing the quality of them.

The new prices will give the Biro range a far wider appeal than ever before. Enormous demand is anticipated, and with it will come greatly increased turnover, and larger profits for you. Trade margins remain, as they always have been, the most generous in the ball-pen field. The terms on which you buy the Biro range coupled with our Super Discount scheme give you really worth-while profits on fast-moving merchandise.

We fully appreciate that your existing stocks are devalued by this operation, and we are therefore giving you this advance notice, together with the opportunity to claim a free special bonus during the month of September. All orders received by us between September 1st and September 30th inclusive, for pens and refills in the genuine Biro price range will be invoiced at the new trade price. All orders must be for immediate delivery. The goods will be delivered to you, plus a free bonus of the same goods ordered by you equivalent to the difference between the old and the new retail value of your order. We feel that you will appreciate that this method of adjustment causes you the least effort, and is absolutely straightforward and fair to you and all our customers ....

The National Advertising starts on September 14th and continues until Christmas. We know that it will create enormous demand for the genuine Biro ball-pen, and at the same time ensure repeat business in refills. You can save in this demand simply by stocking up, displaying, and selling the genuine Biro range.

Yours faithfully,

Sales Manager
BIRO SWAN LIMITED

refill cartridges in the medium-priced BIRO line. Pen reductions were to range from 33⅓% off on the BIRO MINOR (old retail price: 3/-, new price: 2/-) to 7½% off on the BIRO MAGNUM (old retail price: 19/-, new price: 17/6d). Retail prices of refill cartridges were to be cut in half. Prices of the low priced BIC line were to remain unchanged. Exhibit 6 shows Biro Swan's new price list.

Dealer margins on each unit in the BIRO line were to remain the same from a percentage point of view, but would be reduced in absolute money terms. To compensate for the resulting devaluation of stocks presently in the hands of wholesalers and retailers, Biro Swan proposed a special "bonus" offer (see Exhibit 6). A London Financial Times newspaper article announcing the price change also indicated that Biro Swan had plans to launch a £250,000 advertising campaign to introduce the price cuts to the public.

Excerpts of the letter which Biro Swan's management sent to the trade to announce the forthcoming price cuts are reproduced in Exhibit 7.

Italy

4

The Moderno Oil Company

The Moderno Oil Company (A)*†

GENERAL SALES ORGANIZATION PROBLEMS

The Moderno Oil Company was the principal administrative and distributive company for the Italian operations of an international petroleum company. The Moderno company's Italian operations, which included exploration, shipping, manufacturing (refining) and marketing of petroleum products, were carried out by a number of closely related companies.

With sales of over Lit. 100 billion in 1956, Moderno was the market leader in Italy. This included a total of 3,200,000 tons of petroleum products or over 20% of the Italian market. The products included automobile gasoline and gas oil (white products), which accounted for over one-third of the volume, and fuel oils (43% of volume), bitumens, bunker oil and lubricants.

The Italian petroleum market, fourth largest in Europe, was increasing at the rate of about 10.5% per year and competition was keen among the major oil companies to increase their market shares.

A simplified organization chart of the marketing organization of late 1957 is shown in Exhibit 1. In addition to being the marketing company for Moderno operations in Italy, Moderno also centralized most of the functions related to personnel, public relations and financial matters for Italian operations.

The Moderno marketing organization was based on 20 sales districts within which approximately 150 salesmen sold the company's products to retail service stations and to industrial and heating consumers. These two major groups of customers accounted for the bulk of petroleum sales and they were usually sold directly by the Moderno salesmen, although some specialized middlemen were also Moderno resellers.

The first group comprised retail service stations which handled Moderno gas and oil. The service stations could again be divided in two groups the official Moderno posts, which were owned by the company, and the more numerous stations which were independently owned. The Moderno-owned station carried only Moderno gas and oil, while the independently owned stations carried not

†Names, places and figures disguised.
*Copyright 1958 by l'Institut pour l'Etude des Méthodes de Direction de l'Entreprise, Lausanne.

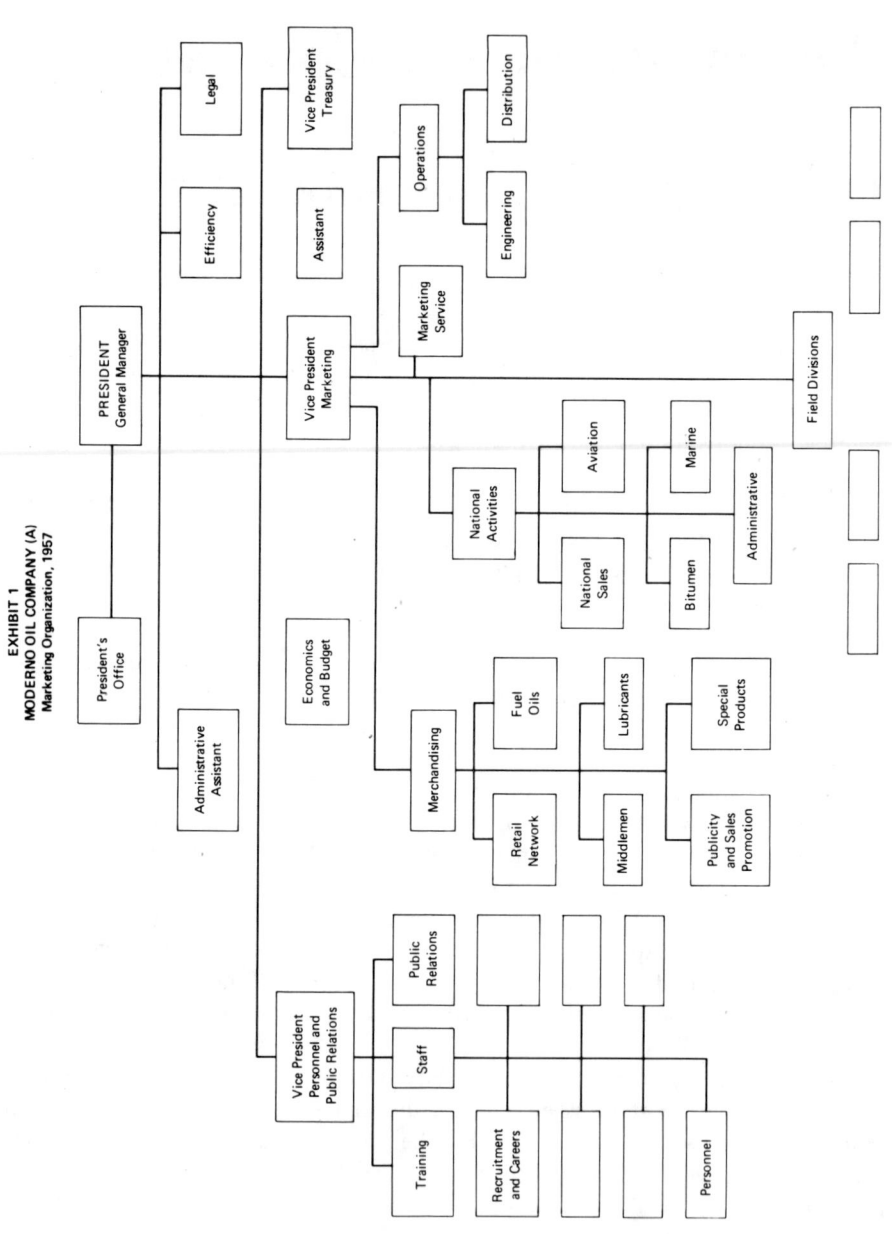

The Moderno Oil Company (A)

only Moderno gas but several competing brands of oil in addition to Moderno oil. Moderno oil was also sold in independently owned stations carrying competitive gasoline. The consumer group of customers included industrial consumers who were customers for the entire range of Moderno products, and central heating customers who purchased only one product, fuel oil.

The 20 sales districts were supervised by four divisional managers who reported directly to the vice president of marketing. In addition to these four territorial divisions there was another division, for national activities, which sold to some major customers and certain categories of customers (such as marine and aviation) on a national basis. The manager of national activities also reported directly to the vice president of marketing. To provide the marketing vice president assistance in carrying out his responsibilities for sales operations several staff departments operated as extensions of his office. The staff departments included Economics and Budgets, Operations, Marketing Service and Merchandising.

The Merchandising Department, which was the largest staff office, was divided into six sections as is shown in the organization chart in Exhibit 1. Three of the sections were clearly product-oriented: Fuel Oil, Lubricants and Special Products. The supervisors of these sections were product specialists who closely followed the problems related to their products and offered assistance, advice and new ideas to the vice president of marketing and to the field sales organization in carrying out the sales of their products. The two sections "Retail Network" and "Middle Men" were specialized according to channels of distribution. "Retail Network" was concerned with the service stations while the "Middle Men" section was concerned with small consumers (agricultural and heating consumers) of petroleum products. These two sections were not concerned so much with specific products as with providing assistance in obtaining the best sales results for all products through the various channels of distribution and to the various customer groups. The section "Publicity and Sales Promotion" was the advertising department. It embraced all products, channels of distribution and customers and was responsible for mass media advertising as well as for recommending and preparing sales promotion programs and materials to be utilized by the sales force and by the retail service stations.

In 1957 the manager of the Merchandising Department recommended that several changes be made in the organization of his department (see Exhibit 1 for organization of the department in 1957). One of these changes related to the establishment of a section in his department which would be specifically responsible for "white products" just as there were already sections responsible for the other main product classifications. He felt that problems related to this important classification of products could be more efficiently handled through one section carrying specific responsibility for it. Under the present arrangement he was forced to delegate various problems in regard to white products to these two sections and this sometimes resulted in confusion, especially since these sections were at the same time assigned responsibilities for other products.

He further suggested that the two sections "Retail Network" and "Middle Men" be combined into one section since they were both concerned with white products.

In addition to his staff responsibilities related to the products and their means of sale, the chief of the merchandising department was also assigned the duty of advising the vice president of marketing and the field sales organization on questions related to the sales force such as selection of salesmen, recruitment, training, compensation and work methods. Under the existing Moderno organization many of these functions were discharged by various departments not necessarily within the sales organization. For example, "Training" and "Recruitment and Careers" were departments reporting to the vice president in charge of Personnel and Public Relations. These departments performed these functions not only for sales personnel but for all personnel within the Moderno organization. Documentation of the sales force, that is the furnishing of literature and printed matter on various products, was carried out primarily by the Publicity and Sales Promotion Department.

Because of the distribution of these responsibilities among many departments, it was essential that the sales organization be represented by a liaison officer or spokesman who would carry the sales organization point of view in both receiving and offering information and advice. This was particularly true in regard to recruitment and training, the policies and programs for which originated outside the sales organization. The chief of the Merchandising Department was responsible for this coordinating job, but in view of his many other responsibilities he felt that the existing arrangement left much to be desired. The responsible officers in other departments lacked a central coordinator for the sales department with whom they could confer, and members of the sales organization lacked an effective means of communicating their problems and ideas to the officers outside their department. To improve this situation the chief of the Merchandising Department proposed that an executive be attached to his department whose responsibility would be to coordinate the functions relating to the sales force performed by various departments. The merchandising chief stated that the responsibilities of the new section would be:

1. To carry out studies in liaison with all the other interested departments and services, giving them the sales department's point of view on problems concerning

    - recruitment of salesmen
    - initial and follow-up training
    - selection and replacement
    - promotions
    - compensation
    - methods of work and improvement of efficiency

The Moderno Oil Company (A)

2. To work with the field sales organization managers learning their problems and assuring the implementation of the above-mentioned policies established by the company.

He envisaged the office not only as an expediter of communications between the sales department and other departments on problems related to the sales force but also as an important counselor within the sales department. The man chosen should be one of successful experience in selling and sales management with the organization. One of his most important tasks would be to help the company make plans for its future sales force to assist in determining the type of salesmen to recruit for replacement and expansion. This would require extensive visiting with the field organization in order to learn exactly what types of salesmen the company now had, what problems were arising, and, on the basis of this information, what type of salesmen the company wanted in future years.

The Moderno Oil Company (B)*†

ORGANIZATION OF THE MILAN SALES DISTRICTS

Moderno Milan Sales Organization

The Moderno Oil Company distributed the following products in the whole of Italy: gasoline (regular and super); gas oil (for diesels); light fuel; motor oil (lubricants); industrial lubricants and a large number of special products.

Its field sales organization consisted of four divisions which were subdivided into districts. The Milan division supervised five districts, of which two (Milan-North and Milan-South) comprised the greater Milan area. The greater Milan area was highly industrialized and densely populated; in this area Moderno sold 18% of its total Italian tonnage. The two Milan districts, furthermore, accounted for 71% of the sales and for approximately 70% of the personnel from the whole Milan division. Sales to some very large national accounts were made directly through the head office and were not within the responsibility and the competence of the field sales organization.

In all divisions, except Milan, the districts centered around the Moderno depots. It was argued that the customer had the closest and most frequent connections with these depots because he was above all interested in delivery which, furthermore, occurred generally more frequently than salesmen visits. The district borders were determined on the basis of the cheapest delivery zone from a given depot. The cost of delivery consisted of the transportation cost to the depot by water or by rail and of the cost from the depot to the customer by road, and it might vary with changes in volume, products, etc. In the Milan division the situation was different; all depots were concentrated around the city of Milan and some of them specialized in one product.

Out of a total of five depots:

> 1 stored white products (gasoline), heavy products (fuels) and lubricants
> 1 stored heavy products and special products
> 1 stored only heavy products
> 2 stored white and heavy products

Because of this depot concentration and specialization, it was impractical to use transportation cost calculations in the Milan division in order to determine the shape of the districts since different zones for the different products would

---

†Names, places and figures disguised.
*Copyright 1958 by l'Institut pour l'Etude des Méthodes de Direction de l'Entreprise, Lausanne.

The Moderno Oil Company (B)

result. The district structure, therefore, had to be devised according to different criteria.

This different depot set-up also was reflected in the divisional organization. Normally the division manager was assisted by two assistant managers, one in charge of sales and the other in charge of distribution (see Exhibit 1). The

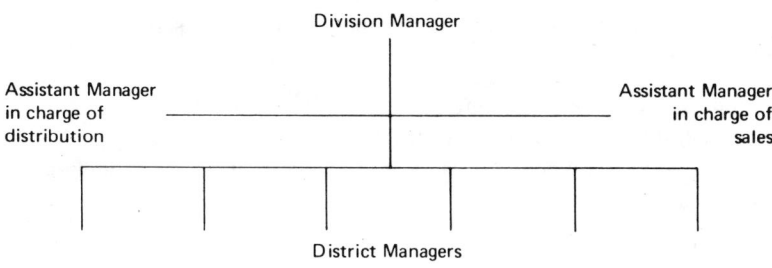

EXHIBIT 1
MODERNO OIL COMPANY (B)
Normal Sales Division

(in charge of sales and distribution, each district having one depot)

district managers, who reported directly to the division manager, were in charge of both selling and distribution and, therefore, had to cooperate with the two assistant managers. In Milan, however, the assistant manager in charge of distribution headed directly the five depots. (See Exhibit 2). The district managers

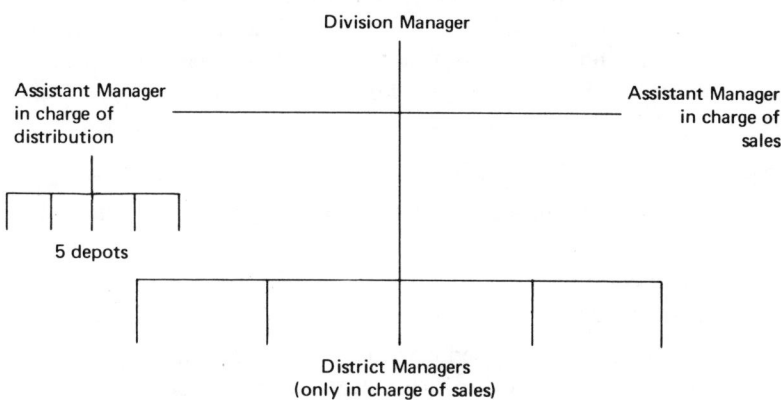

EXHIBIT 2
MODERNO OIL COMPANY (B)
Milan Sales Division

only dealt with sales and thus only cooperated with the assistant manager in charge of selling.

Early in 1957 the districts Milan-North and Milan-South were organized along identical lines. Each district manager was assisted by three assistant managers: one in charge of office work, one in charge of retail service stations and one in charge of central heating and industrial customers. The only difference between Milan-North and Milan-South was that in Milan-South the Moderno salesmen only covered part of the area. Moderno used for the southern, mostly rural, area, two commission agents (representatives).

The sales organization was thus tailored on the basis of the distinction between retail service stations and consumers. The retail service stations were divided by the Moderno organization into four groups:

1. Moderno-owned service stations.
2. Independently-owned service stations using Moderno pumps.
3. Independently-owned Moderno pumps of smaller size than service stations (small garages, cafés).
4. Competitors (service stations and smaller pumps).

Groups 1, 2 and 3 made up the Moderno "*network*" of pumps; Group 4 was called outside-network. The network service stations only purchased two kinds of products from Moderno: gasoline and oil. The outside-network stations only bought Moderno motor oil. (Although in Italy gasoline stations carried one brand of gasoline, they sold several brands of motor oil. The consumers were subdivided into two groups: central heating and industry. The central heating direct customers bought only one product: fuel oil for central heating. Customers within this sub-group were the state, provincial and local administrations, real estate agents in charge of running a whole group of houses, heating specialists and small individual customers. The industrial direct customers might require the whole range of Moderno products which they used for various purposes (see Exhibit 3). According to Moderno sales executives, the distinction between retail service stations and consumers was justified by their different nature. Besides the obvious difference that the retail service stations re-sold the products which they purchased and that the consumers were direct users, there were many other differences which led the company to differentiate its handling of the two groups:

- The number of retail service station customers and prospects was relatively small compared to the number of industrial and central heating consumers.
- It was comparatively simple to identify and classify customers in the retail group while for the consumer group this offered intricate problems.
- The retailer group purchased only two products, gas and oil, while the consumer group was a customer for all Moderno products.

The Moderno Oil Company (B)

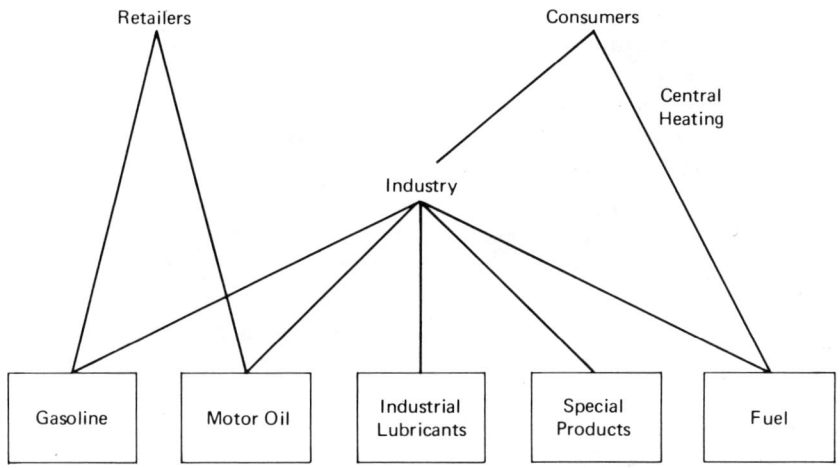

EXHIBIT 3
MODERNO OIL COMPANY
Customer Groups and Products Purchased

- Prices for the automotive gas and oil sold to the retail network were relatively fixed because competition in this field was primarily on the basis of new site construction, service and financial aid to station operators. In contrast, prices on the wide range of products sold to the consumer group were greatly affected by competition.
- Technical problems were negligible in the sale of white products to the retail network while technical assistance was an important aspect of sales to the industrial and central heating customer group. Advertising and promotion comprised an important element of sales through the retail network but had only minor importance in the sales to the consumer group.

Problems in Early 1957

Early in 1957 several problems had arisen in the two Milan districts.

One problem had arisen because some Moderno customers were carrying out their business in both districts. They did not care much whether Moderno had subdivided their territory or not. This was particularly the case for gasoline chains having stations in both districts or real estate agents serving buildings with central heating both in Milan-North and Milan-South. As a result, the selling activities of the two districts were partially overlapping. This resulted in the two district managers coming to the division manager in order to straighten out these problems, which caused some concern on the division level. If the two district managers did not appear, however, the division manager might be even more worried because he might then assume that the overlapping and coordination problems were being ignored.

Another problem in the two districts had arisen because the assistant division manager in charge of "sales" had started to sell to consumers through middlemen. Although, according to one executive, this responsibility was not assigned to him he had assumed it because nobody else was doing or would have done the job. In this kind of activity he did not respect the district frontiers because some middlemen might operate in the two districts. Furthermore, the assistant division manager was centralizing this kind of activity, thus causing, according to company officials, some disturbance on the district level. District managers received detailed orders from above which they had to execute without knowing what had been discussed during the negotiations. They felt that they were often uncertain about what the assistant division manager had negotiated, which made the correct execution of the order difficult. Furthermore, the district managers were disturbed by the fact that middlemen were taking away some of their customers, although this happened with the consent of superior officials. In spite of the problems of morale caused by these "extracurricular" activities, most higher executives approved the actions of the assistant division manager.

While analyzing the situation in the two Milan districts, top management had discovered that Moderno's sales increase was lagging behind that of competitors as shown below:

Increase in Sales between 1954 and 1956
for the Greater Milan Area

	All Companies	Moderno (without direct sales to very large customers)
Gasoline	+ 17%	+ 11%
Gas oil	+ 22%	+ 23%
Light fuel: central heating	+ 40%	+ 50%
Light fuel: industry	+ 40%	+ 15%
Total	+ 43%	+ 39%
Heavy fuel	+ 8%	+ 18%

The increase in light fuel for central heating could be ascribed to a large extent to the middlemen (20% of the increase). The direct sales to very large customers (which were negotiated by the head office) did not compensate for the lag in sales of light fuel to industry; on the contrary the increase of Moderno in direct sales was only 30% compared with 45% for the market. The heavy fuel market consisted mainly of direct sales; the field sales force consequently had little responsibility in this sector.

Although the sales in tonnage had increased by 61% since 1952 and the number of invoices by 48%, the number of personnel had remained unchanged.

The Moderno Oil Company (B)

In view of the problems that had arisen in the two Milan districts, top management was considering whether any action should be taken. The problem was the more important as this market was expanding rapidly and increased competition and reduced margins seemed to be ahead. By March, 1957, the Efficiency department of Moderno had received the assignment to investigate whether organizational changes in the two Milan districts would be justified.

The Moderno Oil Company (C)*†

INVESTIGATION BY THE EFFICIENCY DEPARTMENT OF THE RETAIL SERVICE STATIONS

Introduction

In March 1957 the Efficiency Department of the Moderno Oil Company had been given the task by top management of investigating whether organizational changes would be required or useful in the districts Milan-North and Milan-South.

From the outset of its investigation, the Efficiency Department had decided to adopt the distinction between retail service stations and consumers (see Moderno Oil Company (B)), and then make separate preliminary studies on the two groups.

Classification of Moderno Retail Service Stations

The Efficiency Department of Moderno started its investigation by a classification of the service stations. The following information, which had to be obtained from the customer files and from interviews with salesmen, was presented. The two Milan districts, where Moderno sold direct, included about 2,000 retail stations. Approximately 225 were unknown to Moderno and 483 were prospective customers; 1038 gas stations had competing pumps but purchased Moderno motor oil and, finally, 254 stations sold both Moderno gasoline and motor oil. The two representatives (commission agents), who sold in the souther part of Milan-South, had as customers: 16 service stations, 69 other pumps, of which 39 purchased less than 10,000 liters per month, and 93 competing stations which bought Moderno motor oil. The representatives accounted for 17% of the gasoline and 13% of the motor oil sold in the two Milan districts.

The direct accounts were subdivided as follows: for gasoline, 83 service stations sold in 1956 57,900 m^3 or 71% (compared with 57% for the rest of Italy), 76 pumps, which averaged over 10,000 liters a month, sold 18,750 m^3 or 23% and 95 pumps, averaging less than 10,000 liters a month, sold 5,300 m^3 or 6% of total sales.[1] For motor oil the figures were: 83 service stations accounted for 942 tons or 45%, 76 pumps accounted for 235 tons or 11%, 95 pumps accounted for 122 tons or 6% and 1038 stations, which sold gasoline of competitors, sold 801 tons of Moderno motor oil, or 38% of total sales.

†All names, places and figures disguised.
*Copyright 1958 by l'Institut pour l'Etude des Méthodes de Direction de l'Entreprise, Lausanne.
[1] One m^3 = 1000 liters = 264.18 gallons.

The Moderno Oil Company (C)

The Sales Set-Up for Retail Service Stations

By 1957 the two districts employed 8 salesmen (5 in the North, 3 in the South District), 2 representatives (commission agents), 3 demonstrators, 2 technical agents and 1 panel truck driver. This personnel was supervised in each district by an assistant district manager in charge of retail service station sales and by the district manager.

The Moderno salesmen were not specialized when hired: most of them acquired some technical knowledge on the job. He visited on the average 11 service stations (with a range of 5-18), 23 other pumps (range 8-23) and 138 competitors for motor oil only (range 82-213), and he drove on the average 1510 kilometers per month or 60 km. per day. Of his time per week the salesman spent on the average 1.8 days in the office and 3.7 days visiting 37 customers of which 11 were service stations, 10 other pumps and 16 competitors. This information was obtained by the Efficiency Department through a study of the work of 5 salesmen for a total number of 203 weeks. The frequency of the salesman's visits were for service stations once a week, for other pumps once every 2½ weeks and for competitors once every 9 weeks. It was calculated that for each 100 Lit spent on a salesman the company spent 556 Lit. on investments and 333 Lit. on publicity.

The representatives, who were supervised by one Moderno salesman, sold both to retail service stations and to consumers in the southern area of the Milan-South district. Each of them had an exclusive territory assigned to him. According to one executive, they had been in their sectors for a long time and were making a good deal of money. They seemed to be satisfied with what they had and they knew their customers well enough to handle most of their business by telephone. They were paid a commission on the basis of tons sold.

The demonstrators had to explain to the personnel in the service stations and the other posts how to sell gasoline and how to grease cars. Their duty did not include any technical advice or sales training. They simply had to demonstrate to the personnel how to do their manual work properly. The demonstrator stayed on the average two weeks at the same station.

The technical agents had to supervise the construction of new stations. This included dealing with architects, seeing that the proper arrangement was made and that the required colors were used, watching that enough storage space would be constructed, etc. The number of contracts signed in 1955 and 1956 were for:

	1955	1956
New stations	6	7
Modernizations	36	38

On the basis of 18 samples the Efficiency Department calculated that a technical study required 1½ months and the actual construction 2½ months. Between the study and the start of the construction the average delay amounted to 5½ months.

The panel truck driver sold only standard cartons of one and two liters of motor oil. He drove around in his panel truck and served about 400 customers, averaging 90 weekly visits.

The Moderno policy in respect to service stations was strongly centralized. Little initiative was vested in the salesmen who followed instructions from above. Special selling programs and promotions were planned at the head office and at the divisional level.

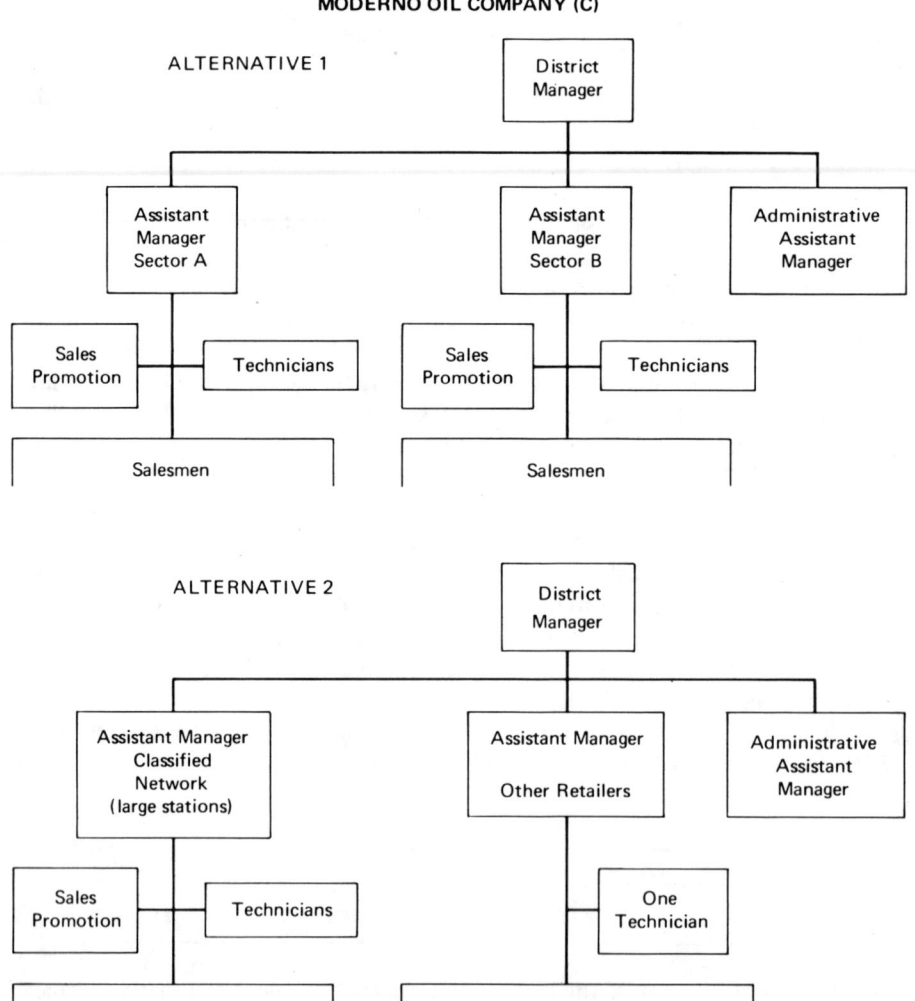

EXHIBIT 1
MODERNO OIL COMPANY (C)

EXHIBIT 1 (Continued)

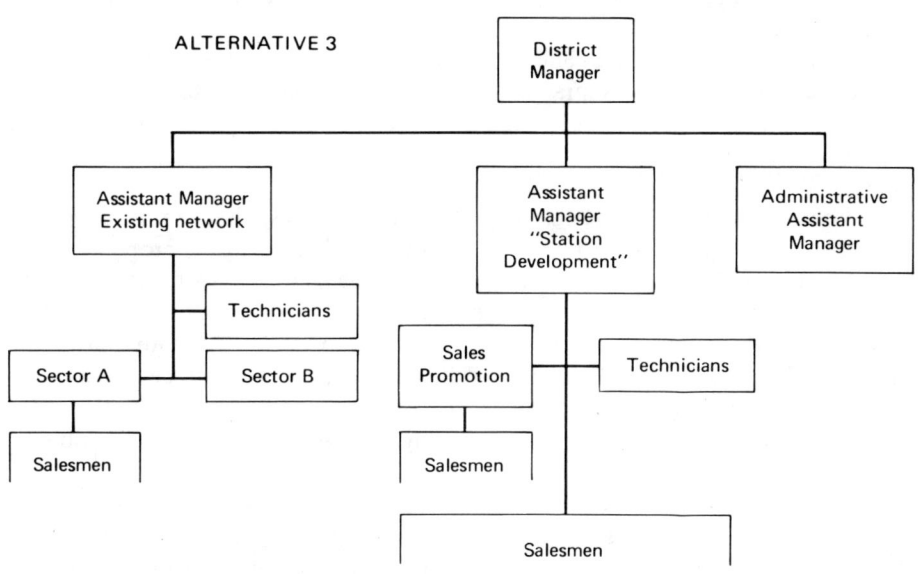

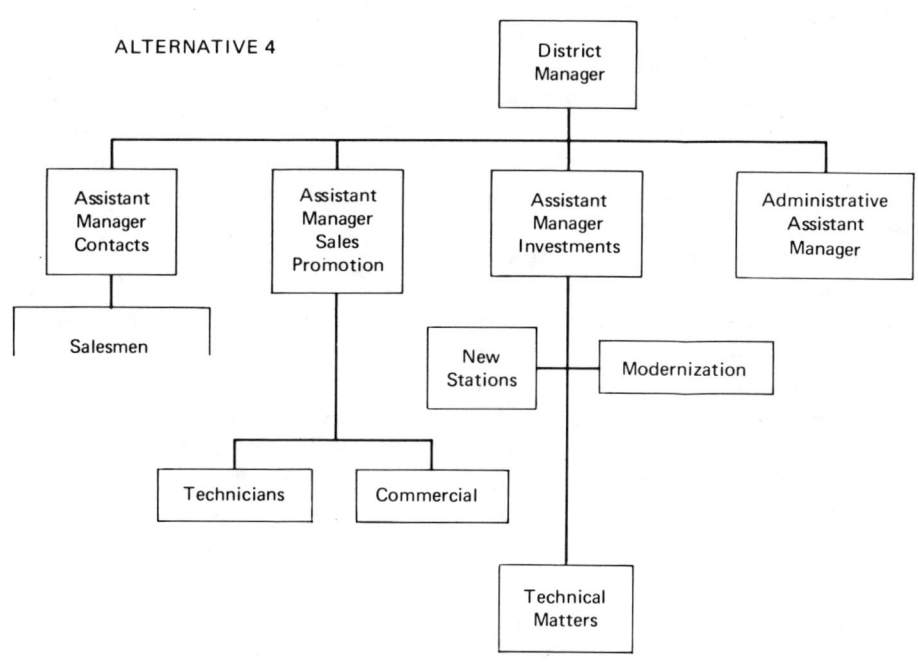

Competition between oil companies was fierce in respect to new privately owned service stations. The companies did all they could, e.g. through financial incentives, to convince the independent, who was planning the construction of a new station, to take their gasoline.

Price competition was practically non-existent on the retail level, partly because of the small margin in relation to the selling price.

Possible Organizational Changes

While discussing the possible organizational changes, the two members of the Efficiency Department to whom the study had been assigned proposed four alternatives. The first alternative was based on a geographical specialization, the second on the division between large and small customers, the third on the differentiation of station development[2] and daily operation. The fourth alternative was a variation of the third, sub-dividing daily operations into daily contacts and promotional activities. (Exhibit 1 gives the organization charts for the four alternatives). As an aid to the decision-making, the task chart shown in Exhibit 2 had been devised.

The items on the upper side of the chart included first: *market study and sales targets* (estimates of sales increase and sales quotas), second *station development* (ideal network = choice of locations where the company liked to build its station; investment decisions; selection and investigation of sites for stations; technical and profitability studies for newly conceived, transformed or modernized stations; contracts to be signed; and supervision of the execution of the construction), third: *operations* (daily contacts with customers, publicity, commercial and technical sales promotion and technical advice), fourth: *motor oil sales* to *stations with competing pumps* and fifth: control of the *results*. Two different signs indicated where the conceptual work had to be done and who had to execute the decisions. On the left side of the chart the persons in question were to be found, whereas the lines below the chart indicated to what kind of stations the various activities related.

The two members of the Efficiency Department thought that this chart might serve as a basis for decision in favor of either of the alternatives. They had further compiled some arguments pro and contra the various choices. Their general feeling was that the tasks one man had to perform, the easier he could be found. Furthermore, they said, a man with a great variety of duties has to be paid more and will be less efficient. The difficulty with the present system, they argued, was that one man nad to do selling, promotion and creation. As most efforts went into selling, the other tasks were easily forgotten. If one would appoint three different men for the three different tasks, a better individual job might be accomplished, but at the price of great problems of coordination at the customer level. If the salesman would be assisted at the sales office in the two

---

[2] Station development included all those activities required in planning new service stations or in modernizing existing ones.

The Moderno Oil Company (C)

EXHIBIT 2
MODERNO OIL COMPANY (C)

O = Conception
X = Execution

	Market Study	Ideal Network	Investments	Land (Sites)	Technical Study	Profitability Study	Contracts	Execution of Works	Daily Contact	Publicity	Commercial Sales Promotion	Technical Sales Promotion	Technical Problems	Oil Sales to Competitors	Control of Results
Station Development									**Operations**						
Head office			O	O			O								
Division manager	O		O	O		O									O
Asst. Div. manager										O	O				
Real Estate (Div)				X											
Technical (Div)					X			X							
Marketing (Div)							X								
District manager	O	O	X	O	O	O	O	O	X	O	O		O		O
Asst. manager	X	O	X		X	X	O	X		X	O		X	O	O
Salesmen	X	X			X	X			X	X	X		X	X	
Demonstrator												X			
Technical agent					X			X							
Architects					X			X							

Large stations
Small stations
Competitors

other tasks, he would be the only person to contact the customer, but this would raise coordination problems in the sales office itself. Furthermore, it was said, under these circumstances it might be difficult for the salesman to draw the proper problems to the attention of his colleagues.

As of May 1957, the two members of the Efficiency Department were wondering what they should propose to their superiors.

The Moderno Oil Company (D)*†

INVESTIGATION BY THE EFFICIENCY DEPARTMENT OF THE DIRECT USERS

Introduction

Early in 1957 the Efficiency Department of the Moderno Oil Company had received from top management the assignment to investigate whether organizational changes in the districts Milan-North and Milan-South might be appropriate. From the start of its investigation the Efficiency Department had adopted the current distinction between the two customer groups of retail service stations and consumers (see Moderno Oil Company (B)) and decided to make separate preliminary studies on the two groups.

Preliminary Problems of Classification

The first problem the Efficiency Department ran into was how to subdivide the consumers. Two major classifications seemed to be possible: 1) customers with or without technical problems, 2) customers divided according to the number and the uses of the products they purchased.

The first classification seemed, according to an internal report, hardly satisfactory. The following reasons were given:

Before the first contact one cannot classify a customer. Furthermore, a large number of customers have not yet been listed.

The same customer may purchase certain products which do not raise any important problems and other products which do.

Such a classification would require that each salesman would be familiar, not only with the customers he has to visit in a certain sector, but also with those he does not have to visit.

A customer who has no technical problems today, may have some tomorrow and vice versa.

Even in the case of a product which raises technical problems such as industrial lubricants, we (the Efficiency Department) have found that very often the personality of the customer leads to a purely commercial discussion. A sample of 251 important customers for industrial lubricants taken from 5 salesmen gives the following distribution among the different kinds of persons making the purchasing decision:

Commercial buyer	42%
Commercial buyer with technical knowledge	19%
Commercial buyer and a technician	26%
Only a technician	13%

†All names, places and figures disguised.
*Copyright 1958 by l'Institut pour l'Etude des Méthodes de Direction de l'Entreprise, Lausanne.

The Moderno Oil Company (D)

The report concluded that under these circumstances such a classification could only be arbitrary.

The second classification, according to the report led to the notion of customers with only one product and use and "multiproduct" customers. This gave the following results:

Non-industrial central heating customers...53%

The rest, multiproduct customers..47%

The advantage of this solution is to divide the customers into two almost equally large groups. Another advantage is that the classification between these two types of customers is very easy.

One group bought one single product to be used for one single purpose which raised few technical problems. The other group purchased various products for various purposes causing many technical problems. The Efficiency Department then decided to adopt the second classification.

The Moderno Central Heating Customers

The total number of customers in this sector was estimated at over 8,500. Moderno, however, had only 1,782 prospective and 1,349 actual customers on its files. An analysis on the basis of yearly sales gave the following results:

Number of Customers Purchasing	Total Purchases by Each Group of Customers
Administration (26 purchasing offices) = 1.9% of customers	7,770 tons = 24.9% of total
16 customers purchasing over 200 tons per year = 1.2% (Half of them are real estate agents)	6,074 tons = 19.4%
40 customers with purchases between 100 and 200 tons = 3%	4,285 tons = 13.7%
164 customers with purchases between 26 and 99 = 12.1%	6,010 tons = 19.2%
182 customers with purchases between 13 and 28 tons = 13.5%	2,984 tons = 9.5%
921 customers with purchases below 13 tons = 68.3%	4,165 tons = 13.3%

The selling procedure varied with each category. For the administrations, Moderno had to submit bids, which was done by the division. The real estate agents often served buildings all over Milan; they, however, preferred to discuss the purchasing of fuel at their office. For this category, therefore, the location of discussion and not the location of consumption was important while selling fuel oil. The small customers, finally, had to be visited at the location where they consumed the oil. Special problems were raised by buildings under construction. Several visits had to be made to architects, installators and owners in order to convince them to use the fuel heating.

The Moderno Industrial Customers

The Efficiency Department had been unable to estimate the total number of customers. Moderno had 1,545 prospective and 1,208 actual customers on its files. An analysis on the basis of yearly sales provided the following result: 640 (53%) customers consumed less than 50 tons of fuel and (or) less than 24 m^3 white products. 568 (47%) customers consumed more. The 53% small customers purchased only 11.8% of the light fuel, 2.3% of the motor oil, 11.8% of the industrial lubricants, 13.5% of the gasoline, 3.5% of the gas oil and 9.2% of the special products. On the other hand, the 47% large customers purchased 92% of the total tonnage.

The Efficiency Department attempted to classify the industrial customers according to industry and to the products they consumed as indicated by the following chart:

Industry \ Products	White Products	Fuels	Motor Oil	Industrial Lubricants	Special Products	No. of Various Products
Metallurgy		X		X		2
Foundry		X				1
Machinery		X		X		2
Automobile industry	X	X	X	X		4
Electrical industry		X		X		2
Transportations	X		X			2
Construction material	X	X	X			3
Public works	X	X	X	X		4
Agriculture	X	X	X			3
Food industry	X	X	X		X	4
Chemistry		X		X	X	3
Paint industry					X	1
Maintenance	X	X	X		X	4
Paper		X			X	2
Average						2

Given the fact that most industries consumed at least two products, it was, according to the Efficiency Department, difficult to differentiate between major categories such as transformation industries (consuming mostly fuel and industrial lubricants), transportation industries (consuming mostly white products and motor oil) and chemical industries (consuming mostly special products).

A classification of the customers simply according to the products they consumed gave the following results:

The Moderno Oil Company (D)

26% consuming essentially white products and motor oil
22% purchasing mainly special products
52% buying most industrial lubricants and/or fuels

The difficulty of this classification according to the Efficiency Department was that in the first group one quarter of the customers (or one quarter of the 26%) also consumed other products in important quantities. In the third group one-fifth of the customers (i.e. one-fifth of the 52%) also bought large quantities of white products and motor oil. Furthermore, given the rapid expansion in fuel oil, the composition of these groups might be subject to continuous changes.

The Importance of the Consumer Group

The consumer group purchased in the two Milan districts 21% of all gasoline sold, using the figures for all oil companies. For Moderno, however, the industrial customers only purchased 11% of the total.

The total industry sales of fuel as well to central heating as to industrial customers had almost doubled from 1953 to 1956. Moderno had increased its sales at the same rate as its competitors in the central heating field but was lagging behind substantially in the industrial area.

The direct users' market was highly competitive. Rebates were frequently given, especially by small companies. Moderno with its well established name according to one executive could sell its products partially on the basis of its brand. Other small competitors, however, with unknown brands used price deals in order to break the brand preference. As rebates were most successful with medium-sized to large customers, price competition was mainly fought on that level. Moderno as one of the largest distributors could not always move as fast as the small competitors, resulting in the paradoxical situation that the small oil companies had a large percentage of medium-sized to large customers, whereas the big oil companies served a large share of small customers. Furthermore, Moderno salesmen had a tendency to prefer the small accounts where they could sell more easily.

This was looked upon by top management with some concern as the selling costs with these small customers was obviously considerably larger than with big customers. Furthermore, the present sales force was insufficient to cover adequately the number of small customers. Nevertheless, the increase in small customers was far more substantial than the increase in large accounts.

The Sales Set-Up for Consumers

The total Moderno sales force in the Milan districts for the consumers consisted of 2 technical salesmen, 12 ordinary salesmen (7 in the north and 5 in the south), 2 representatives (the same people selling to retailers) and a few panel truck drivers. These people took care of the direct sales. The company, however, also used some middlemen: 4 bulk depositors, 2 bulk distributors,

2 heating specialists and 3 fuel dealers. This sales force accounted for total sales as follows:

	White Products	Fuels
Salesmen	76%	66%
Representatives	14%	11%
Panel truck drivers	—	4%
Bulk depositors	10%	5%
Bulk distributors	—	5%
Heating specialists	—	6%
Fuel dealers	—	3%

The salesmen were on the average in charge of 498 customers, 265 of which were for central heating and 233 for industry. Of the 265 central heating customers, 25 were on the average customers with over 100 tons purchases per year and 240 bought for less than 100 tons per year, accounting for only 42% of the total central heating sales of the salesmen. Of the 233 industrial accounts, 95 represented large (of which 47 were actual and 48 prospective customers) and 138 small accounts (58 actual and 80 prospective clients). The salesman spent on the average 1.5 days per week in the office and 3.8 days on the road visiting 18 active accounts, 10 prospective customers and 10 people, eventually customers, for various unforeseen purposes (e.g. repeat visits, obtaining credit information, etc.). The salesman travelled on the average 1120 km per month. His cost to the company amounted to roughly 2,000,000 Lit. in salary and fringe benefits and Lit. 750,000 travelling expenses, totalling Lit. 2,750,000 per year.

The representatives, who were supervised by one Moderno salesman, sold almost all Moderno products both to retail service stations and consumers in the southern rural area of the Milan-South district. Each of them had an exclusive territory. According to one executive, they had been in their sectors for a long time and were making a good deal of money. They seemed to be satisfied with what they had and they knew their customers well enough to handle most of their business by telephone. They were paid a commission on the basis of tons sold.

The technical salesmen were acting in an advisory capacity. One was in charge of central heating only since January 1, 1957, and had the following tasks: study of storage problems, advice for new installations, relations with constructors and installers of heating equipment, taking care of complaints, relations with architects. Two technicians were in charge of industrial customers. On the average they spent half of their time in the office and half on visits. They made approximately four visits a day. Their activity was divided as follows:

	North	South
Network of retailers and white products	5%	5%
Fuel	20%	15%
Industrial lubricants	70%	40%
Special products	5%	40%

The Moderno Oil Company (D)

The technicians for industry visited their customers when asked by the head or divisional office, by the salesman or by the client himself. They went out very seldom together with the salesmen. During the time spent in the office they gave advice by phone, took care of their correspondence and made studies.

The panel trucks carried fuel to bakers. The bakers required a special distribution set-up for two reasons: (1) They only bought in small quantities every month, and (2) they had to be seen very early in the morning while baking.

The bulk depositors were jobbers who had a depot and their own trucks. They sold to a large number of very small customers, such as farmers, small businesses and private homes who normally purchased small quantities of a great variety of products.

The bulk distributor had his own trucks but no depot. Moderno usually lent him money to purchase the truck and gave him a list of customers. The distributor, in addition, had to be actively looking for new customers. He only sold fuel oil to central heating customers. Both bulk depositors and bulk distributors invoiced on Moderno paper.

The heating specialists took care of the heating of several buildings all over Milan, such as maintenance, provision of supplies, etc. They purchased their total requirements in bulk.

The "fuel dealers" bought fuel oil in bulk and filled small jerry cans to be sold to small users through regular coal dealers.

The Cost of Selling

The Efficiency Department made a study of the cost of selling to the different categories of central heating customers, including the cost of the salesmen, the cost of delivery and the administrative cost. The total cost also included the discounts customary for customers ordering more than 100 or 500 tons per year (respectively 200 and 475 Lit. per ton). The following figures were derived:

Customers According to Volume	Cost* per Ton in Lit. (between parentheses = average cost of the salesmen)	
0-12 tons	1500 Lit.	(700)
13-25 tons	900 Lit.	(230)
26-100 tons	700 Lit.	(185)
101-500 tons	750 Lit.	(45)
501 tons and over	925 Lit.	(10)

*Figures have been rounded and disguised.

The cost of new customers was calculated in an internal memorandum as follows: "Calculations have been based on a sample of 11 salesmen studied over 208 weeks for 1,108 visits. These 1,108 visits have yielded 80 new customers which amounts to 13.7 visits for each new customer. The cost[1] of the visit amounting to 1,350 Lit., this new customer has cost 18,500 Lit. As the average Moderno customer consumes 26 tons per year, the average cost to get an additional ton is 710 Lit."

Possible Organizational Changes

In June 1957, the two members of the Efficiency Department studying the possible organizational changes were wondering what to recommend to their superiors. They felt that the huge concentration of population in a relatively small area allowed a very considerable specialization. They thought that the differentiation between central heating and industrial customers should be adopted, but they were unclear as to what further specialization could be implemented. Various possibilities were discussed such as on the basis of size, on the kind of industry, on the type of products used and on the difference between technical problems encountered.

[1] Figures have been rounded and disguised.

5

G. Ottolini & Co., S.p.A.*†

Mr. Alberto Maserati, who had been appointed General Manager of the Ottolini company less than a year earlier, had become increasingly concerned with the inadequacies of the firm's production control system. He was therefore reviewing what he knew about the plant situation before deciding what action he might take.

THE GENERAL NATURE OF THE PROBLEM

Earlier, Mr. Maserati had approved a considerable increase in both plant equipment and raw material inventories in an attempt to reduce customer complaints about deliveries. The number of complaints had not diminished, however, and Mr. Maserati became even more impressed with the company's deficiencies when he investigated some very large projects. Although some of these pieces of equipment had left the factory almost a year earlier, the customers had still not paid their accounts.[1] Mr. Maserati discovered that the reason for non-payment in each case was that some portions of the equipment had not actually been completed because of missing parts and missing sub-assemblies. Currently, the company's inventories (raw materials, work-in-process and goods in process of installation) totalled about 2.5 billion lire[2]; total annual sales amounted to about 5.5 billion lire.

Mr. Maserati was disturbed not only because there were large amounts of capital tied up in these accounts but also because of the customers' dissatisfaction with such long delays. He believed that ability to meet customer delivery requirements was a major factor in competing for equipment orders, at least during periods of economic expansion when Ottolini sometimes had as much as nine to twelve months backlog. This being so, he felt that ability to make installations quickly and completely would add significantly to Ottolini's competitive effectiveness.

---

*This case was compiled by Professor Powell Niland as a basis for class discussion. The names used are fictitious.

†Copyright 1963 by l'Institut pour l'Etude des Méthodes de Direction de l'Entreprise (IMEDE), Lausanne, Switzerland.

[1] Only 20% of the contracts called for advance or progress payments. In all other cases, nothing could be invoiced until the customer's plant manager signed his acceptance of the installation.

[2] 1,000,000 lire equals about U.S. $1,600.

Mr. Maserati tried to find out why the missing parts had been held up. He received a variety of answers, including (1) "the part wasn't in stock," (2) "engineering was late," (3) "purchased parts weren't delivered," (4) "the customer's premises were not ready for installation," (5) "some of the sub-assemblies had been diverted to another job" and (6) "the installers were pulled off the job because of a lack of material."

In some of the cases, a lot of the parts required had been scheduled for fabrication (or delivery from a vendor) during the succeeding several weeks, but because the finished assemblies were bulky and the floor space was required for other orders, the equipment involved had been shipped from the factory and installed in the customer's plant, with the intention of supplying the missing parts at a later date. The installation crews had finished as much work as they could and then had moved on to other customer plants. They were therefore otherwise engaged when the missing parts actually became available.

FACTORY ORGANIZATION AND OPERATION

Ottolini manufactured, to customers' orders, a line of industrial equipment for a segment of the electrical industry. Its plant, employing about 800 men and women in the factory and 100 to 150 more in installation activity off the premises, was located in a major Italian industrial center. The Ottolini firm fabricated the piece parts; assembled major portions of the equipment in its assembly department; and installed the equipment complex in the customer's plant. The average order required at least a nine-months' cycle comprised of three to four months to develop specifications in the Technical (Engineering) Department; another three to four months to fabricate and assemble major portions of the equipment; and two to three months for shipping, installation and testing. Individual orders from customers typically ranged from 30,000,000 lire to 300,000,000 lire each. In accordance with industry practice, the customer did not pay for the installation until it was complete and had been tested satisfactorily.

Every equipment installation performed the same general function but each one had to meet somewhat different specifications as to capacity, size, shape and operating characteristics. Some represented an expansion of the customer's existing facilities, and so had to be designed to be compatible with the existing installation.

An installation was composed of a complex variety of electrical circuits. The Technical Department had in current use some 5,000 different circuit designs. On the other hand, certain principal components, such as relays and switches, were standardized and were wired together to make a great variety of circuits. Furthermore, some of the principal circuits were "modules" which were repeated many times to build up to capacity of a completed piece of equipment.

Ottolini had specification for about 14,000 different mechanical piece-parts

G. Ottolini & Co., S.p.A.

and about 3,000 sub-assemblies. Some of these were used infrequently because the typical customer's order did not require them, but many were common to a large proportion of orders, and some were common to every order received. Of the common parts, a few (such as relay components) were used in large quantities (several thousand pieces) in every piece of equipment, while others were used in small quantities (from one to ten pieces). Each completed equipment installation used a wide variety of purchased parts, a few of which were quite expensive. The bill of material for a typical equipment installation listed about 750 parts.

In the Fabricating Department the principal operations were press work (punching and stamping); sheet metal work; and a variety of metal machining operations. The chiefs of these sections reported to the Factory Manager. Assembly operations involved mechanical assembly (of such items as switches and relays); wiring (including soldering) and welding major sub-assemblies of electrical circuits; and testing electrical circuits as major sub-assemblies were completed. All assembly operations were under the direction of one foreman.

The Factory Manager, Mr. Roggo, aged 53, was a university graduate in mechanical engineering who had held his present position for many years. He had begun his career as a tool designer and his first love was the machine shop, in which he would not tolerate sub-standard workmanship. Exhibit 1 shows the

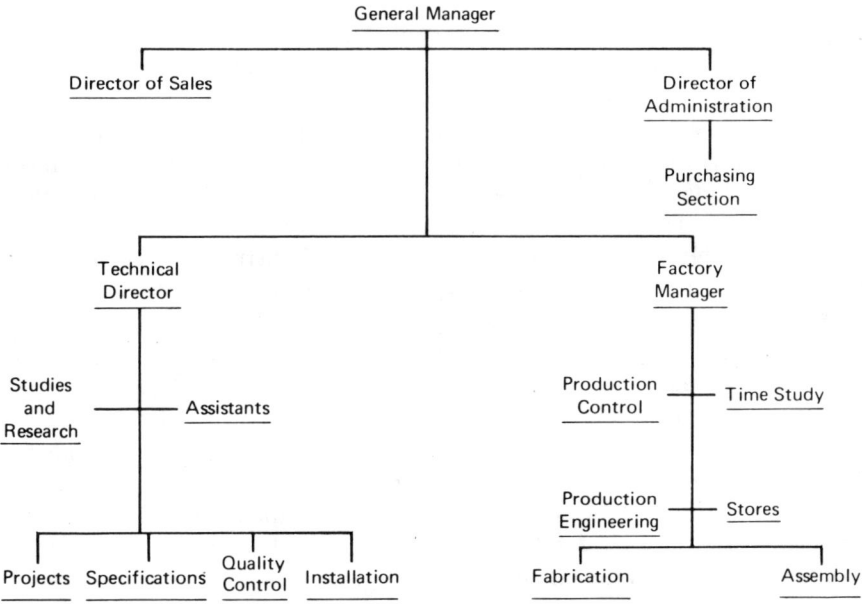

EXHIBIT 1
G. OTTOLINI & CO., S.p.A.
Partial Organization Chart

principal factory function under his direction. Mr. Roggo had complained that although Mr. Erni, the Production Control Supervisor, was supposed to report to him, he felt that he had little control over what Mr. Erni did.

Installation was performed in the customer's plant by crews of electricians and mechanics, working in crews of four to eight under the direction of a leading man. Because it was the first time that the whole complex, including many fragile parts, had been fully assembled, testing was complicated and important. For testing guidance, the installation group relied upon the Quality Control Section of the Technical Department.

The installation crews reported to a chief who in turn reported to the Technical Director. Because of continued customer complaints, Mr. Maserati more recently has been conferring directly and frequently with the Installation Chief on the assignment and progress of installation crews. Exhibit 1 sets forth the organization of the Factory and the Technical (Engineering) Department.

PRODUCTION CONTROL PROCEDURES EMPLOYED

Mr. Erni, who had formerly worked for several years as a member of the installation crews, personally did all of the production scheduling for the plant. Aged 46 and a mechanic by training, he had a wide knowledge of parts and various types of equipment, as well as of the electrical circuitry involved in complete installations. According to his associates, he was hard-working, somewhat reserved, sensitive to criticism, and inclined to use few words. Mr. Erni had had frequent absences because of illness; Mr. Maserati suspected that the cause might be a heart condition.

As far as Mr. Maserati could determine, Mr. Erni had been given only a few policies and a minimum of written procedures to employ. Mr. Erni did have available, in a file for each order, a parts list showing both manufactured and purchased components required for every assembly of standard design, and an operation sheet for each standard manufactured part which showed the processing steps required to manufacture it; the kind and amount of raw material required; time standards for both the equipment set-up and running time; and the assembly operations needed. The Technical Department prepared similar documents for all special parts also whenever they were needed, but in these cases Mr. Erni had to estimate the set-up and running times.

An annual plan was prepared during the last quarter of each year, covering the production activities for the succeeding twelve months. Mr. Erni based his production planning upon an annual sales forecast sent to him by the Commercial Department. This forecast did not give any monthly data nor any information about the expected types of installations, but showed merely the expected total number of installations for the entire year and the estimated average value (at selling price) of each. Mr. Erni therefore estimated the types of installations which would be made, the number of each type, and the kind and number of the sub-assemblies which would be needed to produce them. In making this forecast,

G. Ottolini & Co., S.p.A. 71

Mr. Erni based his estimates on the characteristics of the actual shipment made during the prior year.

Mr. Erni used his annual forecast to prepare a monthly assembly schedule by distributing the requirement for various types of sub-assemblies evenly throughout the year, so as to maintain a steady work load in the factory. To establish the month in which assembly should start, he assumed that two months would be required for assembly and three months for installation.

Mechanical parts were scheduled independently. Mr. Erni first developed the annual requirements for each standard mechanical part, based on his annual forecast of installations and the parts lists for each type of sub-assembly involved. He then divided the total annual requirements for each part into lots in a way which would insure a balanced load throughout the year on the presses and the machine tools, and also avoid uneconomically small lots. In making these decisions, he assumed a uniform monthly consumption of each part. He usually established a lot size equal to one month's usage, but when the expected monthly demand was relatively small, the lot size was increased in order to minimize costly set-ups. Mr. Roggo sometimes instructed Mr. Erni to combine the requirements for two consecutive months in order to keep presses producing the same part for several days. When only a very small number of a particular part would be used during the course of a year, Mr. Erni scheduled shop order releases so that the entire year's requirements would be made in only one or two lots.

Mr. Erni then compiled a Date Book, which listed the lot size and the week during which shop orders should be released in order to fulfill the expected consumption in the Assembly Department. In doing this, Mr. Erni assumed a two months' lead time; that is to say, parts required for assembly during March would be released for manufacture the first week of January.

Stock cards were maintained which showed for each standard part both the actual physical balance on hand and the total number reserved. Reserved parts were those which had been allocated to assembly orders in process, but which had not yet actually been withdrawn. On the date established by the Date Book for ordering a particular item, Mr. Erni checked its stock record card. If the unreserved balance were dangerously low, he would increase the quantity ordered; otherwise, he fixed the ordered amount equal to the previously determined lot size.

After he had completed the Date Book, Mr. Erni prepared a departmental task plan based upon the Date Book, which he sent to the Factory Manager, for distribution to the Fabricating and Assembly Chiefs. These departmental task plans were used in planning the hiring of personnel and the acquisition of new equipment so that the factory would be able to keep its capacity to produce in balance with expected market demand.

Mr. Erni did not do any planning in connection with special parts, which comprised about 10% of all shop orders issued. Instead, he reviewed the files on customers' orders scheduled for assembly, two months before the Assembly

Department started to work on them, to determine the special parts required. As he identified each of these, he prepared a shop order and sent it to the Stores Section along with the day's releases of shop orders for standard parts. For example, he would make up shop orders to produce special parts in, say October for a piece of equipment which the Assembly Department would start assembling in December, and which would be expected to be completely installed by the end of May.

Under Italian law, it was possible to shorten the work week for permanent factory workers from 48 hours to 44 hours without any cost or administrative difficulties. Permanent lay-offs, on the other hand, could be made only after application to a government agency and demonstration that they were absolutely necessary. It was possible to hire temporary workers who would work for several months and then be laid off, but this type of labor naturally included the least trained and least desirable type of workers, and they were much less productive on the job than Ottolini's regular employees.

Mr. Erni also used his annual forecast of mechanical parts required to develop the requirements for raw materials (such as steel, copper, and wire). For each raw material he then made out and forwarded to the Purchasing Section a set of purchase requests which divided the annual total requirement into an appropriate number of lots, and specified delivery a month in advance of its estimated consumption by the Fabricating Department. Mr. Maserati knew that the current investment in raw material inventories was about 600,000,000 lire, and he judged that on the average it turned over about twice a year.

The Purchasing Section, which was part of the Administration Department, put these sets of purchase requests in a "tickler file" and once each month placed purchase orders with suppliers. The same procedures were followed for parts or sub-assemblies which were to be purchased rather than manufactured. Delivery of parts and sub-assemblies was requested for the month before their estimated use in the Assembly Department. Mr. Roggo and Mr. Erni had complained from time to time that the Purchasing Section was unnecessarily slow. In response, the Purchasing Section had continually pressed for additional personnel.

PRODUCTION RELEASE PROCEDURES

During each week, Mr. Erni released shop orders on the parts scheduled in the Date Book for that week. He sent all shop orders to the Stores Section. The Stores Section kept a shop order until the required raw material was available, at which time the order was forwarded to the foremen as an indication that fabrication could begin. In practice, each foreman wished to work with a backlog of shop orders equal to four to six weeks' production, in order to make the most efficient allocation of work, according to the variations in the competency of the workers and the characteristics of the equipment in his department. Mr. Maserati believed that there was some tendency to do the easiest work first

G. Ottolini & Co., S.p.A.

in order to realize high piece-work earnings. When the shop order was completed, the finished parts were returned to the Stores Section and kept in stock until they were withdrawn for use by the Assembly Department.

Customers' orders were habitually processed through the Assembly Department in the order in which they were received from the Technical Department, although occasionally an order was given priority in order to meet a customer's urgent need. As a minimum, the backlog of actual customer orders ahead of the Assembly Department was equivalent to three or four months of full-time production by the Assembly Department. Typically, it was six to eight months in size. For efficient production, it was necessary to have a sizeable backlog because there was considerable variation in the rate at which customers placed orders. Except for the replacement parts orders (which made up less than 1% of total sales volume), most orders represented large and infrequent expenditures for Ottolini's customers, and there were periods of several weeks in which no orders were received as well as other periods of a few weeks in which several orders were received.

The Assembly Department Chief checked on parts availability with the Stores Section before his department began assembling units for a particular piece of equipment.[3] Ideally, all parts required would be available in the Stores Section, but often both special and standard parts were found to be missing. Outstanding shop orders for the missing parts were traced so they could be classified "rush," or new orders issued if they could not be found. If no order was found to be outstanding, then a "rush" shop order was issued for the quantity required. Mr. Erni estimated that perhaps 5% of the shop orders he issued were for rush orders. Sometimes assembly operations were begun on the assumption that the required parts would be supplied at a later date.

Mr. Maserati found out not only that there were sometimes shortages of standard parts but also that there were large excess stocks of other parts. Investigating these latter cases, he found some instances in which Mr. Erni's assumption about the probable mix of sub-assemblies to be made was quite different from the actual mix of customer orders, with the result that expected withdrawals of certain parts had not occurred or had been much lower than the quantity forecasted. In other instances, supplies of a particular part had been made obsolete by a new design's being originated by the Technical Department. The fact that a change in the design of a part had occurred was sometimes not discovered until parts of the new design were called for during the assembly operations.

ORGANIZATIONAL CONSIDERATIONS

Mr. Maserati considered it essential that there should be a suitable person directing the production control function. He was not convinced that Mr. Erni

[3] The Technical Department furnished the Assembly Department a list of the parts required for each order, as well as finished parts and assembly drawings, at the same time as Mr. Erni received his file on the orders.

viewed his activities with a broad enough scope, nor was he sure that Mr. Erni possessed either the interest or the basic qualifications to the extent that he could be easily trained to supervise this function adequately. On the other hand, Mr. Maserati recognized that Mr. Erni did possess an extremely thorough knowledge of parts and various types of equipment, and, although he possessed very few records, he carried in his head considerable valuable experience.

Mr. Maserati considered the possibility of finding someone from another department to head the production control function. He believed that Mr. Livotti, who was working in the Technical Department as Chief of Quality Control, might be such a person. Mr. Livotti had demonstrated considerable personal competence in connection with several engineering projects, with some of which Mr. Maserati was personally familiar. Likewise, he had earned the praise of his superior, the Technical Director. Since the Technical Director was only about 12 years older than Mr. Livotti, the latter's prospects for ultimate advancement to the post of Technical Director were remote. Furthermore, unlike the majority of university-trained engineers with whom Mr. Maserati was acquainted, Mr. Livotti had expressed some interest in considering a management career rather than a technical one, even though he had not had any formal management training. In Mr. Maserati's opinion, the Ottolini company, although employing several younger men of considerable technical skill, had few showing great managerial promise. He had been trying to recruit someone (thus far, unsuccessfully) from outside the company to act initially as his assistant, but who some day might become his second in command and supervise both the Technical Department and the Factory.

A third possibility was to attempt to recruit a person from outside the company to head up the production control function. In view of the tight labor market throughout Italy for managers of all types and his own lack of success in recruiting someone for a higher position, Mr. Maserati thought that this course of action might be difficult at this time.

As he was mulling over the foregoing possibilities, Mr. Maserati also wondered whether the company's organization for production and inventory control was the most suitable one which could be devised. The lack of coordination in production activities and the practical impossibility of fixing responsibility for the continual delays suggested that there might be some weaknesses in the way in which Ottolini was organized to perform these functions.

QUESTION

1. Suggest a course of action for Mr. Maserati to help alleviate the inadequacies of the firm's production control system.

6

Frassati Company

Frassati Company (A)*†

On the 1st May, 1959, Dr. Mazzini, the Personnel Director of the Frassati Company was considering the position that he should take at a meeting with the Internal Commission of the company. This meeting, scheduled for the 5th of May, was a fortnightly meeting at which the chairman of the Internal Commission had asked to discuss the unsatisfactory state of affairs in the special tool section of the Cedano plant. In September 1958, management had extended its system of job evaluation and incentive payment into the Cedano plant where it had met with an unenthusiastic reception. Despite increased productivity in the department, there had been continual grumbling by the workers concerned and this grumbling had finally been brought to management's attention through the representations of the Internal Commission.

THE FRASSATI COMPANY

The Frassati Company had been founded by P. R. Frassati at the end of the 19th century. Originally, the company had been exclusively a fabricator of light iron and steel products for use in general engineering. Under aggressive leadership of its founder and his son, the company had expanded rapidly and successfully and now operated eight plants throughout Italy with a total work force of about 16,000 men. In 1959 the company produced a wide variety of iron and steel products ranging from heavy structural steel girders to small nuts and bolts. A substantial percentage of total output was exported and, in common with most Italian industry, the company had enjoyed a period of rising sales and profits through 1958 and 1959.

The largest of the company's plants, employing about 8,000 workers, was situated at Valate, just outside Milan. This plant produced the full range of the company's products and was the largest and most important plant in the company. The remaining plants in the company were smaller and were widely dispersed throughout the country. Each of these smaller plants tended to be

---

*Copyright 1961 by l'Institut pour l'Etude des Méthodes de Direction de l'Entreprise, (IMEDE), Lausanne, Switzerland.

†This case was prepared by Basil W. Denning under the direction of Professor Stephen H. Fuller as a basis for class discussion. All names have been disguised.

more specialized in its production. One of these smaller plants at Cedano was essentially a satellite of Valate and was situated just a few kilometers away from it.

In 1946, the company had organized a Central Personnel Department under Dr. Mazzini. Before the war he had been personnel manager for another well known Italian firm and during the war had been active in the Resistance. Under Dr. Mazzini's leadership the personnel office had grown into a department employing over 300 people with responsibility for labor relations, personnel policies and welfare services. Frassati Company was highly regarded by the rest of Italian industry as being a leader in the development and practice of enlightened personnel management.

Due to the importance of the Valate plant in the company's overall organization, and the fact that developments at this plant tended to act as precedents for the other plants, the personnel policies at this plant were directly controlled by the Central Personnel Department. In particular, the Central Personnel Department carried full responsibility for relations with the Internal Commission representing the Valate and Cedano plants.

This Internal Commission consisted of 15 members elected by the workers, four representing salaried employees and eleven representing hourly paid workers. Management believed that eight of these members were affiliated with the CGIL union, five with the CISL union and two with the UIL union. Management's relationships with the Internal Commission were kept on a strictly formal basis. Discussion was restricted to the provisions of the collective contract and to the detailed requirements of the labor laws in Italy. Meetings were held every other week to discuss complaints or questions about workload changes, production benefits or incentive earnings, etc. Dr. Mazzini normally delegated responsibility for these meetings to a senior assistant, but would attend himself on important questions. In addition, various operating managers from the plant at Valate would be invited to take part in the discussions if their specialized knowledge could contribute to the effectiveness of the meeting.

About 2,300 (30%) of the company's workers in the Valate and Cedano plants were thought to be active dues-paying union members. Of these it was estimated that 1,100 men were members of the CGIL union; 600 were members of the CISL union and 600 were members of the UIL union. As is characteristic of the Italian labor structure, there was no *union* organization inside the factory, and the majority of management-union discussions or negotiations were held with the appropriate union officers in the provincial Chambers of Labor in Milan.

LABOR POLICIES

The company had clearly defined personnel policies particularly in two areas—incentive wages and strikes. For many years the company had followed the practice of paying workers incentive wages whenever possible. Each worker

Frassati Company (A)

was guaranteed a base wage in accordance with the current collective agreement signed by the unions. However, for production above a certain stated minimum, increased payments were made to the worker based on his additional production. Maximum increments to pay were 30% of the base rates.

In the Valate plant base rates and incentive rates had been set for many years on the basis of scientific job evaluation except in the Maintenance Department where the difficulties of establishing a sound basis for work measurement had been the greatest. It had also not been possible to devise a satisfactory system for use at the Cedano plant.

Consequently, in the Maintenance Department and at the Cedano plant, while incentive pay was used, the rates were for many years based on standards which had come to be set by practice and custom. In 1952, management had started to introduce standards set by time study measurement for the Maintenance Department and by 1958 over 600 highly skilled craftsmen employed on maintenance were being paid on the basis of scientific job measurement.

Management had found that on each occasion of introducing the new system one important factor which had constantly to be kept in mind was the overall internal structure of wages. Inside the company there was a well-established monetary grading of jobs which was known by the workers. Any serious alteration in the relative pay for jobs which carried a historical position in this grading system would have serious repercussions on the entire wage structure and spread discontent over a wide area.

As far as strikes were concerned, management had also adopted a clear policy. This policy had been established in 1952 in defense against the wave of political strikes which had swept the country. Participants in a political strike would be punished; participants in a strike for economic reasons would not be punished. In this connection management distinguished clearly between a strike in which workers failed to report for work and a protest movement with some element of "go-slow" involved. A strike according to Italian practice is a refusal of workers to report for work. This is legally permitted. On the other hand, a "go-slow" or "sit-down" protest movement is not legally regarded as a strike, but rather as an act of non-collaboration. Hence management regarded participation in such activity as a punishable offense. For example, in 1953 the workers in a particular plant had made a "declaration of non-collaboration with management," and management had reacted by cutting all wages by 15%.[1]

THE CEDANO PLANT

The Cedano plant was a satellite of the main Valate plant; it was sited only a few kilometers away, and was solely concerned with the production of light structural steel parts. While some of the parts manufactured were standard items

[1] The assumption is made in Italian law that, if a worker reports for work, he will do a full day's work under the direction of management. Failure to do this by some concerted protest action is not a strike, but an act of non-collaboration.

such as steel brackets and small steel fittings for general use in construction, this plant also carried out a significant proportion of special order work. The plant was supervised by Mr. Rita, a mechanical engineer, who was generally regarded as an efficient manager and a good leader. Under Mr. Rita were four separate sections, assembly, adjustments, materials and special tools. Each section had a section supervisor with four or more foremen who reported to him.

In 1956, a study had been carried out at Cedano to see whether productivity could be increased by the application of more efficient methods and the use of time standards. The study itself was kept secret from the workers and the lower line management. The results of this study clearly indicated that substantial savings could be made. For example, it was estimated that for an expenditure of about five million lira, savings of over 20 million lira per year could be obtained.

The study had included three separate steps:
1. Methods and work simplification, standardization of particular steps in the job, analysis and standardization of the tools to be used, and the introduction of new procedures for ordering work.
2. The application of time standards.
3. The introduction of incentive payments related to these standards.

As a result of the study made, the company decided that a piecework system based on a well-known American type formula would be most suitable. One characteristic of this system was that it allowed some elasticity in setting standards, thus reducing the effort involved in estimating costs for a particular job. The whole system was fully discussed with the Central Personnel Department to check whether introduction of the system would contravene the collective agreements with the unions, or the plant rules negotiated with the Internal Commission. The Personnel Department offered no objections, but one result of these discussions was that it was decided to introduce the same incentive curve[2] at Cedano as had already been applied elsewhere in the company.

The new system was first introduced into the adjustments section of the Cedano plant. The company ran a special index of productivity which showed that productivity jumped from a figure of 93 to 133 within a year. Normal productivity was represented by a figure of 100.

In the special tooling section special jigs and tools for use throughout the company as well as for extra-company sales were manufactured. In this section there was a fairly stable workforce of 350 men, including 140 lathe operators and skilled fitters (finissagio). These 1440 men received higher pay than the remainder of the workers in this section. They were long service workers, and they were generally acknowledged as the key men in the section, both by management and fellow workers.

[2] The incentive curve is the curve relating production above the minimum with the additional wage paid as an incentive.

Frassati Company (A)

In accordance with company policy, a system of incentive pay had been operating in this section for many years. No job measurement or time study work had been carried out in setting standards. The levels of production for minimum rates of pay had been established on the basis of what management knew of past practices and performance. For the two years 1956 and 1957, the workers generally earned the maximum incentive pay that was permissible under the system.

Early in 1958, Mr. Rita was reviewing the operations in this special tool section and felt that the time had come to introduce the new methods and incentive system. Accordingly, he approached Dr. Mazzini to discuss such a step. Following this discussion, Mr. Rita went ahead with his plans, and methods and time study men from the Central Time and Motion Study Department of the company came down to the plant to set the standards in this section.

In September 1958, Mr. Rita reviewed the results of the work done by the methods and time study men. As a result of this review he decided to introduce the system forthwith and gave the appropriate instructions to the special tool section supervisor. New types of work sheets were issued out to the foremen with instructions that they were to be used for future computation of wages. By the end of the month, the system was in full operation.

The nature of the new system of work sheets was fairly simple in concept. Each job was pre-planned to the extent that a detailed routing of the job with instructions about the work to be done at each stage were specified. Each operation was given a standard time based on the results of the time studies. Completion of the job within this time limit automatically qualified a man for his base rate, and if the job was completed in a shorter time he qualified for different amounts of incentive pay in accordance with a predetermined scale called the incentive curve.

During the subsequent months, productivity rose and labor and wage costs in the section were lowered, although no workers had to be laid off. Under the new arrangements of better organized and more systematic work, many workers were in fact working harder since delays in the flow of work were largely eliminated. Most workers took time to adjust to the new required rate of working and they found that their wages were falling below their previous levels. The average drop in actual earnings throughout the section was 4-5%, while productivity, according to the index, increased by 50%.

The section supervisor and foremen noticed that there was a certain amount of grumbling by a number of workers. Typical complaints were based on such things as machine interference preventing the worker from achieving maximum productivity, or differences in quality of raw materials which affected the volume of output. Some workers complained that they had old machines with a slower rate of operation than other workers with new machines and that this fact prevented the workers on the old machines from earning full incentive pay. Individual cases of this type were referred by the foremen or supervisor to the methods and time study men for reassessment. No *formal* complaints or grievances were registered until February 1959.

At this time the whole question was discussed at a meeting of Dr. Mazzini with the Internal Commission. The Commission protested against the system on grounds of principle, saying that management had no right to introduce the system, the system was inequitable, and it must be eliminated. Management took the following position:

1. Management refused to discuss its right to introduce a new system.
2. Management was perfectly prepared to discuss the equity of the new arrangements at those positions where there were particular complaints. These positions could be discussed on a case by case basis between management or the time study men and the operator, any worker's committee, and the Internal Commission.

Dr. Mazzini stated subsequently that he made it plain at the meeting that he was prepared to discuss the complete method and timing of any particular job but that he was not prepared to discuss the system. The Internal Commission rejected this approach by management stating that the whole new system was unacceptable. No further discussion of the matter took place with the Internal Commission although a few individual cases of difficulty were solved within the section with the assistance of the methods and time study men.

On the 30th of April 1959, the Chairman of the Internal Commission informed Dr. Mazzini in writing that at the next meeting of the management with the Internal Commission on the 5th of May, the Internal Commission wished to discuss the situation in the special tool section at Cedano. He stated that as a result of complaints which had been forwarded to him and his own investigation of the situation, the Internal Commission must insist on the following points:

1. The new system of job measurement and incentive pay in the special tooling section was unfair to the workers in that section and was totally unacceptable as a system.
2. If elimination of the system was not possible, a substantial increase in incentive pay was required as compensation for such an inequitable system.

Frassati Company (B)*

At the meeting on the 5th of May 1959, in reply to the demands of the Internal Commission, Dr. Mazzini restated the position which had been taken in February. This position was that he would not discuss management's right to introduce the system but that he was prepared to discuss individual situations on a case by case basis. No additional offer was made. The members of the Internal Commission rejected management's offer to discuss the application of the system and no agreement on any future procedure was reached.

Work continued in the special tool section where management noticed that the increased level of productivity was sustained and costs remained lower. Management recognized that the workers were in fact working harder and that the general level of pay was still averaging 5% below previous levels. Management noticed also that the grumbling of the workers had not significantly decreased, but there were no more official complaints or representations by the Internal Commission until July 1960.

During the summer of 1960, among others, the Communist and Socialist political parties had been growing increasingly dissatisfied with the national government of Signor Tambroni, the Prime Minister. This dissatisfaction arose from the fact that Signor Tambroni relied on the votes of the M.S.I. pro-Fascist parliamentary representatives to maintain his majority, with a somewhat more right wing government policy as a result. When the M.S.I. party announced that it would hold a national convention in Genoa in June 1960, protest riots took place in a number of Italian cities. As a further demonstration, the CGIL planned a one-day national strike in protest against M.S.I. participation in the government. This strike was called for July 9th and the large majority of Frassati workers throughout the country obeyed the strike.

All the workers in the special tool section of the Cedano plant, however, stopped work on the 8th of July and stayed out for three days, resuming work on the 11th of July.

*Copyright 1961 by l'Institut pour l'Etude des Méthodes de Direction de l'Entreprise (IMEDE), Lausanne, Switzerland.

Frassati Company (C)*

The CGIL representatives in the Provincial Chamber of Labor noted that the workers in the special tool section of the Cedano plant had struck for three days and they interpreted this action as a significant measure of the dissatisfaction with the new incentive payment scheme. Accordingly, they contacted the provincial CISL and UIL representatives and made a joint request to the employers' representatives at Confindustria to arrange a meeting with the management of the Frassati Company on July 21st. Dr. Mazzini, reluctant to have a meeting so soon after the strike and desiring to separate company problems from political ones, agreed to meet with the union representatives on July 29th.

At this meeting held between the provincial organization of Confindustria and the three Provincial Chambers of Labor, the unions were represented by noted regional and national labor leaders in the metal-working industry. Indeed, the presidents of the CISL and UIL federations of metal-working unions headed their respective delegations because of the importance which any agreements reached with the Frassati Company might have as precedents in other companies in the industry.

At the meeting Dr. Mazzini restated management's position as outlined in February 1959. Although he continued to refuse to discuss management's right to introduce the new system, he did say that management would conduct an intensive survey of all the work which had been carried out to see if any errors could be found or any corrective measures could be taken by management to improve the system. For example, he suggested that management would thoroughly investigate the extent to which foremen were attempting to iron out difficulties as they arose. He also mentioned the possibility of calling in an outside consultant.

As a result of these various suggestions, Dr. Mazzini said that he felt that the unions were beginning to signal a shift in their position by arguing about the technical merits of the system rather than about the right of management to introduce it at all. While no formal agreement on future procedure was reached, it was agreed to hold a further meeting in two months time at which management would offer the results of its survey. All outstanding issues could be discussed in the light of this survey at that time.

The following day the union leaders called a meeting of the workers of the special tool section outside the plant at which they announced the results of the discussions of the previous day. They recommended that the workers cooperate with management in the survey being made and then bring up any issues which

*Copyright 1961 by l'Institut pour l'Etude des Méthodes de Direction de l'Entreprise (IMEDE), Lausanne, Switzerland.

Frassati Company (C)

remained unresolved in time for the September meeting. The workers refused to accept this recommendation and stated that they were not satisfied that the union had adequately represented their interests. It was apparent that they were still thinking in terms of militant action to force abolishment of the system in their section.

Frassati Company (D)*

Although no final agreement was reached at the meeting on July 29th, management proceeded on the basis of the tentative understanding which they felt had been reached with the unions. Accordingly, the survey of the whole new system, as it had been applied in the special tool section, was carried out.

The most significant findings arose in the general area of communications between the supervisor, foremen, methods and time study men, and workers. Since the supervisor and the foremen had not been adequately instructed in the details and operation of the new system, when faced with a complaint, they had been forced to call in the methods and time study men to iron out the difficulty. This had resulted in an apparent diminution of their authority and appeared as a reflection on their ability to supervise production. As a result of their feelings about this situation they resented the methods and time study men almost as much as the workers did, and thus were not giving their full cooperation either to the time study men or to the workers. Various actions were taken by management to improve this situation including a redefinition of the supervisor's and foremen's responsibilities which laid particular stress on the fact that they were ultimately responsible for the productivity of their men. The methods and time study men retained the responsibility for the times, and individual discussions were held with each methods and time study man to understand his difficulties. One important result of these various discussions was that the methods and time study men who had been working at Cedano were permanently transferred to the Cedano plant to work under Mr. Rita. In addition, management arranged for a careful recheck of all jobs carried out during the previous year. This reexamination revealed that about 2% of all jobs were actually in dispute. In these cases management initiated adjustments as necessary and, in management's opinion, these measures significantly improved the climate in the section.

However, on the 22nd and 23rd August all men in the special tooling section at Cedano went on strike. They also declared and carried out a second strike on the 26th August. Neither of these strikes were sponsored by the union. Management did not punish any of the strikers.

At the meeting between management and union leaders on the 9th September, the unions agreed that the situation had much improved as a result of management action. Hence, the union leaders stated that they would accept the situation and adopt the proposed consultation procedure outlined by management at every meeting since February 1959. However, they also demanded that each worker should be given a cash grant of 10,000 lira as an indemnity. They

*Copyright 1961 by l'Institut pour l'Etudes des Méthodes de Direction de l'Entreprise, (IMEDE), Lausanne, Switzerland.

Frassati Company (D)

justified this demand by drawing attention to the hardships imposed on the workers during the period of difficulty and argued that these hardships could have been avoided if management had introduced the system in a more effective manner. Management felt that the objections of the unions would be heard no more if they granted the 10,000 lira.

Frassati Company (E)*

At the meeting on the 9th September management firmly rejected the union demand for 10,000 lira per man.

At a further meeting between the union representatives and management on November 3rd, the union leaders withdrew their demand for the 10,000 lira cash indemnity. At this meeting the unions accepted the new incentive pay system. In addition, agreement was reached on a consultation procedure to be used in case of disagreement about any particular job. This agreement was spelt out in two documents. The significant portions of the two agreements are attached as Appendix 1.

APPENDIX 1

Minutes of Agreement

1. In accordance with the general conditions governing incentive and piece work rates and agreements previously reached it is agreed between management and the Internal Commission that:
    (a) When it becomes necessary to issue or revise any rates, the appropriate company officials will inform both the workers concerned and the Internal Commission in advance. The giving of this information in no way changes the normal procedure for making time studies or setting rates.
    (b) When the rates for new or revised standards are established, the rates will be exhibited on the notice board and, at the worker's request, explained in detail to him.
    No new or revised standard will be brought into force until 15 days have elapsed from the time of exhibiting this notice on the board.
    (c) At the end of the 15 days, the new rates will automatically be introduced. For the first 20 days, payment of at least 53% of the maximum incentive pay will be guaranteed. After 20 days have elapsed, the rates will be enforced without the guarantee. Nevertheless, disagreement about the new rates may still be registered via the grievance procedure separately agreed.
    (d) Where there is no disagreement about the new rates, the 15 days notice period may be reduced at the request of the Internal Commission. When this occurs, the new rates will be introduced immediately and there will be no guarantee of 53% of maximum incentive pay.
    (e) Unresolved disagreements between workers and management at the shop floor level will be referred to the Internal Commission.
2. It is further agreed that:
    (a) Should a noticeable drop occur in the earnings of any worker on piece work or incentive pay, the worker concerned or the Internal Commission

*Copyright 1961 by l'Institut pour l'Etude des Méthodes de Direction de l'Entreprise (IMEDE), Lausanne, Switzerland.

Frassati Company (E)

may submit the case within 15 days to management in order to determine the cause of the reduction in pay.

(b) Whenever, as a result of the examination of grievances submitted by the worker or by the Internal Commission within the 15 days time limit, an incentive or piece work rate is altered, final payment for the work which provoked the grievance shall be made on the basis of the finally agreed rate.

India

7

The Universal Parts Company*

In January, 1957, two of the three partners of the Universal Parts Company were rather worried. The third partner, Mr. Davidsky, had decided to migrate to Australia by December, 1957. In a meeting of the partners, Davidsky stated that he wanted to sell his share of the business. The partners were uncertain as to what type of financial arrangement to make, what organizational changes would be required, whether a qualified person could be found to fill Mr. Davidsky's place, what further financial changes would be required, what effect his departure would have on the company's sales, profits, employee morale, customer relations, production, and the various other areas which fall within the managerial scope.

The discussion regarding all of these important decisions caused the partners to trace the progress of their company from its conception in 1950 to the time when Mr. Davidsky dropped his bombshell.

The Universal Parts Company was a foundry business formed to manufacture standard parts for oil mills and special parts on a jobbing basis. The foundry was located in Kurla, about 16 miles from Bombay. The Company was a three-way partnership. The partners were:

Mr. Jaimshed Mehta, who provided the initial idea for the foundry, played the enterpreneur's role in setting it up and assumed the major managerial responsibilities. A university graduate with an M.A. in economics, he had worked for over three years (1947-1950) as the general manager of a foundry owned by three of his friends. Not considered a partner, his salary, which was 10% of the net profit, averaged about Rs. 600 a month. In 1950, he was 28 years old.

Mr. Nikola Davidsky was a refugee from Poland and had been in India since 1947. The meeting between Mr. Mehta and Mr. Davidsky was accidental, but it led to a warm friendship. Since Mr. Davidsky had had wide experience as a production worker and as an engineer in various foundries in Poland, they had interests in common. In 1950,

*Dr. Maneck S. Wadia is grateful to Stanford University and to the Ford Foundation for their support in developing the case studies for India.

Mr. Davidsky was about 34 years old. Although he had a limited formal education, he had worked in a foundry since the age of 20, and was well versed in the technical side of the business. Since his arrival in India, he had been working as a spinning master in a cotton mill but was dissatisfied with his job.

Mr. Pheroze Dastur was a college friend of Mr. Mehta and about the same age; the son of a wealthy businessman and relatively well acquainted with the financial aspects of running a business. He had a B. Com. degree and experience as an accountant. He worked for his father but was always on the lookout for good business investments.

FINANCE

The following financial arrangements were made for setting up the foundry: The estimated cost was about three lakhs of ruppees (Rs. 300,000). They expected to take about one year to set up their business. It was decided that each person would have an equal partnership across the board, in ownership as well as in profit and loss. Each partner invested Rs. 50,000 in the business, and Mr. Dastur made the financial arrangements for the remaining money through his father. His father gave a nine-year loan of Rs. 150,000 to the Universal Parts Company at 7% interest.

The partnership came into effect in February 1950, the loan was secured in the same month, and in March 1950, ground-breaking ceremonies were performed in Kurla.

Initially, it was decided that each partner would continue with his past job while the foundry was under construction. They had hired an independent contractor. In July 1950, however, the partners found that the contractor was not doing the type of work they had expected of him and that the partners had not properly planned for the problems in securing various necessary items for construction, such as cement, proper water and electrical connections, etc.

While they were planning the foundry in 1949, Mr. Mehta had agreed to assume responsibility for securing the necessary permits. With great foresight, he had secured an import license early in 1949 for the equipment and materials received from abroad, mainly the United Kingdom. These materials and equipment, worth about Rs. 170,000 when ordered in mid-1949, had already arrived in Bombay by July 1950. The contractor found it difficult, however, to secure the necessary construction materials such as cement, and the water and electric facilities were found to be inadequate.

In August 1950, the partners realized that the construction of the foundry was behind schedule. Mr. Mehta felt that if he devoted full time to this project, the construction would meet the deadline. He resigned from his job in August and devoted all his energies to the construction project; he estimated that he was sacrificing about 5 months of his income, about Rs. 3,000.

The Universal Parts Company

But Mr. Mehta had underestimated the red-tape jungle of bureaucracy. For the next fifteen months, he was shuttled from one government agency to another, from one supplier to another. Construction became irregular, slow, or nonexistent when supplies were lacking, and rapid when the supplies flowed freely. A rather remarkable logistics problem arose in coordinating the flow of supplies, but finally, in November 1951, the foundry was ready for operation, with all the necessary tools and equipment and all of the necessary facilities.

Taking stock of the company in November showed that the company had borrowed an additional Rs. 60,000, a nine-year loan at 8% interest, from Mr. Dastur's father and that setting up the foundry had cost them Rs. 360,000 including interest. Though Mr. Mehta's expenses were paid from company funds while setting up the foundry, he had lost over fifteen months of the income he would have had if he had continued in his old job as the other two partners had done.

Three things made the picture brighter. The land value had increased by about 15%. Because of stricter import regulations, the firm's imported tools and equipment had increased, on the average, about 30% in value. Also, through the effort of all three partners and their friends, the enterprise had accumulated a backlog of orders, mainly from oil mills, worth about Rs. 86,000. The partners felt that if they were to sell the foundry at this time, they would get at least four and a half lakhs of ruppees for it.

The "murat" ceremony for the opening of the foundry was performed on December 18, 1951. By January 1, 1952, the other two partners left their previous jobs to devote full time to the foundry. Other than the usual beginning troubles of a new enterprise, the company started off smoothly. The partners realized that every year they would have to pay Rs. 15,300 in interest to Mr. Dastur's father. They had until 1959 to repay the load. The partners wondered if it would be best to repay part of the loan every year, and, if so, how much.

At first, they decided that they would devote 50% of their yearly profits toward retiring the loan. At the end of 1952, the partners felt that the interest rate on the loan was quite reasonable. They also felt that before the nine years were up they might need further capital to expand and then perhaps they could extend the loan. Mr. Davidsky was of the opinion that they should repay the loan as soon as possible, but he was overruled by the other two partners. It was decided that the interest on the loan would be part of administrative overhead, that each partner would be responsible for having Rs. 70,000 ready by 1959 for the repayment of the loan, and that each partner would receive his share of the profits to do with as he pleased.

By the end of 1956, the partners agreed that their business would be able to expand by at least 50% in the next five years. They realized that they would need to expand their foundry capacity by 50% or require 50% overtime work. In order to expand plant capacity, they would need further capital. Though no commitment was made, Mr. Dastur's father seemed willing to extend his loan for another nine years.

The partners were pleased by the progress their foundry had made. As of December 31, 1956, they estimated the value of their net worth at Rs. 437,433, including current inventory of Rs. 34,638. Though it was estimated that they had lost Rs. 47,205 in terms of depreciation, they had more than made up for it in profits as shown in Exhibit 1.

EXHIBIT 1
THE UNIVERSAL PARTS COMPANY
Comparative Profit and Loss Statements, December 31, 1952-1956

Sales	1952 Rs. 210,498	1953 Rs. 203,394	1954 Rs. 169,101	1955 Rs. 219,216	1956 Rs. 273,287
Sales	100%	100%	100%	100%	100%
Cost of labor	5.5	6.1	8.7	7.2	7.5
Cost of materials	41.5	47.9	38.6	45.2	46.6
Manufacturing and administrative overhead	27.8	25.9	28.5	23.8	26.3
Profit	25.2	20.1	24.2	23.8	19.6
PROFIT	Rs. 53,045	Rs. 40,882	Rs. 40,922	Rs. 52,173	Rs. 53,564

ORGANIZATION

Each partner was considered equal in all respects. But, mainly because of their backgrounds, each partner assumed varying degrees of responsibility and authority in certain areas during the years that followed.

Mr. Jaimshed Mehta. Since leaving his job in August 1950, Mr. Mehta had been the one most closely affiliated with the affairs of the Universal Parts Company. Many of his personal ideas and plans were incorporated into the construction of the foundry as well as into the landscaping. Though the architect had already planned for office space, Mr. Mehta had a small one-bedroom apartment constructed above the office at the cost of Rs. 18,000. He also had some space cleared on the company's property with the hope of eventually constructing some form of housing for the workers.

Since August 1951, he had played the dominant role in hiring the company's employees. He had hired an assistant manager, 37 of the 43 workers, 2 of the 3 foremen, and a "chokidar" (security guard). Eight of the workers and one foreman, among those hired, had worked for him in his previous job as the general manager of a foundry. The chokidar was an old servant of his family. Mr. Mehta also developed a salary structure for these workers. Later, when more workers were needed, he hired them.

After the factory was in operation, Mr. Mehta assumed the full authority of a general manager, and, though he often consulted with the other two partners, most of his decisions were carried through. In the day-to-day operations of the business, he not only interpreted for Mr. Davidsky but also translated his suggestions into a language which the workers could understand and follow. He was the chief source of communication between the owner-managers and the employees of the company.

Only about half of the workers had any foundry or similar work experience, and only eight, those who came from Mr. Mehta's previous foundry, were considered properly trained and expert at their jobs. With the help of one of his foremen and the assistant manager, Mr. Mehta devoted much time and effort to training the workers. The workers were grateful for this opportunity to learn, especially in view of the shortage of trained workers in the foundry line.

During 1953, Mr. Mehta also began to take a more active part than the other partners in securing orders for the foundry. He travelled around India about three months of the year, secured orders, and set up a part-time sales force in various areas. By 1956, though he had reduced his traveling, he was mainly responsible for the company sales. Because of his previous experience and the new responsibilities he now assumed, Mr. Mehta became a "jack-of-all-trades and master of few" in this foundry.

Mr. Nikola Davidsky. Mr. Davidsky had become a part of this venture mainly because of his technical knowledge. Even prior to the formation of the partnership, it was realized that he would not be much help in running the business, since he had no nontechnical interests, spoke halting English and no indigenous languages, and had few, if any, business or government contacts.

In his technical capacity, Mr. Davidsky did an excellent job. He developed furnaces, molding techniques, and mixtures that were more efficient than those used in other small foundries. Moreover, his association with the company paid off an unexpected and substantial dividend to the company in many areas because of his European background.

Nikola Davidsky was husky and six-foot three-inches tall. His blond hair and blue eyes gave him the added appearance of the stereotyped "superior" European, a fetish which continued to persist in India. The workers were respectful toward him. Though they hardly ever communicated directly with him, they always paid greater attention and worked harder if they felt that the orders originated with their "German" engineer. Soon, the workers even began to feel a strong affection toward him, since he often worked by their sides, felt no taboos against menial tasks, and had no aversions to the dirt and hard work of a foundry. What he could not communicate by words, he showed by deeds in helping to train the workers.

His being labeled a "German" engineer first came about for the sake of convenience. Few people knew about Poland, and he could not be called an Englishman or American because of his language problem. The only other Europeans well known to the common man, especially since the war, were the Germans, and the respect for German technical know-how had been prevalent in India for quite some time. Hence, without any effort on the part of management, the workers provided the company with an excellent public relations and sales promotion personality—the German engineer. But the last thing Mr. Davidsky wanted to be called was a "German."

It was not long before the partners realized the usefulness of the "German" engineer image. It was used in all sales pitches, and wherever possible he was introduced to potential customers. A whole legend developed about the time and effort that the foundry had spent securing his services, about his background, about his work, and about his relationships with the workers.

The businessmen in general, as well as the foundry's customers, were as susceptible, if not more so, to the German engineer image as were the workers. Mr. Davidsky himself realized this and, though he did not like it, played his role for all it was worth. At the same time, he continued to perform effectively in his production and technical capacities.

Mr. P. Dastur. At the outset, Mr. Dastur was approached by Mr. Mehta and Mr. Davidsky to become a partner in this venture mainly because he could secure the necessary money to set up the foundry. In initially securing the loan at such a reasonable interest rate, Mr. Dastur certainly provided valuable service. Later, when construction was bogged down and more money was needed, Mr. Dastur came through with flying colors.

In January 1952, when he began devoting full time to the foundry, Mr. Dastur took full responsibility for the purchasing, financial, and accounting aspects of the business and did his best to help out in the other areas. He recruited six workers and a foreman, and, while the foundry was under construction, he secured about seventy percent of the Rs. 86,000 order which the foundry had prior to its opening for business.

During the first year of the foundry's operation, Mr. Dastur made several trips all over India to secure orders as well as to make purchases. However, though Mr. Mehta made fewer trips he was more successful in securing orders. Mr. Dastur gradually began losing interest in sales and let Mr. Mehta assume major responsibility for it. But he continued to assume the finance and purchasing responsibilities.

During the middle part of the second year of the company's existence, Mr. Dastur, without prior consultation with the other partners, hired a young full-time clerk, fresh out of commerce college. Since his salary was rather nominal, the other partners did not object when the young man, Mr. Mohmed, came to work for the company in June 1953.

Mr. Dastur felt that the accounting and bookkeeping aspects of his job assignments were too routine for him. He gradually trained the new accountant to take over the responsibilities for accounting. The bright new accountant also assumed the authority for this function and gradually started taking over some of the purchasing and other aspects of Mr. Dastur's work.

Mr. Dastur came to the company's office regularly until about a year after the hiring of Mr. Mohmed. Around the end of 1954, he hardly ever came to the office—about twice a month was average—and began devoting most of his time

The Universal Parts Company

to his father's business, though he continued to spend time on the purchasing of items for special orders and on important financial problems.

The Assistant Manager. Mr. K. V. R. John, the assistant manager, was hired by Mr. Mehta. John, as everyone called him, was working for a small foundry in Karuvatta, Kerala, when he first met Mr. Mehta. Learning of the new foundry which Mr. Mehta was going to start, he offered his services. He had a bachelor's degree in arts, and four years of experience in the foundry business. When he joined the Universal Parts Company, he was only 27 years old.

In the beginning, Mr. John worked as an assistant to all three partners and helped each one in the performance of his duties. Soon, however, he served primarily as an assistant to Mr. Mehta. Though he continued to assist the other partners, Mr. John spent over 80 percent of his time on the tasks assigned to him by Mr. Mehta—mainly coordinating and supervising the work of the three foremen and inventory control.

The Foremen. All three foremen—here designated as A, B, and C—had varying degrees of experience in the foundry business, and two had previous experience as foremen. Foreman A had worked at the same foundry in which Mr. Mehta formerly worked and foreman B used to be one of the best workers there. Foreman C had 12 years of foundry experience—5 of these as a foreman in a foundry which specialized in parts for oil mills.

Foreman C was in charge of 24 workers concerned chiefly with the parts production for oil mills. Foreman A, with 10 workers, was concerned mainly with special orders such as plumbing equipment, barbell sets, lathe shafts, custom ordered parts for machinery, roller wheels for lifts (elevators), etc. Foreman B, with the remaining workers, took charge of overloads from Foreman A's and C's teams and was mainly responsible for preparing the molds, for checking inventory, and for maintenance. Foreman B also played an active role in training all workers.

Mr. F. Mohmed. In June 1953, Mr. Mohmed was hired as a clerk by Mr. Dastur to help him with the purchasing and accounting aspect of the business. Mr. Mohmed's hiring came as a surprise to the other two partners, but he soon found favor with them by his excellent work, especially the routinized aspect of it.

Mr. Mohmed had recently graduated with a B. Com. degree. He was 22 years old when he joined the company. He was hired mainly to help Mr. Dastur. During the first six months, he took over not only the accounting and bookkeeping responsibilities of Mr. Dastur, but within two years he also became quite adept in the routine purchasing aspects of the business. With the gradual, though never complete, withdrawal from the company scene of Mr. Dastur, the partners began to rely more and more on Mr. Mohmed. Nevertheless, he was still considered and treated as a clerk. Though he never made any major decisions on his own, he was practically always consulted by the partners in matters concerning the financial and purchasing aspects of the company.

The partners found that many of their duties overlapped and that even in

1956 they had never really pinpointed their jobs nor those of most of their employees. In 1956, they first discussed the possibilities of developing an organization chart and some sort of an organization manual. They were uncertain, however, as to whether the chart and manual would be an asset to their organization, nor did they feel qualified to develop a chart and manual.

PRODUCTION

Mr. Davidsky was considered the only real expert in this area, and he had the final word in all matters concerning production. After the first few months, Mr. Dastur was never consulted in these matters, but Mr. Mehta helped out as best he could in the performance of this function and, by 1956, became quite expert himself in the production area.

The usual policy was to let Mr. Davidsky know what and how much was needed and then to give him a free hand in fulfilling the production requirement. He developed the production plans and schedules, worked on new product designs, improved old ones, and made sure of all control factors.

As mentioned in the discussion of the foremen, production was divided into three departments, each under the supervision of one foreman. Foreman C, with 24 workers, was in charge of the standard parts of oil mills, mainly grinders. The grinders were cylinders of various standard sizes with heavy spiralling rims. Once the monthly sales forecast was made, these cylinders and other oil mill parts were produced on a continuous production basis.

The production of these grinders, with the heavy flow of orders, became a continuous production process which was soon highly standardized. These grinders and other standard parts accounted for about 80% of the company's sales volume. After the first year, their production was relatively routinized and posed no major problem for the company except when the orders became very heavy.

When the orders were heavy, foreman B and his group would take up the extra load. This would happen approximately every two months and would last from one to two weeks at a time. Usually, the production of foreman B's group was comparatively slow and the number of discards due to poor quality was about three times as high as foreman C's group. Though Mr. Davidsky tried hard, he could not remedy this situation.

Whenever customers rejected or complained about the grinders, it became common practice on the part of foreman C and his group to blame foreman B and his team for the poor workmanship. Mr. Davidsky also found that during the periods when foreman B and his team were working on the grinders, foreman C's team produced larger quantities, but the quality suffered considerably—though not up to the point where there would be greater rejections. He brought this to the attention of the foreman, but neither of them could solve this problem.

Foreman B and his team spent most of their time in making castings and

The Universal Parts Company

molds, in checking inventory, and in general maintenance of the foundry. They fired the furnaces, hauled the coke, kept the foundry clean, counted and watched the inventory, etc. They were usually sufficiently ahead of schedule to help out team A and C whenever necessary.

Foreman A had the majority of the skilled workers on his team. They were mainly in charge of the special orders. After the first year, Mr. Davidsky spent most of his time with the production aspect of the business which concerned foreman A. For special orders, new designs and methods had to be developed. Also, some experimentation was required. There was greater concern over cost and more planning was required, since the manufacture of certain special products had no precedent for the company.

It was estimated that special orders accounted for about 20% of the company's sales volume. The customers of these special orders always had high praise for the workmanship. Mr. Davidsky found this aspect of his work the most interesting and challenging and often said that this part of his job was what kept him going. Both Mr. Davidsky and Mr. Mehta felt that the special orders were worth the extra labor and time mainly because they brought prestige to their organization. However, Mr. Dastur did not share their opinion. He felt that the special orders took up too much of his and Mr. Davidsky's time and that the special order business was not large enough to compensate for it.

By 1956, the foundry was operating at full production capacity on a six-day, 8-hour per day basis. Except for 1954, there were about 20 to 30 days in a year when the workers, especially those concerned with special orders, worked overtime. In 1956, the partners realized that if their business expanded above Rs. 300,000 sales, they would need to expand or have more overtime.

SALES

The partners realized that, by and large, the business they were in had a seller's market, provided the product was reliable and the price competitive. Yet, they felt some sort of a sales organization was needed to take full advantage of the seller's market and be prepared for the time when market conditions would not be as favorable.

While the foundry was being built, Mr. Dastur traveled to various places in India mainly to contact those organizations with which Mr. Mehta had dealt in his former job. Mr. Dastur continued the sales effort during the first year of the foundry's existence. During that year, Mr. Mehta also made a few trips which were more successful than Mr. Dastur's. At the end of the first year, Mr. Mehta took over the major responsibility for sales.

During the second year, Mr. Mehta had developed a six-part territorial division of the company's market. The territory in and around Bombay was the largest in area, present sales, and future potential and was reserved by Mr. Mehta solely for personal exploration. In the other five territories, he secured the services of salesmen, manufacturing agents, and purchasing agents of customer-companies, on a straight 8% commission on gross sales. The manufacturer's agents were selected for their experience in the foundry line, the purchasing agents came from the companies which had already bought some of the foundry's products, and the individual salesmen were selected on a come-one come-all basis.

This sales force was free to get orders from anyone, anywhere in their territory, on a commission basis. Each person who offered his services as a salesman was provided with a brochure which contained the necessary information—including descriptions of products, prices, and order forms. No limit was set on the number of salesmen per territory. No records were kept of their progress, except in the case of purchasing agents of customer-companies and the manufacturer's agents, since they were the only ones who provided a relatively steady flow of orders.

Once the sales force was assembled, no sales promotion was attempted by mail or advertising. Mr. Mehta continued to visit the different territories during the second year to maintain customer relations, to seek new customers, and to increase sales from old customers. But when his trips became very infrequent in 1954, sales fell, and Mr. Mehta realized that he would never be able to avoid making these trips or even to cut them down substantially.

The orders which these salesmen were to secure were for grinders and standard parts only. Whenever a special job was to be done, both Mr. Mehta and Mr. Davidsky felt that it required face to face communication with one of them and preferably both. Hence, the jobbing aspects of the business were confined mainly to the Bombay territory once Mr. Mehta cut down on his travels. Very often, the company had to refuse orders for special jobs from territories other than Bombay.

As each new company was added to the foundry's customer list, usually a new purchasing agent from that company was appointed as salesman for the foundry. The commission given to the purchasing agents of customer-companies posed a rather delicate problem. Most of these agents either overtly or covertly suggested that the bill sent to the company by Universal Parts should not show the 8% commission and that it should be paid directly to the purchasing agent. The partners could not arrive at any definite and general policy regarding this matter, and they tried to treat each case individually. The responsibility for this decision was placed on Mr. Mehta, and he felt it to be an immense problem because of the overtones of bribery connected with this situation as well as the potential danger to sales and the problems it created in bookkeeping and taxes.

By 1956, the company had a "sales force" of 134 persons. Of these, 38 were purchasing agents, four were manufacturer's agents, and the rest were other individuals interested in selling for the company. The majority of the last group did not send in a single order and only 5 were considered good salesmen for the foundry's products. Two of the four manufacturer's agents and 29 purchasing

The Universal Parts Company

agents sent in a relatively steady and predictable flow of orders as did the customers from the Bombay territory. The other two manufacturer's agents, the remaining purchasing agents, and some individual salesmen sent in orders that were unpredictable and accounted for the heavy load of production at certain times.

PRICING

Both Mr. Mehta and Mr. John had worked for successful foundries, which produced and sold the same line of goods as the grinders and standard parts that concerned about 80% of the Universal Parts Company's business. Since it was anticipated that many of the Universal Parts Company's customers would be previous customers of the foundries where Mr. Mehta and Mr. John had worked, it was decided that the prices of the products of Universal Parts would be competitive with those of their former employers.

Regarding the special orders, the pricing policy could not be so easily dismissed. Mr. Dastur set up a pricing formula based on estimates rather than any factual data. He decided that the cost of a special order would be direct cost of labor plus the direct cost of materials, plus half the amount of that total, for manufacturing and administrative overhead and 40% of that total for profit.

Hence, for example, the price of hypothetical product X would be:

Direct cost of labor	25
Direct cost of material	75
	100
50% of total for manufacture and administrative overhead	50
	150
40% of total for profit	60
Final price	210

Initially, Mr. Mehta and Mr. Davidsky felt this pricing policy to be inadequate and unrealistic, but they were unable to come up with anything better than what Mr. Dastur had provided. Mr. Dastur said that he had figured this formula out, though he did not explain how, and that the formula took adequate consideration of all the necessary factors. Eventually the two other partners accepted this formula, and, by 1956, no one in the company questioned the validity of this pricing formula.

PURCHASING

When the foundry was ready in December 1951, Mr. Dastur was placed in full charge of all purchasing from pencils to steel. During the first year, he explored the market to find suitable suppliers. By the end of the first year, he maintained steady suppliers, and felt that there was no longer any need to explore the market or get various bids.

By the end of the first year, the three partners set down the minimum and maximum limits for the inventory of all items. It became the job of foreman B and his group to keep periodic checks on the inventory. When the minimum or close to minimum inventory standard for a given item was reached, foreman B orally informed Mr. Dastur, and since 1954, Mr. Mohmed. Mr. Dastur and later Mr. Mohmed then ordered the necessary items.

These policies applied only to the standard items purchased by the foundry, and, by mid-1954, this aspect of the business was highly routinized. In spite of the routinization, the information regarding minimum inventory often did not reach Mr. Dastur, and later Mr. Mohmed, on time. They blamed foreman B, who in turn blamed his workers, who in turn blamed each other for this. Though the company continued to use this method, they did not find it very satisfactory.

In case the items required for special orders, Mr. Davidsky made out a list of all the items required for a given order. This list was submitted in writing to Mr. Dastur, who checked this list against what was already in the foundry's inventory. He explored the market for the items that were not available and tried to purchase them at the most advantageous price.

As mentioned earlier, by the end of 1954, Mr. Mohmed had taken over most of the work load of Mr. Dastur. However, Mr. Dastur continued even in 1956 to do the purchasing for special orders. Also, whenever there was a market shortage of items required by the foundry, Mr. Dastur's services were called upon, and, by hook or by crook, he usually succeeded in securing these items.

CONCLUSION

In 1956, Mr. Davidsky married an Australian woman. In January 1957, he told his partners that he had applied for immigration to Australia. He felt that it would take about six months to clear his immigration requirements but that he was willing to stay on a little longer if necessary. At first, the partners tried to dissuade Mr. Davidsky from leaving. But his decision was based on personal reasons and there was nothing the partners could offer to keep him in their business.

This crucial decision of Mr. Davidsky led the partners to make a full analysis of their past and present problems and to analyze the future nature and progress of their company.

8

S.G.H. Products Company

"You can sum up our company's progress like you can the progress of India. We have had success, but not as much as was possible and before we can progress further we have to face up to enormous problems."

Some of the problems Mr. Shah, the owner-manager faced, were tied in with organizational changes and others with business-government relationships.

In 1945, Mr. Shah experimented with manufacturing and bottling a variety of syrups[1], from a treasured family recipe, for his relatives and friends. Initially all the manufacturing and bottling was conducted in the basement of his vast mansion in Poona. Being independently wealthy he had no commercial interests or intentions for his syrup. However, it became so popular with his family and friends, that upon their urging he invested Rs. 35,000 in a small bottling plant in Poona. The plant started its operations on June 4th, 1946 and its product found a rapid market.

With the steady growth of this venture, Mr. Shah took in two relatives, Mr. Gandhi and Mr. Harkisandas, as "sleeping" partners. Each of them invested Rs. 85,000 for a 24% interest each in what was now known as the S.G.H. Products Company.

With the advent of this partnership in February, 1947, the bottling plant in Poona was closed and a new plant was opened in the outskirts of Bombay. The new operations included not only the bottling of syrups, but also the canning of fruits, especially mangoes, and the bottling and canning of edible oils and shortening (ghee). The canning aspect of production was mainly mechanized; edible oils and shortening were partially mechanized and the production of syrups followed time-honored practices.

The steady growth of the S.G.H. Products Company along with the rapid and enormous changes that India underwent since 1947 posed problems for the company especially in the realm of organization and business-government relationships.

ORGANIZATION

With the inception of its Bombay operations with 190 employees, the company hired a retired army officer, Captain Jones, as general manager, Mr. Jones

---

[1] Syrup is called sherbet in India. It is a concentrated mixture of sugar and fruit juices, both natural and artificial, as well as essence of rose, vanilla, almond, etc. A small quantity is mixed with water or milk, usually with ice, for a refreshing soft drink. It is also used in flavoring desserts.

was in his mid-sixties and had some canning experience on a farm in England. From the reminiscences of Mr. Shah it appeared that Captain Jones was mainly interested in the canning aspect of the business, had some interest in syrups, but was little, if at all, interested in the ghee or edible oil products. From a functional point of view, his interests and capabilities were also varied. He took great interest in sales and public relations, some interest in production, but very little in finance and accounting. Mr. Shah offered Captain Jones a relatively free hand in the areas of Jones' interest and took over sole or partial responsibilities of the other areas depending on the degree of Jones' interests in them.

Though no formal organization chart was developed or made by the company, from Mr. Shah's recollections, the following picture emerges, as shown in Exhibit 1.

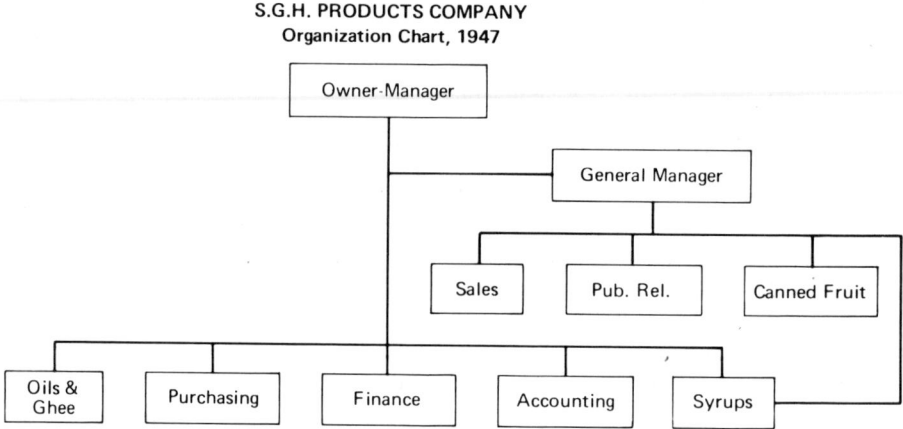

EXHIBIT 1
S.G.H. PRODUCTS COMPANY
Organization Chart, 1947

Though no formal statement to this effect was made in 1947, the company envisioned itself as consisting of eight departments—three on product basis and five on functional basis.

In 1949 Captain Jones suggested new canning machinery. About the time the machinery arrived in 1950, Captain Jones departed for England.

After Captain Jones' departure, Mr. Shah took over full management responsibility but within two months he hired a relative, Mr. Mehta, an engineer, as his assistant. In spite of new machinery the company was now employing over 200 persons, and Mr. Shah had been burdened with two new departments—engineering and plant maintenance. If there was an organization chart in late 1950, Mr. Shah agreed it would have been similar to the one in Exhibit 2; and this was the type of organization he had until 1955.

Mr. Shah felt that during this period (1950-1955) his plant was capable of doubling its output, and that there was more than sufficient demand for his products to meet this output. Though he realized this potential as early as 1951, he felt that the transition from Captain Jones to Mr. Mehta was bogging him down. Though he added more personnel to his organization it did not lead to

S.G.H. Products Company

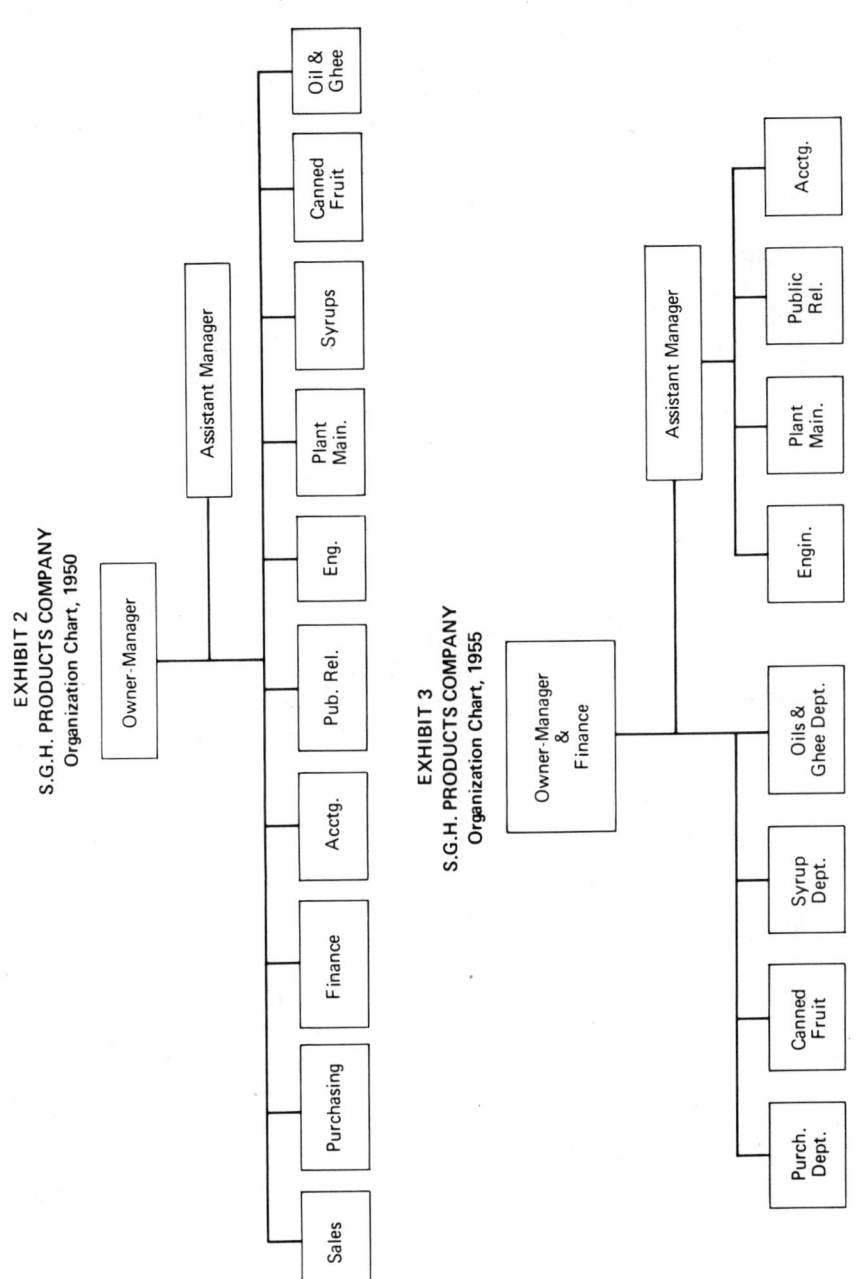

compensatory advantages in efficiency or profit. He realized that in spite of all his efforts he could not efficiently bring about the growth of his company.

By 1955, Mr. Mehta had taken over all engineering plant maintenance and public relations duties. He also became an expert accountant and took over those duties as well. Mr. Shah realized about his time that informal department heads had emerged in the areas of sales and purchasing as well as in each of the product areas. Mr. Shah continued to take full responsibility for the finance area and still maintained his role as general manager. These changes gradually brought about a new organization structure which Mr. Shah said was established and stabilized in 1955 as shown in Exhibit 3.

Each of the five departments now had a formal head and the assistant manager's duties were better delineated. The S.G.H. Products Company continued expanding. In 1957 a new line was added—the canning of pillau, curries, and other prepared foods. Mr. Shah took full responsibility for this area as he did for the hiring of all personnel.

In 1957 two competing canning and bottling companies had achieved some prominence, and Mr. Shah took upon himself the responsibility of advertising and market research.

In 1960 the S.G.H. Products Company had 340 employees. There was still 25% idle capacity in the canning plant, and room for growth in the other products. However, Mr. Shah felt that in spite of new personnel and better methods of production, his company was not making the progress it should. After attending a number of management conferences in Bombay, Mr. Shah realized that his organization structure might be one of the major variables to hinder the growth of his company.

Mr. Shah felt that there was a need for a formal organization structure for his company that would lead to greater efficiency and take into consideration the growth potential of his organization.

BUSINESS-GOVERNMENT RELATIONSHIPS

Another important area in which Mr. Shah felt that he was faced with difficulties was what he called the socialistic approach of the Indian Government. He believed that the policies pursued by the government presented an unfavorable climate for the growth of his company. He felt that there was a general feeling that management in India was out to make a quick profit at the expense of the workers and the public, and that being in business for oneself was not considered a very respectable occupation. He believed this lack of respect stemmed from the fact that there were so many laws and regulations that restricted managerial freedom, with the result that no business could survive for long without breaking some of these laws. He also felt that many government officials who enforced these laws were incompetent or corrupt or both, and that every businessman, at one time or another, had to resort to some form of bribery or "baksheesh."

S.G.H. Products Company

This practice of bribery was a great mental stress. In many cases bribery is considered a criminal offence, subject to fines and imprisonments. Every so often a businessman is apprehended on charges of bribing a government official, often fined and sometimes imprisoned. Though these cases are rare, most businessmen feel a little guilty and many spend restless nights thinking they may be next.

Another problem area for Mr. Shah was the government policy on foreign exchange. Mr. Shah was faced with the problems of the lack of foreign exchange to buy parts for the machinery involved in his canning operations, to buy new machinery to plan for the growth and expansion of his operations, and to convert his largely manual and antiquated bottling operations to a modern well-equipped plant.

Mr. Shah felt that given proper equipment and time, his company could sell its products abroad, especially to countries which had a large Indian population. However, he felt that without the foreign exchange needed for modern and expanded manufacturing operations, as well as foreign exchange for visiting and exploiting international markets, he could not successfully compete abroad. He cited the example that at one time he received a substantial order from the United States for his bottled syrup. However, his whole shipment was returned when some of the bottles were found to contain foreign matter. Out of a shipment of 2 gross bottles, five had one or more hairs, two had pebbles and four had insects. Mr. Shah was assured that unless he had better bottling equipment, such problems would continue to exist. Like many medium-sized business owners, Mr. Shah held the opinion that to earn foreign exchange, one would first have to spend some foreign exchange. The Indian Government's policy was not well established in this respect, was usually not conducive to the possibilities of a foreign market for the S.G.H. Company's type of products, and the government officials were not sympathetic to the medium-sized businessman's pleas.

Most European and American businessmen envy the Indian businessman because of the sellers' market most products have in India and because the hourly wages in India are extremely low.

The current trend in average hourly labor costs, including wages and fringe benefits, in manufacturing industries, is estimated as:

Britain	$ .85
France	.83
Germany	.94
India	.21
Italy	.66
Netherlands	.66
Sweden	1.29
U.S.A.	2.85

Mr. Shah felt that Indian businessmen undoubtedly have the advantage of lower labor costs. However, he feels that this advantage is off-set by the fact that the productivity of Indian labor is not as high as their counterparts in Europe and the United States. Fuel costs in India are higher, the selling prices are lower, and raw materials are rarely cheaper and usually more expensive.

He stated, for example, that bottles are not cheaper in India and cans are more expensive than in Europe or the United States. Fruits, a major raw material in his products, are often more expensive and the wholesale price of sugar, another important raw material, is practically the same.

The S.G.H. Company's products no longer have a sellers market and there is strong price competition. Even if the S.G.H. Company had a monopoly, the low income level of the Indian consumers would automatically put a ceiling on the price, which would be far lower than in Europe or the United States. Hence Mr. Shah felt that the greatest growth potential, especially from the profit point of view, would be to sell his products abroad. How to develop an export market was considered a major problem by Mr. Shah.

9

Bharat Company

Bharat Company (A)

The Bharat Company had begun operations in Dadar, a suburb of Bombay, in November 1950. It was owned by three persons but most general administrative decisions were made by one man, Mr. J. J. Divecha.

The company employed about 45 workers, three foremen and an assistant manager. All the foremen and most of the workers had been with the company since its inception. As the company progressed, the employees received increases in salaries but there was no regular bonus system.

Instead of the bonus system, the company rewarded employees individually or in terms of their needs. For example, if a worker produced exceptionally good products, or made special efforts to meet a deadline, Mr. Divecha rarely failed to reward him, either with money, an extra day off, a raise in pay or a gift. If a worker had financial troubles, Mr. Divecha was always sympathetic and either gave him money or a loan at very little or no interest. In sickness, the employee could rely on the company to pay his medical bills; in marriage, he could be certain of a gift.

All these decisions were handled by Mr. Divecha, and other than for loans or raise in salary, he rarely kept any records. The outside accountant was always worried that the income tax investigation authorities would not look too favorably on this practice and complained that it made his job more difficult. Also, the amount of money spent on employees in this manner varied from year to year and had no relationship to the profitability of the company. One of the partners felt that it would be difficult to continue this practice in lean years. The third partner felt that since only some of the employees got rewarded in this system and since the company followed no set policy in this respect, it was unfair to the employees, especially to those who could not convince Mr. Divecha that they had special problems, or whose special efforts did not come to the attention of Mr. Divecha. However, there was never a major complaint regarding this system from the workers.

In mid-1958, the partners met with the accountant to decide what changes should be made in this policy.

Bharat Company (B)

In December, 1958, Mr. Divecha, at the coaxing of the accountant and his partners since the earlier meeting, decided to change from the present system of "rewards" and "handouts," to a year-end bonus system. They all agreed that the simplest way would be to share 20% of net profit, by dividing it equally among all employees. They decided to pay this bonus in January of each year starting with 1960. The partners estimated that the bonus system would cost the company a little more per year than the old system. However, they felt it worth the extra cost in terms of savings in time and effort by Mr. Divecha and the accountant.

Mr. Divecha called a meeting of all employees in the early part of January 1959. One of Mr. Divecha's partners introduced the accountant as an outside authority. The accountant explained the advantages of the new bonus system, how it would cost the company more, how it would be more equitable and take all workers into consideration, how important government regulations were regarding this matter, etc. Finally, a partner of Mr. Divecha delivered a short speech, saying that none of the employees should bother Mr. Divecha with their problems since he was a busy man and besides he would no longer give extra days off, or money, either in the form of loans or gifts for a job well done, or for special problems. He concluded by imploring the workers to work hard together because from now on they were all partners in the company and they would all share equally.

During the days that followed, all went well and the partners even sensed a greater effort on the part of the employees. In mid-February, one of the workers came to Mr. Divecha's office bringing a small gift and a big smile. He announced that he had just become a father for the third time since his joining the company. During the first occasion, he had received Rs. 15, and at the birth of the second child, Rs. 20, from Mr. Divecha. This time Mr. Divecha did not give him a single paisa. The worker left his gift and his smile in Mr. Divecha's office. A few weeks later, another worker became a father, but did not even inform Mr. Divecha.

A few days later, one of the foremen came to Mr. Divecha to request a loan of Rs. 100 to send his wife to visit her family in their village. This foreman had worked for Mr. Divecha even prior to the establishment of the present company and Mr. Divecha felt rather embarrassed to refuse him this loan. He suggested to the foreman that he seek his loan elsewhere and that if he did not succeed, Mr. Divecha would think of something else. Mr. Divecha felt like giving the man a loan from his own pocket but did not want to set such a precedent. Though he refused, he had no doubt in his mind that the relationship between him and the foreman was rather strained.

Bharat Company (B)

A few days later, Mr. Divecha went up to a worker and praised him for a job well done. The worker replied (though jovially with a typical 'yes-maybe-no' head movement of the Indians), that working hard makes little difference any more, since hard workers and lazy workers get the same rewards.

After various such incidents, Mr. Divecha realized that their plan was definitely not working well. The other partners began to notice this also, not only in the workers' efforts, but also in their morale.

In January of 1960, the partners began to wonder what they did wrong in introducing the new bonus plan and what steps they would have to take to remedy this situation.

10

Korewala Kwality Kore Mills

The Korewala Kwality Kore Mills is a family owned textile mill with headquarters in Bombay. It was founded in 1911 and enjoyed consistent earnings except for small deficits during the two years preceding the Second World War. The mill had its peak sales year in 1957. Since then sales had been slowly, but steadily on the decline as evidenced by the data in Table 1.

TABLE 1
Comparative Profit and Loss Statements, December 31, 1956-1962

Year	1956	1957	1958	1959	1960	1961	1962
Sales	Rs.591,422	693,378	621,632	582,739	579,911	573,343	558,093
Sales	100%	100%	100%	100%	100%	100%	100%
Cost of Materials and Mfg. Overhead	42.6	38.7	41.9	43.8	45.7	47.0	46.1
Salaries, Commissions, Wages and Adminis. Overhead	19.4	18.6	19.2	18.3	19.7	18.4	19.0
Other Overhead Costs	23.8	25.9	22.7	19.8	17.2	15.7	14.7
Profit	14.2%	16.8%	16.2%	18.1%	17.4%	18.9%	20.2%
Profit	Rs. 83,981	116,487	100,704	105,475	100,904	108,361	112,734

In February 1963 the Board of Directors of Korewala Kwality Kore Mills called a special meeting to discuss: (1) the ways and means whereby the mill could improve its sales, (2) the status of the sales organization, (3) certain problems with salesmen, and (4) policy decisions regarding the mill's relationship with the government.

ORGANIZATION

The KKK Mills is owned by the Shah family who also own a number of other business concerns. Though the KKK Mills did not have an organization chart, Exhibit 1 endeavors to present a partial chart of the organization.

The Shah family members comprised the board of directors. They appointed a manager, Mr. Ram, who had an assistant manager. The fourth level in the organization structure consisted of department masters (example, spinning master), who reported directly to the managing agent. Under the assistant man-

Korewala Kwality Kore Mills

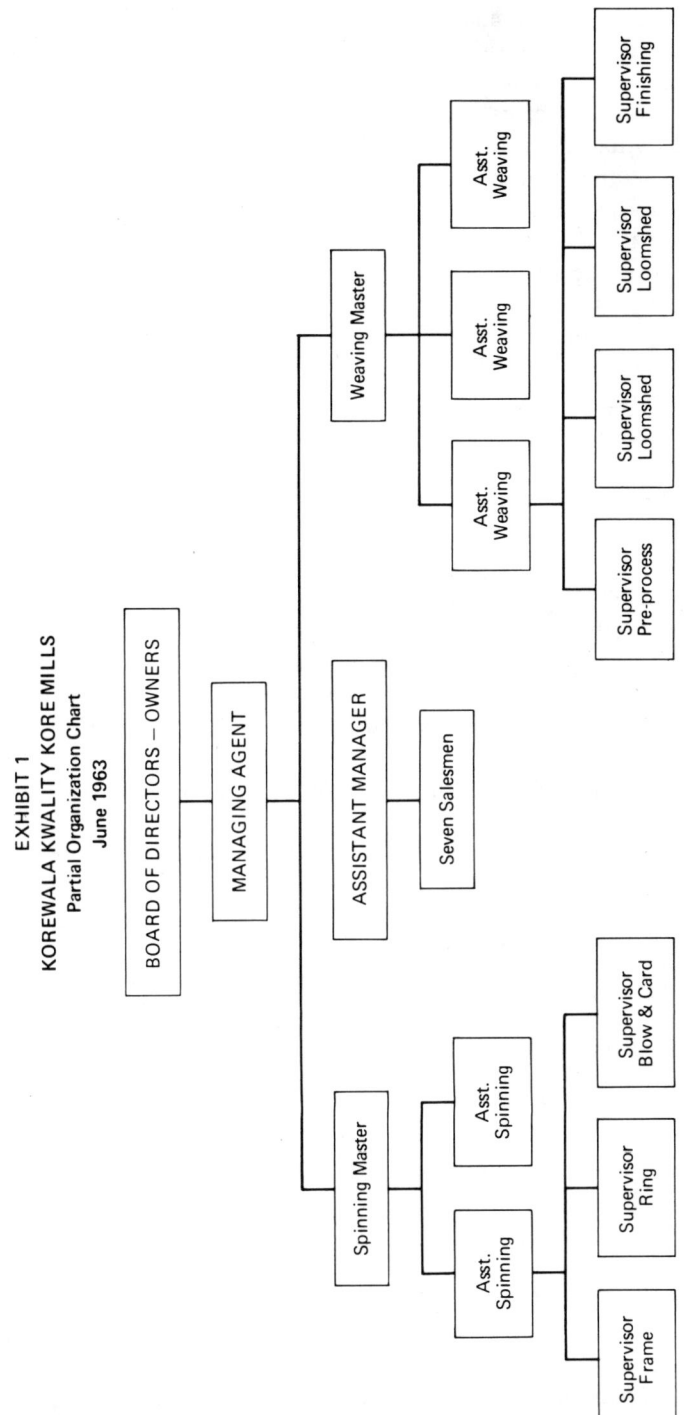

EXHIBIT 1
KOREWALA KWALITY KORE MILLS
Partial Organization Chart
June 1963

ager there were seven salesmen who reported directly to him. Under the department masters there were assistants. Under the assistants there were supervisors, and finally the production workers.

The board of directors established the overall major policies and objectives of the firm, after consultation with Mr. Ram, and usually after some consultation with the other managerial staff members affected by these decisions. The manager, who held this job for 16 years, was responsible for the day to day operations of the KKK Mills and for the implementation of the board's policies. The assistant manager aided the manager in these tasks but his major duties were that of an accountant and supervisor of the company salesmen.

The board of directors routinely met at KKK Mills on the first Monday of each month to study the mill's progress, to make suggestions, and sometimes to set new policies and objectives. On important, but rare, occasions they called a special meeting such as the one in February, 1963.

THE MILL

KKK was a composite mill for the manufacture of borders (Kore in Gujerati), with 30,450 spindles and 450 looms. Once the raw materials had been purchased the mill performed the spinning, weaving, dyeing and/or bleaching, as well as the finishing operations. A considerable amount of handwork was also required in manufacturing, especially that involving complicated borders. The mill employed about 195 persons, and it sold all its goods to wholesalers under the KKK brand.

Both the owners and the managers felt that KKK Mills had its strongest point in the fact that it emphasized and delivered quality goods. KKK had built a solid reputation in the market as well as the industry for consistently high quality. The owners as well as management spared no effort in maintaining this reputation.

One of the marks of quality in Kore manufacturing was to maintain a uniform edge and width. In order to do this, loom speeds at KKK were slower than in other mills. They could still compete on the basis of price because most of the loom operators were old expert employees and were willing to tend more looms than was usually the practice. Morale among the workers was also much higher than usual in this industry.

THE PRODUCTS

KKK Mills specialized in borders for saris, petticoats, blouses, bed spreads, decorations, etc. The borders were made of cotton, art silk, synthetic yarns or a combination thereof. These yarns were woven into intricate designs, in various lengths and widths. A single design often embodies as many as twenty-five different colors. The Kore was woven on special looms which had interchangeable beams so that different widths and styles of borders could be manufactured.

The smallest length manufactured, of a particular design of kore, was 100 yards. All borders were manufactured in increments of 100 yards, (i.e., 100, 200, 300, 500, 700, etc.) up to 1,000 yards. The width could vary from an inch to nine inches. However, most Kores were plain. Others were manufactured in three basic designs: geometrical, flowers, and birds and/or animals. Geometrical designs were most popular. Though the mill introduced new designs from time to time, the majority of the Kores designs were based on about a hundred standard patterns developed by the mill. However, different color combinations and minor pattern changes were quite common.

THE INDUSTRY

There were no large mills in Bombay that specialized solely in borders. However, there were many mills that manufactured borders, either separately or as an integral part of the larger product. For example, many saris were manufactured with borders, as were blouse pieces, table cloths, curtains, etc. Hence, the border industry was highly competitive and though the demand for textile products was increasing, so was the supply. As in all textile mills in India, the margin of profit was relatively low, as compared with other manufacturing industries.

Traditionally, textiles had been the backbone of India's industrial development. After the American War of Independence, cotton was one of the major exports of India. "The first cotton mill in India was built in Calcutta in 1818, but the real beginnings of the industry were made in Bombay in the year 1854, with predominantly Indian capital and enterprise."[1] The first capitalists in India were textile magnates. In many cases it was the textile industry which provided the capital and management know-how that spurred the growth of other industries in India.

Today the textile industry continues to play a major role in the Indian economy. Approximately 5.5 percent of India's outlay on industries during the second five year plan went to the textile industry.[2] The percentage increase in production of cotton yarn in 1960-1961 over 1955-1956 was 19.6 percent and in cotton cloth 29.2 percent.[3] The growth of the cotton textile industry in the twentieth century is shown in Table 2.[4]

There were nearly 500 cotton textile mills in India in 1961, which represented an investment in excess of Rs. 120 crores and which employed nine lakh workers.[5]

In the textile industry, various types of marketing channels were used by manufacturers. The seven important alternative marketing channels in the textile industry are shown in Exhibit 2 in an increasing order of importance.

[1] *India 1962* The Publications Division, Ministry of Information & Broadcasting Government of India, New Delhi, India, p. 295.
[2] *Ibid.*, p. 306.
[3] *Ibid.*, p. 309.
[4] *Ibid.*, p. 314.
[5] *Ibid.*, p. 315.

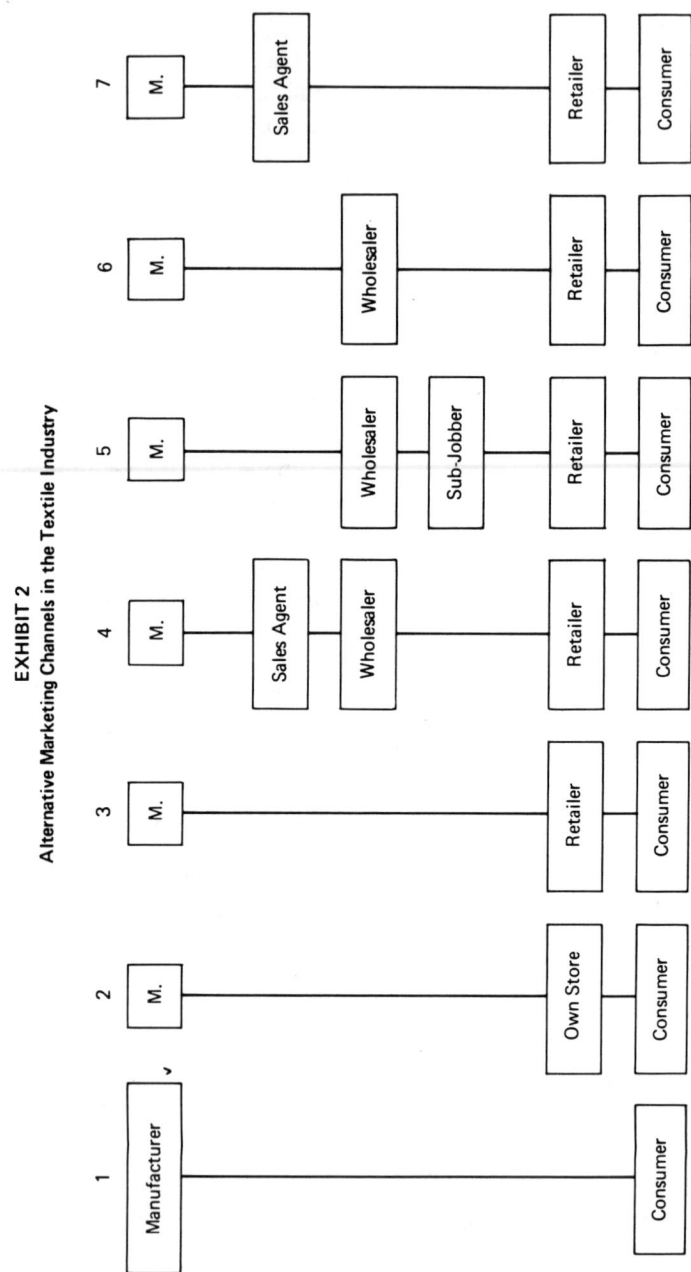

EXHIBIT 2
Alternative Marketing Channels in the Textile Industry

TABLE 2
Production of Cotton Yarn and Cloth

Year	Production (lakh lbs)	
	Cotton yarn (lakh lbs)	Cotton cloth (lakh yds)
1901	57,30	12,00
1911	62,50	26,70
1921	69,40	40,30
1931	96,60	67,20
1941	157,70	109,30
1947	129,60	376,20
1950	117,48	366,70
1955	163,08	509,40
1956	167,12	530,66
1957	178,01	531,74
1958	168,54	492,70
1959	172,28	492,54
1960 (provisional)	171,00	504,40

Some mills relied solely on one of these alternative channels but most combined two or more methods in the distribution of their goods. The trend was toward textile mills opening their own stores without abandoning their previous channels of distribution. This was especially true of large textile mills who opened retail stores in the large cities. However, smaller mills could not do this, since good store locations were difficult to find and very expensive to maintain.

INDUSTRY-GOVERNMENT RELATIONS

The textile industry was highly regulated by the government. Some of these regulations were in terms of "codes of conduct" rather than laws. These codes were developed by the government of India in consultation with various industry representatives and industry organizations. Among these codes was one to maintain existing prices.

In terms of the effectiveness of these codes they were, for all intent and purpose, very akin to laws because of the Industries (Development and Regulation) Act of 1951. "Under the Act all new and existing undertakings and any substantial expansion of existing undertakings were required to be licensed. The government was authorized to examine the working of any industrial undertaking and to issue such directions as they considered necessary. If the undertaking continued to be mismanaged, the government was empowered to take over its management or control."[6]

[6]*Ibid.*, p. 301.

In 1961, 162 industries, including the textile industry, fell within the scope of this act. Though the law was sensibly enforced, it was by reason of this act that the "codes of conduct" were so effective. Not following the code could be construed as "mismanagement," giving the government the right to take over the management of a company or the entire industry, if necessary, under the power granted the government by the Industries Act of 1951.

There was a strong feeling in the textile industrial circle that small mills need not worry too much about government laws and codes. However, the owners and management of KKK Mills were divided in this respect. The owners believed that KKK Mills had little to worry about in terms of government regulations. Management felt that not only were they legally obliged to obey the government laws and codes, but that such regulations, and compliance to them, was essential for the survival of small and medium sized mills and for the survival of competition within the industry. The owners, on the other hand, felt that government interference affected them adversely and their philosophy of business lead them to pseudo compliance to government codes or to no compliance to the codes if the code affected them adversely.

To date, the KKK Mills had no trouble with the Indian government nor did they foresee any in the near future. However, management felt that the board should establish a firm policy in this area, whatever that policy might be. Management would prefer a policy ruling that would require compliance to all regulations, but thus far the board had been unwilling to commit itself. To convince the board to establish such a policy was considered by management to be a major problem. The manager felt he should discuss this during the special meeting called by the board.

CUSTOMERS

During the early years of its existence, KKK Mills sold its products to whomever would buy them. In the 1940's, the company began to make greater use of wholesalers. In the early fifties KKK Mills decided to sell to wholesalers only. By 1954-1955 it sold its products through 30 to 35 wholesalers. In late 1958, the customer policy was changed again and KKK Mills decided to sell only to those who were service wholesalers to some degree. These wholesalers soon became the sole connecting link between KKK Mills and the retailers. They had their own salesmen who contacted a wide variety of retailers. Also, these wholesalers provided the transportation and paid the costs thereof, from the KKK Mills godowns, to their own warehouses. Most of the wholesalers had their own storage facilities. Some of them also extended credit to retailers and KKK Mills' management was of the opinion that these wholesalers were more prompt in paying their bills to the mill than retailers would be.

However, what the management of the mill really appreciated, from the use of wholesalers, was the fact that they bought ahead and were in an excellent position to advise the mill on the trends in the market. According to management, this reduced costs as well as risks for KKK Mills.

In 1963 the mill had 22 relatively major customers, and nine customers who purchased their products occasionally and usually in small quantities. All 31 customers were wholesalers, most of them specializing in textile products. Most of these customers bought KKK Mills' products for many years, and KKK Mills enjoyed an excellent relationship with its customers. All of these wholesalers were located in Bombay and vicinity.

The wholesalers were not only pleased with the mill's products but also appreciated the fact that KKK sold exclusively to wholesalers. Most mills had recently started selling directly to retailers or manufacturer's agents, which had adversely affected the general textile wholesalers. What was worse, from both the wholesalers and the retailers point of view, was the growing trend in the textile industry for mills to have their own retail outlets. As a result, the power and the number of wholesalers, especially service wholesalers, in the textile industry was dwindling in recent years. It was, therefore, not surprising that the wholesalers left no stone unturned, to promote products of mills, such as KKK Mills, that sold exclusively to wholesalers.

From KKK Mills' point of view, the major advantages of selling only to wholesalers were (1) The wholesalers understood the market, and normally ordered well in advance so that KKK Mills could schedule its production systematically, (2) The wholesalers were steady customers. Thus there were no significant ups and downs in the mill's operations, (3) Other than having a small sales force, the mill was involved in no major marketing operations, since KKK Mills only used wholesalers that performed these services.

Though all the wholesalers were located in Bombay and vicinity, KKK products reached retailers, though not to any appreciable extent, in every state of India. However, the possibility of deeper exploration of the Bombay area had never been seriously considered by the mill's owners. It was felt by the owners that Korewala's products sold mainly because of their high reputation, and this reputation was only well known in the Bombay area and therefore their market area was limited. However, management felt that by employing more salesmen the mill would successfully enlarge its sales by getting wholesalers in other territories to carry their products.

Though the management of KKK Mills had never scientifically calculated what additional costs they would incur if they were to sell directly to retailers, it was estimated that if the KKK Mills were to sell directly to retailers, it could increase its selling price by at least 15 percent. The owners felt that most of this 15 percent would be profit. However, the management feared that the cost of selling to retailers would involve a large number of additional activities and costs which would exceed the 15 percent increase in selling price.

The board of KKK Mills, at the meeting held in February 1963, asked management to consider the possibility of changing its customer policy from selling to wholesalers only, to selling to both wholesalers and retailers, and also investigating other possible channels of distribution. The owners felt that if they could implement this change there would not only be an increase in sales and profits, but that they would be able to better control the price at which retailers sold the KKK products.

The manager, Mr. Ram, was given the responsibility for preparing a report to show what effect such a change would have on the mill's marketing operations, and whether such a change would be justified. He had no data on the number of retail outlets that existed for KKK Mills products nor did he have an estimate of the total market for border.

SALES FORCE

In the late forties KKK Mills employed about 30 salesmen. In the fifties it employed about 13. In 1963, the company had 7 salesmen. Five of these salesmen had been with the company for a number of years (15 to 30 years), one had been with the company for about eight years and the seventh, Mr. Singh, had recently joined the sales force.

The salesmen received no salaries or expenses. All salesmen sold directly to wholesalers for a 5 percent commission. They had no special territories. Each of the older salesmen had brought some of the present customers to KKK Mills, and most of them still retained the same customers as well as some others. Though there were no territorial or other divisions for the salesmen, they seemed to have an unwritten agreement among themselves of exclusive rights over the customers they brought in and/or retained at present.

Since the number of service wholesalers were dwindling in the textile industry, and since the older salesmen had the agreement mentioned above, it was difficult to increase sales by hiring new salesmen. In the past seven years 12 salesmen had joined the mill's sales force and quit within a year.

When Mr. Singh joined the sales force in late 1962, he was very unsuccessful in securing orders. However, about a month or so after his employment he decided to share part of his 5 percent commission with the wholesalers. Through this method he managed to get some new customers for the KKK Mills' products and also managed to convince 2 or 3 older customers to share in his commission. This soon came to the attention of the other salesmen who complained to the assistant manager. When Mr. Singh was called in to discuss this matter with the assistant manager, he said that he was unaware of the fact that he had violated the salesmen's code. He argued that the mill had not suffered through his action and that he had brought in new customers. He stated that the code followed by the salesmen was bad for KKK Mills. Because the older salesmen had steady customers they did not work hard on finding new ones and that without a salary, it was not sufficiently rewarding for a new salesman to join KKK Mills since it took time to develop new customers. Mr. Singh told the assistant man-

Korewala Kwality Kore Mills

ager that the older salesmen were relying on their previous efforts without making new efforts to sell the Mills' products. The assistant manager realized that there was some truth in what Mr. Singh had to say. He asked Mr. Singh to desist from "poaching" any further. He knew that he was faced with an important decision regarding his sales force. He therefore went to the manager, Mr. Ram, explained his problem and sought advice.

PRICING

In the textile industry the cost of raw materials and manufacturing overhead amount to an average of 45 percent of the manufacturers' sales price to wholesalers. Salaries and wages to employees and administrative overhead amount to about 20 percent of the sales price. This leaves about 35 percent of the selling price to wholesalers for various other overhead costs and profit. The margin of profit for a mill was most crucially affected by this additional overhead cost which usually amounted to about 20-25 percent in the industry.

At KKK Mills these costs were slightly lower than in the industry. The overhead cost had been substantially reduced from 23.8 percent in 1956 to 14.7 percent in 1962. Five percent of selling price to wholesalers was paid as commission to the KKK Mills' salesmen, which finally left the mill with a profit margin of 15 to 20 percent on selling price.

The wholesalers sold the KKK Mills products with a 10 to 25 percent mark up on the price they paid for it, depending on the quantities and conditions under which they sold to the retail outlets.

The wholesalers sold the KKK Mills products to various retail outlets, from door-to-door salesmen to department stores, and from small tailors to tourist shops. All wholesalers quoted the same price, and KKK Mills did not in any way dictate to the wholesalers to whom and at what price they should sell. It is not known at the KKK Mills how many and what type of retailers carry their products. Though they have a general idea of the approximate retail price, it varies from retailer to retailer, sometimes by as much as 20 percent.

At the special meeting of the board of directors and management, the owners said that a quality product such as theirs, should sell at a fixed retail price and asked management to report on what steps would have to be taken to put this into effect and to give the pros and cons of such a change in policy.

QUESTIONS

1. Suggest ways in which the KKK Mills can improve its sales picture.
2. Do you approve of the mill selling exclusively through wholesalers? Should the mill follow the trend in other textile mills of selling direct to the consumer; or should it sell to both wholesalers and retailers? What marketing channels do you recommend? Why?

3. What management policy would you recommend regarding compliance with government laws and codes?
4. Do you consider it advisable for KKK to extend its marketing operations beyond the greater Bombay area?
5. What would be the best strategy to effect such wider distribution?
6. Do you consider Mr. Singh's conduct contrary to KKK Mills' interests?
7. Do you support the policy of retail price maintenance?

11
Entrepreneurship In Village Culture*

Maneck S. Wadia

INTRODUCTION

This paper is a combination of research in the behavioral sciences and in the field of administrative behavior, concerning the realm of change in village culture.

The research findings have been formulated in terms of a case study. This has been done because the research lends itself admirably to such a format, because anthropologists have been interested in case studies,[1] and because innovation follows certain patterns[2] which may be conveniently and usefully traced in the format of a case.

The central theme of the paper reflects a theoretical treatment of an important, though often neglected, aspect of management—namely, that culture strongly affects the activities of business administration. Many authors seem to recognize this phenomena and Pfiffner and Sherwood have treated the subject in some detail. They state that cultural awareness gives management better understanding, ability to predict behavior, vicarious experience, and aid in facilitating change.[3] Few writers, however, have exemplified this through research studies.

The following research study makes specific examination of the various characteristics of village culture in general, and particularly in India, and their effects on the management of an enterprise.

---

*Selected as award winning paper in national competition sponsored by the *Academy of Management*. Presented at the annual meetings of the *Academy of Management*, December, 1963, and published in the *Proceedings of the Annual Meetings*, 1963. Reprinted by permission.

[1] Edward H. Spicer, *Human Problems in Technological Change*, New York, Russell Sage Foundation, 1952.

[2] Maneck S. Wadia, "The Administrative Function of Innovation," Brussels, *International Review of Administrative Sciences*, XXVIII, 1962.

[3] John M. Pfiffner, and Frank P. Sherwood, *Administrative Organization,* Englewood Cliffs, New Jersey, Prentice-Hall, Inc., 1960.

STATISTICAL BACKGROUND

Over seventy percent of India's population is rural and dependent on agriculture for its survival. Agriculture and allied village activities account for half of the country's national income.

The lot of the Indian farmer is indeed a sorry one, nor has it improved much since independence. Two important studies, covering occupational structure, wages, consumption, and the cost of living of agricultural labor were conducted by the Government of India. "The first Agricultural Labour Enquiry was conducted in 1950-51 in 800 villages covering a sample of 11,000 agricultural labour families. The second Agricultural Labour Enquiry was conducted in 1956-57, in 3,600 villages and data on employment, unemployment, wages and earnings, income, expenditure and indebtedness were collected from 28,560 sample agricultural labour households."[4]

These studies were summarized in *India 1961*,[5] (See Appendix I). The following is an abstraction of some salient points from that report.

The comparative statistical data for 1950-51 and for 1956-57 point to an adverse trend in the life of the Indian peasant. The average daily wage of male farm workers decreased from Rs. 1.9 nP (about US 0.22) to .96 nP (about US 0.19). The average annual income of an agricultural labor household decreased from Rs. 447 in 1951-52 to Rs. 437 in 1956-57.

Yet, the average accumulated debt per household increased from Rs. 47 to Rs. 88. Of the total debt, 46 percent was incurred for meeting the consumption expenditures and 24 percent for social purposes which are closely related to consumption expenditures for special occasions. Of this total debt, 34 percent was borrowed from money lenders, often at exorbitant rates of interest, 44 percent from friends and relatives, 15 percent from employers, 5 percent from shop-keepers and 1 percent from cooperatives.

RESEARCH DATA

Located in the state of Maharashtra, India, the village of Bhima was primarily a Marathi-speaking community of farmers.

Compared to the general standard of living in village India, Bhima was progressive. Its total population of approximately 650 persons constituted about 110 families. The village was well supplied with water by four old-fashioned wells and one modern well with a pump.

The majority of the families made their living by farming. Some supplemented their income through handicrafts. The village also had certain specialists, whose trade was usually based on their caste. There was a "Suthar" (carpenter) family, two "Chamar" (leather tanner) families, five families of "Bhangis" (scav-

---

[4]*India 1961*, The Publications Division, Ministry of Information and Broadcasting, Government of India, New Delhi, India, p. 258.
[5]*Ibid.*, pp. 258-260.

engers) who clean out-houses, streets, etc., and six families of "Banyas" (traders) whose family tongue was Gujerati. The Banya families owned the two small stores in the village. There was also a small school with a part-time teacher from Poona.

The majority of the people in the village belonged to one major caste group. Through rules of endogamy and other caste customs, this majority of approximately 80 families was interrelated, and, in many respects, they considered themselves as a large joint family. Among them, smaller joint family groups lived together under the same roof. A portion of these 80 families owned most of the land in Bhima, and their patriarch was also the informal head man of the village. They were the major customers of the stores in Bhima, since the others had practically no cash income.

Of the two small stores in Bhima, one mainly carried food staples such as rice, ghee, oils, grains, and, sometimes, fresh fruits and vegetables. The second and larger shop was a general store which sold household goods such as cloth and pots and pans. Both of these stores, however, featured only a limited line of goods, and their prices were usually higher than for similar goods in Poona. In the past, the store owners had made barter arrangements with the villagers. Gradually, a cash economy emerged in the village, and now most of the commercial dealings were in cash or on the basis of short-term loan accounts.

This village had moved towards greater prosperity since India's independence. The villagers had been strongly influenced by Ghandi, and, even after his death, the followers of the Mahatma continued to take interest in village affairs. The Ghandian influence had been especially effective in the development of village handicrafts and the weaving of Khadi cloth. This emphasis on handicrafts had brought greater self-sufficiency to the village. The self-sufficiency, however, was not of the type that Ghandi envisioned. Rather than leading to an exchange among villagers of their fruits of labor, the handicrafts mainly found an outside market and brought in cash.

Another element conducive to prosperity, a cash economy, and greater contact with the outside world was the growth of new industries in the nearby Poona (Pimpri) area. At least 15 families had one or more members working in industry. Small as the amount may be, these workers brought a regular pay check and a different set of values to Bhima and their families.

With the advent of this prosperity, the two stores in Bhima, no longer satisfied the needs and growing aspirations of many villagers. The very poor villagers, such as the Bhangis and the Chamars, who were rarely customers of the village stores, were still poor and perhaps worse off than they had been.

Most of the former customers of the two village stores, however, had more money to spend than ever before. The two stores were unable to satisfy their needs. The customers often preferred to buy in Poona where the prices were a little lower and where they could get a wider selection. Besides, going to the city always seemed a special event.

There were no cars in Bhima, but eight families had bullock carts which could carry eight or more people to Poona and back. About two score individuals, all males, owned bicycles. There was a morning and afternoon bus to Poona and an afternoon and evening bus back. The bus stop was just a short distance from the village. While the bus trip took about half an hour one way, the bullock cart or bicycle took between an hour and a half to two hours. The bicycle was the most popular mode of travel to the city, followed by bus trips. Bullock carts were now rarely used except in cases of very important trips for the whole family, especially on festive occasions, such as marriage, Divali, or mela (fairs).

Most of the housewives went to the city about once a week for shopping and/or excursions. The men travelled to the city more often and sometimes did the shopping. When the family ran short of items which the two stores in the village did not supply, special trips to Poona sometimes became necessary. In these instances, travelling eighteen miles to buy something in Poona was considered a great nuisance. During the monsoon season, about four months of the year, trips to Poona were greatly curtailed, and the stores in Poona were sorely missed.

The owners of the village stores complained about the villagers shopping in Poona, but they showed no signs of improving their facilities nor of reducing their prices. They were still making profit and were not worried about any competition. Traditionally, only the Banyas ran stores in the villages of this area and the present stores, with few changes, if any, had been in business for many years.

In the summer of 1959, Mr. Pandu, the son of the village patriarch, thought of opening a store in the village. He felt that a more modern store, carrying some of the goods the present stores carried, plus the goods for which the villagers went to Poona, would attract the villagers. He felt that such a store would be a boon to the villagers since they would not be spending time and money to travel to Poona. At the same time he hoped to earn a good living. Having worked in a store in Poona, he knew how and where to buy his goods wholesale and had had experience in many facets of the business. His employment in the city and his membership is one of the richer families in the village provided him with sufficient money to start a reasonably well-stocked store.

Mr. Pandu discussed his idea with some of his many friends and relatives in the village. Some of the elders were disturbed. They said that it was bad enough his working in the city, but at least that was away from the village. For an elite Maharashtrian to start a store in the village was completely unheard of; they said that it would bring shame to his family and nothing but trouble to him. Most of the others, however, indicated that they would patronize his store and that his store would be a great help to the village, since it would carry items for which the villagers now had to go to Poona. They also suggested that a small refreshment stand would be very successful.

In 1960, just after the monsoons, Mr. Pandu opened a small store and refreshment stand. The store featured mainly those goods which its competitors did not carry, such as soap and ready-made clothes. The refreshment stand

Entrepreneurship In Village Culture

served mainly tea, cold soft drinks, biscuits, and some Indian sweets which its customers consumed while squatting outside the shop.

Most of the people who patronized the store were relatives of the owner or worked for his family and had little cash to spend. Hence, Mr. Pandu found it very difficult to refuse credit to his customers. Because no books were kept, it became increasingly difficult to remember who owed what amount. It was also not the custom to have people sign promissory notes each time they bought something on credit. In any case, the 70 to 80 percent illiteracy, made such a system unfeasible. Within a few months, the credit situation became such that Mr. Pandu started keeping records of it and had to spend an increasing amount of time and effort in trying to collect what his friends and relatives owed him.

During the first few months, everyone in the village agreed that Mr. Pandu's store was a great boon to the village—that his prices were fair, and that his goods were of good quality. For about three months, many villagers patronized his store. Though many of the purchases were on credit, the customers intended to pay, though few specified when. With rare exception, they agreed to pay the debts as shown in Pandu's books. Practically no one refused to acknowledge his debt to Pandu, and Pandu continued to extend credit to those who asked for it.

Yet, after the first few months, business at Pandu's began to taper off. The villagers used every excuse to go to the city to purchase many of the goods carried by Pandu's store. They began to say that Pandu was getting too rich and powerful, that he charged higher prices, that his goods were of inferior quality, and that his records were inaccurate. They gave various other reasons as well for not patronizing his store. Within seven months, the villagers who patronized the store had bought nearly as much on credit as they had paid for. The number of customers also dwindled substantially, and even the monsoon did not help to increase his business. Persons who had been friends began to avoid Mr. Pandu and, later, his family. They seemed to feel that Pandu was a threat to them; that he was smarter and would therefore cheat them.

Mr. Pandu found that it was much more profitable and peaceful for him to find a job in Poona than to run a store. Pandu's store went out of business fourteen months after it was opened.

It has been nearly two years since the store has been shut down. The people of Bhima still complain of the expense and trouble of the shopping trips to Poona. Mr. Pandu still wonders why his venture failed, and how a new store could be successfully operated in Bhima.

APPENDIX 1

Occupational Structure

1. The estimated number of agricultural labour households was 1.63 crores in 1956-57 as against 1.79 crores in 1950-51, i.e., a fall of 16 lakhs. This reduction might be mainly due to conceptual difference in the definition of the term "agricultural labour households" adopted during the two enquiries.

2. The landless agricultural labour households in 1956-57 accounted for 57 per cent of the total as against 50 percent in 1950-51.

3. The proportion of attached and casual agricultural labour households was 10.90 in 1950-51. In 1956-57 attached labour households accounted for about 27 percent of the all-India total, the remainder being casual labour households. The increase may, to some extent, be due to resumption of personal extates for self-cultivation by the erstwhile intermediaries like zamindars, jagirdars, talukdars, etc., in the different States.

4. The average size of the agricultural labour households rose slightly to 4.40 in 1956-57 from 4.30 in 1950-51. The average number of wage earners was 2.03 per household, comprising 1.13 men, 0.74 women and 0.16 children. The corresponding figures for 1950-51 were 2.0 wage earners, comprising 1.1 men, 0.8 women and 0.1 children.

5. The estimated number of agricultural labourers during 1956-57 was 3.3 crores, composed of 1.8 crore men, 1.2 crore women and 30 lakh children. The corresponding figures for 1950-51 were 3.5 crores, consisting of 1.9 crore men, 1.4 crore women and 20 lakh children.

Employment and Unemployment

1. Casual adult male workers were employed, on an average, for wages for 200 days in 1950-51 and for 197 days during 1956-57. They were self employed for 75 days in 1950-51 and for 40 days in 1956-57.

2. Casual adult female workers were employed on wages for 134 days during 1950-51 and for 141 days during 1956-57.

3. The wage-employment of children increased from 165 days in 1950-51 to 204 days in 1956-57.

4. Casual adult male workers were unemployed for 128 days in 1956-57, as compared to 90 days in 1950-51.

Wages

1. About 76 percent of the average income of agricultural labour households was derived from wage-employment in agricultural operations as well as from non-agricultural occupations during 1950-51, as against 81 percent during 1956-57. About 56 percent of the man-days worked were paid for in cash in 1950-51 and 48.7 percent in 1956-57. Payments made entirely in kind accounted for 31.3 percent in 1950-51 and 40.5 percent in 1956-57. Wage payments made partly in cash and partly in kind related to 9.8 percent of the total man-days worked in the first enquiry and formed 10.8 percent in the second enquiry.

2. The average daily wage rate of adult male workers decreased from 109 nP in 1950-51 to 96 nP in 1956-57, and the average daily wage rate of adult women also fell from 68 nP in 1950-51 to 59 nP in 1956-57. Child Labour received an average wage of 70 nP in 1950-51 and 53 nP in 1956-57.

3. The estimated wage-bill in agriculture worked out to roughly Rs 520 crores in 1956-57 as against Rs 500 crores in 1950-51. The increase was mainly due to the proportion of attached labour households being considerably higher (above 27 percent) in 1956-57 as compared with 1950-51 (about 10 percent) and the average annual income per attached labour household and also of all households taken together from agricultural wage employment in 1956-57 being higher than in 1950-51.

Household Income

1. The average annual income of an agricultural labour household in 1950-51 was Rs. 447, while in 1956 it was Rs. 437.

2. The average income derived from different sources during the first and second enquiries by agricultural labour households is given in Table 1.

TABLE 1
Sources of Income*

	1950-1951 Rs. nP	1956-1957 Rs. nP
Cultivation of land	59.90 (13.49)	30.07 (6.87)
Agricultural Labour	286.97 (64.2)	319.55 (73.04)
Non-agricultural Labour	53.19 (11.9)	34.94 (7.99)
Others	46.94 (10.51)	52.91 (12.10)

*Figures in brackets are percentages to total income from all sources.

Income from farming and non-agricultural labour declined during 1956-57, but that from agricultural labour had increased.

Consumption and Cost of Living

1. The average annual consumption expenditure of agriculture labour households increased from Rs. 461 in 1950-51 to Rs. 617 in 1956-57. The percentage expenditure on different consumption groups is given in Table 2.

TABLE 2
Consumption Expenditure (percentage to total)

Consumption Group	1950-1951	1956-1957
Food	85.3	77.3
Clothing and footwear	6.3	6.1
Fuel and lighting	1.1	7.9
Miscellaneous and service	7.3	8.7

2. The average income per household during 1956-57 was Rs. 437 while average consumption expenditure was Rs. 617. The deficit was thus Rs. 180. This deficit, to a considerable extent, would seem to have been met from past savings, sale of stocks, remittances received and loans.

Indebtedness

1., About 64 percent of agricultural labour households was indebted during 1956-57 as against 45 percent in 1950-51. The average accumulated debt per household increased from Rs. 47 in 1950-51 to Rs. 88 in 1956-57.

2. The average debt per indebted household also rose from Rs. 105 in 1950-51 to Rs. 138 in 1956-57. One of the reasons for the higher percentage of

indebted households as also the higher volume of debt in 1956-57 was the higher proportion of attached labour households, some of whom were under debt bondage and/or tie-in-allotment.

3. The total estimated volume of indebtedness of agricultural labour households in 1956-57 was Rs. 143 crores as against Rs. 80 crores in 1950-51.

4. Of the total debt, about 46 percent was incurred for meeting the consumption expenditure. Social purposes accounted for 24 percent and productive purposes for 19 percent, the remaining 11 percent of the total debt being incurred for meeting the expenditure on other miscellaneous items.

5. Of the total loan, 34 percent was taken from money-lenders, 44 percent from friends and relatives, 15 percent from employers, 5 percent from shopkeepers and one percent from cooperatives.

These statistics give a general idea of villages in India as a background for this research study in the village of Bhima.

BIBLIOGRAPHY

Banfield, Edward G., *The Moral Basis of a Backward Society*, Glencoe, Illinois, The Free Press, 1958.

Carstairs, G. Morris, *The Twice Born: A Study of a Community of* High Caste Hindus, Bloomington, Indiana, Indiana University Press, 1958.

Dube, S. C., *Indian Village*, Ithaca, New York, Cornell University Press, 1955.

Foster, George M., "Interpersonal Relations in Peasant Society," *Human Organization*, XIX, 1960-61.

Gouldner, Alvin, "The Norm of Reciprocity: A Preliminary Statement," *The American Sociological Review*, Vol. XXV, No. 2, April 1960.

Hosclitz, Bert F., *Sociological Aspects of Economic Growth*, New York, The Free Press, 1960.

India 1961, The Publications Division, Ministry of Information and Broadcasting, Government of India, New Delhi, India.

India 1963, The Publications Division, Ministry of Information and Broadcasting, Government of India, New Delhi, India.

Lawrence, Paul R., "How to Deal With Resistence to Change," *Harvard Business Review*, May-June 1954.

Lewis, Oscar, *Life in Mexican Village, Tepoztlan Restudied*, Urbana, Illinois, University of Illinois Press, 1951.

Lewis, Oscar, "Some of My Best Friends are Peasants," *Human Organization*, Volume 19, Winter 1960-61.

Malinowski, Bronislaw, *Crime and Custom in Savage Society*, London, Paul, Trench, Trubner, 1932.

Pfiffner, John M., and Sherwood, Frank P., *Administrative Organization*, Englewood Cliffs, New Jersey, Prentice-Hall, Inc., 1960.

Spicer, Edward H., *Human Problems in Technological Change*, New York, Russell Sage Foundation, 1952.

Wadia, Maneck S., "The Administrative Function of Innovation," *International Review of Administrative Science*, Brussels, XXVIII, 1962.

Egypt

12

Standard Refrigeration Company*

In June of 1961, Standard Refrigeration stood as the manufacturer of the most complete line of industrial cooling and air handling equipment in the United Arab Republic. Most of the manufactured products were used by the contracting end of the company which bid usually on large jobs for air conditioning factories, hospitals or offices. As a result of import restrictions and the rapid growth of industrialization of the country which necessitated many air handling installations for new factories and office buildings, the market for locally manufactured equipment had grown very rapidly and in 1961 Standard Refrigeration had approximately £E 1,250,000 in order backlog. Since jobs took about two and a half years to complete, between the time tenders for airconditioning were invited and buildings were completely air-conditioned, this represented about £E 500,000 in annual sales. This rapid growth had taxed very heavily the production and financial resources of the company, and was putting a very heavy burden on its executives and employees, and in June 1961 the company was still engaged in a general reorganization which was started in 1959.

COMPANY HISTORY

The company was founded in 1944 by Mr. Mohammed Kamel who was a mechanical engineer with ten years of experience in air conditioning. The company was engaged from the beginning in contracting for air handling and cooling installations, and Standard Refrigeration imported most of the equipment it used except for some of the sheet metal components which were manufactured in the company's workshop. This situation lasted until 1952 when the Government began to establish some import restrictions and the company began to manufacture more of the components it used in its contracting business. With the increasing difficulty of obtaining import licenses, Standard Refrigeration's product line increased gradually, until it included in 1961 all of the items shown in Exhibit 1. Since 1955, the great increase in the company's manufactured products had been taxing its production facilities very severely and the manage-

*Reprinted by permission of the National Institute of Management Development, Cairo, United Arab Republic.

EXHIBIT 1
STANDARD REFRIGERATION
Company Product Line

AIR HANDLING UNITS: using chilled water or D.X. refrigerant. Horizontal type (CH) from 1000-27,500 cfm-Vertical type (Cv) from 1000-15,000 cfm. Zone Vertical or Horizontal type (CVZ,CHZ) from 2000-27,500 cfm.

FLOOR: Using chilled water or D.X. refrigerant, type (FU) 250,400 600 cfm. With decorative Sheet Metal or Formice Covers.

CEILING UNITS: Using chilled water or D.X. refrigerant, type (CU) 500, 750, 1000, 11250, 1500 cfm.

WATER COOLED CONDENSERS: Shell, Tube (WC-S) from 15-175 tons refrigeration. Double tube type (WC-T) from 1-7,5 tons refrigeration.

AIR COOLED CONDENSERS: Type (AC) from 1-50 tons refrigeration.

EVAPORATIVE CONDENSERS: Type (ECD) from 3-125 tons refrigeration.

COOLING TOWERS: All Metal Packed Forced Draft type (CT-M) from 3-100 tons refrigeration, Spray Filled Forced Draft type (CT-S) from 40-900 tons refrigeration.

AIR WASHERS: For high efficiency humidification type (AWH). type (AWC) for high efficiency cooling from 6000-270,000 cfm.

CENTRIFUGAL FANS: Single or Double Suction, Forward Inclined type (FI-S.SD.S.) from 500-13500 cfm., 0,25-3 S.P. Backward Inclined (BI-S.S.D.S.) from 750-134,000 cfm., 0,25-3 S.P.

AXIAL FANS: Type (AF) from 1700-60,000 cfm, 0,25-3,25 S.P.

BOILERS: For Hot Water type (WB) or Low Pressure Steam type (SB) from 1000,000-1,500,000 Btu hr.

OIL BURNERS: Gun type (OB) for the above boilers range.

HEATING COILS: Type (HC) for Steam or Hot Water.

UNIT, JET COOLERS: Type (UC), (JC) from 300-1750 Btu. hr. 1 F temperature difference.

REACH-IN REFRIGERATORS: Type (RR) from 15-100 cu. ft.

CONDENSING UNITS: Type (CDU) 1,5-2-3-5-7,5 tons refrigeration.

PACKED AIR CONDITIONERS: Water Cooled type (P.U.) 3, 5-7,5-10-15 tons refrigeration.

WATER CHILLERS: Type (WCH) from 30-200 tons refrigeration.

HEAT EXCHANGERS: Type (HX) from 30-200 tons refrigeration.

OIL SEPARATORS: Type (OS) from 50-150 tons refrigeration.

GRILLES: Stamped (STG) 3-12 width x 8-60 length, Strip (SG) 2-20 width x 6-60 length, Vaned Curved (VG) 4-60 width x 8-138 length. Available Throttling Device.

WALL OUTLETS: Types (SO) 3-12 width x 6-60 length, Bar (Bo) 4-10 width x 8-60 length. Available Straightners, Throttling Device.

CEILING DIFFUSERS: Type Multi-Ring (MR-D) sizes 6-33, Half-Multi-Ring (HMR-D) same sizes, Multi-Flush Cones (FC-D) sizes 6-24. Half Flush-Cones (HFC-D) same sizes and Multi Stepped Cones (SC-D) sizes 6-24.

DAMPERS: Type (D) blades sizes 4, 5, 6, 8, frames 18-48 x 22-98

TANKS: For oil (OT) or water (WT).

CHEMICAL DRIERS, STRAINERS: Type (DS) up to 200 tons refrigeration.

WINDOW CONDITIONERS: Type (WU) 1.1,5 H.P. available (1960)

EVAPORATIVE AIR COOLERS: (EC) from 1000-15,000 cfm.

---

ment began considering a move into more spacious quarters. By 1958 a parcel of land of two feddans had been acquired at Shubra el-Kheima near Cairo, a new plant was built, additional machinery was purchased, and the move to the new facilities was completed in 1959.

Although Standard Refrigeration had little competition at the manufacturing end of the business, there were many contractors for air handling equipment, the largest of these being the General Supplies Company, a large general contracting company which had been acting as representative for American air conditioning equipment manufacturers and had a large and diversified contracting business.

Standard Refrigeration Company

Because of the scarcity of components General Supplies decided in 1960 to set up its own manufacturing facilities and make most of the necessary components under license from foreign manufacturers.

A tentative agreement was reached however in 1961 between Standard Refrigeration and General Supplies whereby Standard Refrigeration would separate completely its manufacturing and contracting activities; a new company would be formed to take over the manufacturing facilities and the shares of the new company would be owned 50% by Standard Refrigeration and 50% by General Supplies. The agreement for the new company had not yet been signed however. It was decided that the new company would carry on the same manufacturing activities and that it would sell its products to any potential purchaser. The only limitation put on the new manufacturing company's activities was that it would not enter the contracting business. An official of Standard Refrigeration estimated that in 1960, Standard Refrigeration and General Supplies had about 35% and 25% respectively, of the industrial air conditioning field, the rest being divided between five or six smaller competitors. Exhibits 2 and 3, are comparative income statements and balance sheets for the company from 1956 to 1960.

PRODUCTION SYSTEM

Because of the great diversity of products manufactured by the company and the limited market for each type of equipment taken individually, production orders were usually handled in small lots. The company's basic product line included approximately 40 main assemblies, each one made up of at least four or five sub-assemblies and the whole product line being available in many different sizes.

Furthermore, each sub-assembly would include anything from five to twenty components, and each component would undergo several manufacturing operations. In addition, most of the products were manufactured for custom installations and many variations were possible according to the conditions of each job; Cooling units could be refrigerant or chilled water cooled, air filters might or might not be necessary, heating coils could be included at the customer's request and the control system utilized could be designed to suit his specifications.

The great number of different components to be made, the many different operations which each component had to go through, and the fact that production orders were in small lots caused the company many production planning and scheduling problems.

Before the move to the new factory was made and when production volume of manufactured parts was small, Mr. Kamel, who had accumulated much engineering know-how, used to explain to the workshop manager what he wanted, and the latter would follow individual production orders through the various machining and assembling operations. With the increase of production, this be-

EXHIBIT 2
STANDARD REFRIGERATION
Comparative Income Statements, 1956-1960

	1956		1957		1958		1959		1960	
Sales (Total contract value)		339.130		273.207		462.861		436.982		413.697
Cost of sales	293.780		234.655		426.699		397.734		383.644	
Depreciation of auxiliary equipment	407		755		282		222		610	
Automobile expenses	2.093									
		296.280		235.430		426.981		397.956		384.254
Gross profit from contracting	42.850		37.777		35.880		39.026		29.443	
Gross profit of maintenance workshop	2.158		7.153		6.418		10.736		9.977	
Gross profit from export sales*	230		743		2.968		8.161		20.199	
Gross profit of factory operations	—		8.993		11.431		17.713			
Total gross profit		45.238		45.672		54.259		69.354		77.332
General administrative expenses	19.148		20.351		16.375		18.357		16.172	
Depreciation	3.085		2.895		3.296		4.074		5.462	
Social insurance	3.205		3.505		4.057		3.975		.432	
Directors fees	500		500		500		750		750	
Stamp duties on shares	1.151		—		219		280		280	
Loss in selling a car	—		134		—		—		—	
Interest on outstanding debentures	—		—		—		2.000		—	
Reserves for employees indemnities	1.000		—		—		3.000		5.000	
Allowance for bad debts	2.000		2.500		4.000		2.500		6.000	
Provision for unforeseen expenses					2.000		6.000		8.000	
		30.089		30.085		30.447		38.396		44.596
Net profit before taxes		15.149		15.585		23.812		30.418		32.736

*This total was made up mainly of export allowances given by the government for sales abroad.

Standard Refrigeration Company

EXHIBIT 3
STANDARD REFRIGERATION
Comparative Balance Sheets, 1956-1960

	1956			1957			1958			1959			1960		
Assets															
Cash			29,025			35,171			8,135			39,417			31,705
Accounts Receivable	265,336			316,070			563,328			224,594			297,233		
Less: Provision for bad debts	7,000			9,500			15,000			10,921			13,421		
Accounts receivable mortgaged at the bank	258,336		289,003	306,570		322,047	548,328		596,609	213,673		257,869	283,812		339,510
	30,667			15,477			48,281			44,196			55,698		
Inventories (valued at cost)		70,030			94,172			78,188			94,461			115,117	
Contracts in Process		104,439			165,353			135,478			110,787			267,581	
Prepaid expenses		3,322			6,259			2,411			4,575			1,737	
Fixed Assets (Not of Depreciation)															
Land, Buildings	16,620			11,554			36,976			45,706			47,898		
Machinery	4,441			19,395			20,927			22,214			33,576		
Furniture				4,688			5,816			6,308			8,349		
Automobiles and Trucks	2,944	24,005		1,987	37,624		1,905	65,624		2,610	76,838		5,543	95,366	
Investments in subsidiary companies (Iraq)		—						12,431			27,056			27,056	
		519,824			660,626			898,876			611,001			878,072	
Liabilities															
Accounts payable		337,231			435,553			555,032			230,172			362,546	
Bank loans		21,593			40,857			56,173			95,462			55,231	
Reserves: for taxes	612			1,384			2,617			5,498			10,220		
for employees' indemnities	14,000	14,612		13,900	15,284		13,650	16,267		15,476	20,974		19,900	30,120	
Accrued expenses		14,664			34,984			84,176			48,085			114,812	
Bond issue															75,000
Equity															
Common Stock	100,000			100,000			140,000			140,000			150,000		
Reserves	16,364	116,364		17,879	117,879		23,069	163,071		44,300	184,300		56,905	206,905	
	213			484			346			4,590			722		
Profits reported from previous years	15,147	15,360		15,585	16,069		23,811	24,157		30,418	32,008		32,736	33,458	
Net profits for the year		519,824			660,626			898,876			611,001			878,072	

came impossible and at first attempt at standardization was made. Standard drawings were to be made for each part, standard manufacturing process sheets were to be made showing the detail and order of various operations, and standard jigs and fixtures were to be designed to facilitate the different machining operations for individual parts. By June of 1961, this work had been completed for only a few parts since the technical staff was constantly under pressure to get production out at whatever cost and could not devote its time to the designing and planning of operations. Another limitation was that most of the engineers had not yet accumulated enough experience, and both manufacturing and production planning relied heavily on Mr. Kamel's judgment. This, apart from the technical help that Mr. Kamel had to provide at the contracting end to advise his systems engineers about the suitability of different components for each installation.

Another related production difficulty was that of machine scheduling. No standard times were available for individual operations and it was difficult to predict the future workload on various machines and production orders and thereby very difficult to determine exact delivery dates. In the words of Mr. Kamel: "Assuming that time and motion studies had been completed for each operation, a gigantic task in itself, we would still have a very difficult scheduling task with the number of assemblies, sub-assemblies, components and machining operations we have and keeping in mind that we only make a few parts of each kind thus having to change constantly jigs, fixtures and machine set-ups." Mr. Kamel estimated that the factory had to process yearly from 1,500 to 2,000 manufacturing orders for assemblies and sub-assemblies.

In June of 1961, two I.L.O. production consultants on loan to the Department of Productivity, Ministry of Industry, were helping Standard Refrigeration solve its planning and scheduling problems. They had been working since the summer of 1960 designing a new integrated system with the relevant forms to be utilized in order to give Standard Refrigeration the necessary planning, scheduling, follow up and cost accounting information.

Exhibit 4 is a routing sheet showing the preparation of individual operation slips for a single manufacturing order.

Before the assignment of individual machines to individual operations can be made, the sales department checks with the planning department on a tentative delivery date. To do this, planning has to make a first check on a general factory loading chart (by department and not individual machines) and to check on materials and purchased components availability. If the order is not of a standard type, a further check has to be made with the Design, Drawing and Prototype Departments and a tentative delivery date is set.

If the order is approved, the steps shown in Exhibit 4 have to be taken in order to prepare individual operation slips for each machine or worker involved in this manufacturing order. If no changes in standard design are required, the Product Processing Department sends a Standard Process Master Sheet showing the individual operations to be performed and the standard times for each oper-

Standard Refrigeration Company

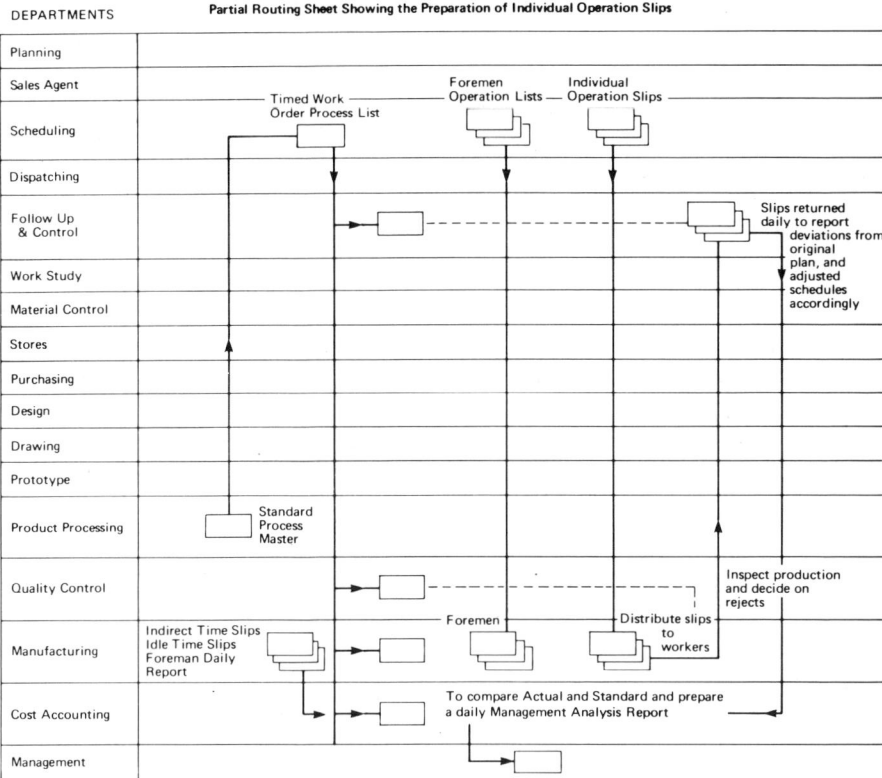

EXHIBIT 4
STANDARD REFRIGERATION
Partial Routing Sheet Showing the Preparation of Individual Operation Slips

ation to the Scheduling Department. The Scheduling Department translates these standard processes into actual start and finish times for individual operations on individual machines according to a General Machine Loading Chart.

A timed Work Order Process List is then made and copies of this list are sent to the following departments:
  Follow-up and Control
  Quality Control
  Manufacturing
  Cost Accounting

This Work Order Process List is also broken down by the Scheduling Department into Foremen Operation Lists for the work assigned to each manufacturing department and into Individual Operation Lists for the work within each department, and these are sent to Manufacturing for assignment to foremen. Production then starts on individual operations and Quality Control checks on the daily production according to its Timed Work Order Process List. Slips are then sent to Follow-up and Control, to make any readjustments in production orders if necessary, and the slips showing the actual time taken for each operation are sent to the Cost Accounting Department which makes an analysis of the deviations between actual and standard and issues its reports to Management.

A similar procedure was followed to control the issuing of raw materials according to standards set.

The new system also required the making of time and motion studies for each of the standard machining and assembling operations and the company had not yet had time to complete this task. Mr. Kamel and Mr. Dessouki, the factory's production manager, believed however that the system was quite good if the appropriate people could be trained to assemble first the necessary data (standard drawings, schedules, time and motion studies) and then utilize the system successfully.

SALES POLICY AND PRODUCT LINE

Standard Refrigeration used the lowest American F.O.B. prices as a guide to decide on a transfer price between manufacturing and contracting. In the managing director's opinion, this was a valid assumption since there was no local competition at the manufacturing end, and if one of the contracting companies was able to obtain an import license for components, it had to pay customs, insurance and freight in addition to the American F.O.B. price. In his opinion, European prices could not be used since few European manufacturers were engaged in this type of production, and their prices were not much lower than American prices.

The company's product line, shown in Exhibit 1, included everything it could make with its available machinery and know-how in the industrial air handling field. It was impossible for the company to manufacture only the most profitable items and import the rest, since import licenses were not easily available. Moreover, a big contracting job could be held up for the lack of a small component which the company had to produce to secure the big profits at the contracting end. In the words of the managing director: "Even if I could use my import licenses to import components which are unprofitable to manufacture now I would still manufacture the whole product line in order to accumulate experience on all components since I am looking ahead to the time when imports will be absolutely impossible."

In addition to the industrial air handling components, the managing director began in 1959 to work on the development of a window-type air conditioner and in 1960 the company produced and sold 200 units. In view of this success which was achieved largely on the company's reputation in the air conditioning field, and without any consumer advertising, the company planned to produce 750 units in 1961. These units were sold directly from contracting to individual users, largely on the basis of personal contacts with the company's executives. This was the only product manufactured on an assembly line basis in batches of 50 units. These window air conditioners were sold at retail for £E 180 which

Standard Refrigeration Company

was about £E 20 cheaper than the Ideal air-conditioner, the largest selling window-type unit in the United Arab Republic. This sale price of £E 180 left a large profit margin to Standard Refrigeration.

The managing director felt that "he would like to make anything he could sell" and which would leave him a good profit margin. He felt that refrigerators were completely outside his line since they needed heavy manufacturing equipment, but he forecast a big market for water coolers and ice cream cabinets. For such products as air conditioners and water coolers the managing director felt that he was in a much better competitive position than Ideal, the largest Arab manufacturer of metal furniture, refrigerators and window air-conditioners. "We have our own *know-how*," he said "consequently, we can design products which are suited to our local conditions and produce them with manufacturing methods which are suited to our limited facilities; as for Ideal or Frigor, they import a foreign design together with foreign manufacturing methods and try to use this with our local conditions. For an air conditioner, for example, they might import stamping presses and dies for a value of £E 100,000 in order to manufacture 200,000-300,000 units. On the other hand, I would use sheet metal components produced in any sheet metal shop without having to go into the expense of importing large stamping presses and expensive new dies for each different model."

Standard Refrigeration did not have any salesmen as such since most of their work came from tenders for which the contracting company submitted its bids. Very little advertising was done, except for large billboards which were posted on the sites of buildings for which Standard Refrigeration had been awarded air conditioning contracts. Most contracting bids were handled by the company's general manager although technical specifications, especially for large jobs, were often reviewed by the managing director. Both managing director and general manager had a long experience in the industrial air handling field and final bids for large air conditioning installations were reviewed by both of them to ascertain the adequacy of the price asked.

COSTING AND FINANCE

As was mentioned previously, products were sold to the contracting division at the lowest American F.O.B. price available. In order to get the approximate cost, and therefore the profitability of each order, direct labor and raw materials spent on each order were added up. To this total a general manufacturing overhead was added, this overhead being allocated on the basis of direct labor. All manufacturing expenses shown in Exhibit 5 except direct labor and raw materials were added up and calculated as a percent of direct labor. This was done every three months and the percent derived used for the following three month period, and adjustments were made in the consolidated profit and loss account at the end of the year to account for overabsorbed or underabsorbed manufac-

EXHIBIT 5
STANDARD REFRIGERATION
Details of Factory Costs and Gross Profits, 1956-1960

	1956	1957	1958	1959	1960
Raw Materials	37.600	49.842	74.303	83.058	112.284
Direct Labor				9.848	11.503
	7.225	10.052	15.033		
Indirect labor & Salaries				7.844	6.573
Medical care			376	71	439
Transportation of goods	315	290	296	1.427	2.427
Office Supplies			600	274	1.292
Water and electricity	1.006	1.025	1.503	1.679	1.855
Telephone & Telegraph			540	582	809
Insurance			3.373	4.003	3.378
Deport permits			30	202	1.751
Bank Charges				59	8.555
Rent	1.667	1.453	1.648	1.013	307
Advertising				442	
Furnitures				406	
Trucks & Automobiles Expenses			2.493		
Custom Duties			134	112	
Maintenance and Repairs	2.760	2.908	4.199		
Miscellaneous	57		506	1.140	2.035
Adjustment for unforeseen expenses			840		
Total Factory Cost	50.630	65.570	105.874	112.146	153.408
Gross Profits of Factory Orders	–	–	8.993	11.431	17.713
Transfer Price to Contracting*			114.867	123.577	171.121

*This transfer price was determined by taking the lower of factory cost or lowest American F.O.B. prices when these were available.

turing overhead. When the cost of each order was arrived at, a factor of:

$$A/S = \frac{\text{American F.O.B. price}}{\text{Standard Refrigeration F.O.B. cost}}$$

was calculated in order to have a measure of the comparative profitability of different items manufactured. The results, segregated by product type, were collected in a manufacturing costing book for the use of the factory manager and the managing director of the company. Because of the pressure of work, however, and the scarcity of competent cost accountants at the plant, the book was often out of date. Exhibit 6 is a copy of the plant costing book for water cooled condensers.

In the financial manager's office, who was also responsible for cost accounting, the same type of information was collected for each order. It was easier to

Standard Refrigeration Company

EXHIBIT 6
STANDARD REFRIGERATION
Factory Cost Accounting Book
Condensing Units Single and Double Tube

Form No. Req. No.		Date of Completion Promised	Date of Completion Actual	Labour £E	Manhours	Materials £E	Labour% Materials	Total F.O.B.	American F.O.B.	A/S%
683	One 15 Ton Unit without reservoir	15/10/58	2/2/59	61.5	408	531	11.5	592.5		
650	One 7½ ton without compressor	15/10/58	8/6/59	73.5	489	116.9	61.5	190.31	190	9
954	Two 7.5 ten units	12/7/59	31/1/60	239.739	2101	990.4	24	1275.8	896	7
1183	Three 1.5 ton unit	25/4/60		47.7		56.6	86	105.3	105.3	1
924	One 5 ton unit	25/6/59	4/10/59					220	235	1
1008	One 7½ ton unit	5/8/59	15/12/59					405	315	1
1066	One 5 ton unit								490	7
56/60	1½/2/3/5 ton units	30/5/60		111.8		2122.5		2430.9	3450	
100/60	Two 10 ton units	30/5/60	30/8/60	100.826	848¾	521.117	19.3	621.9	966	1.5
96/60	One 2 ton unit	30/5/60	30/5/60	35.4	252	283	12.5	318.5	400	1.2
235/60	Two 2 tons units	30/9/60		19.7		243.5		298	365	1.2
195/60	Two 5, 7½ Tons Units	18/8/60	18/8/60	21.67		479.32		538.98	591	1.1
179/60	One 7½ ton unit			30.4		44.3	64.2	77.8	78	1
178/60	One 3 ton unit	8/5/60		2.5				2.5	2.5	1
238/60	Two 7½ ton units	18/9/60	18/11/60	24.68		238.8		309.7	630	2
275/60	One 7½ ton unit	20/8/60							346	
211/60	One two ton unit	3/1/61		13		114.2		150.1	150.1	1
276/60	One two ton unit		31/1/60	1.5		98.1		102.4	182	1.7
278/60	Four 2 & 3 ton unit		31/12/60			98.1		98.1	182	1
53/60	29 double tube 5 T. Unit	15/4/60	30/8/60	437.4	4367½	1201.48	36.3	1638.6	1888	1.1
136/60	30 double tube 5 T. Unit	15/5/60	23/4/60	527	534¼	120.06	43.9	172.8	200	1.1
241/60	15 Standard water cooled double tube	31/11/60		50.3		208.5		347.9	440	1.2
270/60	Six double tube units	15/12/60	15/1/61	71.35		257.85		457.96	549	1.2
970/60	One double tube water			4.5				17.6	17.6	1

compile this in his department since all labor cards and materials requisitions came to his office in Cairo for use in the financial accounts of the company. The only difference was that order costs were not segregated according to the product manufactured since within each class of products you could not compare the cost of one order with that of another which had some slight modifications. "In order to control our costs, we need to break down each order into standard elements with standard manufacturing times and standard raw materials issues. Only then can I make the operating people responsible for the quantities of raw materials used and the direct labor spent on operations. Hopefully, this will be possible when time and motion studies have been made and standards established for each manufacturing operation, a work which is already being done for

EXHIBIT 7
STANDARD REFRIGERATION
Cost Accounting Information: Financial Manager

Production Order	Contract No.		Raw Materials	Direct Labour	Direct Expense	Allocated Expenses	Standard Refrigeration cost	American F.O.B. Prices
			£E	£E	£E	£E	£E	£E
1/60	1157	15 Sets of Copper Tubing for cooling coils	9			13	31	31
2/60	2259	1 Distribution Panel size No. 5 140x190x35 complete with connections	258	72		126	456	456
5/60	1157	20 Double Supports for copper Tubing outside diameter 10.125" five of which have guides. 7 Double Supports of copper tubing outside diameter 8.125" 15 Double Supports for copper tubing outside diameter 6.125 two of which have guides. 25 Double supports for copper tubing outside diameter 5.125" four of which have guides	112	44	1	77	235	235
9/60	2658	One 50 ton cooling tower	205	61	1	107	374	487
11/60	1258	3 Cast Iron Pulleys 14 19/64"	158	1	-	2	161	162
17/60	356	2 Galvanized stainers	1	2	-	4	8	9
50/60	1959	20 Ceiling Diffusers types 5.27 with 4" straightner necks	73	9	-	16	99	296
51/60	1959	Air ducts lined with 1" Microlite	404	52	-	92	550	1003
52/60	660	One water cooled shell and Tube Condenser model No. 40	307	59	-	103	471	860
124/60	1360	16 Vaned Curved Return Grills 31 Ceiling Diffusers Type P.S.	65	16	-	28	111	115
....	....							
....	....							
....	....	etc., etc.						
		Total for the year	62518	14539	246	26274	103638	134154

Standard Refrigeration Company

our new planning and scheduling system." The financial manager felt that a comparison with American F.O.B. prices was not a suitable indication of operating efficiency since conditions were very different in the United Arab Republic. Raw materials, for instance, could be twice as expensive as in the United States while labor and general overhead were much cheaper. Exhibit 7 is an illustration of the manufacturing costs record compiled by the financial office.

Most of the financial manager's time was consumed by trying to remedy to the company's constant shortage of cash. The increase in contract volume and manufacturing operations without a corresponding increase in capital was putting the company in a very difficult position financially. The financial manager explained that he constantly had £E 1,200,000 of contracts between backlog and work in process with about £E 500,000 worth being completed each year. In addition, accounts receivable were very slow since many air conditioning installations were made for government factories and the government was very slow in paying its bills because of the administrative routine involved. Some bills for government contracts terminated in 1957 had still not been paid. The company also had to carry a very large inventory of raw materials since most of these were imported and a long time was needed between applying for an import license and receiving the goods in Cairo.

The financial manager was trying to remedy his difficulties by getting bank loans and by trying to receive some advance payments on some of the contracts in process. There was a limit, however, to the amounts the banks were prepared to loan in view of the relatively small capital of the firm and its large volume of business. A temporary solution was reached in 1960 when the company floated a bond issue of £E 75,000 but this had still not been enough. The financial manager felt that many of his difficulties would be overcome if an agreement with the General Supplies Company was reached. The new manufacturing company would pay Standard Refrigeration approximately £E 40,000 for its goodwill and manufacturing knowhow and in addition, the association with such a large company would facilitate bank loans for Standard Refrigeration.

PERSONNEL AND ORGANIZATION

One of the main bottlenecks of the company's expansion had been to find suitable people to staff its technical and administrative positions. The lack of good engineers, to take over some of the managing director's technical work, had been troubling him for some time. "In another country I would have no trouble in hiring the engineers needed by paying the price they would be worth to me. Here, however, with our system of allocating engineers to different organizations I cannot get either the number or the quality I need." In his efforts to alleviate this problem, the managing director used to supervise most of the development work in manufacturing and the design work for contracting, explaining every time to the engineer in charge the reasons for the changes he made. "All I succeed in doing, however, is to develop good draftsmen but not resourceful engineers who will use their own judgment."

Many of the company executives filled different functions because of the lack of sufficiently trained personnel. The managing director, because he supervised much of the technical work of the company, had to travel often to Europe and the United States to keep abreast of the latest developments. The general manager, who was also an engineer and who had worked with Carrier Egypt at the same time as the managing director, came to Standard Refrigeration in 1957 after having filled several executive positions, first with a cement company and then with a refrigeration company. Most of his time was taken up by customer contracts and follow-up on the various contracts in process. His work was mainly on the administrative rather than the technical side of the business.

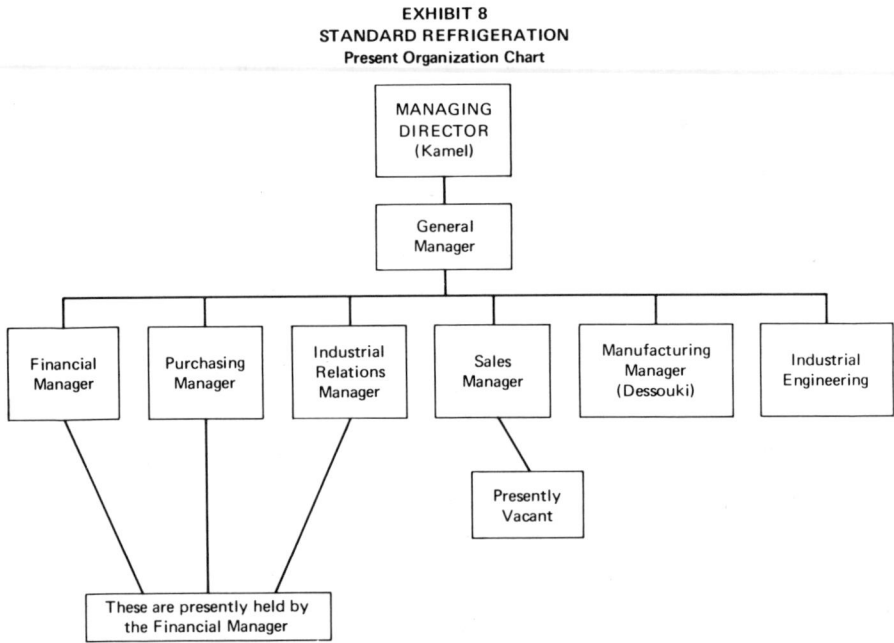

EXHIBIT 8
STANDARD REFRIGERATION
Present Organization Chart

The financial manager because of the lack of personnel, was also supervising purchasing, sales and industrial relations; in the latter department he had recently hired a young man as his assistant, and he hoped to develop him for the position of industrial manager. Exhibit 8 shows the present organization chart of the company for all its activities (manufacturing and contracting) and Exhibit 9 is the proposed organization chart suggested by the I.L.O. consultants for the separate manufacturing division.

Standard Refrigeration Company

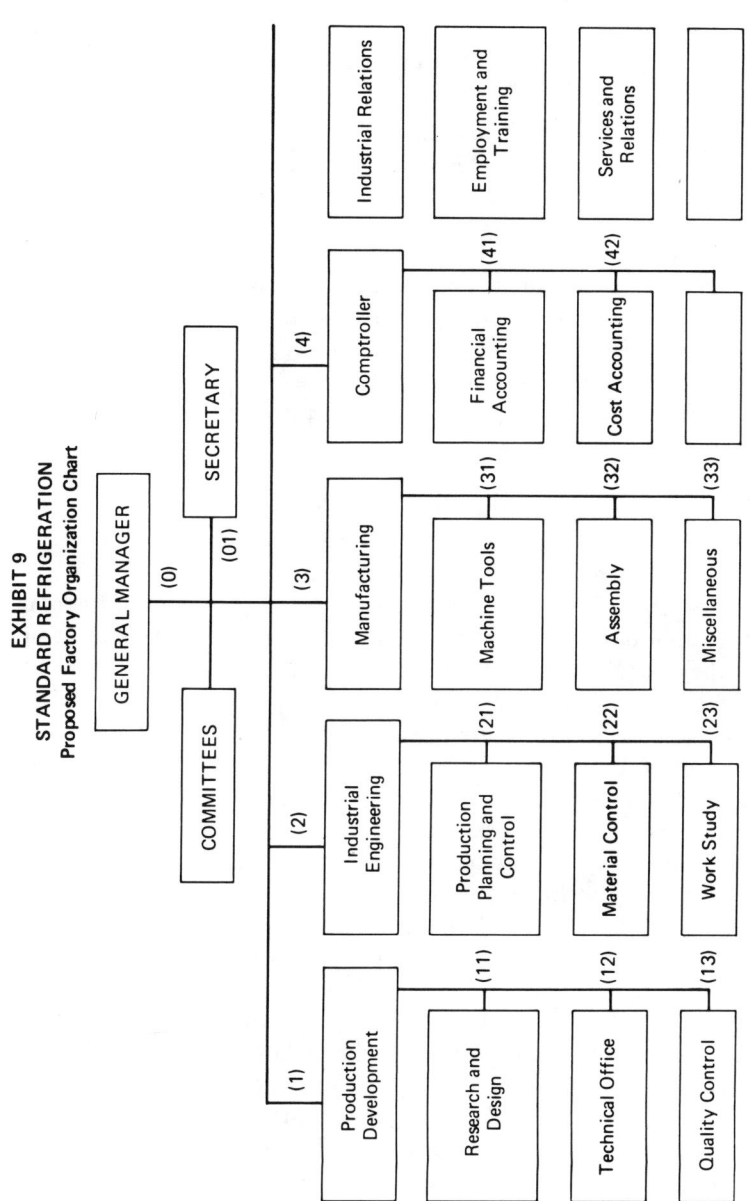

EXHIBIT 9
STANDARD REFRIGERATION
Proposed Factory Organization Chart

13

Gomhouria Tobacco Company*

In January, 1960, Nadim Hamdi, 52, managing director of the Gomhouria Company, Cairo, in a discussion with other members of the company's executive committee outlined his plans for a new strategy in marketing the company's tobacco products. Hamdi suggested that funds be allocated for advertising to stimulate the overall consumption of tobacco products. This was a major change in the existing strategy which was to focus advertising effort on a few major brands.

In addition to this suggestion, Hamdi proposed to concentrate more marketing effort on the low income market. Because of the large percentage of the Egyptian population contained in this group, Hamdi forecast that the future expansion of demand would come largely from this segment of the population. He also pointed out that the company's cheaper products were more profitable because they required less processing and could be manufactured from low grades of tobacco which were more easily obtained than high grades. These suggestions were a part of Hamdi's marketing philosophy to maintain company leadership in the Egyptian market and to offset the slow decline in sales which had taken place in the preceding two years.

Hamdi's ideas were opposed by J. B. Balian, 69, chairman of the board, and his son, Philip Balian, 36, production manager who did not want to change the existing strategy. (See Exhibit 1 for organization chart). The existing policy was largely that of J. B. Balian and his close friend and associate Pierre Melikian, 71, general sales manager. Both Balian and Melikian were well known throughout the industry and were held in high regard because of the successful sales record of the company. Hosney Zohdy, the industrial relations manager, was the fourth man on the executive committee. All major policy decisions were made by this committee and were often presented as reports or directives circulated to each member for his signature. A missing signature meant that the officer in question disagreed with the proposal and could call a meeting to discuss it. Hamdi had been promoted to managing director from general manager and was made a member of the committee in late 1957.

Gomhouria Tobacco Company was founded in Cairo in 1897 by J. B.

*Reprinted by permission of the National Institute of Management Development, Cairo, United Arab Republic.

Gomhouria Tobacco Company

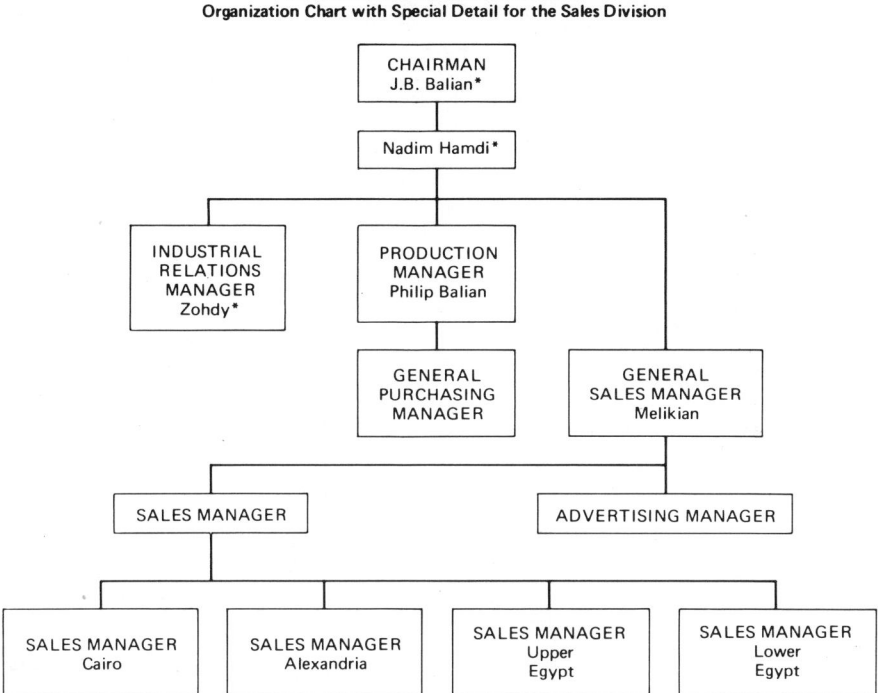

EXHIBIT 1
GOMHOURIA TOBACCO COMPANY
Organization Chart with Special Detail for the Sales Division

*Members of the Executive Committee

Balian's father. Throughout its history, the company had been the leading manufacturer and distributor of tobacco products in Egypt. (Exhibits 2 and 3 show the 1959 balance sheet and profit and loss statement of the company).

In 1959, over 4,000 employees were working at the company's single plant in Cairo. A new addition was being built at this time to house production equipment for the manufacture of filter cigarettes and plans had been made for expanding office facilities.

The company sold three main types of tobacco products: cigarettes, roll-your own cigarette tobacco, and a special tobacco called moassal for use in the hubly-bubbly pipe. Smaller amounts of madgha (a chewing tobacco), standard pipe tobacco, and cigars were also manufactured and distributed. Shipments of these products from the company's factory from 1954 to 1959 are shown in Table 1. The sales record for the year ending September 30, 1959 is given in a quotation from the company's report in Exhibit 4.

EXHIBIT 2
GOMHOURIA TOBACCO COMPANY
Balance Sheet as of September 30, 1959

ASSETS

I. Current Assets

    A. **Cash**

In hand an in transit	£E 303,601		
At banks	4,150,932	£E 4,453,993	

    B. **Accounts receivable**

Customers	42,678		
Less: Provision for doubtful debts	25,000		
	17,678		
Prepaid to suppliers	672,295	689,973	

    C. **Inventories** (At average cost or under as certified by officials of the company)

Leaf and other raw materials	5,954,675		
Goods in process	573,954		
Manufactured goods	643,694		
Supplies	294,878	7,467,201	

    D. **Government securities** (At cost) (Market value LE 182,750)

		200,000	£E 12,811,167

II. Trade Investments (At cost or under)   2,546

III. Share Holdings in Subsidiary Companies (Including goodwill resulting from their complete legal amalgamation)   3,476,305

IV. Government Securities (Purchased in accordance with law No. 7 of 1959)   104,215

V. Prepaid Expenses and other Debit Balances   378,904

VI. Fixed Assets

	At Cost	Accumulated Depreciation		
Freehold Land	£E 61,696	—	61,696	
Building	960,263	204,948	755,315	
Plant & Machinery	1,625,917	1,108,560	517,357	
Welfare Equipment	57,074	41,320	15,754	
Furniture & Fixtures	161,641	118,285	43,356	
Vehicles	64,665	33,651	13,014	
	2,913,256	1,506,764		1,406,492

TOTAL ASSETS   £E 18,179,629

Gomhouria Tobacco Company

EXHIBIT 2 (continued)

LIABILITIES AND NET WORTH

I. Current Liabilities

Customers	£E 228,689		
Suppliers	340,034		
Sundry creditors	95,720		
Accrued liabilities	113,153		
Dividends	1,682,829		
Taxation	272,543		
Due for subsidiary cost	1,696,868		
Total current liabilities		£E 4,429,836	

II. Long-Term Liabilities

Pensions and indemnities	1,060,064		
Sundry	20,926		
Total long-term liabilities		1,080,990	
Total liabilities			£E 5,510,826

III. Net Worth

Capital Stock (Authorized and issued)			4,000,000
Retained Earnings			
Provisions, appropriations and reserves			
Sequestration expenses		164,000	
Renewals		982,900	
Contingencies		769,016	
Amortization of goodwill		200,000	
Legal reserves		653,344	
Reserve for purchase of govt. sec.		208,658	
Reserve for replacement of assets		2,732,000	
Reserve for dividend equalization		100,000	
Reserve (General)		2,810,000	
Total restrictions of retained earnings		8,619,918	
Unrestricted retained earnings		48,885	8,668,803
TOTAL LIABILITIES AND NET WORTH			**£E 18,179,629**

THE EGYPTIAN TOBACCO INDUSTRY

Raw materials necessary for the manufacture of tobacco products were not available in Egypt in 1959 and practically everything that went into the making of a cigarette (raw leaf tobacco, cigarette paper, aluminum foil, card-board, filters and cork tipping) had to be imported.

EXHIBIT 3
GOMHOURIA TOBACCO COMPANY
Income Statement for Year Ending September 30, 1959

SALES LESS COST OF GOODS SOLD: GROSS PROFITS				£E 3,363,730
Less:	Operating expenses			
	Depreciation			
	Buildings			
	Plant, Machinery etc.		208,302	
	Welfare equipment			
	Furniture and fixtures			
	Vehicles			
	Administrative expenses		242,456	
	Pension and indemnities		218,934	
	Total operating expenses			669,692
				£E 2,694,038
TRADING PROFIT				
Add:	Miscellaneous income			
	Revenue from trade investments		11,331	
	Miscellaneous receipts		34,531	
	Non-recurring profits		242,996	£E 288,858
				£E 2,982,896
Less:	Miscellaneous expenses			
	Amortization of goodwill		100,000	
	Taxation (on profits, income, prop.)		287,507	387,507
	NET PROFIT FOR THE YEAR			£E 2,595,389

Statement of Changes in Retained Earnings
for Year Ending September 30, 1959

Retained earnings October 1, 1958—unrestricted		£E 48,844
Retained earnings October 1, 1958—restricted		7,704,570
Total retained earnings, October 1, 1958		7,753,414
Add: Net profit per income statement		2,595,389
		10,348,803
Less: Dividends proposed		1,680,000
Retained earnings, September 30, 1959		8,668,803
Restricted retained earnings (per Balance Sheet, Sept. 30, 1959)		8,619,918
Unrestricted retained earnings, September 30, 1959		48,885
TOTAL RETAINED EARNINGS, September 30, 1959		£E 8,668,803

Gomhouria Tobacco Company

EXHIBIT 4
GOMHOURIA TOBACCO COMPANY
Quotation from Annual
Report for the Year Ending September 30, 1959

The total quality of leaf tobacco withdrawn from bonded warehouses and cleared through customs, during the fiscal year under review, amounted to 11,30,479 kilograms, as against 11,877,564 kilograms during the previous year, viz: a decrease of 0.62% for the year 1958/1959 as compared to the year 1957/1958, whereas the decrease in the percentage of the company's clearances, compared to total clearances of the whole tobacco industry, was of the order of 0.99% during the year under review as compared to last year.

The per capita average of tobacco consumed during the year 1957/1958 (taking the population of the Egyptian Province as 22,600,000) is estimated as 526 grs. as against 515 grs. for the year 1958/1959 (with a yearly increase in population estimated at 300,600).

We estimate, on the above basis, the annual per capita expenditure on smoking in the Egyptian Province at £E 2.748 for the year 1957/1958 and £E 2.776 for the year under review, i.e. an increase of 1.02% in the latter.

It should be pointed out that part of this increase is due to the higher prices charged after the duty increase imposed as from 2nd July, 1959, whereas the previous year suffered nothing of the like.

The cigarette output of your company, divided between Oriental and Virginia brands, the latter including both the American blended and the English types, for the last two financial years is as follows:

	Year 1957/58 %	Year 1958/59 %
Cigarettes of Oriental brands	11.1	10.7
Cigarettes of Virginia brands	88.0	89.3
TOTAL	100.0	100.0

Proportions in the above totals of 10.4% and 22% respectively, represent the output of filter tip cigarettes (the production of the latter increased by 104.63%, as compared to last year) the remainder being regular cigarettes. Percentages of 0.016% and 0.01% represent the output of handmade cigarettes all the remainder being machine made. The total cigarette output of the company during the year 1958/1959 decreased in the proportion of 2.4%, as compared to the output of the preceding year, this decrease being due to many smokers shifting to packet tobacco.

The total quantities of the company's output of manufactured tobacco during the two financial years under review are divided as follows:

	Year 1957/58 %	Year 1958/59 %
Packet tobacco (Cut)	78.3	78.6
Moassal	19.1	18.7
Pipe tobacco	0.8	0.6
Madgha (Chewing)	1.8	2.1
TOTAL	100.0	100.0

The total quantities of the company's manufactured tobacco output during the year 1958/1959 have increased in the proportion of 10.54% as compared to the total output of the preceding year, the major part of this increase is concentrated on packet tobacco and to a much lesser extent on moassal. The reasons for this have been set out above.

The company's exports during the year under review, including supplies of ships stores, attained 20.3% of the total exports of tobacco products of the Egyptian Province, as against 21% during the previous year. The total export of the Egyptian Province during the year 1958/1959 decreased in the proportion of 18.8% as compared to last year.

The particulars of both the balance sheet and income and expenditure in the profit and loss account, as described under their various headings, are self-explanatory, and there is nothing of special significance to report. We would, however, draw your attention to the general tendency towards price increase of leaf tobacco, as well as all other raw materials during the year under review, such increases were consequently reflected in a corresponding increase in our production costs.

TABLE 1
Gomhouria Tobacco Company Annual Shipments
1954-1959

Brand	1954	1955	1956	1957	1958	1959
Individual LVM* Type Cigarettes (000,000)						
Arrow	...	...	...	...	...	272
Bol Air	...	...	...	...	1	25
Mohammed Ali	...	...	...	...	1	8
Assouan	2,945	2,884	3,042	3,564	4,274	3,301
Service	81	80	90	68	15	6
Lewa	45	58	78	58	2	...
Sunrise	...	121	336	390	480	1,539
Nile	618	877	1,233	1,434	833	662
Nefertiti	123	144	179	232	245	176
Askari	242	240	279	341	308	175
Ramses	206	244	302	320	230	136
Tewfik	...	...	...	8	23	24
Lord	...	3	3	19	24	17
Total LVM Type	4,260	4,651	5,542	6,434	6,435	6,341
Individual Oriental Type Cigarettes (000,000)						
Sami	133	128	136	121	124	147
Fellah	13	7	2	...	...	...
Maden	16	11	4	...	...	...
Sabet	1,216	1,093	1,017	765	566	486
Shams	17	10	5	...	...	...
Hekmat	2	1	1	1	1	1
Lattakia	45	32	23	14	11	10
Alexandria	13	10	8	6	5	5
Semiramis	8	6	5	4	4	4
Salah El Din	4	2	1	...	...	...
Amal	68	86	94	97	90	66
Total Oriental Type	1,535	1,386	1,296	1,008	801	719
Kilograms of Packet Tobacco (000)						
Small packet tobacco	1,226	1,313	1,425	1,537	1,394	1,548
Large packet tobacco	89	99	104	117	161	209
Total Packet Tobacco	1,315	1,417	1,529	1,654	1,555	1,757
Miscellaneous Other Products (000)						
Moassal packets	1,709	1,773	1,257	600	357	432
Madgha packets	50	49	40	28	38	49
Cigars	3	3	2	...	...	...
L.V.M. pipe tobacco	23	21	21	22	14	13
OM pipe tobacco (imported)	2	2	1	...	...	...
Total Miscellaneous	3,102	3,265	2,850	2,304	1,964	2,251

*LVM stands for Local Virginia Manufacture, a name used to distinguish company manufactured cigarettes from imports. There were practically no imported cigarettes in 1959. LVM covered all classes of non-Oriental type cigarettes: Straight Virginia or English blends such as the Ramses and Askari brands and American blends such as the Sunrise, Nile and Assouan.

Gomhouria Tobacco Company

Raw tobacco leaf was by far the largest item of value in this list. The amount imported by Gomhouria in 1959 was over 8,000 tons.

Duties on this tobacco were about 650-700% of the value and provided the largest single source of duty revenue in Egypt.

Cigarettes were made from mixtures of different types of tobacco.

The main tobacco types were Virginia, burley and oriental, and came mainly from the United States, India and Greece. Government restrictions favored the importation of the oriental types which came from soft currency countries. The prices of raw leaf at the factory exclusive of import duties in 1959 were approximately as follows:

>Oriental : £E 0.60-0.70 per kilogram
>Virginia : £E 0.65-0.75 per kilogram
>Burley : £E 0.70-0.80 per kilogram

Customs charges were on a weight basis irrespective of the value. A Tobacco plant had four useable types of leaves called cutters, leaf, lugs and primings. Each leaf type could have up to 20 grades thus giving the tobacco blend for a particular cigarette "blend."

A Gomhouria official estimated that 29 per cent of the Egyptian population smoked cigarettes. Table 2 shows an estimate of the income structure of the Egyptian population.

TABLE 2
Estimated Per Capita Income of Egyptian Population

Group	Income per Year	No. in Group	Percentage of Total Population
Low income	£E 30 to £E 70	18,375,000	75%
Middle income	£E 70 to £E500	4,900,000	20%
Higher income	Over £E 500	1,225,000	5%
Total		24,500,000	100%

It was the lower income group made up of the fellahin on which Hamdi wished to concentrate more of the company's marketing effort. The smoking habits of this group were closely correlated with the success or failure of agricultural crops: when crop prices were high, they smoked the cheaper types of oriental cigarettes, but when prices were down, they used more packet tobacco for roll-your-own type cigarettes. In recent years, peasants had begun to smoke filter cigarettes, but they usually bought individual cigarettes rather than packages. An estimated 20 per cent of Gomhouria cigarettes were sold this way: one at a time.

In addition to Gomhouria there were about 25 companies in the tobacco industry. Only six, however, manufactured cigarettes. The others concentrated on roll-your-own packet tobacco and moassal which required less investment in machinery and production equipment. An estimate of the share of tobacco

TABLE 3
Percentages of the Total Market Held by Various Tobacco Companies in Egypt, 1957 to 1959

	1957	1958	1959
Somhouria	69.2%	66.6%	66.8%
Middle East	13.0	14.9	14.4
Hosney	1.9	2.1	1.7
Arab	1.5	1.7	1.6
Port-Said	2.4	3.0	2.8
Al-Mottahida	1.7	1.8	1.9
Others	10.3	9.9	10.8
	100.0%	100.0%	100.0%

market held by various companies in Egypt prepared by a market research consultant for 1957, 1958, and 1959 is shown in Table 3, and the number of brands manufactured by the three largest companies in Table 4.

TABLE 4
Number of Brands of Cigarettes and Other Products Manufactured by Gomhouria and Principal Competitors: 1959

Company	Product	Number of Brands
Gomhouria	Cigarettes-Oriental	9
	Cigarettes-LVM	11
	Packet Tobacco	6
	Moassal	1
Middle East	Cigarettes-Oriental	17
	Cigarettes-LVM	32
	Packet Tobacco	2
	Moassal	1
Hosney	Cigarettes-Oriental	24
	Cigarettes-LVM	12
	Packet Tobacco	3
	Moassal	3

Competitors created new brands by adding extra tobacco to cigarettes and packing them tighter. These were introduced with special display advertising and extra trade discounts. These promotion techniques were discontinued as soon as brand acceptance had been achieved.

GOMHOURIA SALES ORGANIZATION

An organization chart of Gomhouria's sales division is given in Exhibit 1. Tobacco products were distributed to consumers through agents, wholesalers, and retailers of all sizes. To facilitate distribution, Egypt was divided into four

Gomhouria Tobacco Company

regions; Alexandria, Cairo, Lower Egypt and Upper Egypt. Melikian, the general sales manager, explained the distribution system in the Cairo region in a management report as follows:

> Since April 1, 1959 the distribution of the company's goods in Cairo has been handled by the Nile Company whose paid-up capital is £E 90,000.
>
> This company has 50 partners, all specialized in the sale of tobacco and cigarettes, and has been active in the Cairo market for the last 20 to 30 years.
>
> To secure a rapid distribution of goods, our distributor keeps in store a permanent stock valued at about £E 60,000 to 70,000. Their store is supplied by means of two large 3 ton lorries which make several journeys daily between the factory and the distributor's warehouse.
>
> Cigarettes and tobacco products (amounting to £E 46,000 per day) are sorted out, loaded on eleven vans, and carried to various parts of Cairo and delivered to wholesalers.
>
> The distributor owns a fully equipped garage and has specialized technicians who take care of the maintenance of the two lorries, eleven vans and 250 bicycles used by the company and wholesaler salesmen to distribute products from the wholesalers to small retailers. There are 18,000 in Cairo who are supplied once or sometimes even twice daily.
>
> The distributor issues invoices to the wholesalers and is responsible for collecting them.
>
> The bicycle and tricycle salesmen collect the orders and deliver them, and collect payment. All this work is carried out by a staff of 93 individuals employed by the distributor.

TABLE 5
Regional Distribution of Gomhouria Products for the Months of June 1954 and June 1959*
(Sales figures in £E 000's)

	LVM		Oriental		Packet		Madgha		Moassal		Other[†]	
	Sales	%	Sales	%	Sales	%	Sales	%	Sales	%	Sales	%
June 1954												
Cairo	530	41	24	8.0	13	3.42	0.3	1.95	33	26.6	12.04	52.5
Alexandria	217	16.8	5	1.67	9	2.37	1.0	6.6	17	13.7	5.5	24.0
Lower Egypt	370	28.6	22	7.23	285	75.28	2.0	13.1	26	21.0	4.0	17.4
Upper Egypt	177	13.6	249	33.1	72	18.93	12.0	78.35	48	38.7	1.4	6.1
Total	1,294	100	300	100	379	100	15.3	100	124	100	22.94	100
June 1959												
Cairo	1,276	39.4	8	4.85	34	4.2	...	...	...	...	2.0	46.5
Alexandria	461	14.2	3	1.82	28	3.40	...	...	...	...	1.0	23.3
Lower Egypt	799	24.7	7	4.25	563	69.5	0.2	...	25	41.6	1.0	23.3
Upper Egypt	702	21.7	147	89.08	186	22.9	21	100	35	58.4	0.3	6.9
Total	3,238	100	165	100	811	100	21.2	100	60	100	4.3	100

*Between 1954 and 1959, customs duties on tobacco increased from £E 3,000 per Kilogram to £E 4,000 per Kilogram.

†This included all other products manufactured or imported by the company such as pipe tobacco, cigars, and cigarettes.

TABLE 6
Retail Prices of Gomhouria and Competitive Products
January 1960

Product and Brand	Small Size		Large Size	
	Size of Package	Retail Price (Piasters)	Size of Package	Retail Price (Piasters)
Gomhuria Products				
Oriental Cigarettes				
Sabet	......	...	100 cigs.	1 per 3 cigs.‡
Shams	......	...	18 "	7½
High Lattakia	......	...	20 "	10
Semiramis	......	...	20 "	11½
Amal	10 cigs.	6	20 "	12
LVN Cigarettes				
Assouan	10 "	5	20 "	10
Arrow*	10 "	5	50 "	0.5 per cigs.‡
Nefertiti	10 "	5½	20 "	11
Nile	10 "	6	20 "	12
Lewa*	10 "	6	20 "	12
Service†	10 "	6	20 "	12
Sunrise*	10 "	6	20 "	12
Askari	10 "	6½	20 "	13
Ramses	10 "	7	20 "	14
Tewfik	......	...	20 "	15
Lord	......	...	20 "	16
Packet Tobacco				
Omda	......	...	25 gms.	2.5
Moassal				
Sakia			25 "	1.0
Middle East Products				
Oriental Cigarettes				
El Fallah	17 cigs.	7	......	...
High: El Nakhla	9 "	4½	18 cigs.	9
El Rais	10 "	6	20 "	12
El Kaed	10 "	6	20 "	12

Gomhouria Tobacco Company

Brand				
LVM Cigarettes				
Olympia	100	1 per 4 cigs.‡	500	1 per 4 cigs.‡
Universal	100	1 per 3 " ‡	500	1 per 3 " *
Splendid			20	9
Belair	10	5	20	10
Marshal†	10	5	20	10
Capri*	100	1 per 2 cigs.‡	500	1 per 2 cigs.‡
Himalaya*	10	5½	20	11
Temptation*	10	6	20	12
Hawaii	10	6½	20	13
Glory	10	7½	20	15
Packet Tobacco				
Samara			25 gms.	2.5
Mazag			25 "	3.0
Moassal				
Ala Kaifak	20 gms.	1	60 "	3.0
Hosney Products				
Oriental Cigarettes				
El Gamal	100	25		
El Shaab	50	17½		
Port-Said	21	8	100 cigs.	0.4‡
High: Angle			17	10
Sofia*	10	5½	20	11
El Mamoura			17	11
Shephard's			17	12
Beghdad	10	6	20	12
Orabi			20	15
LVM Cigarettes				
California	10	5½	20	11
Jet*	10	6½	20	13
Special*	10	7	20	14
Packet Tobacco				
Nasser			25 gms.	2.5
Moassal				
Shater Hassan			40 gms.	2.0

*Filter tip
†Cork tip
‡Cigarettes sold individually at retail.

It should be remembered that cash collected daily-amounting to about £E 64,000- consists mainly of very small notes which must be counted, sorted out, and paid into the bank each day. This alone requires a certain number of employees.

The wholesalers, who supply the 18,000 retailers of the Cairo market through the medium of tricycle and bicycle salesmen, have invested approximately £E 150,000. They possess 52 distribution centers which must be stocked with all necessary brands in order to provide prompt supply of the market.

For internal work, they employ 128 men and women and bear all the risks of the credit which they grant to satisfy their customers needs.

The distributor and the wholesalers, all work in the market to develop sales, fight competition, and assure the constant freshness of our stocks on the market.

From the above it can be seen that the part played by the Cairo distributor and wholesalers is far from being a sinecure.

This distribution requires considerable sums to maintain lorries and vans and to pay the large staff necessary to handle successfully the business.

We may add that the distributor as well as the wholesalers are under the constant supervision of the sales personnel of the Gomhouria Company and that the slightest error is immediately reported to management.

Total costs of distributors and wholesalers are about 1.1 per cent of our sales.

The sales manager explained that the same distribution system was followed in the other three regions but that in some of these the distributor's role was filled by the company itself until a reliable distributor could be found.

The distribution of the company's major products among the four regions in June 1954 and June 1959, is shown in Table 5.

Each major region was subdivided into a number of divisions called inspectorates. There were, for example, 7 inspectorates in Alexandria, each of which had a supervisor or chief inspector, a head salesman, and a number of junior salesmen. It was the function of the latter to call upon retailers, take orders, deliver goods, collect payments and inspect displays of stock. The inspectors worked out of the offices of the wholesalers, but were paid by Gomhouria.

Melikian believed that pricing was a very important factor in selling tobacco. In discussing this subject, he had said, "A change of one piaster in the price of a package of cigarettes will have a strong effect on sales. We prefer to have the price of a package divisible by 20 so that the price of an individual cigarette is easy to calculate, since 20 per cent of our cigarette sales are on an individual basis."

Retail price comparisons of Gomhouria and competitive products are shown in Table 6.

Manufacturing consumer tobacco products was largely a converting process of changing raw leaf tobacco to a tobacco blend either packaging it to make packet tobacco and moassal or adding cigarette paper, filters, etc. to make

Gomhouria Tobacco Company

TABLE 7
Cost Comparison of Filter and Plain LVM Cigarettes

	Filter Type	Plain
Size of package	26 X 74 millimeters	26 X 69 millimeters
Cost of tobacco per kilo	482 piasters	482 piasters
Weight of tobacco per 1,000 cigarettes	905 grams	984 grams
	Piasters	Piasters
Manufacturing cost-including raw materials	510.50	512.00
F. C. & I.	1.50	1.50
Selling expense	6.00	6.00
Advertising	1.00	1.00
Total cost per 1,000 cigs.	519.00	520.50
Net selling price per 1,000 cigs.	514.75	541.75
Profit before administrative expenses, etc.	22.75	21.25

cigarette products. A comparison of the profitability of manufacturing a filter and a non-filter cigarette in 1959 is shown in Table 7.

Packet tobacco and moassal were less costly to produce but also commanded lower prices. Moassal was more profitable because of the cheaper grades of tobacco that could be used in manufacturing the product.

In 1959, the company spent about £E 70,000 on advertising. About 60 per cent of this amount was spent on direct advertising of individual brands, the remaining amount being directed to various forms of other company advertising. The heaviest expenditures were for outdoor billboards, gifts and newpaper advertising. The balance was spent on retail storefront displays, samples and office administration. The total advertising expenditures of the company and the amounts spent on direct advertising for the company's main brands are given in Tables 8 and 9.

Melikian had always believed that too much advertising could not be used effectively in Egypt where 40% of the population was still illiterate and media were not well developed. For these reasons his advertising expenditures were concentrated in the urban areas and on the comparatively better brands. Mr. Hamdi felt, however, that the advent of television, especially when it was introduced in rural areas, would provide an excellent medium for mass advertising.

Marketing information was supplied mainly through salesmen's reports. A small three-man department handled the compilation of statistical information, sales reports, shipping orders and sales forecasting. The company did not use an advertising agency.

Hamdi suggested a number of basic changes in the company's marketing

TABLE 8
Total Advertising Expenditures Gomhouria Tobacco Company
1954 to 1959 (September 1 to August 31)

Media	1954	1955	1956	1957	1958	1959
Press & sundry	9485	18572	23557	9038	10592	13202
Screen*	6740	6171	3159	...	...	...
Outdoor*	19684	28114	30558	28076	18082	19241
Retail shops*	2287	827	8316	131	6255	6428
Gifts*†	16750	15641	18421	14323	11448	13775
Free samples	642	165	...	...	...	5417
Departmental‡	8171	12564	14664	11832	10374	9386
Total	63759	82053	98675	63399	56752	68449

*Advertising expenditure identifiable with a specific brand.

†Includes such items as diaries, calendars, pens etc...with individual brand names of cigarettes printed on the gift.

‡Largely made up of the administrative expenses of the advertising department.

strategy. First, he wanted a larger share of advertising and promotion effort to be directed to the low class market. "New inexpensive products," he said, "should be introduced to appeal to the middle and low income groups." Promotions which would appeal to this group should be used. The increased sales of lower class products would, he said, enable the company to expand its overall sales without additional filter-assembly equipment which was expensive and difficult to obtain. In addition to the £E 50,000 to £E 100,000 invested in each filter-assembly machine, the expensive filter cigarettes also required promotion. The promotion cost could be as much as £E 10,000 to £E 20,000 during the introductory period for a new brand. Contrary to Hamdi's suggestions, the com-

TABLE 9
Direct Advertising Expenditures
for Gomhouria's Main Cigarette Brands
1954 to 1959 (April 1 to March 31)

Brand	1954	1955	1956	1957	1958	1959
Assouan	32908	39607	29496	29979	28541	35178
Sunrise	...	3134	1013	776	1583	7019
Ramses	*	*	*	8892	7876	8582
Nile	*	*	*	10490	7541	8853
Sibet	2796	2234	1033	1317	736	1052
Askari	*	*	*	1399	1203	2805
Tewfik	*	*	*	409	246	2320
Amal	*	*	*	1526	932	2026
Lord	*	*	*	52	396	535
Omda (packet tobacco)	*	*	*	3857	2988	4310
Sakia (moassal)	*	*	*	1967	1354	1778

*Data not available.

pany's marketing policy was proceeding in the opposite direction. Moassal, for example, was being withheld from the market and J. B. Balian wanted to completely discontinue the product line by the end of 1960.

Hamdi's other major disagreement with the company's marketing philosophy was in the relationship which had been established between direct and indirect advertising. More attention, he said, should be given to building up the image of the Gomhouria Company and the pleasures of smoking than to the advertising of specific brands.

"Advertising," he said, "had obviously done nothing to prevent the sales decline of the Assouan brand between 1958 and 1959, and the Sabet brand between 1954 and 1959."

14

Standard Trading*

The Standard Trading Company produced refrigerators and airconditioners for sale in the Egyptian market. In 1961 it planned to add vacuum cleaners to its product line. As a start, the company imported 500 kits of vacuum cleaner parts which were to be assembled and put in cabinets made in Egypt. Only about 12 cleaners had been assembled by February 1962 when a change in top management took place and the new managing director suspended the vacuum cleaner operation.

HISTORICAL DEVELOPMENT

Standard Trading started its activities as a purely commercial enterprise. During World War II, the company engaged in some light manufacturing activities and a small factory was established at Shoubra for that purpose. After the War, these activities were discontinued.

In the early 1950's, the management's interest in industrial operations revived. The Shoubra factory was overhauled and equipped for the purpose of partly assembling and partly manufacturing refrigerators. In 1954, the company signed a licensing agreement with a German manufacturing firm under which the Egyptian firm would manufacture refrigerator cabinets and a few other parts, while the German firm would provide the motor and most other components.

The factory went into production toward the end of 1954, with an output of five to eight units per day. Total production amounted to 114 refrigerators during the remainder of 1954, but expanded in the following years. Table 1 shows the production and sales of refrigerators for the period 1954-1961.

The company had five show rooms in Cairo, four of which were also sales branches. It had three sales branches in Alexandria, one in Luxor, and one in Mansourah. Non-exclusive agents sold Standard products in the other governorates on commission basis. These agents were also merchants or agents for other products besides those made by Standard.

Cairo accounted for roughly 75% of refrigerator sales, while Alexandria and the provinces accounted for about 12½% each.

Cash sales amounted to about 30% of total refrigerator sales; the other 70%

*Reprinted by permission of the National Institute of Management Development, Cairo, United Arab Republic.

Standard Trading

TABLE 1
Standard Trading Company Production and Sales of Refrigerators and Airconditioners

Year	Refrigerators		Airconditioners	
	Production (units)	Sales (units)	Production (units)	Sales (units)
1954	114	113		
1955	2402	1947		
1956	4289	3938	94	94
1957	2016	2584	—	—
1958	3104	2413	3	3
1959	2687	3421	612	278
1960	9533	9308	1185	912
1961	17184	14589	1842	1770

SOURCE: Company's records.

were made on a credit basis with payment extending over periods of 12 to 20 months.

In 1955 Standard Trading started thinking about building a new factory for the production of a wide range of appliances such as airconditioners, radio and television sets, electric irons, cookers and burners. By the end of 1955, a licensing agreement was reached with an American manufacturing company according to which Standard was authorised to produce the American company's line of products, particularly airconditioners, oil burners and radio and T.V. sets.

As a beginning, Standard assembled airconditioners at its Shoubra factory; ninety-four units were completed and sold before the Suez Crisis forced the company to discontinue operations.

In 1958, the project was reconsidered with the objective of producing airconditioners locally without having to secure a licence. The technical department designed a set which was approved by the management. Production began late in 1958; foreign sources supplied the motor and certain other components, while Standard manufactured the cabinet and some other parts. Table 1 shows production and sales of airconditioners since 1956.

In 1958, the company began a study of electrical household appliances to find others that might be added to its line. One of the items considered was the vacuum cleaner. The company decided to experiment with this product, and imported 500 unit kits (a kit contained the motor and most other parts of the vacuum cleaner with the exception of the case and few parts which were to be produced locally). The shipment arrived in July 1961, and the production-assembly of vacuum cleaners began shortly afterwards. Shortly therafter the market research unit was asked to make a study of the local market for vacuum cleaners. The study was completed and a report was presented by the research unit dated 23rd December 1961. A summary of the report is given below.

A SUMMARY OF THE MARKET RESEARCH REPORT ON THE LOCAL MARKET FOR THE ELECTRIC VACUUM CLEANER

Objective

The study aimed at determining the market absorbing capacity and its development in the future as well as helping the sales department to draw up its selling and promotion policies for the vacuum cleaner.

Brands Available

1. *Super:* This is a local make which had a 400-watt motor and sold for £E 49. This brand gave a better performance and had a wider scope of use than Standard's cleaner. But Super had a poor finish and a relatively high price.

   Super was one of the most important competitors of Standard's vacuum cleaner because Super was locally made and also because the present capacity for its production was about 2,000 units a year, even though only 400 units were produced in 1961.

   Super had not been selling well because of the above mentioned factors, and also because the promotion and advertising policies were not enough to attract a large volume of sales.

2. *Other Brands:* These were all foreign makes which were imported in very limited quantities:

   (a) *Progress:* A German brand; 350 watts, retail price £E 55, with 10% discount for each cash sale.

   (b) *General Electric:* An Italian model; about the same size as Standard's model; retail price £E 46.50.

   (c) *Hoover* and *Philips:* These had not been available since 1956.

Selling Methods

The importing firms usually sold to dealers on credit for a period of 10-12 months. Most sales to consumers were made for cash.

Average Annual Sales

Data necessary to determine average annual sales of vacuum cleaners in Egypt were lacking. Estimates made by the main vacuum cleaner agents for sales before 1956 were used as the best measure of market potential. These estimates indicated a market for about 1,200 units annually.

Sales during 1956-1961 could not be taken to represent the absorbing capacity of the local market because of the lack of imports of vacuum cleaners during that period.

A Study of the Consumer

Who would be the potential customers of the new vacuum cleaner? Three basic factors determined the size of the potential market:

Standard Trading

1. Availability of electricity.
2. Availability of a certain minimum of income.
3. Certain habits and ways of living.

Ownership of private cars was taken as an indicator of families with the above characteristics. In other words, those who owned private cars would be considered potential customers for the vacuum cleaner.

An interview was conducted with 47 private car owners in three Cairo districts.

Garden City	Zamalek	Manial El Roda
20	17	10

Out of the 47, only 19 owned vacuum cleaners. From these 19, the following information about their vacuum cleaners was obtained:

1. *Type of Use:* 58% used the vacuum cleaner in cleaning carpets only, while 42% used it in cleaning curtains, chairs and the floor as well.
2. *Frequency of Use:* 58% used the vacuum cleaner once a month; the rest used it more frequently.
3. *Price Paid for Vacuum Cleaner:* 33% paid less than £E 20; 50% paid £E 20 to 30; 17% paid more than £E 30. (Prices paid were primarily those prevailing before 1956 when imported vacuum cleaners were much cheaper due to lower import duties and to less rigid import restrictions).
4. *Order of Priority of Main Household Appliances:* The vacuum cleaner owners were asked to classify the refrigerator, the gas cooker, the electric washing machine, and the electric vacuum cleaner in the order of priority which suited them.

First priority was the appliance they wanted most, the second priority was the next most wanted, etc. Points were assigned as follows:

> First priority .... 4 points
> Second priority .... 3 points
> Third priority .... 2 points
> Fourth priority .... 1 point

The following results were obtained:

> Refrigerator .... 39 points
> Gas cooker .... 37 points
> Washing machine ...... 16 points
> Vacuum cleaner .... 16 points

5. *Replacement Market Potential:* The sample was then asked whether they would be prepared to buy the Standard vacuum cleaner. The purpose of this question was to throw some light on the "replacement" market potential. 92% said they would not be prepared to buy a new vacuum cleaner; only 8% stated that they would.

This answer was explained by two factors:

(a) A high proportion of vacuum cleaner owners did not make much use of it because of their unawareness of the benefits that could be obtained by using it.

(b) Over half the sample population used the vacuum cleaner only once a month; this lengthened the life of the product.

The replacement market open to the new vacuum cleaner was limited; this phenomenon would become of substantial importance at a later stage when the non-replacement market approached a saturation point.

To expand the replacement market, efforts should be made to increase the utility of the vacuum cleaner, so that the consumer could be convinced that it would pay him to replace his old vacuum cleaner with a new one.

The 28 respondents who did not own a vacuum cleaner at the time of the interview, were asked about:

1. Their attitude with regard to using a vacuum cleaner. The following table classifies their answers:

	Zamalek	Rodah
Anxious to have . . .	44.5%	17.0%
Has no objection . .	44.5%	50.0%
Does not want	11.0%	33.0%
Total	100%	100%

A higher percentage of those who did not want a vacuum cleaner occurred in Rodah than in Zamalek. This confirmed the hypothesis that the vacuum cleaner should be introduced gradually, beginning with the areas characterized by a relatively high level of income.

2. Who would use the vacuum cleaner in case it was bought?

	Zamalek	Rodah
Housewife	66%	79%
Servant	22%	21%
Not mentioned	12%	. . .
Total	100%	100%

The majority preferred the housewife to use the vacuum cleaner. There was a common belief that servants did not use vacuum cleaners properly.

3. The prices non-owners would be prepared to pay for a new vacuum cleaner were as follows:

>40% would pay less than £E 20
>40% would pay £E 20-30
>20% would pay more than £E 30

4. The order of priority of buying household appliances was determined. The following results were obtained:

>Refrigerator . . . . 55 points
>Gas cooker . . . . 50 points
>Washing machine . . . . . . 20 points
>Vacuum cleaner . . . . 20 points

Standard Trading

Conclusions

The Standard vacuum cleaner model was of the cylinder type with several attachments for different cleaning jobs; it was simple to set up; and was relatively low priced. There was another, bigger model on the market which had a larger base, was more powerful, faster, and more efficient in cleaning carpets, but it was more expensive than the cylinder type cleaner.

Since it was likely that the middle and above-middle classes would become more and more significant, the market would require a versatile and a cheap vacuum cleaner.

Long-term plans should be made to improve the Standard model by raising its efficiency. The following specific improvements were suggested:
1. Redesign the carpet nozzle to enlarge the base; make it smoother and eliminate the sharp edges so that it may have an easy run over the carpet.
2. Improve the motor to give the cleaner a greater suction power.
3. Attach an accessory for polishing parquet floors. *Super* offered this facility.
4. Lengthen the cord: the cord in competing makes was 6.5 meters long on the average.

CHANGE OF TOP MANAGEMENT

A change in Standard's top management took place in February 1962, by which time only about a dozen vacuum cleaners had been assembled. The new managing director instructed the factory to suspend vacuum cleaner production until further notice.

The change in management took place according to the decrees nominating the boards of directors of public sector companies. (Standard Trading was merged into the public sector in July 1961). The company's new board now consisted of Ali Kamel, managing director, who had been a member of the board since November 1961; Ahmed Moursi, general manager, previously the general manager of an engineering company; and Labib Hanna, production manager, who had been production manager for the last six years. The employees' and workers' representatives on the board were yet to be elected.

Ali Kamel, the managing director, made a quick study of the "small production" section (small production referred to production of airconditioners and vacuum cleaners which were produced in relatively small quantities) as soon as he took over, and discovered a lack of trained employees and improper organization of work in that section. He did not go in detail to determine the minimum quantity of vacuum cleaners which would be economical to produce. However, he considered that it would not be economical to produce as few as 300 or 500 units a year. Apart from this, the company, in Kamel's opinion, faced a number of problems more important and urgent than the introduction of the vacuum cleaner.

First, the firm was trying to recruit more factory staff to fill in the gap which existed, partly as a result of the expansion of production without any corresponding increase in the factory's labor force, and partly because ten of the twenty highly skilled technicians in the company left.

Second, there were defects in the refrigerator; customers' complaints had been received in connection with the performance of certain components of the refrigerator, such as the handle, thermostat button, and the door. The staff had been trying to remedy these defects, but the managing director thought that their efforts had not been completely successful.

TABLE 2
Complaints Received Regarding the Refrigerator

Period	Number of Complaints
October 1961	2,021
November 1961	1,695
December 1961	1,117
January 1962	1,071

SOURCE: Company's records.

Most complaints were made in person at the company's showroom. A substantial number of these complaints was received when individuals came to pay their monthly instalments. About 15% of the complaints were not specific; customers simply asked for a general inspection of the unit. The result of virtually all inspections of this kind was negative.

Third, Kamel also believed that there were defects in the airconditioner. Complaints had been received about the mechanical operation, and he personally thought the cabinet should be redesigned.

Kamel believed it was very important to remedy these defects, especially from the point of view of the export market where the refrigerator, as well as the other products, were bound to meet fierce competition.

Fourth, the company did not have a complete and efficient maintenance and repair department for the refrigerator and airconditioner, and no plans had been made for maintenance of vacuum cleaners. Efficient servicing was necessary to the successful marketing of products. "Even a good product becomes bad," Kamel said, "if no proper preparation for maintenance and service is made in advance."

Finally, the managing director considered the vacuum cleaner a luxury for Egypt, as it was still a luxury for many countries, including some of the advanced countries. The company was also finding it difficult to obtain import licences for vacuum cleaner parts, because of the shortage of foreign exchange which was needed to import more vital goods for basic industries. Kamel was also of the opinion that household labour was still cheap in Egypt, and that the Egyptian housewife still had plenty of time for household cleaning.

Standard Trading

In view of all these factors, Kamel thought it necessary to order the suspension of vacuum cleaner production. However, as soon as he had enough staff and enough space (the company was constructing a new factory due to be completed in 1963), he would plan a new start with the vacuum cleaner. At that time, technical research would be done to adapt the vacuum cleaner for use under Egyptian conditions and with household labour capabilities. "Real market research" would also have to be undertaken. In the light of the results of these research activities, production would again be undertaken. But Kamel estimated that it would be over a year at the minimum before vacuum cleaner production was resumed.

Kamel decided to assemble the 500 vacuum cleaner kits and to sell them, at cost, to the company's employees and a few other people. The product would not be offered for sale in the open market. These instructions, however, he did not plan to give until current re-organization problems in the maintenance department had been solved. He estimated that this would take about three weeks.

Ahmed Moursi, the general manager, thought that the decision to suspend production of the vacuum cleaners was necessary in view of the defects found in the refrigerator and the lack of technicians from which the company suffered. He also was not sure that the Egyptian housewife was at present ready to accept the vacuum cleaner as a useful and necessary household appliance. However, he was optimistic regarding the future prospects of the vacuum cleaner in Egypt. Factors such as education and the increasing problem of obtaining household labor were likely to make the vacuum cleaner a success in Egypt in the near future. Thus, he thought the question was mainly a matter of timing.

Labib Hanna, the production manager, had a different opinion. He believed that assembly and completion of the vacuum cleaner units should go ahead. He believed that the sale of the present stock of vacuum cleaners (once they were completed) would require very little effort, because of the shortage in the local market as a result of import restrictions, and because the cleaner would be sold at £E 20-22. Competing foreign brands were selling for about £E 40. The Standard vacuum cleaner would cost about £E 16 to assemble; £E 10 for the kit and £E 6 for local materials, labor and factory overhead. The company would thus avoid incurring the loss which would result from not selling those on hand. Moreover, the launching of this limited quantity into the market should, in his opinion, be regarded as an experiment and should be used as a device to feel the "pulse" of the market and explore its potentialities. Although market research had already been undertaken, the best method to test the market, according to Hanna, was to actually introduce the product to the consumer.

The production manager also estimated that production of the vacuum cleaner did not require additional labor force or equipment. On the contrary, this activity would fill in the time gap which sometimes existed between orders. In fact, he thought that only one assembly man, a semi-skilled worker, could be given the relatively simple job of assembling the vacuum cleaners. Assembly and testing of one vacuum cleaner took one man approximately 30 minutes. In addition, the market potential was satisfactory because of the increasing shortage of household labor. Lastly, Hanna believed that the fear of maintenance problems was unfounded. Every product would require maintenance service. This fact should not deter the company from producing the vacuum cleaner, especially since vacuum cleaner service was simple. Standard's vacuum cleaner was a successful product in England in both local and export markets and, hence, should have few service problems.

Hanna was also not in favor of the idea that the vacuum cleaner should undergo further technical and market research before it was introduced to the consumer. His opinion was that there was no basic defect in the vacuum cleaner in its present form.

The company's sales manager, Alfred Nicholas, and the assistant manager, Adel Hassan, were of the opinion that the firm should go ahead now with vacuum cleaner production. Their argument was that the vacuum cleaner was in the company's product line and that no additional sales staff would be required.

"Providing there is good sales effort, the vacuum cleaner should be a good seller. We are now selling about 20,000 refrigerators a year, so I am convinced that we can sell about 5,000 vacuum cleaners a year, although annual sales may range between 1,500 and 3,000 for the first two years," Nicholas stated. He proposed that the vacuum cleaner be sold on credit with monthly payments in the order of £E 1.20-1.50. This, he thought, was likely to influence sales favorably.

In a memorandum submitted to the managing director, the sales department proposed the following advertising media:

1. Direct mail, in which the potential customer would be offered a free demonstration of the vacuum cleaner at his house and without any commitments on his side.
2. Television.
3. Cinema.
4. Magazines.

Daily newspapers would be used only to a limited extent in order to inform the public about the addition of the vacuum cleaner to the company's line of products.

The sales department also stated in the memorandum that £E 5,000 would be required for each of the first three years to finance effective advertising and selling campaigns.

The vacuum cleaner would be sold through the same branches and agents that sold the company's refrigerator and airconditioners.

15

The Egyptian Motors Company*

The Egyptian Motors Company was established in Egypt in 1926 and has operated continuously since then. In 1961 a situation developed which caused the management to reappraise the firm's long-term objectives. At that time Egyptian Motors had on hand well over 3000 cars in knocked-down condition which had been imported at an unusually high foreign exchange premium. No additional import licenses for passenger cars were available and none appeared likely in the foreseeable future.

Instead of importing cars, the Egyptian Government decided to have the Nasr Car Company produce a car under a franchise agreement with the Fiat Company of Italy. In 1961, the Nasr Car Company announced its first cars would be on the market by July 1962 and would sell for approximately £E 700, a price far below the import cost in Egyptian Pounds of Egyptian Motors stock. However, their stock was of a larger vehicle.

From 1924 until 1939, Egyptian Motors operated as a parts and accessories warehouse depot and a central sales and service office for 26 countries in the Balkans, Near East, and Africa. In 1936 it established in Alexandria what was still in 1961 the largest engine reconditioning plant in Egypt. From 1939 through World War II, the Company assembled small trucks and conditioned cars for delivery received built up from sources abroad. In 1950 it erected the only automotive assembly plant in the Near East at Alexandria. This plant had a potential daily capacity of 15 units. From 1950 to 1959 the company assembled 1000 to 1200 trucks per year and 700 to 1000 tractors. The latter was a less complex operation than the assembly of passenger cars. No cars were assembled during this period, because the savings achieved by shipping assembly parts and components instead of complete cars were more than offset by the high costs of assembling cars in small quantities.

Exchange controls which were instituted in 1952 made it impossible for the firm to serve the other countries in the area and, thereafter, all activities were restricted to Egypt. The importation of cars became increasingly difficult as the Government in its effort to speed the country's development, limited the use of

*Reprinted by permission of the National Institute of Management Development, Cairo, United Arab Republic.

foreign exchange for consumer goods. By 1959 the direct importation of cars had been virtually eliminated and Egyptian Motors, like all the other automobile importers in Egypt, was virtually without any product to sell. Importation of cars, however, was still possible under barter arrangements in which the importer first arranged for the sale of Egyptian goods to cover the foreign exchange required for the import.

In September 1959, an important Egyptian business man approached the company with a proposal. He had obtained a very large import license that could be used on a barter basis. He proposed to sell the passenger cars imported by virtue of this license to Egyptian Motors at a premium of 120 per cent. This would make the cost of importing the smallest European-type car about £E 1140 instead of £E 500 at the official rate of exchange. This was a heavy premium to pay, but the business man reported that no other licences to import cars were available and rumours were rife that importation of cars had been stopped and would not be resumed for years. Under the circumstances and despite the fact that it has never sold more than 1200 cars in Egypt in one year and normally imported only 400 small cars and 300-400 big cars per year, the company contracted to purchase the cars covered by the import license of 4,000 cars.

Under the terms of the agreement between Egyptian Motors and the business man, the latter was to deliver the cars in Egypt and the company would pay in Egyptian pound. The license was issued in early 1959 and was good for 12 months, but such licenses were normally extended for 6 months or more. Towards the end of 1959, the government announced there would be no more import license extensions; Egyptian Motors had to get all the vehicles into the country before the end of February 1960. The firm made immediate contacts with all the manufacturing branches in Europe and was able to obtain the 4,000 cars before the deadline. This rush, however, necessitated the acceptance of a mix of vehicles in various stages of assembly and types not necessarily the most desirable for the Egyptian market. The distribution of the imports was as follows:

- 250 small size-cars, semi-knocked down
- 2000 medium-size cars, completely knocked down
- 300 small-size cars, completely built-up but in need of conditioning for delivery
- 1450 medium-size cars, completely built-up, but in need of conditioning for delivery

The Egyptian intermediary arranged to deliver the cars in Alexandria and was paid by Egyptian Motors a flat price of £E 1140 per car regardless of make, type, or condition after he had made the proper settlement in foreign currency to the suppliers of the 4000 cars. The import wholesale and retail prices established for different cars in 1960 are shown in Table 1.

In concluding the business deal with the Egyptian intermediary, the man-

The Egyptian Motors Company

TABLE 1
Price Schedule Established in 1960
for Cars Imported by Egyptian Motors under the
Business Deal

	Small-Size Cars		Medium-Size Cars	
	Source A	Source B	Source A	Source B
Import Cost	£E 1140	£E 1140	£E 1140	£E 1140
Wholesale price	1191	1255	1466	1718
Retail price	1350	1437	1721	1463

ager of Egyptian Motors had hoped to establish a firm position in the market and to ensure the continuity of the Company during the transitional period under the Government manufacturing program. However, other major importers were able to obtain import facilities for other makes amounting in total approximately to 4000 cars at premiums believed to be lower than those paid by Egyptian Motors.

PRODUCTION

When Egyptian Motors imported the 4000 cars, it had neither the equipment nor the assembly line for cars as such and immediately set about adapting the existing premises to the assembly of cars. This took six months, an additional investment of about £E 5000, and the addition of 55 additional workers. The resulting assembly line had a capacity of 6 cars per day. A complete second shift was not possible because of the shortage of skilled workers. However, the main production bottlenecks were in the body welding and paint sections. A second shift of skilled workers, there, plus some semiskilled workers added to the rest of the line, would enable the firm to increase daily output to 13-15 cars on a single shift. The assembly line was laid out as shown in Exhibit 1.

The direct labor required to condition a built-up car was 12 to 23 hours depending on the model; to assemble a completely knocked-down car, 125 hours; an 8 ton truck about 75 hours; and 50 HP. tractor, 23 hours. This quantity of labor represented a relatively inefficient use of labor which was the result of the small scale not permitting tooling normally employed with higher volumes. In Denmark where about 40 cars were assembled each day, 45 hours of direct labor per car is required, and in Germany where 1000 cars were assembled each day the direct labor per car is only 32 hours.

All cars were kept in the custom zone area; the Alexandria plant itself being included in a free zone area. Vacant land was rented for storing the built-up cars under custom bond. Import duties did not have to be paid until cars were withdrawn from the free zone.

Built-up cars represented a problem. To protect the upholstery, the windows of these cars were painted and they were moved regularly to protect the

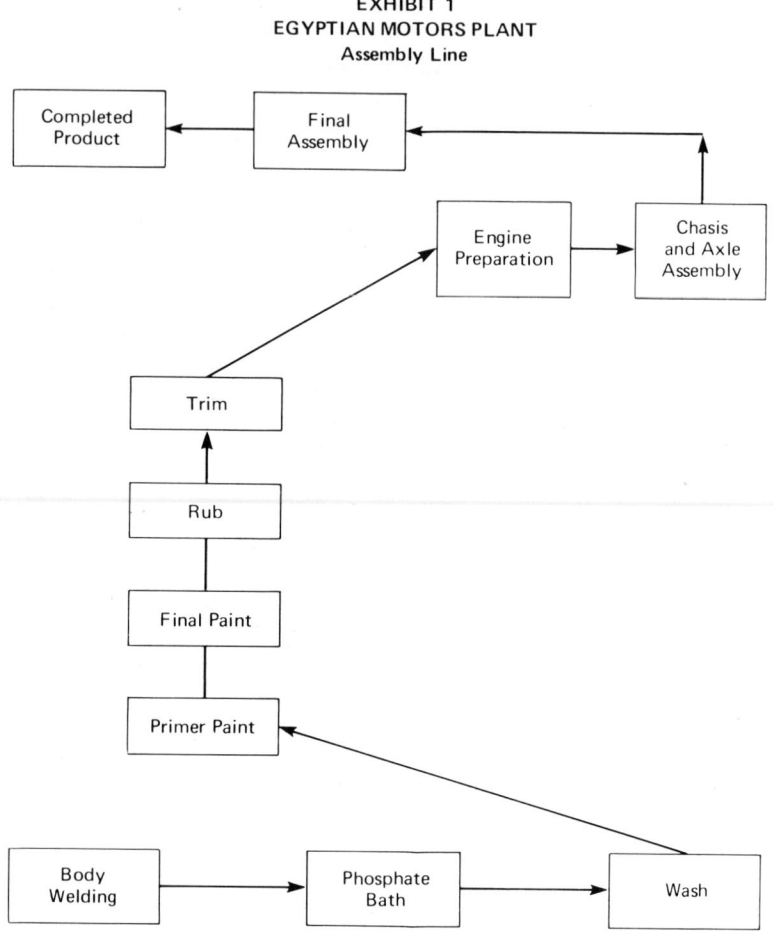

EXHIBIT 1
EGYPTIAN MOTORS PLANT
Assembly Line

tires and maintain engine lubrication. Nevertheless, some rubber parts decayed and had to be replaced from the manufacturing source before the cars would be sold. For this reason, emphasis was put on conditioning and selling the built-up cars first.

FINANCE

Huge sums of money were involved in the import deal of 1959/60 and Egyptian Motors had to make special arrangements for financing. The total debt incurred was £E 5,800,000. Bank loans of £E 2,800,000, were obtained locally and the parent company outside Egypt guaranteed the repayment of an additional £E 3,000,000 worth of dept. Interest costs came to £E 30,000 per

The Egyptian Motors Company

EXHIBIT 2
EGYPTIAN MOTORS COMPANY
Income Statement, 1956-1960
(in thousands of Egyptian pounds)

	1960	1959	1958	1957	1956
Gross Profit	346	793	648	333	744
Administrative and Commercial Expenses	251	227	208	178	364
Depreciation	22	22	24	28	28
Interest charged & Other expenses	327	60	35	24	—
Miscellaneous charges	20	23	37	52	31
Total Charges	620	332	304	282	423
Operating Profit	(274)	461	344	51	321
Other Income	35	21	15	27	32
Other Deductions	—	—	—	—	54
Net Profit Before Taxes	(239)	482	359	78	299
Provision for Income Taxes	—	57	78	18	64
Net Profit After Taxes	(239)	425	281*	60†	235‡

*A write back of prior year provisions of £E 29,366 took place in the year, but is not included in data above.
†A write back of prior year provisions of £E 101,380 took place in the year, but is not included in data above.
‡A write back of prior year provisions of £E 46,841 took place in the year, but is not included in data above.

month. Annual financial statements for selected years are shown in Exhibits 2 and 3. Egyptian Motors helped its dealers by shipping cars to them for a down payment of only 20 per cent. The balance was due in 60 days, or upon retail sale of the unit whichever occurred first but interest was charged in the meantime.

ORGANIZATION

In mid 1960, a new manager, Mr. Smith, arrived in Alexandria to take over the company in its difficult situation. The firm was in debt to banks for £E 5,800,000. Four thousand cars, both built-up and knocked down, were on hand as were about 4,000 diesel engines imported at the same time as the cars. A limited number of knocked-down trucks and tractors were also in stock, but no further import licenses were available. The organization as it existed is shown in Exhibit 4.

Smith had been in the automobile business for many years and had had experience in 11 different countries under many different circumstances. His experience had taught him that circumstances were apt to change rapidly in countries undergoing rapid change, such as Egypt was. He was inclined therefore, not to rush into any decisions even though the situation was quite difficult. Within Egypt there was the question of disposing of the cars on hand which had

EXHIBIT 3
EGYPTIAN MOTORS COMPANY
Balance Sheet, 1956-1960
(In thousands of Egyptian pounds on December 31 of each year)

	1960	1959	1958	1957	1956
ASSETS					
Property, Plant & Equipment, at depreciated value:					
Land and improvements	95	95	96	96	96
Buildings & Construction in progress	254	253	272	291	310
Machinery, durable equipment & Office Furniture	30	10	11	17	24
Net property plant & equipment	379	358	379	404	430
Marketable securities at cost less provision for losses	37	16	—	—	—
Current Assets:					
Commercial Inventories (at lower of cost or market)					
Work in process	2,882	14	486	16	284
Finished product	1,757	1,434	842	310	540
	4,639	1,448	1,328	326	824
Current Receivables, less provisions for doubtful accounts	178	2,106	742	612	537
Cash	195	1,052	60	61	212
Total Current Assets	5,012	4,516	2,130	999	1,573
Other Assets:	114	135	147	183	14
TOTAL ASSETS	5,542	5,025	2,656	1,586	2,017
LIABILITIES					
Captial stock, authorized and issued	405	405	405	405	405
Reserves, and Prior Years Profits	815	658	556	487	606
Current Liabilities:					
Bank Overdraft	3,950	2,784	753	208	494
Accounts Payable	123	68	168	51	55
Total Current Liabilities	4,073	2,852	921	259	549
Other Liabilities included Dividends	488	685	465	274	175
Profit and Loss Account—Current Year	(239)	425	309	161	282
TOTAL LIABILITIES	5,542	5,025	2,656	1,586	2,017

EXHIBIT 4
EGYPTIAN MOTORS COMPANY
Organization Chart, 1960

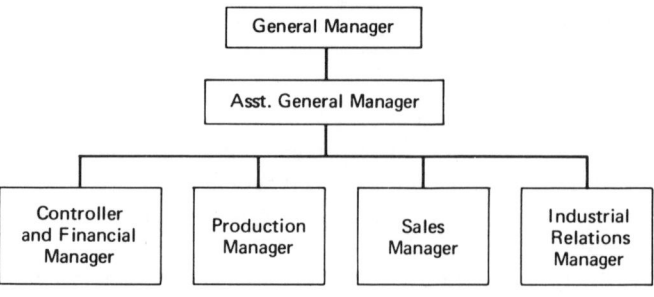

The Egyptian Motors Company

been imported at high prices. This was worsened by the frantic efforts of the other cars distributing agencies to dispose of the 4000 cars they had imported at slightly lower prices than Egyptian Motors, and by the Government's announced plan to produce the Nasr car on a franchise from Fiat. This problem became crucial in August 1961 when the Government announced that the first 700 Nasr cars (the Fiat 1100) would be available in July 1962 and would sell for about £E 7000. Thereafter, 800 Nasr cars would be produced each month.

The Nasr Car Company had been in operation for several years producing trucks and buses under license from a German firm. The plant was constructed in the first five year plan to produce 3500 trucks and an additional 500 diesel engines annually of 4 to 5 ton capacity. In 1960 a plan was announced to expand this factory to produce 2000 diesel trucks annually with 10 to 12 ton capacities. Another announcement in 1960 was that of the plan for the factory to produce diesel engines as follows:

1. Cylinder with 12 horsepower .... 1500 engines
2. Cylinder with 20 horsepower .... 750 engines
3. Cylinder with 40/50 horsepower .... 750 engines
4. Cylinder with 80/100 horsepower .... 2000 engines

The 80 to 100 horsepower engines would be for replacement in trucks. The smaller engines would be used in industry and agriculture. Another factory was announced in the Second Five-Year-Plan to build 1500 agricultural tractors or 40 to 50 horsepower per year per shift with output to be expanded to 2700 in two shifts as rapidly as possible.

The Egyptian-Fiat agreement was a five-year contract that specified that Fiat would help the Nasr firm achieve 95% local (Egyptian) production by the end of the contract. Smith was doubtful that this could be achieved and was also doubtful that the Nasr Company could achieve a rate of production of 800 cars per month even by the end of 1962. In his opinion a rate of half that number was more likely. If Fiat failed to meet these plans, there was a possibility that its contract might not be extended at termination.

Smith believed that Egypt was not a large enough car market to make manufacture there profitable. There was a possibility, however, that an Arab League market or an Afro-Asian Common Market might develop which would be large enough to support a manufacturing plant. Since Egyptian Motor's Alexandria plant was the only plant in the area, except for the new Nasr Company plant, there was a possibility that Egyptian Motors might be able to capture a strong position in any such market by assembling cars in the Alexandria free zone custom area. The profitability of this operation would depend, of course, on the magnitude of preferential treatment Egyptian Motors may enjoy in such a market.

Regardless of the future, Egyptian Motors faced two other serious problems. For one thing, early in 1961 the Government ordered a "custom freeze" on all cars in custom zone areas. The purpose was to investigate the validity of import licenses covering about 1000 cars in custom areas at that time. These developments halted sales of Egyptian Motors for almost four months.

Another major development seriously hampered company sales. Following the nationalization of insurance companies in July 1961, these companies stopped insuring retail credit. As a result, all sales of durable goods, particularly automobiles, were badly hit. The establishment of the Nasr Car Company also raised a lot of questions and speculations about the future availability of spare parts and accessories of other car makes. This too adversely affected Egyptian Motors car sales.

Smith's philosophy as a manager was to delegate authority and then to interfere as little as possible in the execution of the authority. He almost never called meetings except when a specific problem arose, but he had a regular daily meeting with his sales and finance managers and fairly frequent meetings with his technical and labor relations managers. Smith particularly prided himself on the fact that he had always been able to maintain a peaceful atmosphere in his plants. He gave a lot of attention to personal relations, although he was not inclined to get well acquainted with every body in his plant or even to learn the names of other than those with whom he worked directly i.e., managers and supervisors. He reviewed all salaries once a year.

Smith specified that reports coming to him should not be more than one to one and half pages in length. He had a number of these reports that came to him on a regular schedule as follows:

Daily Reports (with cumulative total for the month)
- Sales by car type by dealer to whom sold
- Orders from dealers by car type
- Retail sales by dealer by car type (wired in by dealers each day)
- Scheduled production by type of car
- Production by type of car

Weekly Reports
- Inventory on hand by item and showing number of month's supply
- Status of customs clearance documents
- Bank overdrafts outstanding
- Estimated balance sheet
- Analysis of cash flow

Monthly (with cumulative total for the year)
- Inventory of cars by type in plant and in dealers' hands
- Forecast of sales by car type
- Complete balance sheet with attached schedules
- Expense budget, actual, and variance

THE EGYPTIAN CAR MARKET

The total number of cars in Egypt had grown steadily over many years to a high of 73000 in 1955. Since that time it had declined to about 70000 as a

The Egyptian Motors Company

result of import restrictions that kept the additions below the loss resulting from scrappage. The firm's sales planning department estimated that the average car was transferred to the second-hand market at the end of five years and was scrapped at an age of 10 years or somewhat more. The Ministry of Industry estimated that there was one car per 295 persons in Egypt in 1955.[1] The number of cars per population had declined since that date, but was expected to return to that ratio by 1965, and to reach one car per 280 persons by 1975. These increases were based on the increase expected in national income. The above ratios combined with population forecasts led the Ministry to estimate that the total number of cars in Egypt in 1965 would be 94900 and in 1975 would be 125000.

Egyptian Motors' sales in Egypt over the last 14 years are shown in Table 2.

TABLE 2
Egyptian Motors Company Sales in Egypt (1948-1961)

Year	Cars	Trucks	Tractors	Total Units
1961	943	70	0	1,013
1960	948	1,022	354	2,324
1959	1,381	960	30	2,371
1958	551	840	183	1,574
1957	229	629	87	945
1956	390	921	223	1,534
1955	577	946	431	1,954
1954	425	432	372	1,229
1953	375	253	321	949
1952	647	466	574	1,687
1951	748	598	1,228	2,574
1950	678	480	1,151	2,309
1949	1,363	579	720	2,662
1948	944	849	776	2,569

Cairo and Alexandria accounted for about 80 percent of the car market in Egypt in the estimation of Egyptian Motors' executives. Therefore, the firm made particular efforts to study these markets and maintained statistics on both Egyptian Motors and Competitive sales there. Such data for 1961 are shown in Table 3.

Total sales of cars in Egypt had varied considerably over the years as a result of changes in demand and in the limitations on importation. In only one year, 1951, had sales exceeded 7,000 cars. The countries from which cars were imported also had varied from year to year, although United States had accounted for 50 percent in most years.

Large cars, i.e. all American cars and the larger European cars, had taken widely varying shares of the Egyptian market over the years, partly as a result of changes in total demand and partly as a result of shortages of hard currency and import restrictions. Table 5 shows these variations for typical periods.

[1] Central Ministry of Industry, Second Five-Year Industrial Plan, (Jan. 1960), p. 97.

TABLE 3
New Car Registrations in Cairo and Alexandria (1961)

Month	Egyptian Motors Sales in Units		Egyptian Motors Percentage of Market		Cairo and Alexandria
	Cairo	Alexandria	Cairo	Alexandria	
January	54	11	30%	34%	30%
February	59	11	31	50	33
March	65	20	31	54	35
April	62	19	34	54	37
May	55	28	29	79	36
June	36	7	18	29	19
July	47	5	28	17	26
August	21	14	14	39	19
September	42	13	24	35	26
October	41	11	24	48	27
November	53	12	26	57	29
December	40	&	29	64	31

TABLE 4
Sales of Cars in Egypt by Countries of Origin (1947-1959)

Year	U.S.	U.K.	Germany	France	Others†	Total
1959	n.a.*	n.a.	n.a.	n.a.	n.a.	4,000†
1958	648	611	1,621	186	1,051	4,117
1957	421	9	140	99	75	775
1956	989	216	122	154	100	1,681
1955	2,068	352	1,233	315	300	4,268
1954	571	220	955	292	150	2,188
1953	502	49	875	229	150	1,805
1952	1,431	881	742	324	50	3,428
1951	3,522	1,453	1,638	506	50	7,069
1950	2,561	2,083	847	641	50	6,082
1949	3,284	1,934	41	672	...	5,931
1948	1,221	3,058	...	1,287	...	5,564
1947	2,484	1,204	...	1,176	...	4,864

*n.a. = not available
†Estimated

TABLE 5
Share of Egyptian Market Obtained by Large Cars: Selected Years

Period	Market Share Obtained by Large Cars
1935-1938	68%
1947-1951	44
1952-1954	34
1955	49
1956-1957	58
1958	16

The Egyptian Motors Company

Data on the size of the cars market in other Middle Eastern countries were scarce but there were some data for the various countries for different years during the middle 1950's. Working with these data, Egyptian Motors estimated the average annual volume for the various countries in the early 1960's. These estimates are shown in Table 6.

TABLE 6
Estimated Annual Car Sales in Middle Eastern Countries: Early 1960's

Country	Estimated Annual Volume in Units
Syria	2,700
Jordan	400
Lebanon	3,000
Kuwait	2,500
Bahrain	500
Yemen	30
Saudi Arabia	3,500
Iraq	3,600
Sudan	700
Libya	1,200
Total	18,130

In trying to estimate the volume of car sales in Egypt and the Middle East, Egyptian Motors took the following points into consideration:

1. Egypt's economic planning called for doubling the national income within 10 years.
2. No more imports of cars would be permitted.
3. Prices of cars produced in Egypt would be regulated to a low level.
4. The demand for cars would increase as incomes rose; as a new group of purchasers such as engineers, lawyers, officers, and teachers have credit facilities available to them; and as more small business men used cars in their work.
5. Upper income people would no longer be able to buy large luxury cars and so would buy more than one small car.

Only limited information was available on the distribution of the Egyptian population by income groups, but one estimate showed 500,000 families with annual incomes over £E 625. The numbers in this bracket would expand as the national income rose, but it was hard to predict at what rate. Similarly Egyptian Motors executives expected the demand for cars to increase in the other countries of the Middle East, but no basis for estimating the rate of increase was available.

MARKETING

Car, truck, and tractor sales in Egyptian Motors were handled by a sales department, and parts and accessories and service were handled by separate departments all reporting to the General Sales Manager. The following organization chart (Exhibit 5) show how each of these divisions was set up.

EXHIBIT 5
EGYPTIAN MOTORS COMPANY
Organization of the Sales Offices

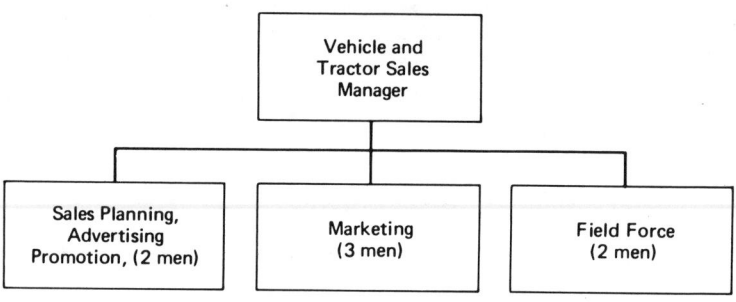

PARTS AND ACCESSORIES DEPARTMENT

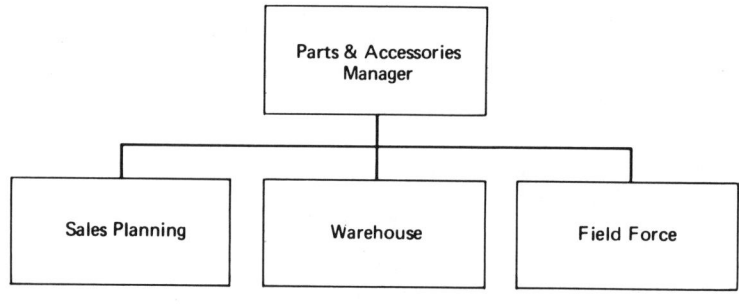

SERVICE DEPARTMENT

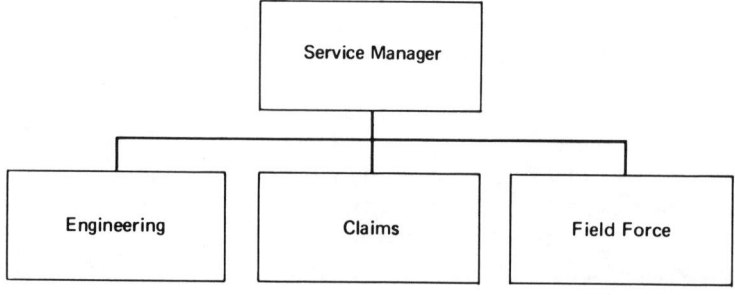

The Egyptian Motors Company

In the Sales Department, the marketing section handled dealer orders and production scheduling; the field force maintained personal contact with dealers and helped them in their selling activities. The parts and accessories and service department also had field forces that worked with the dealers relative to their activities. Sales planning, advertising, and promotion within the sales department were also separate from similar activities in the parts and accessories department.

There were 11 Egyptian Motors dealers in Egypt, two in Cairo, one in Alexandria, and eight in the other leading cities. In addition to selling cars, trucks, and tractors, these dealers also maintained stocks of parts and accessories and offered repair and maintenance services. Egyptian Motors believed that these dealers should make 15% to 18% return on their investment capital and worked with them to help do this. Cars were shipped to dealers on cash except as previously explained.

Egyptian Motors had always spent modest amounts on advertising and promotion, but had been increasing these amounts in recent years. The budgets for the last three years are shown in Table 7.

TABLE 7
Egyptian Motors Advertising and Promotion Budgets
1959-1961

Item	1961	1960	1959
Advertising	£E	£E	£E
Press	6,488	215	4,000
Slides and films	1,750	250	600
T.V. and Radio	960	880	0
Direct mail	0	900	0
Outdoor	1,450	440	600
Institutional	250	500	0
Miscellany	3,260	1,050	0
Sales promotion			
Fairs and exhibitions	500	0	2,500
Sales training	300	375	0
Dealers meeting	200	200	0
Miscellany including duty on catalogues	775	515	1,250

PERSONNEL

Of the 379 persons employed by Egyptian Motors towards the end of 1961, there were 248 that were hourly employees and 131 that were salaried. The pay scale was relatively high for Egyptian firms averaging 9.4 piasters per hour for those paid by the hour and £E 54.50 per month for salaried employees including high cost of living allowance. One tenth of the company personnel had been with Egyptian Motors for 25 years or more and the average length of service was 10 years for both hourly-paid and salaried individuals.

Termination of employment had run at the annual rate of about 3.5%

among hourly workers, but increased with the increase in employment in 1960 and 1961 to 12.2% in the latter year. The rate for salaried employees followed a similar pattern, but was a little higher, standing at 13.6 in 1961.

Absenteeism, not including paid leave, had been consistently below one-half of one percent for a number of years. The management considered the morale of the plant to be high. A suggestion system had been in operation for a number of years, but only 4 suggestions had been received in the last four years and a total of £E 25 had been paid for these.

GENERAL

In the latter part of 1961, Smith, The General Manager, was faced with the need to make some clear cut decisions about the future of Egyptian Motors. The Nasr car was to be on the market in less than a year and the price for the smaller model (Fiat 1100) had just been announced as in the vicinity of £E 700. Egyptian Motors had a large inventory of cars imported at prices far above the £E 700 level. The two dealers in Cairo, the largest for the company, informed Egyptian Motors that they had signed contracts to handle the Nasr Car, and a total of 22 dealers throughout the country was announced by the Nasr Company. All of these things made the future look uncertain for Egyptian Motors, but the company had a good plant, good management, and a skilled labor force, all of which were in short supply in Egypt. Smith believed that the government would not want to let these assets be dissipated.

16

The Nasr Bicycle Manufacturing Company*

Early in June, 1962 the Nasr Bicycle Manufacturing Company was studying the marketing policies which it could adopt after October 1962 when the contracts concluded with its distributors terminated.

Marketing policies had been given earnest attention by the Management since the inception of the Company and the commencement of production. This has been responsible for several changes in that policy consequent upon the circumstances and the difficulties with which the Company had been confronted. What rendered the plan to be pursued by the Company's Management after October 1962 all the more important was the occurrence of important developments connected with the doubling of the Company's production and the introduction of large-scale expansions as a result of the addition of more products to the list of the Company's manufacturers. The plan was also rendered more important still by the vital role entrusted to the Company as supervisor of the import trade of bicycle spare parts.

GENERAL FRAMEWORK OF BICYCLE MARKET

The bicycle being a means of transport by different categories of individuals of various professions, incomes, sexes, and ages, is designed in several ways reflecting themselves in different shapes and sizes, so that every class or category of consumers may find the type that suits its tastes and requirements. This necessarily requires the existence of homogeneous assortment of bicycles reflecting many important aspects such as size, type, color and other features.

The shape and frame of a bicycle may change according to special requirements; thus we find certain types of bicycles such as the one with the front basket, the tricycle, the racing and sports bicycles and the children's bicycles, etc. However, sales of the 28 ordinary bicycles constitute between 70% and 80% of the total annual sales of bicycles in the Egyptian market.

*Reprinted by permission of the National Institute for Management-Development, Cairo, United Arab Republic.

It is to be noted nevertheless, that the relative importance of the 28 ordinary type bicycle changes somewhat from one district to another. Another noteworthy feature is that the sports model and smaller sizes are used less in rural than in major urban districts. Certain consumers of the latter districts care less for the durability than the good appearance and availability of what they consider to be vital supplementary parts such as dynamos, horns, back bag, etc.

The economic importance of the bicycle market could be shown through the study of the development of Egyptian imports of bicycles and spare parts for the years 1951-1960 as shown in Table 1.

TABLE 1
Imports of Bicycles and Their Spare Parts

Year	Number of Bicycles	Value in Pounds (CIF)	Value of Spare Parts in Pounds
1951	26,263	192,003	106,077
1952	17,242	143,157	95,605
1953	12,986	100,547	93,052
1954	22,727	177,610	101,929
1955	26,838	203,356	129,219
1956	23,463	182,955	118,479
1957	19,966	142,872	90,151
1958	36,495	227,439	91,868
1959	10,547	68,689	98,589
1960	13,617	89,179	53,389
Total	210,144	1,527,887	1,078,358
Annual Average	21,014	152,781	107,837

SOURCE: Department of Statistics, Cairo.

The bicycle market comprises several categories of consumers, namely the hire and repair shops, government organizations, companies, and individuals.

The hire and repair shops represent only a small proportion of the total demand for new bicycles which does not exceed 15% of that demand. They are considered an important buyer in the replacement market however, in that they offer bicycle owners the easiest means of selling their bicycles irrespective of their conditions. They are also the most important purchasers of spare parts since they are the natural place for maintenance and repairs. Bicycle merchants do not normally offer these services on a large scale while the ordinary consumer lacks the technical experience and the facilities enabling him to handle repairs and maintenance by his own means. In smaller towns and rural districts these shops engage in hire, repairs and marketing. In major towns and urban districts however, a hire and repair shop is not a natural outlet for the sale of bicycles because of the availability of commercial establishments specializing in the sale of bicycles.

Certain government organizations represent an important customer in the bicycle market, and normally secure their annual requirements through tender or

Nasr Bicycle Manufacturing Company

private treaty, according to the size of the sale. Government tenders often provide a scope for speculation, strong competition and the beating of prices. Through these practices a leading merchant might aim at spreading his influence and creating the impression that he is the main source for the supply of certain government quarters' needs of bicycles.

Demands by certain companies have concentrated on particular types of bicycles which are consistent with the nature of their work such as tricycles, and the bicycles with the front basket. Companies get their needs of such types from traditional bicycle dealers. Transactions are normally effected in cash. Companies' requirements of ordinary bicycles are obtained from both traditional merchants and certain leading department stores.

Individuals represent the largest section of bicycle consumers; the most important categories being workers and students. Members of these categories normally buy bicycles in instalments from bicycle merchants or leading stores.

Demand for bicycles distinctly rises in summer because of the mild weather and suitable roads. It also increases after the release of examination results and at the opening of the school year. Members of those groups buy their bicycles in instalments from bicycle dealers or commercial firms.

A total of 742 establishments are engaged in the trade of bicycles and their spare parts as shown in Table 2.

TABLE 2
Number of Wholesale and Retail Establishments Dealing in Motorcycles and Bicycles and Their Spare Parts in 1957, Distributed Geographically

District	Wholesale Trade		Retail Trade	
	Motorcycles and Bicycles	Spare Parts	Motorcycles and Bicycles	Spare Parts
Cairo		11	40	315
Alexandria	1	3	15	114
Canal			23	30
Lower Egypt		2	39	196
Upper Egypt			13	87
Total	1	16	130	742

SOURCE: Department of Statistics, Cairo.

The small size firm is the prevalent type in this trade. Among every 130 retail establishments there exist 118 employing less than five persons each. Of all the firms engaged in the bicycle trade, only four have an average annual sale of over 2,000 bicycles.

Cairo is deemed the main centre for the trade of bicycles on the Egyptian Market for it includes the leading importers and wholesalers whose activities spread all over the national market. In the country, there exist 6 establishments with a wholesale trade figure representing 50% or over of their total sales. Of these six establishments there exist 4 firms serving a wide geographical sphere which occasionally covers the whole local market.

The traditional distribution outlet is not specialized in marketing functions. An importer merchant does not confine his activities to import, for he also performs the functions of the traditional wholesaler. He also often acts as a retailer. Likewise, a number of medium size firms combine the characters of wholesalers and semi wholesalers. At a time when certain establishments imported part of their requirements of bicycles from outside sources and acted as wholesalers, they obtained their needs of certain types of bicycles as well as spare parts from leading importer merchants.

Large wholesale establishments were successful in the course of years in linking small retail firms in the local market to their wheels in such a way to render them completely dependent on them in both their activities and trade. The big merchant is considered for instance the only source for the supply of the spare parts that constitute the life artery for small dealers. Big merchants also assume an important role in financing small dealers and affording them credit facilities.

Retail firms are lacking in capital and, with the small size of the market they serve, have only a slender volume of sales. They normally sell to individual consumers in cash or difficult credit terms.

With the changing import policy there have been several sources of bicycle imports. The volume of imports also fluctuated from one year to another as shown in Table 1. This has given rise to a variety of types on the market and to anomalous prices seen in Table 3.

TABLE 3
Brands and Prices of Foreign Bicycles on Local Market

Mark	Average Wholesale Price	Average Retail Price
Philips	£E 18,000m/ms	£E 24,000m/ms
Chinese	13,400	14,500
Czech	11,500	12,500
Hungarian	13,600	15,500
German	13,500	14,500
Russian	12,000	13,500

SOURCE: Report by Nasr Organization Market Research Department.

The commercial profit margin in the bicycle trade amounts to some 20% distributed between the wholesaler and the retailer. This is compared to up to 25% in the case of spare parts trade which is also distributed between both wholesalers and retailers.

The financing of the bicycle trade represented no major problem to importer merchants. Once import permits were obtained, the merchant concerned opened a documentary credit with a bank. In some cases a small margin of the price had to be deposited with the bank. Shipments of bicycles normally arrived at Alexandria or Port Said in the form of well-packed cargoes containing component parts of dismantled bicycles. An importer merchant found in the customs warehouses suitable space for the storage of the bicycles. All shipment documents were retained by the financing bank.

In the light of this study of market conditions and trends a merchant released part of his consignment through the customs to supply the market according to needs against payment to the financing bank of the value of the part so released. Normally a merchant does not hold a big stock in his firm; but maintains ample assembling facilities to have the bicycles marketed in his own district. Orders by customers in rural districts were customarily dispatched in parts, the assembling process being conducted by the customer himself. This is in order to make use of all transport means and to avoid the possibility of a bicycle being damaged if dispatched completely assembled.

INCEPTION AND ORGANISATION OF NASR COMPANY

The bicycle industry plan was included in the first five-year Industrialization Program. Its execution was entrusted to the Engineering and Car Company which was engaged in its study at the time. A contract was actually concluded between that company and the Czech Techno-Export for the implementation of the plan including the technical study of the project, the necessary equipment and machinery for production and the technical blueprints for three types of bicycles namely:

1. The 28 size double-tube men's bicycle
2. The 26 size bicycle
3. The 22 size children's bicycle

The bicycle plant's productive capacity was estimated at 30,000 bicycles of all sizes per annum on the basis of one-shift operation, apart from 20% of the Egyptian market's requirements of spare parts.

The necessary equipment and materials for the plant were duly supplied and work started by the Engineering and Car Company on the installation of such equipment at Amirieh, a suburb of Cairo in one of that Company's premises formerly used as a warehouse. The plant was scheduled to begin production not later than the end of 1958.

However, the Company was unable to proceed with the schedule due to financial difficulties. The Minister of Industry early in 1959 thus ordered the appointment of a committee to study the project and to suggest proper solutions to deal with the situation. Eventually, in April 1960, an agreement was reached between the Engineering and Car Company on the one hand and the General Authority for the Implementation of the Five Year Plan on the other, whereby the latter would carry out the project, and the former would provide a specific contribution to the capital to the value of its investment in the project. On

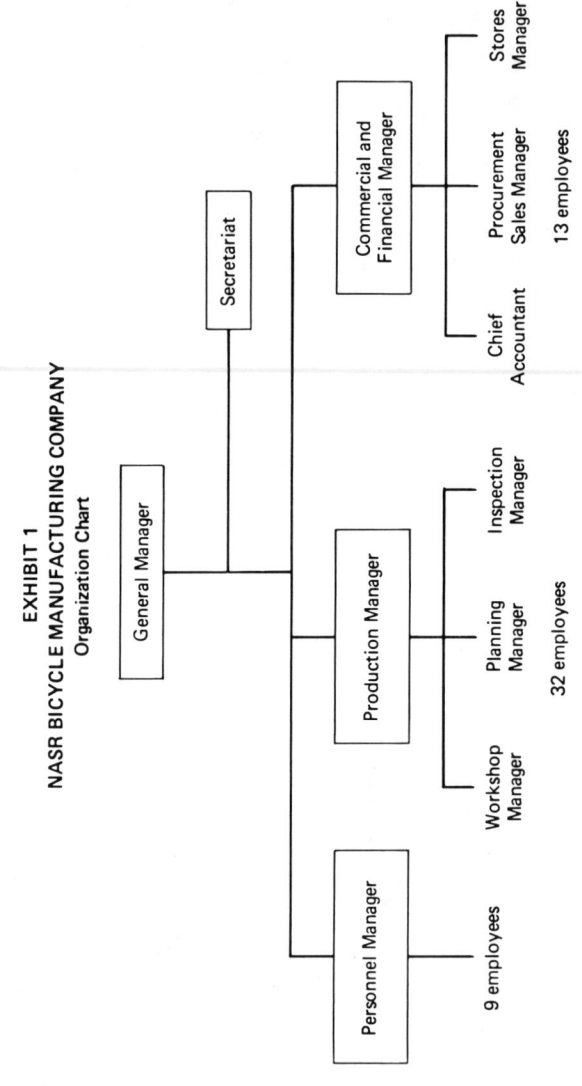

Nasr Bicycle Manufacturing Company

December 26th, 1960, a Republican Decree was issued establishing the Nasr Manufacturing Company with a capital of £E 400,000.

In the initial period the Company's activities included the assembling of 500 bicycles imported from Czechoslovakia in July, 1960, as well as the soldering, painting and assembling the parts of 1000 other imported bicycles. At the same time the Company's various sections were put into operation immediately upon the installations of their equipment and machinery, and the arrival of the necessary imports of raw materials. The sections involved were those for pressing, instruments, metal working, soldering, primary assembling, whetting, phosphatising, painting and final assembling.

The Company's production started with the Nasr 601 bicycle in November, 1960. The proportion of local materials in the manufacture of this bicycle rose to 70% by weight (75% in value) during the first year of operation. The number of workers employed in the different sections of the plant was 159 in June, 1961. Salaried employees totalled 49.

Exhibit 1 shows the Company's set up at that time:

Until the issue in February 1962 of the Republican Decrees setting up boards of directors for industrial establishments, the Company's General manager assumed all top-management duties in the company, in which he was assisted by the production manager and the financial and commercial manager.

DISTRIBUTION POLICY (SEPTEMBER 1960 – FEBRUARY 1961)

Before the start of actual processing operations, and with the arrival of the first Czech shipment of bicycles, the management began considering alternative distribution policies. The management deemed it preferable in the initial stage of the Company's life to concentrate its attention on production as well as technical and administrative questions in order to expedite the completion of the necessary constructions and installations of machinery. As for marketing and sales operations the management considered it advisable to intrust them entirely to the care of distributors so that it might give its full attention to administrative and technical problems.

In implementation of this policy, management decided to have the company's products distributed through a number of exclusive agents to be selected from the Governorates of the Republic. The first advertisement calling for agent distributors appeared in Al-Ahram, Al-Akhbar and Al-Gomhourieh dailies on July 2, 1960. The advertisement required that applicants should have previous experience in the trade of bicycles, must have suitable exhibition premises, and undertake to distribute a minimum of 500 bicycles per annum and fix the territory where he would like to serve. Selected candidates were also required to provide a preliminary deposit in cash equal to one pound Egyptian for every bicycle contracted for.

Up to July 5, 1960 only a car company in Alexandria applied in response to the advertisement with the result that the Company repeated the announcement on July 6, 1960 in the same morning dailies, with a slight amendment in the text of the advertisement to the effect that a deadline for the acceptance of prospective agent distributors' applications had been fixed for July 7th, and that contracts would be made out with applicants up to that date for a period of two years.

In view, however, of the meager number of applications made in response to the second advertisement, management decided to keep the door for more applications open for a further period to enable the greatest possible number of such applications being received from distributors in most governorates.

In the light of applications received up to that date, management decided to divide the Egyptian market into a number of territories in which one or more distributors would have exclusive sales rights. Contracts were duly concluded with 16 distributors on probation for six months starting September 1st, 1960 and terminating the end of February, 1961.

In the contracts the company specified the quantities which a distributor is required to sell within his territory. It made a condition that no distributor shall sell the company's products outside his territory. The selling prices to the consumer and the distributor of both the bicycle and its spare parts were fixed by the company. All sales were F.O.B. the agent's railway station. The contract further required that a distributor shall arrange for a suitable display in his showrooms and that he would maintain adequate service facilities. Distributors were again required to do everything possible to encourage and promote the sale of the company's products in their respective territories.

However, the difficulties experienced by the company in its relations with distributors resulted in the quantities withdrawn during the period from 1st September, 1960, to the end of February, 1961, not exceeding 3199 bicycles against the distributors commitments of 12050 bicycles. It transpired that a number of distributors had exaggerated their estimates of the quantities contracted to secure exclusive sales rights in certain territories. At the same time some 11,000 bicycles imported by merchant's own means during the year 1961 arrived into the country while the stocks accumulating from previous years reached about 5000 bicycles.

The August 1960 price control by the Ministry of Industry had fixed the price per Nasr 601 bicycle at £E 11,250 to the wholesaler and £E 12,250 to the consumer. Most of the distributors raised the point of the insufficiency of this margin to cover their expenses and commercial obligations. On the company's part it was not possible to raise that margin by reducing the selling price to the distributor owing to the fact that average cost per bicycle at the time was over £E 11,250.

Trucks were used by the company in the transport of assembled bicycles to distributors' stores. Consignments were required to be not less than 50 bicycles each to provide a full cargo for the truck. In this connection the company experienced some difficulties on account of the damage sustained by bicycles in

Nasr Bicycle Manufacturing Company

certain cases. Some difficulties were also encountered on the account of the non-availability to leading merchants of sufficient storage space particularly for assembled bicycles, and the inconvenience which merchants experienced in despatching the bicycles to retailers.

Some distributors failed to observe the condition of restricting sales to their territories. There were frequent complaints by distributors over the dumping of their districts by bicycles arriving from other areas especially Cairo and Alexandria. Other distributors did not respect the established price, or used the Nasr bicycle as means of promoting the sale of uncontrolled foreign bicycles by offering it for sale at less than the fixed price.

It also transpired that most distributors had failed to carry out conditions relating to publicity and the provision of proper exhibition space and service stations in their territories. A leading installment-selling store was the only distributor that arranged for publicity in the daily press and used easy credit as means of promoting the sale of the bicycle.

Distributors' failure to withdraw the quantities they had contracted for between September 1st, 1960, and the end of February, 1961, was responsible for the accumulation of stocks in the company's stores. Management tackled this problem by amending production schedules in such a manner as to ensure some equilibrium between production and sales as shown in Table 4 below:

TABLE 4
Production, Sales and Inventories
(August 1960—August 1961)

Month	Production During the Month	Sales	Stock at Month End
August and September 1960	990	532	458
October	432	700	190
November	450	590	50
December	884	567	367
January 61	923	504	786
February	161	547	400
March	1,719	1,119	1,000
April	1,974	1|743	1,231
May	1,080	1,183	1,128
June	2,384	2,373	1,139
July	1,178	1,168	1,149
August	899	1,491	557

SOURCE: Nasr Bicycle Manufacturing Company.

DISTRIBUTION POLICY (MARCH 1961 — JULY 1961)

In view of the difficulties suffered by the company during the first six months of distribution, management decided not to renew distributors' contracts after the trial period which ended in February 1961. Hence after, the company assumed distribution by its own means, and started contracting companies, organizations governorates, cooperative societies and government administrations.

Management was able in that period to create new classes of customers including companies and public sector establishments, with which the company maintained direct contact. It was also possible to dispose of a further number of bicycles through dealers without a written contract and on a basis of direct cash dealings in most cases.

Table 5 shows the company's sales during the period under review:

TABLE 5
Company Sales According to Type of Customer (March–July 1961)

Type of Customer	Percentage of Sales	Comments
Distributor Merchants	50%	
Companies	17%	
Governorates and government bodies	33%	Without contracts 21 merchants

Source: Nasr Bicycle Manufacturing Company.

Two merchants' purchases during the period exceeded half the volume of all distributor merchants' purchases. Only five distributors bought over 300 bicycles each. Government purchases included 600 for the police, 1500 for the Menufieh Governorate, 320 for the Ministry of Agriculture, 300 for the General Petroleum Organization; the balance being for other government bodies and public organizations.

DISTRIBUTION POLICY SINCE JULY 1ST, 1961

Management decided to re-introduce the contract system, and on July 1st, 1961 sent out to the Company's 16 previous distributors fresh contracts running for one year from that date. The distributors were asked to enclose a letter of guarantee representing 15% of the value of their annual contracts. With the contract forms a list of monthly withdrawals was enclosed for every distributor to indicate the quantity he needed per month. This was in order to enable Management to regulate production in line with distributors' orders.

Up to July 30, 1961, only three contracts were received back with the required letter of guarantee attached together with an order for 500 bicycles per annum by each distributor. The contracts were duly signed with all the three distributors but Management started considering the reasons why distributors were not inclined to take out contracts with the Company. This situation was attributed to three main reasons:

1. Distributor's apprehension of contracting for quantities which it would not be easy to dispose of on the market;

Nasr Bicycle Manufacturing Company

2. The insufficiency of the profit margin (£E 1) accorded to the distributor per bicycle which would not cover his expenses especially since a large proportion of retailers' sales are effected on credit. Furthermore, the issue of a letter of guarantee meant the blocking of part of a distributor's capital, and would involve the payment of issue charges.
3. The propensity of merchants to buy in cash in line with market requirements without being committed to an annual figure or a certain production programme.

    They had been used in the past to order bicycles from outside sources whenever they required, and have not as yet been accustomed to the proposed procedure.

On August 20, 1961, an important development in the Company's activities occurred with the promulgation of a ministerial order introducing a supplementary shift duty. This entailed the increase of output to 60,000 per annum. In view of this development management called a meeting of leading bicycle merchants early in September, 1961. The manager explained the new policy governing the Company's production, stressing the enormity of the required figure of production. He then listened to the dealers' demands and their recommendations.

Eventually the meeting decided to make an announcement fixing the quantities to be distributed in each Governorate, and the number of distributors as set out in Table 6.

TABLE 6
Proposed Distribution Areas, Number of Distributors, and the Quantity Allotted to Each

Distribution Area	Number of Distributors	Quantity Allotted to Each Area
1—Cairo Governorate	4	20,000
2—Alexandria	2	6,000
3—Dakahlia, Sharkieh, Gharbieh, and Minia Governorates.	one distributor each	2,000 each
4—Other Governorates (15)	one distributor each	1,000 each

In the middle of September, 1961, the Company announced the new distribution system in the morning press, and called for new distributors for all the governorates as indicated in Table 6. It made it a condition that a letter of guarantee representing 15% of the value of the contract required should be enclosed.

Seven applications fulfilling the announced conditions were received. They sought distribution concessions in the various Governorates for an aggregate quantity of 49,000 bicycles. A committee appointed to open the envelopes and decide on the applications eventually recommended that contracts be made out with the distributors who had so fulfilled the conditions in addition to three distributors with whom contracts had been signed since July, 1961. This brought the total number of distributors to 10 covering all the Governorates who would contract for 50900 bicycles as set out in Table 7.

TABLE 7
Distribution of Contracted Bicycles According to Distributors and Territories

Distributor's Name	Quantity Contracted for (Bicycles)	Territory
1. Hag Ibrahim Mostafa's Co.	17,400	Cairo, Sharkieh, Dakahlieh, Minia, Asswan, Fayum, Beni-Souef, Assiut, Suhag, Quena, New Valley, Sollum, Marsa Matruh and Sinai
2. Mostafa Ibrahim Mostafa	8,000	Cairo, Damietta, Qualiubiah, Kafr El-Sheikh, and Cairo
3. Ahmed Ibrahim Mostafa	8,000	Cairo and Alexandria
4. Said Mahmoud Saadalla	8,000	Cairo, Port-Said Ismailia and Suez
5. Mahmoud Ekaila Mostafa	5,000	Alexandria, Behira and Menufieh
6. Fathi El-Saggan	2,000	Gharbieh
7. SHAHER Co.	1,000	Gharbieh ⎫
8. Abdel-Halim Megahed	800	Dakahlieh ⎪ Contracts expiring in June 1962
9. Misr Agencies Co.	500	Gharbieh ⎪
10. Egyptian Bicycles Co.	500	Ismailia ⎭

In the new distribution contracts care was taken by the Company to benefit as far as possible by previous experience on the one hand, and to make preparations for the foreseen development of production on the other. For instance a provision was included in the contract to the effect that a distributor shall take delivery of the goods from the Company's stores at Amirieh, and that such delivery will discharge the Company's liability. The contract also provided for delivery to be effected in monthly instalments to be determined by the distributor in writing and marked on a schedule printed in the contract form, subject to the Company's approval. Another condition in the contract required distributors to receive 50% of each order in the form of fully assembled bicycles without cases, and the other half in parts inside cases.

It was further decided to allocate 100 m/ms on every sold bicycle for advertising and sales promotion. Half of this amount will be borne by the Company and other by the distributor concerned who shall provide payment thereof upon the receipt of every consignment. The Company is to determine the publicity procedure and shall agree on the cost of advertisement and its settlement. An

Nasr Bicycle Manufacturing Company

adjustment shall be made between the Company and the distributor on the total sales and the amount collected for publicity purposes.

Under the terms of contracts a distributor is required to settle 25% of the value of monthly instalments of bicycles and spare parts he receives, immediately he takes delivery of them. The balance is made payable by equal bills for the six consecutive months following the date of delivery plus annual interest at the rate of 6%. There would of course by no objection to a distributor settling the whole amount in cash upon delivery if he so desires. A distributor is bound to sell at the price fixed by the Company for its products and gets a commercial discount of 10% on the cost of the bicycle involved. He is prohibited to sell outside the area or areas fixed in the contract; the company reserving the right to sell direct to government bodies and organizations at a selling price not less than that fixed for the consumer. This latter condition caused no inconvenience to leading distributors who were still able to get orders from those bodies and organizations through public tenders by cutting down the price a few piastres below that fixed for the consumer.

Since Management has started to develop its output and to turn out different sizes and types of bicycles, it was provided in distribution contracts that distribution of the Nasr 601 (the 28 ordinary type bicycle) shall not be less than 60% of each order, and that every distributor shall mark his orders of other types in the delivery schedule attached to the contract form. Through these monthly terms Management aimed at formulating production programmes in such a way as to ensure the greatest possible measure of efficiency.

Up to the middle of June, 1962 distributors carried out their obligations as laid down in their distribution contracts and on the basis of the monthly delivery schedules agreed upon. At the same time the Company arranged with a publishing house to design an advertising campaign for the Nasr bicycle in Arabic dailies and periodicals. It also agreed with the Societe Egyptienne de Publicite to advertise the Nasr bicycle on posters in main towns, and the principal thoroughfares between them. Cinema houses contributed to the publicity activities planned by Management in the form of short films and other features.

SOME RECENT DEVELOPMENTS

At a time when average withdrawals of the Company's products proceeded according to schedule, the management experienced some problems in relation to bicycle dealers who had not been selected as distributors. Certain wholesalers of Cairo complained of the existence of a 'monopolistic grouping' in the distribution of these products, and that a leading distributor had been able by grouping his relations and other merchants to secure the greatest quota. In view of the approaching data of the expiry of contracts with the seven distributors in October 1962, the Ibrahim Mostafa Company and the other distributors expressed their desire for the renewal of their contracts and offered to market all the

Company's production of bicycles all the year round on such conditions as the Company set for them. It was necessary therefore to balance such renewal which would regulate the Company's production, against the desire to secure more distributors.

At the same time important developments occurred in the trade of bicycle spare parts; the higher authorities having decided that the Nasr Bicycle Manufacturing Company should effectively control that trade by examining merchants' applications for import permits to ascertain that the articles and parts required do not constitute a whole bicycle thereby combating disguised imports of bicycles. The Company was further required to receive consignments of imported spare parts and have them distributed to merchants according to the quotas assigned to them.

Under the second Five Year Development Plan's expansion programme, the Company's capital will be increased to £E 2 million with a view to the addition of more products to the Company's line such as the Mobid, Vespas and motorcycles.

The Company's Management is already studying the proposed large-scale expansions for the next few years.

Japan

17

Carnation Company, Ltd.*†

In March, 1959, the Executive Committee of Carnation Company, Ltd., a leading manufacturer of cosmetics, soaps, and dentifrices, was considering making an important change in the Company's mode of wholesale distribution.

The Company's sales of more than 10 billion yen annually (1958) were obtained through 73 independently owned distribution outlets, termed Carnation Sales Companies, one or more to each of Japan's 46 prefectures. Each such outlet was franchised to act as the sole representative for Carnation products within a designated geographic area. In return for their exclusive franchises, the Carnation Sales Companies agreed not to wholesale competing items, to carry certain inventories of Carnation products, and to perform other usual services of an exclusive representative. The Carnation Sales Companies, in turn, distributed Carnation products and related non-competitive items through several sales channels.

The primary channel was to some 8,000 Carnation "Chain Stores," i.e., a varied array of independently owned retail outlets including drugstores, cosmetic stores, beauty parlors and about 140 department stores, each of which had signed a sales agreement with the appropriate regional Carnation Sales Company. A second channel was directly to some 13,000 retail stores, none of which was bound by a sales agreement. A third was through some 750 wholesalers, each of which had signed a sales agreement with the appropriate regional Carnation Sales Company, to some 100,000 retail outlets, none of which were bound by sales agreements. The full line was distributed through the first channels, while cosmetics were excluded from the second and third channels.

Details of the standardized sales agreements with the Carnation Sales Companies, the Carnation "Chain Stores," and the wholesale outlets are given in Appendixes 1, 2, and 3, respectively. Resale price maintenance was a prime objective of each of these forms of sales agreements.

A diagrammatic sketch of the Carnation distribution system is given in Exhibit 1.

The issue before the Carnation Executive Committee was whether to

---

*This case material has been prepared as a basis for group discussion, and is not intended to present illustrations of either correct or incorrect handling of administrative problems. All names have been disguised.

†Prepared by Frank T. Hartzfeld and Kenneth H. Myers of Northwestern University, Graduate School of Business, assisted by Matsutaro Wadaki and Shoji Murata of Keio Gijuku University and Takeshi Kikuchi and in cooperation with the Japan Productivity Center.

EXHIBIT 1
CARNATION COMPANY LTD. (A)
Carnation Production and Distribution System

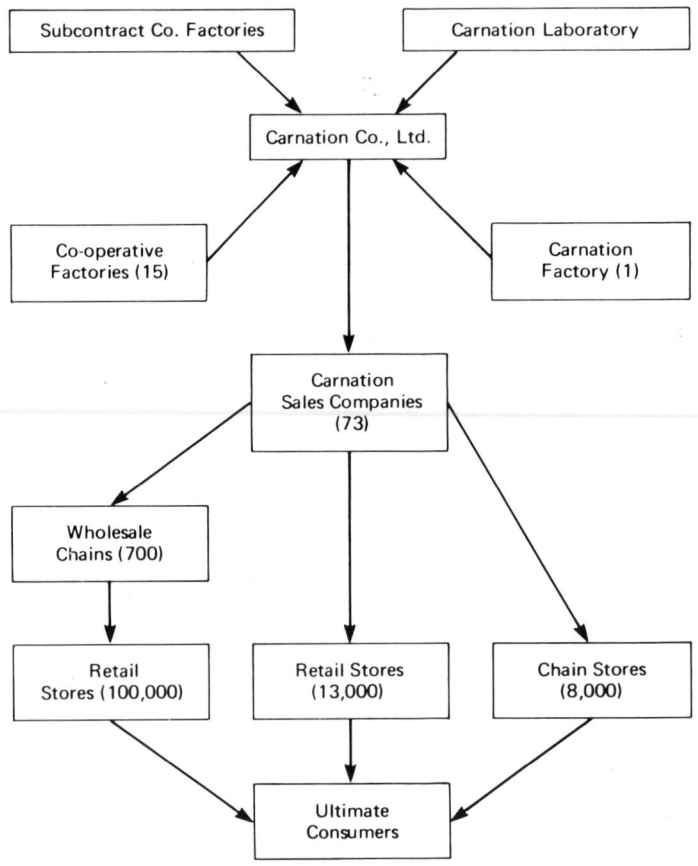

modify this distribution arrangement by withdrawing Carnation soaps, dentifrices, and sundries from the present Carnation Sales Companies, leaving them with Carnation cosmetics as their sole distributive responsibility. Responsibility for distributing Carnation soaps, dentifrices, and sundries would then be transferred to a new distribution outlet. This new outlet would be given exclusive distribution rights in return for which it would be expected to agree to identify itself as a Carnation Sales Company, to distribute Carnation products to the exclusion of competing products, maintain prices, and otherwise to conduct itself in the same general manner as the present Carnation Sales Companies.

Although the separation of the Company's distribution system for cosmetic products from its distribution system for soaps, dentifrices, and sundries had been the subject of sporadic discussion for more than ten years, and although

Carnation Company, Ltd.

there had long been general agreement that the separation of cosmetics distribution from the channels of other products was a desirable objective, there had not yet been a sufficient sense of urgency about the matter to result in concrete action. Recent developments had focused management attention on the subject, however, and M. Hiroshi Hanada, Managing Director for Marketing, had been particularly emphatic in urging that the change be instituted at an early date, preferably within the current year.

HISTORICAL DEVELOPMENT

Carnation Company, Ltd., was founded in the fifty year of the Meiji era, 1872, when Mr. Keizo Tamura opened the Carnation Pharmacy in Tokyo's Kanda area. This was the first western-style pharmacy to do business in Japan.

Within a few years, Mr. Tamura had established several branches for the filling of prescriptions and had expanded his business operations to include the preparation and distribution of general pharmaceutical products to the public. They were sold through his own branches and through other Japanese-style apothecaries.

In time the new drugs, dentifrices and toiletries replaced the old patent medicines and other products which had been produced under the methods of preparation in use at the beginning of the Meiji era.

Mr. Tamura's son, Kazuo, joined his father's business in 1914 and became extremely interested in the cosmetic aspect of the business. In addition to introducing new lines of cosmetics, Kazuo Tamura worked with prominent designers to improve Carnation's packaging styles and to develop its trade mark, the Carnation design. These efforts set the tone of the whole line of Carnation cosmetics in French classical style. Color tones, designs, and package lettering worked out under Mr. Kazuo Tamura's supervision still characterized the entire Carnation line in 1959.

In the year 1921, Carnation introduced its Carnation soap on a small scale. The next year Carnation soap was introduced to the Japanese national market as a result of a business tie-up with Honjo Co., a soap manufacturing firm long known for its high quality products. This established Carnation's reputation in the soap industry and in 1926, the Carnation Soap Co., Ltd., went into business as a joint venture with Honjo Co. In 1930 the soap firm was amalgamated with Carnation Company Ltd.

Meanwhile, Carnation had been separated into Goshikaisha and a separate venture which remained a partnership within the Tamura family.

Goshikaisha carried on the business operations of the old Carnation firm and six years later, in 1927, Gashikaisha merged with Ogawa Co., Ltd., an old established sales agent in the Kansai and other southwestern areas of Japan.[1]

---

[1] This was "mixed" partnership in the sense that some persons have a limited liability for the acts of the business and some assume an unlimited liability.

The manufacturing company and the sales agency became the limited liability company which has borne the name Carnation Company Ltd., since that time.

Because the amount of capital required to manufacture cosmetics economically was small, and because such factors as scent, color, package design, name, beauty or medical claims, and the sheer fact of "newness" were so important in the sale of cosmetics, there were a large number of small companies in the field in the 1920's. Price competition at all levels—manufacturing, wholesaling, and retailing—was keen, and Carnation products, being well known, were the object of much price cutting, especially by retail outlets.

In an effort to control the retail price of its products, the Carnation management intensified its selective distribution policy in the late 1920's, gradually limiting its sales to those retail firms which agreed to maintain prices and to emphasize Carnation products. As already noted, these franchised retail stores were termed "Chain Stores" by the Carnation management. As part of its program to increase control over the promotion and distribution of Carnation products, the Company found it advisable to intensify its selective wholesaling policy also. Exclusive regional wholesaling franchises were granted to firms which agreed to assume the name of "Carnation Company" for a particular area, i.e. Carnation Sales Company, Shizuoka, and to observe the Company's requirements with respect to pricing, inventories, promotion, and so forth.

EXHIBIT 2
CARNATION COMPANY LTD. (A)
Sales Record 1928-1959

Fiscal Period	Year*	Net Sales (000)	Fiscal Period	Year*	Net Sales (000)
1	1928	1,957	23	1949(F)	386,788
2	1929	1,897	24	1949(L)	392,299
3	1930(F)	2,013	25	1950(F)	522,516
4	1930(L)	854	26	1950(L)	716,695
5	1931	3,335	27	1951(F)	875,987
6	1932	2,804	28	1951(L)	865,763
7	1933	3,610	29	1952(F)	1,015,778
8	1934	3,394	30	1952(L)	1,174,128
9	1935	4,681	31	1953(F)	1,386,249
10	1936	5,306	32	1953(L)	1,596,690
11	1937	7,423	33	1954(F)	1,953,504
12	1938	11,606	34	1954(L)	2,119,251
13	1939	16,309	35	1955(F)	2,703,198
14	1940	21,505	36	1955(L)	3,144,937
15	1941	22,261	37	1956(F)	3,616,529
16	1942	23,636	38	1956(L)	3,858,818
17	1943	22,792	39	1957(F)	4,583,012
18	1944	15,144	40	1957(L)	4,369,755
19	1945	13,210	41	1958(F)	5,096,857
20	1946	86,365	42	1958(L)	4,954,492
21	1947	215,303	43	1959(F)	5,702,523
22	1948	428,842			

(F. First Half – June through November)
(L. Last Half – December through May)

*Fiscal period begins December and ends May.

EXHIBIT 3
CARNATION COMPANY, LTD. (A)
Balance Sheets 1949 - 1958 (000,000 yen, as of November 30)

Ref. Short-term Debts (1) due in less than one year

(CREDIT)	1949 Yen	1949 Percent	1950 Yen	1950 Percent	1951 Yen	1951 Percent	1952 Yen	1952 Percent	1953 Yen	1953 Percent	1954 Yen	1954 Percent	1955 Yen	1955 Percent	1956 Yen	1956 Percent	1957 Yen	1957 Percent	1958 Yen	1958 Percent
CURRENT LIABILITIES																				
Bills Payable	92	29.0	221	38.9	233	30.5	301	29.5	430	32.1	552	29.7	889	35.5	1,087	37.8	1,297	36.3	1,302	32.4
Accounts Payable	16	5.0	37	6.6	44	5.8	50	4.9	46	3.4	36	2.0	79	3.1	91	3.2	100	2.8	128	3.2
Short-term Debts	78	24.6	88	15.5	165	21.7	305	29.8	320	23.8	291	15.7	234	9.3	64	2.2	30	9.8	35	0.9
Short-term Debts (1)																	20	0.6	20	0.5
Unpaid Money	27	8.5	27	4.7	39	5.0	46	4.5	1	0.1	2	0.1	5	0.2	6	0.2	8	0.2	9	0.2
Tax Payable									30	2.2	51	2.8	44	1.8	47	1.6	61	1.7	69	1.7
Accrued Expenses					15	2.0	1	0.1	55	4.2	196	10.5	261	10.4	269	9.4	465	13.0	679	16.9
Accrued Interest	1	0.4	2	0.3					3	0.2	5	0.3	7	0.3	10	0.4	8	0.2	9	0.2
Deposits Received					16	2.0	8	0.8	55	4.1	100	5.4	146	5.8	188	6.5	299	8.4	366	9.1
Reserve for Price Fluctuations																				
Others	24	7.5	22	3.9	14	1.9	1	0.1	63	4.7	105	5.6	51	2.0	71	2.5	60	1.7	60	1.5
													137	5.5	149	5.1	213	6.0	175	4.4
TOTAL OF CURRENT LIABILITIES	238	75	397	69.9	526	69.0	712	69.7	1,003	74.8	1,338	72.1	1,853	73.9	1,982	68.9	2,561	71.7	2,852	71.0
FIXED LIABILITIES																				
Long-term Debt	16	4.9	18	3.1	21	2.8	18	1.7	17	1.3	19	1.0	18	0.7	107	3.7	67	1.9	47	1.2
Deposits of Guarantees															17	0.6	16	0.4	16	0.4
Reserve for Pensions Fund									4	0.3	34	1.8	62	2.5	87	3.0	115	3.2	138	3.4
TOTAL OF FIXED LIABILITIES	16	4.9	18	3.1	21	2.8	18	1.7	21	1.6	53	2.8	80	3.2	211	7.3	198	5.5	201	5.0
TOTAL OF LIABILITIES	254	79.9	415	73.0	547	71.7	730	71.4	1,024	76.4	1,391	74.9	1,933	77.1	2,193	76.2	2,759	77.2	3,053	76.0
NET WORTH																				
Paid-in Capital	50	15.8	100	17.6	150	19.7	200	19.6	200	14.9	300	16.2	300	12.0	300	10.4	300	8.4	300	7.5
Capital Surplus			27	4.7	26	3.4	26	2.5	25	1.9	41	2.2	40	1.6	39	1.3	39	1.1	39	1.0
Earned Surplus	13	4.3	27	4.7	40	5.2	67	6.5	92	6.8	125	6.7	238	9.3	375	12.1	503	13.3	675	15.5
Net Profit for the period	(13)	4.3	(27)	4.7	(40)	5.2	(62)	6.0	(91)	6.7	(125)	6.7	(233)	9.2	(300)	10.4	(360)	9.3	(408)	5.0
TOTAL OF NET WORTH	63	20.1	154	27.0	216	28.3	293	28.6	317	23.6	466	25.1	573	22.9	714	23.8	842	22.8	1,014	24.0
TOTAL OF LIABILITIES AND NET WORTH	317	100.0	569	100.0	763	100.0	1,023	100.0	1,341	100.0	1,857	100.0	2,511	100.0	2,907	100.0	3,601	100.0	4,067	100.0

EXHIBIT 4
CARNATION COMPANY, LTD. (A)
Balance Sheets 1949 - 1958 (000,000 yen, for year ending November 30)

(DEBIT)	1949 Yen	1949 Percent	1950 Yen	1950 Percent	1951 Yen	1951 Percent	1952 Yen	1952 Percent	1953 Yen	1953 Percent	1954 Yen	1954 Percent	1955 Yen	1955 Percent	1956 Yen	1956 Percent	1957 Yen	1957 Percent	1958 Yen	1958 Percent
CURRENT ASSETS																				
Cash & Deposit	58	18.3	136	23.9	182	23.8	292	28.5	346	25.7	375	20.2	353	14.1	254	8.9	271	7.6	576	14.4
Bills Receivable	48	15.1	78	13.6	86	11.2	145	14.2	176	13.1	224	12.0	460	18.1	522	18.2	512	14.3	829	20.7
Accounts Receivable	38	12.1	57	10.2	72	9.4	144	14.1	251	18.7	378	20.4	459	18.4	532	9.9	379	10.6	350	8.7
Finished Goods	22	7.0	39	6.9	58	7.6	82	7.9	117	8.7	140	7.5	180	7.2	286	9.9	379	10.6	350	8.7
Raw Materials	72	22.7	95	16.7	100	13.2	87	8.5	95	7.1	148	8.0	195	7.8	249	8.7	288	8.1	288	7.2
Goods in Process					31	4.1	27	2.7	24	1.8	33	1.8	38	1.6	57	2.0	76	2.1	119	3.0
Stores					2	0.3	2	0.3	1	0.1	2	0.1	2	0.1	2	0.1	3	0.1	5	0.1
Suspense Payable									17	1.2			25	1.0			97	2.7	2	0
Prepaid Expenses					3	0.4	3	0.3	5	0.4	7	0.4	10	0.4	10	0.4	17	0.5	23	0.6
Others	45	14.0	85	14.9	115	15.1	109	10.6	126	9.4	241	12.9	373	14.6	438	15.2	466	13.0	407	10.1
Reserve for Bad Debts													7	0.3	19	0.7	15	6.4	27	0.7
TOTAL CURRENT ASSETS	283	89.2	490	86.2	649	85.1	891	87.1	1,158	86.2	1,548	83.3	2,102	83.6	2,369	81.2	2,864	79.3	3,244	79.5
FIXED ASSETS																				
TANGIBLE ASSETS																				
Buildings	5	1.5	19	3.4	23	1.9	22	2.1	23	1.7	56	3.0	55	2.2	95	3.3	157	4.4	174	4.3
Improvable Structures					3	0.4	4	0.4	5	0.4	7	0.4	7	0.3	10	0.4	7	0.2	7	0.2
Machinery & Equipment	10	3.2	29	5.1	35	4.6	40	3.9	59	4.4	72	3.9	87	3.5	150	5.2	174	4.9	205	5.1
Delivery Equipment					1	0.1	3	0.3	6	0.5	10	0.5	13	0.5	13	0.5	12	0.4	17	0.4
Tools, Furniture & Fixtures	3	0.9	8	1.3	7	1.0	9	0.9	12	1.0	20	1.1	29	1.2	42	1.5	64	1.8	68	1.7
Land	2	0.7	3	0.5	3	0.4	4	0.3	3	0.2	7	0.4	9	0.4	12	0.4	75	2.1	91	2.3
Construction in Process													52	2.1	12	0.4	32	0.9	20	0.5
TOTAL OF TANGIBLE FIXED ASSETS	20	6.4	59	10.3	72	9.4	82	7.9	108	8.2	172	9.3	252	10.2	334	11.7	521	14.7	582	14.5
Investments	14	4.4	20	3.5	42	5.5	51	5.0	75	5.6	136	7.4	156	6.2	203	7.1	215	6.0	239	5.9
TOTAL OF FIXED ASSETS	34	10.8	79	13.8	114	14.9	133	12.9	183	13.8	308	16.7	408	16.4	537	18.8	736	20.7	821	20.4
Deferred Accounts											1	0	1	0	1	0	1		2	0.1
TOTAL OF ASSETS	317	100.0	569	100.0	763	100.0	1,023	100.0	1,341	100.0	1,857	100.0	2,511	100.0	2,907	100.0	3,601	100.0	4,067	100.0

EXHIBIT 4. (continued)
CARNATION COMPANY, LTD. (A)
Income Statements 1949 - 1958 (000,000 yen, for year ending November 30)

	1949		1950		1951		1952		1953		1954		1955		1956		1957		1958	
	Yen	Percent	Yen	Percent	Yen	Percent	Yen	Percent	Yen	Percent	Yen	Percent	Yen	Percent	Yen	Percent	Yen	Percent	Yen	Percent
Net Sales	779	100.0	1,239	100.0	1,742	100.0	2,189	100.0	2,982	100.0	4,072	100.0	5,848	100.0	7,475	100.0	8,952	100.0	10,051	100.0
Cost of Sales	676	86.7	1,041	84.1	1,441	82.7	1,758	80.3	2,276	76.3	3,059	75.1	4,263	72.9	5,312	71.1	6,039	67.5	6,599	65.6
Gross Profits	103	13.2	198	15.9	300	17.3	431	19.7	706	23.7	1,013	24.9	1,585	27.1	2,163	28.9	2,913	32.5	3,452	34.4
General Administration & Sales Expense	71	9.1	129	10.4	202	11.6	312	14.3	526	17.7	799	19.6	1,220	20.9	1,798	24.1	2,535	28.3	2,995	29.8
Personal Expenses			(26)	(2.1)	(40)	(2.3)	(51)	(2.3)	(68)	(2.3)	(105)	(2.6)	(117)	(2)	(145)	(1.9)	(173)	(1.9)	(202)	(2.0)
Advertising Expense			(51)	(4.1)	(105)	(6.0)	(192)	(8.7)	(363)	(12.2)	(559)	(13.7)	(944)	(16.1)	(1,368)	(18.3)	(546)	(6.1)	(651)	(6.5)
Sales and Sales Promotion*																	(1,254)	(14.0)	(1,481)	(14.7)
OPERATING PROFITS	32	4.1	69	5.6	99	5.7	119	5.4	180	6.0	214	5.3	365	6.2	365	4.8	378	4.2	457	4.6
Non-operating Revenue	5	0.6	6	0.4	9	0.5	35	1.6	29	1.0	38	0.9	46	0.8	52	0.8	68	0.8	(56)	0.6
Interest & Dividend Re'vd	0	(0.06)	(1)	(0.10)	(2)	(0.1)	(3)	(0.2)	(10)	(0.3)	(17)	(0.4)	(29)	(0.5)	(28)	(0.4)	(20)	(0.2)	(27)	(0.3)
Dividends Received			(1)	(0.05)	(1)	(0.1)	(3)	(0.1)	(4)	(0.1)	(4)	(0.1)	(4)	(0.07)	(6)	(0.08)	(8)	(0.1)	(8)	(0.08)
Rent									(9)	(0.28)	(9)	(0.2)	(7)	(0.01)	(7)	(0.09)	(7)	(0.08)	(8)	(0.08)
Other Revenue	(5)	(0.6)	(4)	(0.3)	(5)	(0.3)	(28)	(1.3)	(7)	(0.2)	(8)	(0.2)	(6)	(0.1)	(11)	(0.14)	(30)	(0.3)	(11)	(0.1)
Non-operating Expenses	24	3.1	48	3.8	68	3.9	92	4.2	118	4.0	127	3.1	178	3.0	117	1.6	86	1.0	105	1.1
Interest & Discount Paid	(20)	(2.6)	(41)	(3.3)	(52)	(3.0)	(68)	(3.1)	(70)	(2.3)	(83)	(2.0)	(64)	(1.1)	(58)	0.8	(52)	0.6	73	0.7
Appropriation of Reserve for bad debts					(1)	(0.03)			(0.4)		(4)	(0.1)	(10)	(0.2)	(17)	(0.2)	(15)	(0.17)	(17)	(0.2)
Appropriation of Reserve for price fluctuation																				
Others	(4)	(0.6)	(7)	(0.6)	(15)	(0.8)	(24)	(1.1)	(36)	(1.2)	(41)	(51) (1.0)	(9) (52)	(0.9)	(20) (23)	(0.26) (0.3)	(19)	(0.2)	(1) (15)	(0.01) (0.1)
NET PROFITS FOR THE PERIOD	13	1.6	27	2.2	40	2.3	62	2.8	91	3.0	125	3.1	233	4.0	300	4.0	360	4.0	408	4.1

*Including expense of special introductory sales promotions.

The war years of 1937-1945 brought first a rapid expansion, as Asian markets were opened to Japanese exports and then contraction, as war induced shortages of raw materials and labor limited production and other aspects of a war economy limited sales. Inflation and the uncertainties and chaos of the early postwar years then took their toll. Moreover, the Company's resale price maintenance agreements were rendered void by a provision of the Anti-Monopoly Law of 1949.

Between 1950 and 1958, however, the Company's condition underwent drastic improvement. Annual sales of Carnation products increased more than ten-fold (Exhibit 2). During this period the Company became more and more involved in the manufacture of non-cosmetic items, especially soaps, and in 1952 it established the wholesale "chain" outlets already described. When a 1953 amendment to the Anti-Monopoly Law eliminated that law's prohibition of resale price maintenance clauses, Carnation immediately reestablished the uniform price system which had been in effect prior to the War.

Balance sheets and income statements for the postwar period are given in Exhibits 3 and 4, respectively.

INDUSTRY POSITION

As indicated by Exhibit 5, Carnation Company Ltd., was active in four fairly well defined product lines; cosmetics, toilet soaps, laundry soaps and

EXHIBIT 5
CARNATION COMPANY, LTD. (A)
Carnation Sales, 1955 - 1958, Classified by Product Line
(Unit: million yen)

	1955	1956	1957	1958
Cosmetic Goods	¥2,910	¥3,640	¥4,680	¥5,490
(percentage of previous year)	129%	125%	128%	117%
Toilet Soaps	¥1,030	¥1,240	¥1,450	¥1,600
(percentage of previous year)	130%	120%	117%	110%
Laundry Soaps	¥1,290	¥1,570	¥1,780	¥1,890
(percentage of previous year)	195%	121%	113%	106%
Dentifrices	¥280	¥440	¥510	¥490
(percentage of previous year)	175%	157%	116%	96%
Other Sundries	¥340	¥590	¥530	¥580
(percentage of previous year)	162%	173%	90%	109%
Total	¥5,850	¥7,480	¥8,950	¥10,050
(percentage of previous year)	144%	128%	119%	112%
Index Number (1955=100)	100	125	161	189

Carnation Company, Ltd.   211

dentifrices. The Carnation management estimated that the Company's share of the total sales of these various product categories during 1958 was about 15 per cent of sales in the field of cosmetics, 11 per cent of toilet soaps, 10 per cent of solid laundry soap, 4 per cent of powdered laundry soap, 1 per cent of detergents, and 6 per cent of dentifrices. (See Exhibit 6.) The management's appraisal of the Company's relative position in the various markets follows.

EXHIBIT 6
CARNATION COMPANY, LTD. (A)
Industry Position, 1958

Products	Industry		Carnation Company, Ltd.	
	Number of Highly Ranked Companies	Percentage of Market Occupation	Rank	Percentage of Market Occupation
Cosmetic goods	10	50%	1	15%
Toilet soaps	6	60%	3	11%
Laundry soaps:				
Solid	6	45%	3	10%
Powder	7	55%	7	4%
Detergents:				
Powder)				
Liquid)	N. A.	N. A.	N. A.	1%
Dentifrices	3	65%	3	6%

SOURCE: Management estimates
NOTE: N.A. means "Not available".

CARNATION'S MARKET POSITION

Cosmetics: Without taking up specific products, which have proved their superiority in the field, Carnation's position in cosmetics might be summed by saying it holds the major position in this country. In addition to the quality of Carnation products, the strong and well-established sales organization which handles its products must be given a major portion of the credit for the Company's accomplishment.

Carnation is the only company which functions as a full-line consolidated cosmetic manufacturer selling through distributors and chain stores. Relatively, the Company's competitors are all doing business on a very small scale.

Soap, Detergents, and Dentifrice: Carnation ranked third in 1958 in sales of toilet soap, cake washing soap and dentifrice.

The companies which were first and second in toilet soap sales are specialists in this field and both have long, solid backgrounds in its manufacture and sales. The firms leading Carnation in sales of detergents and dentifrices are large com-

EXHIBIT 7
CARNATION COMPANY, LTD. (A)
Carnation Sales in Various Product Categories Relative to Total
Sales of Leading Companies in the Same Product Categories
(all figures are for the year 1958 and are in millions of yen)

Product Category	Net Sales	Assets	Paid-in Capital	Number of Employees	Principal Business Lines
Cosmetics					
Carnation Co., Ltd.	¥5,500				
Company "A"	2,000		¥10	6,000	Cream
Company "B"	1,800	¥1,200	150	440	Cream
Company "C"	1,500		45	200	Pomade
Company "D"	1,400		15	420	Toilet water
Company "E"	1,300	600	50	350	Lipstick
Company "F"	1,200	780	30	610	Cream
Company "G"	1,200		10	460	Cream toilet water
Company "H"	1,200	810	33	340	Cream
Company "I"	1,200		10	160	Hair tonic
TOTAL	¥18,500				
TOTAL OF THE FIELD	¥36,500				
Toilet Soaps					
Carnation Co., Ltd.	1,600				
Company "J"	2,400	1,970	80	325	Toilet soaps
Company "K"	2,800	1,850	60	607	Toilet soaps
Company "L"	8,000	5,150	500	1,414	Toilet soaps, detergents Chemicals, Oils, and Fats
TOTAL	¥14,800				
Laundry Soaps					
Carnation Co., Ltd.	1,890				Laundry soaps, margarine
Company "M"	7,540	4,220	1,000	1,134	Chemicals
Company "N"	3,600	2,210	100	973	Laundry soaps, detergent, etc.
Company "O"	2,060	1,320	50	350	Laundry soaps
Company "P"	10,540	9,120	1,000	3,620	Soaps, paints, oils and fats
Company "Q"	7,340	2,230	327	507	Edible oil, oils and fats
Company "R"	3,520	2,600	450	1,005	Industrial and household soaps
TOTAL	36,490				Detergents
Dentifrices					
Carnation Co., Ltd.	490				
Company "S"	2,540	1,560	160	1,070	Dentifrices, tooth brushes
Company "T"	2,300	1,630	150	1,026	Dentifrices
TOTAL					
Carnation Co., Ltd.	10,050	4,010	300	1,030	Cosmetics, toilet soaps, laundry soaps, dentifrices and sundries

NOTES: a. Carnation sales are given for each respective product classification. Total sales for Carnation Co., Ltd., as well as other data, are given at the bottom of the table.
b. "Total of the Field" is the estimated total sales of the respective products. It is not total of all sales of the respective companies in the field.

panies which produce other fat and related products and have high-productivity plant facilities.

More detailed information regarding Carnation's 1958 market position in various product lines is given in Exhibit 7. Carnation sales in these same product lines for the year 1955 and 1958 are given in Exhibits 8, 9, and 10, and those of the respective industries for the postwar period are given in Exhibit 11.

Carnation Company, Ltd.

EXHIBIT 8
CARNATION COMPANY, LTD. (A)
Industry Shipments of Cosmetics by Major Product Categories and Carnation Shipments by Comparable Product Categories, 1955-1958

Year / Product	1955 Carnation* Kg(000)	1955 Carnation* Yen(000)	1955 Industry† Kg(000)	1955 Industry† Yen(000)	1958 Carnation* Kg(000)	1958 Carnation* Yen(000)	1958 Industry† Kg(000)	1958 Industry† Yen(000)
Non-oily cream	19	57,591	1,864	3,152,221	11	35,679	2,026	4,755,915
Oily cream	236	756,631	2,094	5,018,840	354	1,473,993	2,169	6,100,505
Foundation	39	181,898	376	1,326,809	61	257,072	533	2,545,441
Dusting powder	10	76,438	388	1,204,946	23	163,841	346	1,456,225
Dusting powder	5	62,147			12	136,779	52	564,732
Dusting powder	1	2,948	56	320,841	1	1,830	11	23,214
Dusting powder	5	10,600	16	20,711	410	11,492	48	254,659
Toilet lotion	192	344,365	997	1,378,738	245	445,215	1,824	3,039,257
Toilet water	97	182,294	2,410	2,338,551	2	551,695	3,255	3,915,383
Pomade (vegetal)	5	20,185	2,374	2,658,154	1	10,304	2,428	2,831,319
Pomade (mineral)	1	2,121	10	17,679		4,053	15	16,589
Hair Oil (vegetal)	4	22,787	143	193,861	7		113	153,420
Hair oil (mineral)			1,007	1,002,161			1,010	1,076,170
Hair oil			232	465,704			343	612,892
Hair cream			105	138,967	92	124,694	1,055	1,135,787
Hair tonic	0.02	56	858	939,051	4	13,190	1,356	1,558,778
Eau de cologne					0.2	1,302	141	248,668
Lip stick	5	222,373	57	1,355,456	8	309,125	51	1,817,282
Rouge	2	21,682	8	93,951	2	33,804	9	189,274
Eyebrow pencil	2		7	135,951	2	96,399	16	323,874
Perfume	10		174	962,433	19	163,800	67	1,021,744
Manicure	1		28	119,602	6		61	203,755
Washing powder)			260	105,986)			250	120,572
Shampoo)			601	219,942)				
Hair dye)	3	6,746	71	171,456)	27	118,138		
Others)			218	287,953)			1,586	2,537,255
Total	637	2,150,847	14,354	23,630,064	1,291	4,372,562	18,765	36,501,811

SOURCES: *Company records.
†Tokyo Cosmetic Trade Association.

GENERAL ADMINISTRATION

The chief executive of Carnation Company Ltd., was the President to whom reported managing directors for Marketing, Finance, Manufacturing and Engineering, and Advertising. The four managing directors, together with the President, formed the Executive Committee. This committee met weekly to consider general trading trends and to deside upon overall operating policy. Each managing director was also responsible for the administration of one or more departments of the Company.

The Board of Directors, which met twice monthly, was responsible for determining the basic policy of the Company. The first meeting of the month was devoted to policy matters, the second meeting to a review of operating budgets and financial reports. All members of the Board were full-time officers of the Company. (See Exhibits 12 and 13.) Execution of decisions made by the Board of Directors and by the Executive Committee was planned at weekly meet-

EXHIBIT 9
CARNATION COMPANY LTD. (A)
Industry Shipments of Soaps and Detergents by Major Product Categories
and Carnation Shipments by Comparable Product Categories, 1955 and 1958

Year Product	1955			
	Carnation*		Industry†	
	Kg(000)	Yen(000)	Kg(000)	Yen(000)
Toilet soaps	3,740	1,031,374	56,367	11,578,888
Laundry soaps	13,372	1,180,430	179,010	15,236,244
Soaps for textiles			7,406	787,398
Industrial soaps			2,251	206,358
Soap powder	550	49,185	33,373	3,559,095
Other soap			770	105,473
Total	17,635	2,260,989	279,177	31,473,406
Detergent			5,033	827,990

Year Product	1958			
	Carnation*		Industry†	
	Kg(000)	Yen(000)	Kg(000)	Yen(000)
Toilet soaps	5,501	1,651,694	60,396	12,615,840
Laundry soaps	16,566	1,337,655	192,832	15,053,159
Soaps for textiles			6,627	637,469
Industrial soaps			1,821	170,834
Soap powder	3,246	254,791	81,935	7,696,768
Other soap			2,922	256,065
Total	25,203	3,244,140	346,533	36,430,135
Detergent	135	19,310	13,519	1,931,319

SOURCES: *Company records.
†Research Statistics Division, Ministrial Secretariat,
Ministry of International Trade and Industry.

ings of the department heads. Basic policy decisions were made by the Board of Directors and by the Executive Committee. Then the department heads meeting decided the details of execution in conform with the basic policy decided. Attached to the Board of Directors was a Planning Section (not shown on Exhibit 12) which prepared regularized reports and analyses as requested by the Board, and which undertook special investigations at the direction of the Board.

The sources of the Company's manufactured products are indicated in Exhibit 15. As noted therein, there were five plants, not owned by the Company, which devoted their total capacity to the manufacture of Carnation products on a contract basis.[2] Collaboration between these plants and the Company included assistance from the Sales Department in product planning and technical guidance from the Carnation Laboratory. The Managing Director for Production exercised overall control over the Company's relations with the sub-contracting plants.

[2] Called "cooperative factories" in Exhibit 1.

Carnation Company, Ltd.

EXHIBIT 10
CARNATION COMPANY LTD. (A)
Industry Shipments of Dentrifice by Major Product Categories
and Carnation Shipment by Comparable Product Categories, 1955 and 1958

Year / Product	1955 Industry* Kg(000)	1955 Industry* Yen(000)	1955 Industry† Kg(000)	1955 Industry† Yen(000)
Tooth Powder			4,674	749,620
Moist Tooth Powder			6,422	2,337,616
Tooth Paste	350	276,052	5,062	3,724,855
Total	350	276,052	16,158	6,812,091

Year / Product	1958 Industry* Kg(000)	1958 Industry* Yen(000)	1958 Industry† Kg(000)	1958 Industry† Yen(000)
Tooth Powder			2,414	434,373
Moist Tooth Powder	584	204,027	9,270	3,223,993
Tooth Paste	378	291,171	5,649	4,344,944
Total	962	495,198	17,333	8,003,310

SOURCES: †Dentrifrice Trade Association.
*Company records.

EXHIBIT 11
CARNATION COMPANY, LTD. (A)
Industry Shipments Cosmetics, Soaps, Detergents and Dentifices, 1946 - 1958

Year	Cosmetics* Kg(000)	Cosmetics* Yen(000)	Soaps† Kg(000)	Soaps† Yen(000)	Detergents† Kg(000)	Detergents† Yen(000)	Dentifrices‡ Kg(000)	Dentifrices‡ Yen(000)
1946	3,651	499,121	16,882				13,476	88,270
1947	4,403	928,849	7,981				9,240	340,424
1948	5,506	3,148,247	15,147				12,713	753,843
1949	5,921	6,164,356	25,862				8,282	1,060,649
1950	7,144	8,841,467	96,380	18,934,027	579	132,589	7,858	1,336,542
1951	9,814	12,193,639	147,826	15,141,256	2,062	370,299	9,592	2,301,620
1952	9,824	14,881,770	150,243	18,832,776	3,526	603,243	10,865	3,369,867
1953	11,373	17,708,892	191,878	20,573,568	4,193	713,730	13,677	5,039,929
1954	12,420	20,470,295	237,276	25,883,142	3,809	627,679	14,031	5,616,256
1955	14,354	23,630,064	279,177	31,473,406	5,033	827,990	16,158	6,812,091
1956	15,860	26,699,824	296,622	32,676,630	8,542	1,311,956	18,615	8,140,953
1957	18,115	31,595,909	319,731	33,881,538	10,032	1,514,247	18,019	8,055,942
1958	18,764	36,501,811	346,533	36,430,135	13,519	1,931,319	17,733	8,003,310

SOURCES: *Tokyo Cosmetics Trade Association.
†Research Statistics Division, Ministrial Secretariat, Ministry of International Trade and Industry.
‡Dentifrices Trade Association

EXHIBIT 12
CARNATION COMPANY, LTD. (A)
Organization Chart*

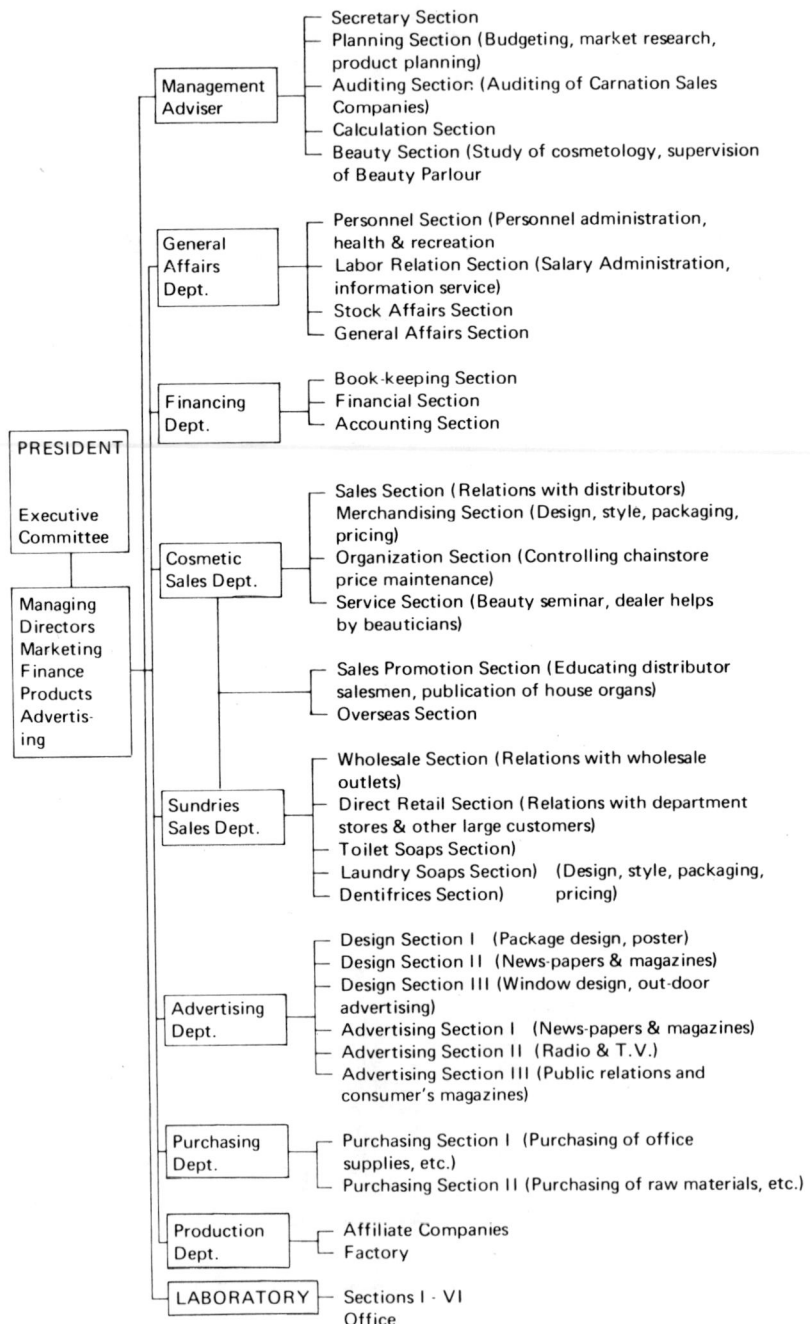

*As drawn by company officer.

Carnation Company, Ltd.   217

Various designated members of the Sales and Production Departments, and from the Laboratory met as a Products Committee, a Color-tone Conference, and a Perfume Conference, respectively. These committees co-ordinated the activities of the Company in respect to the chemical and quality characteristics of Carnation products.

PRODUCTION

The production processes involved in the manufacture of cosmetics are diagrammed in Exhibit 14. As suggested by the diagrams, the preparation of cosmetics was typically a batch process operation which utilized relatively simple equipment and which offered no significant cost savings as the volume of production increased beyond fairly low levels.

Soap manufacture, also diagrammed in Exhibit 14, was largely conducted as a batch process. The equipment required for refining and saponification was somewhat more costly than that required for cosmetic manufacture, however, and a plant having an output of approximately 800 tons a month was considered relatively economical. A plant having half this capacity, for example, might incur costs 3 per cent to 4 per cent higher.

These were traditional cost relationships, however, and new technological developments nearing commercial application seemed likely to swing the balance in terms of production costs more in favor of the large producers. These developments affected both manufacturing methods and basic raw materials. Among the former, the Carnation management reported increased use of continuous process flow techniques in place of batch processing, automation in container filling and packaging, mechanization of intraplant transportation, and automatic control of temperature during production processes. New equipment in operation at the Carnation factory in Tokyo included a Sharpless-type neutral fat continuous saponification machine used in the manufacture of soaps and automatic packaging and filling machines for cosmetics, soaps and dentifrices.

Among the changes in basic raw materials, the Carnation management reported:

> Developments in surface chemistry and synthetics and their application to products made by Carnation are naturally of the greatest interest to the Company. The development of an improved surface activator and improvement of emulsification have contributed to the high quality and stability of the quality of soap products.
>
> High-polymer compounds developed as a result of study and research in synthetic chemistry include synthetic oily materials, synthetic wax, and synthetic mucin. Both synthetic oily material and synthetic mucin have been used in the manufacture of soaps and cosmetics and have been found to be superior in quality to the natural products. Steps are now being taken to improve the quality of toiletries by the introduction of these newly-developed products. For example, Carnation plans to begin the manufacture and trial sale of a soap using a surface

EXHIBIT 13
CARNATION COMPANY LTD. (A)
The Profile of Top Management

President, Ichiro Takeda (62)
- 1927: Appointed Director of Carnation Co., Ltd. from Musashi Co., Ltd., after merger.
- 1941: Held an additional post of Managing Director of Carnation Tooth Brushes Industry Co., Ltd.
- 1948: Appointed Managing Director of Osaka Carnation Co., Ltd.
- 1954: Managing Director of Carnation Co., Ltd.
- 1959: President of the Company above mentioned.

Managing Director, Hiroshi Hanada (63) Marketing
- 1921: Entered Carnation Limited Co.
- 1944: Appointed Director of Carnation Co., Ltd.
- 1948: Managing Director of the Company above mentioned.

Managing Director, Takeshi Ishikawa (59) Finance
- 1926: Entered Carnation Limited Co.
- 1944: Appointed Director of Carnation Co., Ltd.
- 1947: Managing Director of the company above mentioned.

Managing Director, Mamoru Suzuki (51) Production
- 1920: Entered Tamura Carnation
- 1944: Appointed Director of Carnation Co., Ltd.
- 1950: Managing Director of the company above mentioned.
- 1954: Resigned from the post above mentioned and appointed managing director of Osaka Carnation Co., Ltd.
- 1957: Held an additional post of Auditor of Carnation Co., Ltd.
- 1958: Resigned from Auditor.

Managing Director, Kazuo Yamada (60) Advertising
- 1927: Entered Carnation Limited Co.
- 1947: Appointed Director of Carnation Co., Ltd.
- 1950: Managing Director of the company above mentioned.

Director, Taro Kawano (51) General Affairs
- 1927: Entered Carnation Co., Ltd.
- 1944: Appointed Assistant-manager of Carnation Tokyo Factory.
- 1947: Director of Carnation Co., Ltd.

Director, Shigeo Uchiyama (51) Cosmetic Department
- 1924: Entered Carnation Limited Co.
- 1944: Appointed Managing Director of Manshu Carnation
- 1948: Director of Carnation Co., Ltd.

Director, Saburo Tamura (48) Assistant-manager of Laboratory
- 1933: Entered Carnation Co., Ltd.
- 1943: Appointed Assistant-manager of Laboratory
- 1953: Director of Carnation Co., Ltd.

Director, Masao Sato (52) Manager of Factory
- 1933: Entered Carnation Co., Ltd.
- 1943: Appointed Assistant-manager of Laboratory and Chief Engineer of Tokyo Factory consequently
- 1953: Director of Carnation Co., Ltd.

Carnation Company, Ltd.

EXHIBIT 13 (continued)

Director, Hideo Okawa (51)
    1934:   Entered Carnation Tokyo Factory
    1946:   Appointed Chief-engineer of Osaka Carnation Co., Ltd.
    1954:   Director of the company above mentioned
    1959:   Director of Carnation Co., Ltd.

Director, Masaaki Kimura (47) Treasurer
    1933:   Entered Carnation Co., Ltd.
    1956:   Appointed Auditor of the company above mentioned
    1958:   Director of the company.

Auditor, Taijo Kondo (56)
    1920:   Entered Tamura Carnation
    1956:   Appointed Manager of Carnation Parlour Co., Ltd.
    1958:   Held an additional post of Manager of Carnation Paints Industry Co., Ltd.
    1958:   Auditor of Carnation Co., Ltd.

Auditor, Katsuhiko Amano (59)
    1927:   Entered Carnation Osaka Branch
    1947:   Appointed Director of Carnation Co., Ltd.
    1951:   Manager of Carnation Co.,
    1951:   Manager of Carnation Tokyo Central Sales Co., Ltd.
    1957:   Manager of Carnation Parlour Co., Ltd.
    1958:   Held an additional post of Auditor of Carnation Co., Ltd.

EXHIBIT 14
CARNATION COMPANY LTD. (A)
Manufacturing Processes

COSMETICS

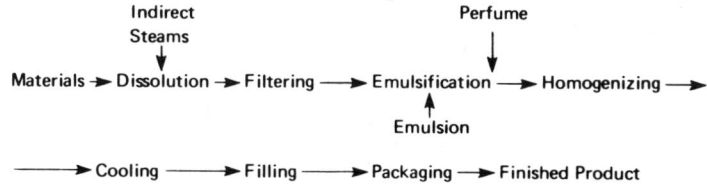

SOAPS

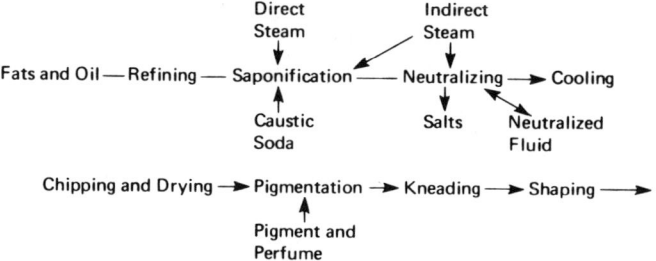

activator as its basic material in lieu of the fatty acid which formerly carried out that role. With the Company's growing production of detergents and its near-introduction of a synthetic soap, it appears that petroleum derivations will soon eclipse fat in the manufacture of washing compounds.

Partly in order to facilitate a shift to the new manufacturing process and new materials, and partly for the purpose of expanding production capacity, the Company was constructing a new cosmetic factory at Matsudo in Chiba Prefecture. When this was completed in late 1959, the Cosmetic Department of the Tokyo factory would move to that location and the present Tokyo factory would be completely renovated and modernized for the exclusive manufacture of toilet soap. It was anticipated that the Tokyo alterations would be completed in 1960. The total program was expected to increase the Company's cosmetic capacity by 100 per cent and its toilet soap capacity by 30 per cent, using 1958 production as 100 per cent. (See Exhibit 15 for the present sources of Carnation manufactured products.)

The soap plant at Tokyo would be set up on an independent accounting system and would undergo a complete reorganization. The existing organization of the Tokyo factory is given in Exhibit 16. Mr. Hanada, Managing Director of Marketing, had recommended that the proposed shift in the Company's whole-

EXHIBIT 15
CARNATION COMPANY LTD. (A)
Manufacturing Source of Carnation Products, 1958

Product Line	Number of Items	Sales Value (total in million yen)	Manufacturing Source		Sales Value (per cent of total)
			Company	Factory Location	
Cosmetic Goods	300	¥5,500	Carnation Co., Ltd.*	Tokyo	4,100(40%)
			Osaka-Carnation Co.*	Osaka	1,400(14%)
Toilet Soaps	50	1,600	Carnation Co., Ltd.*	Tokyo	1,380(14%)
			"X" Co., Ltd.	Osaka	180(2%)
			"Y" Co., Ltd.	Osaka	40(0.4%)
Laundry Soap	65	1,900	"Z" Co., Ltd.	Yokohama	1,900(18%)
Detergents	12	20	"U" Co., Ltd.	Kyoto	20(0.2%)
Dentifrices	8	500	Osaka-Carnation Co.*	Osaka	500(4.5%)
	35	170	Carnation Tooth Brushes Industry Ltd.*	Osaka	170(2%)
Sundries	9	500	"V" Co., Ltd.	Gifu	80(0.9%)
			Others (3 companies)		420(4%)
Total		¥10,190			10,190(100%)

*Prepared by company.

Carnation Company, Ltd.

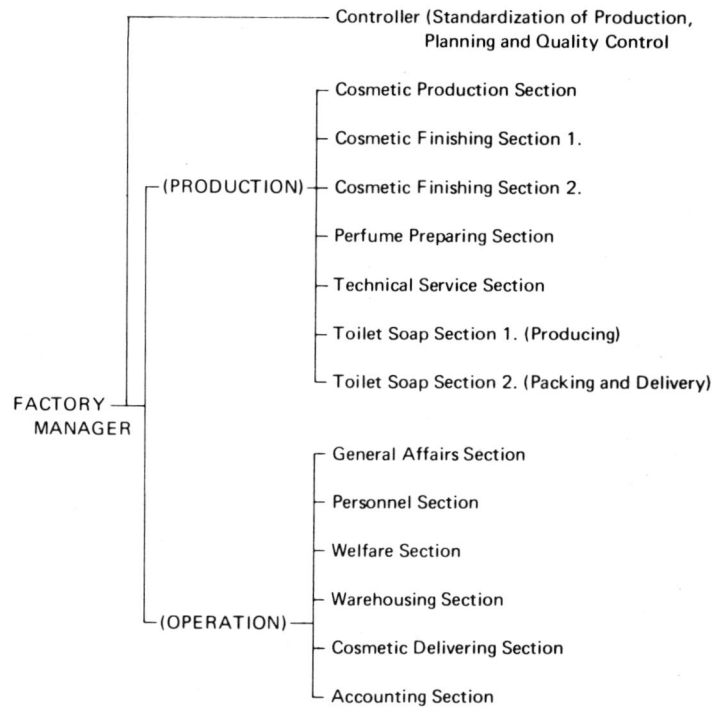

EXHIBIT 16
CARNATION COMPANY LTD. (A)
Organization of the Tokyo Factory* (Spring, 1959)

*Prepared by company.

sale distribution system be timed to coincide with the renovation and expansion of the Company's soap manufacturing facilities.

BRAND POLICY

In respect to brand promotion, it was the Carnation Policy to emphasize the concept of a "Carnation family" of high quality products. All packages and containers, therefore, carried the name "Carnation" in prominent position and bold type, usually second in importance only to the generic name of the particular product. Partial exceptions were dental creams and powders, which carried the trade name "PEARL" in addition to Company name and a generic description, Carnation "DE-LUXE" cosmetics, Carnation "POINT" shaving articles, and other similar combinations. (See Exhibit 17 for brand policy as applied to packaging of cosmetics, toilet soap, dentifrices, laundry soap, and other sundries.) The same policy was applied to the Company's advertising in mass media such as

EXHIBIT 17
CARNATION COMPANY LTD. (A)
Illustration of Product Names

1.	Cosmetics	Carnation Lip Stick "Special"
2.	Toilet Soap	Carnation Soap "Olive"
		Carnation Soap "White"
		Carnation Soap "De Luxe"
		Carnation Soap "Carnation"
3.	Laundry Soap	Carnation Powder Soap
		Carnation "A P"
		Carnation Cleaner
4.	Dentifrices	Carnation Pearl Dental Semi-wet Powder "Echo"
		Carnation Medical Dental Cream "Pearl"
		Carnation Tooth Brush
5.	Sundries	Carnation Safety Razor "De Luxe"
		Carnation "Honey Cake"

newspapers, magazines, and TV. The objective of a connotation of high quality was frequently conveyed by a restrained use of pastel colors and gold tints in what the management referred to as "the classical French style," by a careful selection of style printing, and by the use of high quality materials and well constructed packages. The Company utilized no secondary brands or secondary price lines.

MARKETING ORGANIZATION AND POLICY

As visualized by Mr. Hanada, the organization of the Company's marketing function was as follows:

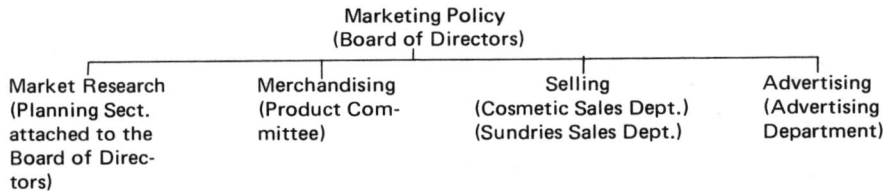

In the Company's marketing procedures for cosmetics, top priority was being given to the establishment of "organized" sales channels, i.e., channels which could be depended upon to produce sales results because of a regularized and continuing relationship between the Company and the purchaser. At the wholesale level this was achieved by the Carnation Sales Companies, exclusive distributors of Carnation products. Selective distribution of cosmetics through Carnation "chain stores" provided stability at the retail level and Carnation-kai, an organization of women customers of the chain stores, represented the Com-

Carnation Company, Ltd. 223

pany's attempt to "regularize" the ultimate users of Carnation products. The Carnation management was well satisfied with the way in which its channels for the sale of cosmetics had been organized. Other firms in both the soap and dentifrice industries, as well the cosmetic industry, used general and specialized wholesalers on a non-exclusive basis to distribute their products.

Mr. Hanada noted that the same system as had been applied so successfully to cosmetics was not entirely appropriate to such items as toilet soaps, laundry soaps, and dentifrices. Women could be induced to patronize selected retail outlets for cosmetics by such devices as beauty care advice, annual gifts (each chain store kept a record of the purchases of its regular customers and provided gifts proportionate to the amount of the purchases), demonstrations and lectures, and printed literature on beauty care. Mr. Hanada thought that such personalized sales effort was not appropriate to most of the other Carnation products, either on a cost basis or on the basis of customer motivation. The Company's other products tended to fall into the category of "convenience goods."

The Company's merchandising activities were outlined by Mr. Hanada as follows:

```
                        Products Council
                   (Composed of all Directors)
        ┌──────────────────────┴──────────────────────┐
Products Committee                          Chemical Committee
(design, packaging, pricing;                (composed of the Directors
composed of Departmental                    and the Managers for
Managers concerned)                         Factory, Laboratory, and
                                            Sales)
```

One of the principal concerns of the Carnation management was new product development. Ideas for product planning were sought with the more than 500 salesmen and 400 beauticians who were employed by the Carnation Sales Companies. The sales Companies and other distributors were also asked to submit periodic reports on consumer trends. The reports and suggestions were analyzed and summarized by the Planning Section attached to the Board of Directors, which also made recommendations. These recommendations were examined by the Sales Departments and then forwarded, with comment, to the Products Committee. The recommendations of this Committee were then submitted as proposals to the Products Council, where final decisions were made. During 1958 some new fifteen products and twenty-eight improved products were proposed to the Products Council. All of these products were adopted. Twenty-eight items were dropped from the Carnation line during 1958. Mr. Hanada was of the opinion that these efforts should be supplemented by consumer panels of some sort, but no action along these lines had as yet been taken.

ADVERTISING

The Company's advertising activities were organized as follows:

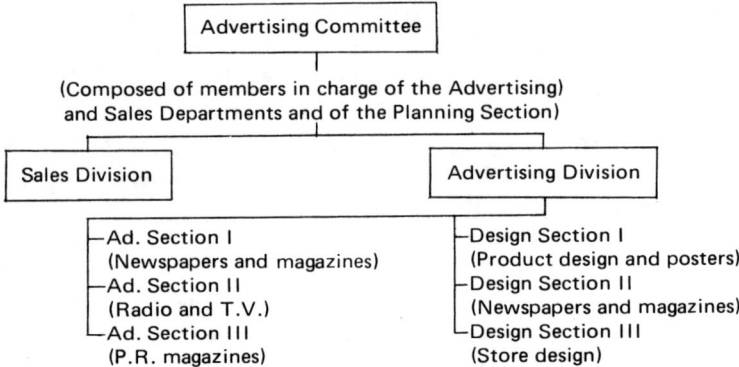

It was the policy of the Company to emphasize the Carnation "tone" in its advertising efforts, i.e. to present the individual products in such a way as to stress high quality and the relationship of the particular product to the family of Carnation products. With the Guidance of the Board of Directors, the Advertising Committee prepared and controlled the advertising budget, which usually approximated 6 per cent of estimated sales. The intensity of competition in recent years had resulted in moderate supplemental appropriations during 1957 and 1958. The distribution of advertising expenditures by type of media for 1957 was as follows: Newspapers, 52.2 per cent; magazines, 9.7 per cent; T.V. 5.2 per cent; Radio, 19.2 per cent; Cinema, 5.1 per cent; Outdoor, 7.5 per cent; Others, 1.1 per cent. Advertising expense classified according to product emphasis was 38.6% for cosmetics, 22.9% for toilet soap, 36.3% for dentifrices, and 2.2% for other sundries.

SALES

The sales organization was as follows:

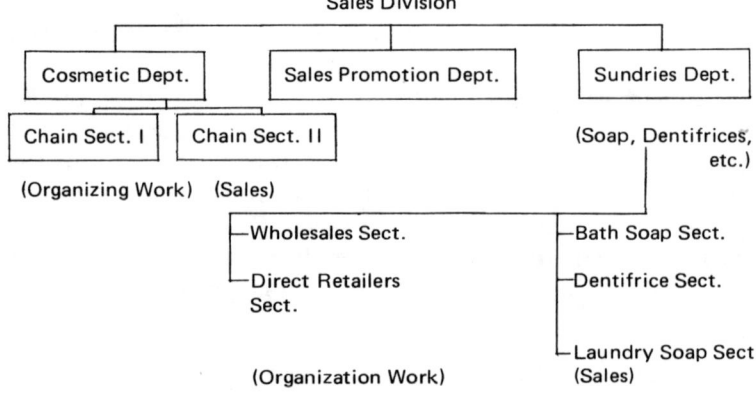

Carnation Company, Ltd.

As outlined by Mr. Hanada:

All of the Company's products are sold through the distribution channels shown above. The 73 Selling Companies, constituting the wholesale system, are independent corporations which are made to maintain certain prices for all Carnation Products, and, what is more, they (the Sales Companies) exchange "Resale Price Maintenance Contracts" with the Chain Stores for Carnation cosmetic goods.

As for products other than cosmetic goods (such as soap and dentifrices), the Sales Companies are now trying to promote sales through general wholesalers to retail stores. Adequate control over the general wholesalers has not yet been obtained, however, in that neither franchise policy nor price maintenance policy have yet been satisfactory applied.

PROMOTION:

Sales promotion at Carnation is the responsibility of the Sales Promotion Department of the Sales Division, and includes the following activities:

Relation with Sales Companies:
Guidance for salesmen including training in salesmanship, in the attributes of Carnation products, and in the use of cosmetics generally.

Instructions for beauticians of sales companies including beauty art, salesmanship, and product information.

Relations with Wholesale Companies or Dealers:
Training for salesmen similar to that given to the salesmen of Carnation Sales Companies.

Sponsorship of contests for salesmen to promote sales and collections. Lectures on management for owners of wholesale houses.

Relations with Carnation Chain Stores:
Lectures on salesmanship, cosmetology, and store management.

Assistance with Sales Promotion to Regular Customers:
Sponsorship of Carnation-Kai, a society of the regular women customers of the chain stores. Free consultation on beauty is offered by visiting Carnation exports and gifts are presented each year. Special sales to regular customers are sponsored, and free samples are made available to them. Visiting Carnation beauticians also provide free beauty advice and sales literature at gatherings sponsored by the individual chain stores.

Publication:

Marketingram	Published for the Sales Companies (24 times annually; 3,000 copies per issue).
Wholesale-Chain	Published for wholesalers 12 times annually, 3,800 copies per issue.
Chain Store	Published for chain stores 12 times annually, 13,000 copies per issue.

The number of people at the Carnation home office engaged in sales promotion were 15 instructors, 4 persons engaged in editing house publications, and 48 beauticians. The budget allocated to the Sales Promotion Department usually approximated 7 per cent of sales, and was typically divided as follows:

Dealer oriented activities 38%
Regular customer oriented activities 39%
General consumer oriented activities 23%

Sales promotion expense for 1958, classified according to type of product, was as follows:

Cosmetics 79
Toilet soap 5
Laundry soap 2
Dentifrices 11
Other sundries 3
                                              100%

In respect to the general marketing situations, Mr. Hanada commented:

> A keen competitive situation prevails in the marketing of cosmetics and a great many different sales techniques are being used. Among them are special sales companies; awarding of premiums with purchases; free samples and gifts for customers; rebates; and special entertainment for wholesalers and retailers. At this particular time there does not appear to be any evidence of unfair competition.

Mr. Hanada did indicate, however, that the Company was concerned about the amount of price-cutting prevalent at retail levels. In this connection he observed that self service outlets of various kinds were growing rapidly in importance and that they were among the prime offenders in respect to price cutting. Carnation's policy was to refuse to sell cosmetics to these outlets either directly or through Carnation Sales Companies. Such sales would, he felt, constitute a breach of faith with the Carnation Chain Stores. Several operators of self-service

EXHIBIT 18
CARNATION COMPANY LTD. (A)
Pricing Structure for Typical Products

Product Categories	Carnation Sales Company Purchase Price	Wholesale Company Purchase Price	Retail Store Purchase Price	Retail Customer Purchase Price
Cosmetics	64.5		75.0	00%
Toilet soaps	69.8	72.0	80.0	100%
Laundry soaps	69.8	72.0	80.0	100%
Dentifrices	65.5	67.5	75.0	100%
Other sundries	63.3	65.3	75.0	100%

EXHIBIT 19
CARNATION COMPANY, LTD. (A)
Sales,* Inventory and Number of Retail Sales Outlets Handling Cosmetics for June, 1956 (000,000 yen)

Reference	Cosmetic Retail Stores			Drug Stores			Apparel and Sundries Stores			Department Stores		
	Sales	Inven-tory†	Number of Stores	Sales	Inven-tory†	Number of Stores	Sales	Inven-tory	Number of Stores	Sales§	Inven-tory†	Number of Stores‡
Hokkaido	112,973	246,094	427	335,272	909,458	1,355	403,617	890,894	1,241	863,859	1,125,471	19
Tokyo	346,016	688,309	1,615	1,036,457	2,165,996	3,696	1,306,866	2,578,831	4,612	7,829,155	6,564,952	25
Kanagawa	110,871	210,789	495	271,365	584,079	935	409,923	959,890	1,355	450,604	863,591	9
Aichi	138,194	298,787	986	262,918	598,760	1,764	480,007	1,042,484	2,471	1,048,202	1,237,450	6
Osaka	245,656	413,244	1,635	472,794	876,184	2,361	575,691	1,048,466	3,188	3,017,137	2,378,021	11
Hyogo	141,494	309,095	1,055	245,507	579,686	1,395	369,863	830,829	2,092	586,895	591,704	6
Fukuoka	128,707	311,457	745	205,568	407,335	1,255	342,165	765,650	1,238	1,145,118	1,743,937	19
Other Pref.	1,147,147	2,841,556	8,721	2,754,403	6,430,226	17,268	4,471,164	12,081,243	22,987	14,940,970	14,505,126	82
Total	2,371,058	5,319,331	15,679	5,584,284	12,551,724	30,029	8,359,296	20,198,287	39,184	29,881,940	19,905,871	177

SOURCE: Research Statistics Division, Ministrial Secretariat, Ministry of International Trade and Industry

* Sales—for the period from June 1 to June 30, 1956
† Inventory—as of July 1, 1956
‡ Number—as of July 1, 1956
§ Total sales of all products and services sold by the outlet, not merely sales of cosmetics.

EXHIBIT 20
CARNATION COMPANY LTD. (A)
Growth of Self-Service Stores 1953 - 1959

Year	1953	1954	1955	1956	1957	1958	1959 (as of July)
Number	1	2	37	99	144	279	530
Average Tsubo			13.1	22.2	22.3	42.3	

SOURCE: Japan Self-Service Association.

outlets had already approached the Company with offers to stock and sell the full line of Carnation products. In view of the continuing rapid growth of the self-service type of outlet, Mr. Hanada said that Carnation was hopeful that some arrangement whereby Carnation products could benefit from this new mode of distribution would eventually be found. (See Exhibits 20, 21, 22 for resume of self-service store growth.)

The pricing structure for typical items of the various Carnation Product lines is given in Exhibit 18.

Additional information regarding possible retail distribution channels is given in Exhibits 19.

EXHIBIT 21
CARNATION COMPANY LTD. (A)
Sales, Gross Margin, and Inventory Data for Medium-Sized Self-Service*
Food Center

June 1957 - May 1958 (thousand yen)

	Sales	Cost of Sales	Average† Inventory	Gross Profit	Gross Profit‡ Percent	Inventory Turnover§
Miscellaneous	8,970	8,046	913	924	10.3	8.82
Fruits	4,077	3,301	24	776	19.0	137.58
Foods	33,169	28,273	1,680	4,896	14.8	16.83
Candies	11,613	10,039	215	1,574	13.6	46.69
Meats	13,276	11,673	184	1,603	12.1	63.44
Fish	6,396	4,942	9	1,454	22.7	549.11
Vegetables	7,956	5,887	23	2,069	26.0	256.00
Cloth	2,864	2,422	222	442	15.4	10.90
Sugar: oil	7,517	7,345	206	172	2.3	24.24
Cosmetics	2,004	1,650	261	354	17.7	6.32
Total	97,842	83,578	3,737	14,264	14.6	22.38

SOURCE: Japan Chamber of Commerce.
*A self-service food center which was organized in 1955 in a city of 100,000 persons. There are now six similar food centers in the city. This particular store now has a capitalization of 2.4 million yen, 42 employees, and 75 tsubo.
†Average end of month inventories.
‡(Gross Profit ÷ Sales) x 100
§Annual sales ÷ average end of month inventories.

Carnation Company, Ltd.

EXHIBIT 22
CARNATION COMPANY LTD. (A)
Income Statement and Sales by Product Category for a Large Scale Self-Service Store

A. Income Statement, Jan. - Dec. 1958

Sales		100%
Cost of goods sold		88%
Gross Profit		12%
Expenses:		
Salaries	2.7	
Packaging	0.9	
Advertising	1.7	
Other expenses	4.2	
		9.5
Net Profit		2.5%

B. Sales by Line Handled in 1958

1. Candy	13.7%
2. Food	29.3
3. Apparel	20.8
4. Cosmetics and Sundries	13.7
5. Footwear	4.0
6. Bag & Office Supplies	1.8
7. Utensils	7.2
8. Clothes	7.4
9. Fruits	2.2
	100.0%

C. Tendency of Sales

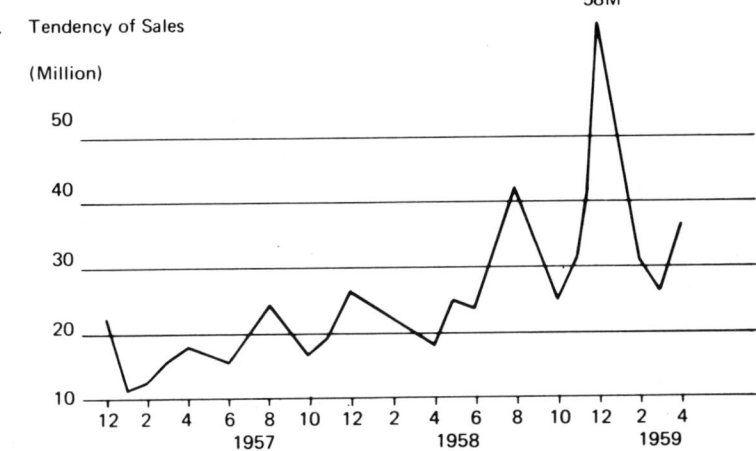

SOURCE: Japan Self-service Association

NOTES: Capital: 8,000,000 Yen
No. of Employees: 116
Average Monthly Sales Turn-over: 1.25
Growth of store space: Expanded from 190 tsubo to 330 tsubo March, 1958.

THE PROPOSAL

As noted more briefly earlier, the question before the Executive Committee was whether to adopt Mr. Hanada's proposal to establish one separate and independent Carnation Sales Company and seven branch offices, each to have a clearly defined territory. This would occur during December, 1959.

EXHIBIT 23
CARNATION COMPANY LTD.
Carnation Chain Stores Sales by Product Line & by Type of Store
June 1958 - May 1959
(in million of yen)

Principal Activity	Number of Stores	Total Sales	Carnation-Type Products			
			Cosmetics		Other Products	
			Carnation Brand	Other Brand	Carnation Brand	All Others
Cosmetics	597	1,986	707	627	163	489
Drugs	2,031	3,636	1,504	1,182	190	760
Apparel and Accessories	3,474	14,528	4,507	5,082	1,630	3,309
Dept.	168	3,654	561	807	503	1,783
Others	1,944	4,926	1,587	1,298	230	1,811
Totals	8,094	28,730	8,866	8,996	2,716	8,152

Then as the first step, the new sales company would take over the distribution of Carnation soaps, dentifrices, and other sundries to the wholesale chains to retail "salesmembers," beginning in 1960. As a second step, the new sales company would also take over distribution of these same products to Carnation chain stores in two or three years.

APPENDIX 1

Summary of Carnation Sales Company Agreement

1. The Carnation Sales Company agrees to handle Carnation products exclusively.
2. The Carnation Sales Company agrees to carry an assessed amount of Carnation products sufficient for proper and efficient sales promotion and service to chain stores and other retailers in the territory granted to sales company by Carnation Co., Ltd.
3. The Carnation Sales Company agrees to sell Carnation products at the wholesale price fixed by Carnation term of payment for the Carnation production purchased from the Carnation Co., Ltd.

APPENDIX 2

Carnation Wholesale Chain Agreement

Agreement is made between Carnation Co., (hereinafter called "A"), party of the first part:_____ (hereinafter called "B"), party of the
(Name of Wholesaler)
second; and Carnation Sales Co., of _____ (hereinafter called "C"), party of the third part. All parties to this agreement hereby accept

Carnation Company, Ltd.

the terms and conditions which follow below and bear the numbers one (1) through nine (9):

1. The "B" with assistance of the "C" will be responsible for advertising, promoting, and developing the "A" Merchandise.
2. The "A" Merchandise is defined as Carnation's line of products excluding cosmetics and other, particularly selected for chain store.
3. The "B" will commit no conduct destructive to the credit of the "A" Merchandise nor conduct detrimental to the mutual benefit.
4. The "A" will receive the order from the "B," and deliver directly to the "C."
5. The "C" will make her best efforts to further development in cooperation with the "B" as the "A"'s substitute agency.
6. The "B" will make payment for each shipment within 30 days after shipment in cash.
7. The "C" will be responsible for all acts of the "B" and make her best efforts to further development in cooperation with the "B" and as the "A"'s substitute agency.
8. The "A" and the "C" will organize a "Carnation Wholesale Chain" signboard prepared by the "A."
9. The "A" may cancel this agreement after consultation with the "B" if considered that the "B" is not giving the necessary cooperation in sales promotion or the sales by the "B" does not reach the level anticipated by the "A."

Three copies of agreement will be prepared and kept by the "A" the "B" and the "C" respectively for achievement of each clause listed.

For Carnation Co.

For _____

For Carnation Sales Co.

APPENDIX 3

Carnation Chain Store Sales Agreement

Agreement is made between Carnation Sales Co. (hereinafter called "B"), and Carnation Chain Store of _____ (hereinafter called "C"). All parties to this agreement hereby accept the terms and conditions which follow below and bear the numbers one (1) through fourteen (14):

And whereas this agreement is fully understood by Carnation Co. (hereinafter called "A") and, notice has been duly filed with the Fair Trade Commission as required by Article 24-2, paragraph 6 of the Anti-Monopoly Law.

1. During the period this agreement remains in force, the "C" will carry a stock of Carnation's Products sufficient for proper and efficient sales promotion and service of customers.
2. The "C" will at all times sell Carnation Products at the retail price fixed by "A" for each item at that time, but the "C" will not sell Carnation's

EXHIBIT 24
CARNATION COMPANY LTD.
Carnation Sales Companies by Product Line
by Type of Outlet (June 1958 - May 1959) (000 Yen)

Carnation Sales Companies	Carnation Cosmetics					Other Carnation Products						Non-Carnation Products Sold at the Retail Stores Dealing Carnation Products					
	Total	Chain Store	Department Store	Wholesale Chain	Other Retails	Other Wholesales	Total	Chain Store	Department Store	Wholesale Chain	Other Retails	Other Wholesales	Total	Chain Store	Department Store	Wholesale Chain	Other Retailers	Other Wholesales
Hokkaido																		
A	104,900	102,070	2,830	—	—	—	141,710	42,620	4,470	84,030	9,010	1,580	1,320,230	243,190	22,390	993,170	61,380	—
B	108,850	98,810	10,140	—	—	—	128,380	34,140	9,010	77,430	7,600	200	1,230,180	211,300	51,840	915,260	51,780	—
C	49,310	48,490	820	—	—	—	55,870	20,600	1,870	29,050	4,350	—	498,540	116,710	8,810	343,390	29,630	—
Tokyo Prefecture																		
A	232,000	232,000	—	—	—	—	306,520	93,230	—	168,050	37,570	7,670	2,619,040	435,030	—	1,932,580	251,430	—
B	247,150	247,150	—	—	—	—	243,240	101,680	—	123,590	17,680	290	2,117,470	577,860	—	1,421,290	118,320	—
C	210,640	210,640	—	—	—	—	186,510	61,850	—	89,930	34,730	—	1,664,970	409,440	—	1,922,480	232,420	—
D	211,210	211,210	—	—	—	—	273,350	81,450	—	171,650	19,670	580	2,591,200	485,610	—	1,973,950	131,640	—
E	200,280	—	200,280	—	—	—	591,080	—	544,190	—	—	47,090	2,490,020	—	2,490,020	—	—	—
F	67,630	67,630	—	—	—	—	91,830	28,390	—	55,590	7,460	490	1,433,700	744,490	—	639,290	49,920	—
Kanagawa Prefecture																		
A	174,230	153,480	20,750	—	—	—	186,890	36,720	54,690	91,100	2,900	1,390	3,899,785	315,210	350,765	3,162,470	35,340	—
B	43,810	43,810	—	—	—	—	46,410	18,560	—	23,460	4,390	—	1,003,840	137,560	—	814,390	51,890	—
C	42,540	42,540	—	—	—	—	47,650	23,530	—	15,520	8,300	200	799,360	159,360	—	542,240	98,110	—
Aichi Prefecture																		
A	71,700	70,980	810	—	—	—	62,380	21,050	2,140	28,310	10,880	—	330,175	104,620	7,005	172,470	46,080	—
B	227,640	202,070	25,570	—	—	—	250,820	47,240	56,070	128,400	15,730	3,380	1,305,680	266,920	189,890	782,240	66,630	—
Osaka Prefecture																		
A	238,770	238,770	—	—	—	—	309,920	133,540	—	133,930	39,390	3,060	1,666,720	543,510	—	937,510	185,700	—
B	110,460	110,460	—	—	—	—	127,820	54,890	—	62,930	1,070	8,930	678,830	233,280	—	440,510	5,040	—
C	110,000	110,000	—	—	—	—	132,180	77,080	—	44,230	10,100	770	648,630	291,410	—	309,610	47,610	—
D	66,400	—	—	68,400	—	—	341,000	—	341,000	—	—	—	1,137,080	—	1,137,080	—	—	—
Hyogo Prefecture																		
A	142,530	134,880	7,659	—	—	—	205,720	48,520	38,560	107,710	3,640	7,290	1,389,990	263,920	146,880	958,720	20,190	—
B	116,330	112,950	3,380	—	—	—	91,080	39,950	18,290	29,360	6,920	1,560	570,800	218,870	51,690	261,330	38,910	—
C	41,980	41,980	—	—	—	—	1,230	17,240	—	21,510	11,540	940	233,870	88,530	—	191,460	64,880	—
Fukuoka Prefecture																		
A	125,330	112,450	12,880	—	—	—	137,110	26,250	32,320	64,430	3,760	10,350	858,860	172,840	128,110	537,720	20,190	—
B	86,910	79,190	7,720	—	—	—	175,830	22,440	20,230	123,980	8,300	880	1,292,120	133,160	79,680	1,034,710	44,570	—
C	64,600	64,160	440	—	—	—	121,480	17,000	2,570	95,760	5,930	220	944,870	104,470	9,370	799,190	31,840	—
D	55,350	52,600	2,750	—	—	—	152,650	9,660	11,990	126,540	2,380	2,110	1,186,560	73,280	44,670	1,055,830	12,780	—
All others	2,963,470	2,884,990	78,480	—	—	—	3,665,650	1,026,720	231,890	1,837,170	472,740	97,040	26,001,600	5,852,010	935,400	16,534,830	2,678,860	—
Total	6,114,210	5,673,310	440,900	—	—	—	8,124,410	2,084,250	1,364,380	3,733,730	746,130	196,020	60,023,990	12,218,230	5,653,600	37,776,740	4,375,420	—

NOTE: "A" "B" and so forth refer to separate Sales Companies within each prefecture.

Carnation Company, Ltd.

EXHIBIT 24 (continued)

Total Sales by Type of Outlet

Carnation Sales Companies	Total	Chain Store	Department Store	Wholesale Chain	Other Retailer	Other Wholesalers	Total	Chain Stores	Department Stores	Wholesale Chains	Other Retailers	Other Wholesalers
Hokkaido												
A	1,566,840	387,880	29,690	1,077,300	70,390	1,580	293	138	3	9	142	1
B	1,467,510	344,250	70,990	992,690	59,380	200	379	164	6	8	200	1
C	603,720	185,800	11,500	372,440	33,980	—	268	73	3	7	185	0
Tokyo Prefecture												
A	3,157,650	762,260	—	2,100,630	289,000	7,670	452	288	0	16	122	26
B	2,607,860	926,690	—	1,544,880	136,000	290	467	326	0	15	125	1
C	2,061,490	681,930	—	1,112,410	267,150	—	535	310	0	5	218	0
D	3,075,760	778,270	—	2,145,600	151,310	580	492	354	0	12	124	2
E	3,281,580	—	3,234,490	—	—	47,090	59	0	37	0	0	22
F	1,593,160	840,410	—	694,880	57,380	490	189	97	0	10	81	1
Kanagawa Prefecture												
A	4,260,905	541,410	426,205	3,253,570	38,330	1,390	332	253	9	14	50	6
B	1,094,060	199,930	—	837,850	56,280	—	157	73	0	6	7	0
C	889,550	225,080	—	557,860	106,410	200	230	66	0	7	150	7
Aichi Prefecture												
A	464,345	1,996,650	9,955	200,780	56,960	—	361	97	2	10	252	0
B	1,784,140	516,230	271,530	910,640	82,360	3,380	423	278	4	11	128	2
Osaka Prefecture												
A	2,215,410	915,820	—	1,071,440	225,090	3,060	432	319	0	7	100	6
B	917,110	398,630	—	503,440	6,110	8,930	259	185	0	9	60	5
C	890,810	478,490	—	353,840	57,710	770	274	189	0	12	72	1
D	1,544,480	—	1,544,480	—	—	—	12	0	12	0	0	0
Hyogo Prefecture												
A	1,738,240	447,320	193,090	1,066,430	24,110	7,290	248	173	4	11	48	12
B	778,210	371,770	68,360	290,690	45,830	1,560	295	102	2	11	170	10
C	438,080	147,750	—	212,970	76,420	940	370	64	0	5	300	1
Fukuoka Prefecture												
A	1,121,300	311,540	173,310	602,150	23,950	10,350	237	110	5	13	76	33
B	1,554,860	234,790	107,630	1,158,690	52,870	880	249	147	3	10	57	32
C	1,130,950	185,630	12,380	894,950	37,770	220	262	85	1	13	162	1
D	1,394,560	135,540	59,410	1,182,340	15,160	2,110	151	80	2	11	48	10
All others	32,630,220	9,763,720	1,245,860	18,372,000	3,151,600	97,040	15,158	4,123	75	466	10,213	281
Total	74,262,710	19,975,790	7,458,880	41,510,470	5,121,550	196,020	22,584	8,094	168	700	13,161	461

Products even at the fixed retail price if such sale will jeopardize the future re-sale of Carnation's Products.

3. The "C" will make no sales of Carnation's Products on credit nor place any Carnation's Products on loan to retail customers.
4. The "C" will cooperate with "B" to stop or prevent any cutprice sales in the territory assigned to the "C" if such selling now exists or occurs any time this agreement is in force.
5. The "C" will make payment for Carnation's Products in cash to "B."
6. The "C" will not allow any kind of discount to its retail customers nor make any sales which entail the giving of the gifts or premiums or allowing any credit toward any gifts or premiums unless the "C" is so instructed by "A."
7. The "B" reserves for itself and "A" the right to change the retail price of Carnation's Products by giving a 30-day notice to the "C."
8. The "C" will exchange or allow credit for returned goods in the event of any defect or deterioration of any Carnation's Products provided such defect or deterioration shall be deemed to have been caused by the "C" or the "B."
9. If any time either party to this agreement fails to carry out this agreement or does anything which in any way breaches any of the terms or conditions of this agreement, either the "C," or the "A" may suspend business transactions with the other party and/or terminate this agreement.
10. Appointments of agents or establishment of branches on the part of the "C" shall not be covered by this agreement. If the "C" moves its sales room to a new location or transfers its rights of business to any party not a member of the family of the principal owners of the "C," the "B" may terminate this agreement at any time.
11. If this agreement is terminated, the "C" will sell and the "B" will repurchase all Carnation's Products held by the "C" at the time of termination. The price of the products shall be net cost of original purchase less ten per cent.
12. This agreement shall be valid only if it bears the signatures of authorized representatives of the three parties and seals of the three parties and shall remain in effect until the end of December, 1959, unless it is sooner terminated by either party.
13. The "A" will furnish all advice, guidance, information and assistance in marketing of Carnation's products that it deems necessary to enable the "B" and the "C" to establish the most desirable sales rooms according to the best methods and systems known to the "A."
14. Three copies of agreement will be prepared and kept by "A," "B," and "C" respectively for achievement of each clause listed above.

For Carnation Co.

For _____

For Carnation Sales Co.

18

Sumiyoshi Corporation*†

INTRODUCTION

In April, 1959, the Executive Committee of Sumiyoshi Corporation, Osaka, was considering the extent to which the Company should expand its output of transistor radios during the coming year. In previous discussion of this subject, various members of the Committee had proposed figures ranging from 75,000 per month to over 100,000 per month. Current production was nearly 50,000 per month, and 12 months previously the figure had been less than 15,000 per month. Ever since the Company's pioneer introduction of transistor radios in early 1956, demand for the Sumiyoshi output of these products had exceeded the Company's production capacity, and, even at the current rate of production, output was being "rationed" among ready buyers.

Transistor radios presently accounted for 50 per cent of the Company's monthly sales volume of 550 million yen, the other major items being tape recorders, 30 per cent, transistors (excluding those used in the Company's own products) 10 per cent; recording tape, 5 per cents and miscellaneous, 5 per cent.

The Sumiyoshi plants and offices were located in Higashi-Sumiyoshi-ku, Osaka, and at Nagoya. Current employment was 2,123 and sales volume for the six month period ending in April, 1959, was estimated at 3,500 million yen. The Company had already experienced three periods of remarkably rapid growth and some members of the management felt that Sumiyoshi might be on the verge of still another wave of rapid expansion. This feeling, which was shared by the Company president, Mr. Masao Ishikawa, was based upon the Sumiyoshi position as a pioneer in the commercial application of semi-conductors, and upon its continuing program of research and development in that field. To illustrate (for the case writers) his concept of the present state of the commercial application of semi-conductors, President Ishikawa drew the diagram shown in Exhibit 1.

OFFICERS, DIRECTOR, AND PRINCIPAL STOCKHOLDERS

Nearly all of the officers and directors of Sumiyoshi Corporation in April, 1959, had been associated with the Company since its establishment in May,

---

*All names have been disguised. This case material has been prepared as a basis for group discussion, and is not intended to present illustrations of either correct or incorrect handling of administrative problems.

†Prepared by Frank T. Hartzfeld and Kenneth H. Myers of Northwestern University, Graduate School of Business, assisted by Nobuyuki Sakurai of Aoyama Gakuin University and Takeshi Kikuchi and in cooperation with the Japan Productivity Center.

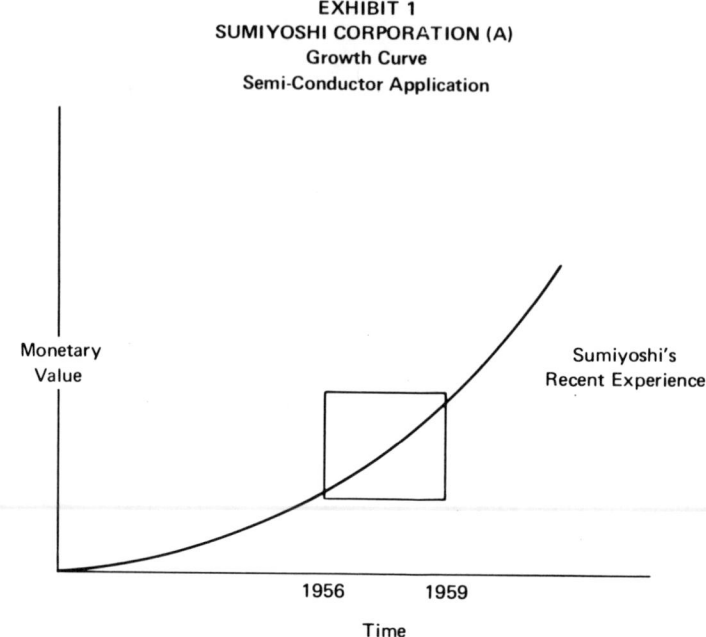

EXHIBIT 1
SUMIYOSHI CORPORATION (A)
Growth Curve
Semi-Conductor Application

1946. Juichi Momose (71) chairman of the Board of Directors since 1951, had acted as an advisor to the Company since its founding. Until recently the chairman of a large Osaka bank and a past chairman of the National Association of Banks, Mr. Momose had devoted much time in his later years to assisting new businesses to become established, particularly those types of enterprises which he felt would make a strong contribution to Japan's postwar recovery. Mr. Momose's interest in such businesses was in freely offering advice and other types of assistance *when asked*; the actual conduct of the businesses was the responsibility of others. See Exhibit 2.

Masao Ishikawa (49), managing director from 1946 to 1951 and president since 1951, was perhaps the person most responsible for the initial founding of the Company and for the direction of its activities thereafter. A graduate engineer, President Ishikawa, had been involved in research and manufacturing of devices for recording, measuring, and amplifying sound and light since 1935 when he had entered a photo chemical laboratory. His last association (prior to Sumiyoshi) had been as vice president and director of a measuring instrument manufacturing company. At the end of the war this Company was dissolved, and Mr. Ishikawa with Mr. Hosoi and a number of other engineers moved to Osaka and started the research and manufacture of electrical communication equipment.

Arata Miyoshi (40), executive director from 1947 to 1951 and managing director since 1951, was, like Ishikawa, a principal in the founding of the Com-

Sumiyoshi Corporation

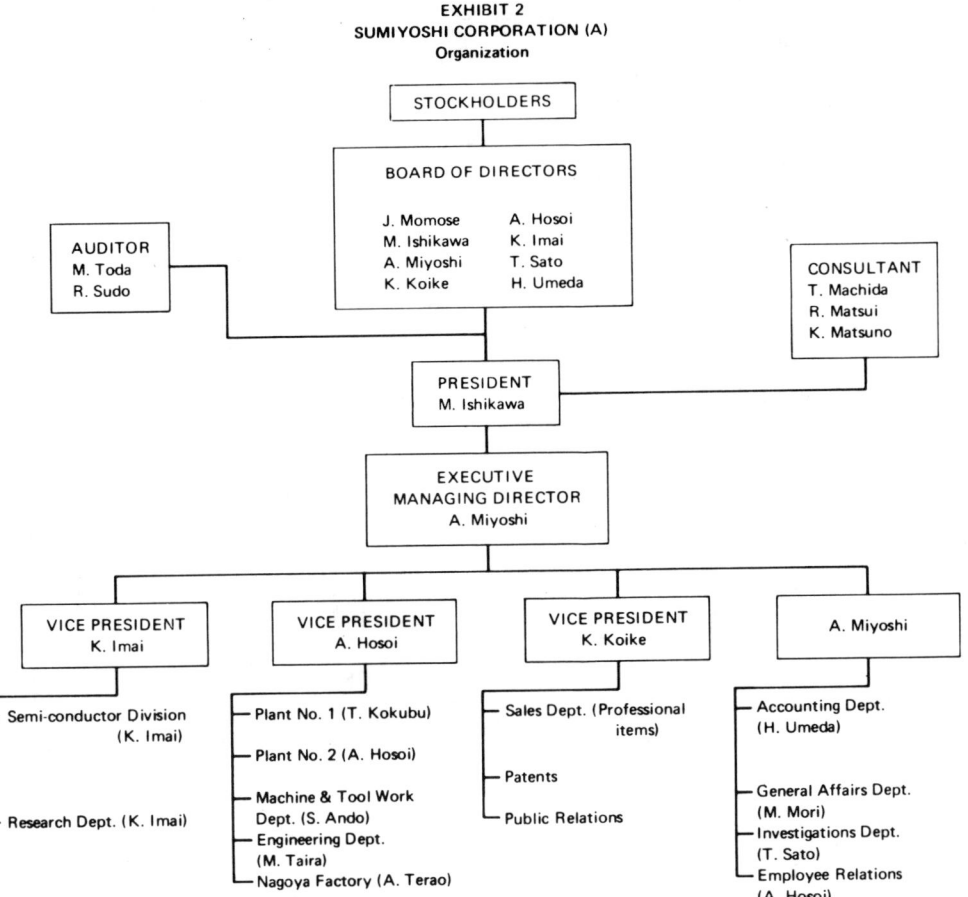

pany and in its direction since that event. A graduate in the physical sciences, Mr. Miyoshi, had been a member of the faculty of a university prior to the establishment of Sumiyoshi.

Kiichi Koike (53), vice president and director, was in charge of sales (professional items), patents, and public relations. A graduate in commerce, Mr. Koike, was one of the few members of top management who had not matriculated in science or engineering. This difference was more apparent than real, however, for Mr. Koike had long been an enthusiastic amateur radio operator and was active in the Japan Amateur-Radio League and the Japan Amateur Television Association. Prior to his association with Sumiyoshi, Mr. Koike had been an executive in the sales department of a large electrical goods manufacturing firm.

Atsuo Hosoi (46), vice president and executive director, was in charge of all manufacturing except that of semi-conductors. Mr. Hosoi was a graduate engineer who, prior to Sumiyoshi, had been associated with Mr. Ishikawa at the measuring instrument company.

Kiyoshi Imai (42), vice president and executive director, was in charge of the Semi-Conductor Division and the Research Department. A graduate in metallurgy, Mr. Imai, had been awarded a research assistantship at Osaka Imperial University following his graduation in 1942. From the time of his association with Sumiyoshi in 1946, Mr. Imai had contributed greatly to the Company's programs of research and development both as a research scientist and as a supervisor of such activities.

Toru Sato (53), director and manager of the investigation department, and Haruo Umeda (59), director and manager of the accounting department, had equally impressive backgrounds in their respective areas. Mr. Sato had been an auditor of Sumiyoshi prior to becoming a director in 1952 and comptroller in 1958. Mr. Umeda had been Sanji (Councilor) at the head office of a large metropolitan bank prior to joining Sumiyoshi in 1957.

As of September 12, 1958, officers and directors held about 11 per cent of the Company's stock with Messrs. Momose, Ishikawa, and Miyoshi holding 4 per cent, 2 per cent, respectively. Other large stockholders included Matsuno Co. (15 per cent) and the Sase Company (3 per cent); a metropolitan bank (4 per cent); an insurance company (4 per cent); and a photo chemical company (4 per cent).

The consultants to the president, Messrs. Taro Machida, Ryoichi Matsui, and Kozaburo Matsuno, had each been associated with the Company since its inception. Mr. Machida, a former high official in the Ministry of Education, had served as president of Sumiyoshi from 1946-1951. Mr. Matsui was president of a photo chemical laboratory. Mr. K. Matsuno, a prominent business executive in the Kyoto area, had actively interested himself in the Company's affairs since 1946. Through his holdings in Matsuno Company and Sase Company, Mr. K. Matsuno was the largest stock holder in Sumiyoshi Corporation.

GROWTH AND DEVELOPMENT, 1946-1959

The formation of Sumiyoshi in 1946 had brought together an usually favorable blend of talents and personalities. Older men provided business acumen, financial resources, and excellent connections; men in their middle years, who had already acquired extensive business experience with firms specializing in the application of scientific research to commercial products, became the operating managers; still younger men who had already demonstrated special promise, usually in a scientific field in which electricity is related to light or sound, brought enthusiasm and scientific talent. Behind the accomplished fact stood Masao Ishikawa, the individual who conceived the purpose of the new Company, who assembled the resources to bring it into being, and who was to direct its operating activities. This highly purposeful collection of well qualified personnel

Sumiyoshi Corporation

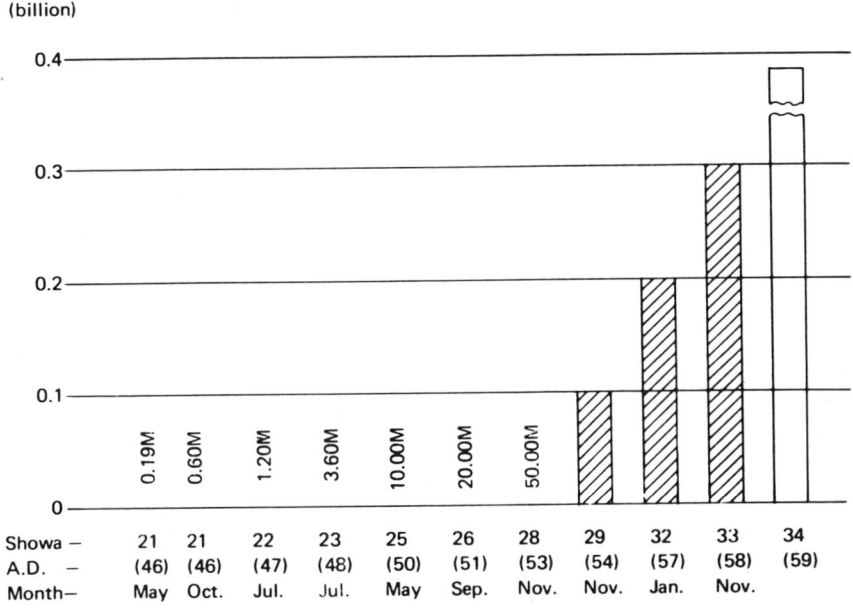

EXHIBIT 3
SUMIYOSHI CORPORATION (A)
Capitalization, 1946 - 1959

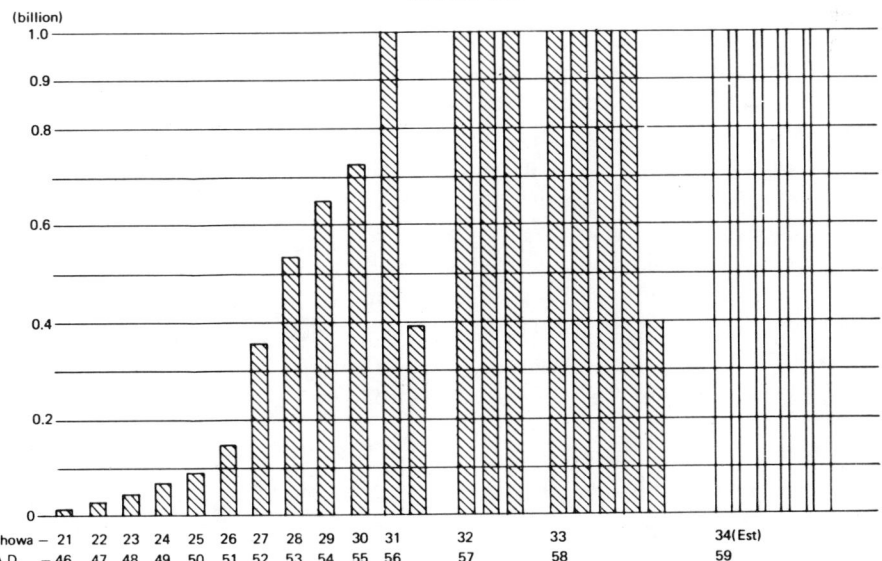

EXHIBIT 4
SUMIYOSHI CORPORATION (A)
Sales 1946 - 1959

began to make its mark very shortly after its founding, as is indicated by Exhibits 3 and 4.

EARLY PRODUCTS

The first products of the Company were primarily connected with the postwar revival of radio broadcasting in Japan and with governmental telephonic and radio communication needs. Among the products were electromagnetic tuning forks, sound oscillators, reluctance type microphones, moving coil type microphones, condenser microphones, and condenser pickups. Sales grew slowly but steadily during this period, and by 1949 some 100 persons were employed.

MAGNETIC TAPE AND TAPE RECORDERS

At this time Mr. Ishikawa became aware of the commercial possibilities in Japan of magnetic tape recorders, and convinced the Sumiyoshi management to "plunge" by mobilizing a special research group to develop designs and manufacturing processes for magnetic tape and tape recorders.

As a result, a task force of 4 physicists, 5 chemists, 20 electrical engineers, and 3 mechanical engineers was assembled to develop a commercially feasible means of producing the new products, neither of which was yet being manufactured in Japan. Since this group absorbed about 80 percent of the Company's engineering personnel at the time, the use of the task force idea in the hope of achieving success ahead of competition represented something of a gamble on the part of management. Magnetic tape production in commercial quantities and quality was begun in mid 1950, and similar results were achieved with tape recorders later the same year.

The "break-through" which Sumiyoshi engineers had accomplished was not immediately rewarded with success in the market place, however, for the application of tape recorder products was still virtually unknown in Japan. A vigorous campaign was undertaken to gain acceptance by radio broadcasting facilities and, concurrently, by educational institutions. These campaigns were followed by promotion of tape recorders designed especially for use in office work in business and government. Especially rewarding was the Sumiyoshi effort to apply tape recorders to audio and audiovisual education. Success brought competition, however, as well as a broadening of the market as the "professional" models of tape recorders were supplemented by lower cost models designed for home use.

As a result of its pioneering efforts, Sumiyoshi was virtually the only domestic producer of magnetic recording tape and of tape recorders for several years. Competition in both fields began about 1952 and by early 1959 there were 3 producers of recording tape and 20 producers of tape recorders in Japan. The 4 largest producers together supplied about 60 per cent of the market for recorders (per cent of monetary value, estimated as of April, 1959). Further information is given in Exhibits 5 and 6.

EXHIBIT 5
SUMIYOSHI CORPORATION (A)
Production of Tape Recorders in Japan
(units — sets)

Period	(A) Industry	(B) Company	B/A x 100 (%)
Jan — Dec 1956	20,997	13,231	63%
Jan — Dec 1957	49,399	28,706	58%
Jan — Dec 1958	102,732	50,157	49%
Jan 1959	14,098	5,201	37%
Feb 1959	15,467	4,339	28%
Mar 1959	14,749	3,535	24%
Apr 1959	16,958	3,912	23%

SOURCE: Company estimates.

EXHIBIT 6
SUMIYOSHI CORPORATION (A)
Production of Recording Tape in Japan
(units — reel)

Period	(A) Industry	(B) Company	B/A x 100 (%)
Apr — Dec 1956	224,943	131,236	58%
Jan — Dec 1957	334,394	202,524	61%
Jan — Dec 1958	509,017	278,522	55%
Jan 1959	72,604	48,093	66%
Feb 1959	70,492	46,676	66%
Mar 1959	70,777	45,010	64%
Apr 1959	75,676	46,056	61%

SOURCE: Company Estimates

Sumiyoshi research in the field of magnetic tape application continued and the product line grew to include a stereophonic tape recording system; a synchronous 35 mm magnetic film recording device; a projector in which film strips or slides run synchronously with recorded materials; and still later, such items as a transistorized, portable, battery operated tape recorder. Developmental work presently underway included an audiovidio tape recorder (Substitute for film reproduction of both sight and sound) and a synchronized bookkeeping machine, tape recorder device, and tape printer which would enable complete bookkeeping records to be maintained on magnetic tape and to be printed selectively.

As a corollary to its work with magnetic tape recording systems, Sumiyoshi developed a patented process for making high quality ferrite cores for magnetic recording heads and other uses. Commercial production of these cores was begun in 1954 in a factory at Nagoya which had been constructed for this purpose. The location was selected because of its proximity to a local university in whose laboratories much of the research was undertaken, and because of the ready availability at low cost of the electric power needed in the ferrite reduction process.

TRANSISTORS AND TRANSISTOR RADIOS

In 1953, Messrs. Ishikawa, Miyoshi, Imai and others of the Sumiyoshi management began to give close attention to technical reports on semi-conductors and to speculate among themselves on their implications. By that time knowledge of the field had progressed to the point where extensive commercial application seemed to depend upon price. At this time transistors still cost $4.00 per unit in the United States and were used mainly in military applications. About the only commercial application thus far was in hearing aids. There was no domestic production. Calling upon their experience with magnetic tape, the benefits of which were now beginning to flow in upon the Company, President Ishikawa and his management resolved to initiate another "crash program," the end result of which would be a commercially acceptable transistor radio using Sumiyoshi-built transistors. By 1954, 40 men, about 60 per cent of the Company's engineering force, had been mobilized for the task. The first Sumiyoshi transistors were produced in late 1954 and the Company's first all transistor radio followed in early 1955, only a few months after the first commercial transistor radio had appeared in the United States. In the meantime, the necessary licensing arrangements had been made with the Western Electric Company, and preparations for commercial production had begun. The first Sumiyoshi transistor radio, a five transistor set, went on the market in October, 1955 and Sumiyoshi enjoyed a virtual monopoly of the product in Japan for the next two years. Sales were limited by the cost, however, and no attempt was made to export the product to the United States market.

During 1955 and 1956 a team of 50 Sumiyoshi scientists and engineers continued to work on improving the quality and size characteristics of the transistor radio, and in April, 1957, these efforts were rewarded. The result was the Company's first all transistor super hererodyne radio with built-in dynamic speaker. It employed six transistors, measured $1\frac{1}{4}'' \times 2\frac{3}{4}'' \times 4\frac{1}{2}''$, and retailed for Y 13,800. The new set caused a sensation not only in Japan but in the world markets to which it was introduced in 1957. The phenomenal growth of Sumiyoshi from April 1957, to April, 1959, was almost wholly attributable to the Company's ever increasing output of high quality transistor radios. During these two years the Sumiyoshi production of such radios went from 3,000 per month to nearly 50,000 per month, and the sales value from approximately

Sumiyoshi Corporation

20 million yen to some 200 million yen. At the same time the Company's line of transistor radios was greatly broadened and by April, 1959, included 15 production models. Among these was a fifteen transistor FM/AM model designed for export, the first commercial model of its kind. It was planned to introduce the new model to the United States market in the summer of 1959, and the management expected very substantial increases in export orders to result.

EXHIBIT 7
SUMIYOSHI CORPORATION (A)
Industry and Company Production of
Transistors and Transistor Radio Sets

TRANSISTORS

Period	A Industry	B Company	C A/B x 100 (%)
1955	N.A.*	N.A.	N.A.
1956	590,000	398,000	69
1957	5,803,000	2,631,000	45
1958	26,736,000	4,586,000	16
Jan. 1959	4,252,000	681,000	16
Feb. 1959	5,229,000	822,000	16
Mar. 1959	5,486,000	731,000	13
Apr. 1959	5,849,000	638,000	11
Jan. 1959 – Dec. Estimate	80,000,000		

TRANSISTOR RADIO SETS

Period	A Industry	B Company	C Market Share B/A x 100 (%)
Jul. – Dec. 1955	7,086	7,086	100
Jan. – Dec. 1956	38,025	38,025	100
Jan. – Dec. 1957	632,749	162,479	25.7
Jan. – Dec. 1958	2,989,806	299,555	10.0
Jan. 1959	380,482	40,964	10.8
Feb. 1959	421,715	50,958	12.1
Mar. 1959	433,933	50,816	11.7
Apr. 1959	482,343	58,189	12.1
Jan. – Dec. 1959 Estimate	8,000,000		

SOURCES: Electronic Machine Industry Association of Japan.

*N.A. — Not available.

EXHIBIT 8
SUMIYOSHI CORPORATION (A)
Industry and Company Exports of
Transistors and Transistor Radios
TRANSISTORS (exports were negligible) and TRANSISTOR RADIOS

Period	A Industry	B Company	C A/B x 100 (%)
Apr. – Dec. 1957	362,517	66,173	18.3
Jan. – Dec. 1958	1,928,860	148,340	7.7
Jan. 1959	148,388	18,490	12.5
Feb. 1959	276,318	27,739	10.0
Mar. 1959	304,624	37,375	12.3
Apr. 1959	342,617	45,131	13.2

SOURCE: 1. Electronic Machine Industry Association of Japan.
2. Ministry of International Trade and Industry.

REMARKS: Unit is set.

Basic to these advances was the Company's production of transistors; all Sumiyoshi radios used Sumiyoshi transistors exclusively. In addition to the production of transistors, for its own products, Sumiyoshi produced transistors for sale. Industry and Company production of transistors and of transistor radios are given in Exhibit 7. Export of transistor radios is given in Exhibit 8. United States production of transistors and transistor radios is given in Exhibit 9.

EXHIBIT 9
SUMIYOSHI CORPORATION (A)
United States Production and Imports of
Transistors and Transistor Radios

Period	Transistors		Transistor Radios	
	Production	Imports from Japan	Production	Imports from Japan
1957			1,740,000	102,240
1958	47,050,000	10,000	2,430,000	1,226,318
1959 (Estimated)	70,000,000	3,220,000	5,000,000	1,800,000

SOURCES: Reports and estimates of the Electronic Machine Industry Association of Japan and of the Ministry of International Trade and Industry.

OTHER PRODUCTS

As already noted, following its "break-through" on magnetic tape and tape recorders, Sumiyoshi Corporation sought to apply the tape recording principle

Sumiyoshi Corporation

to a wide variety of products, among them a substitute for film in audio-visual recording, a magnetic tape bookkeeping system, and synchronous audio-visual slide projection. After its success with transistors and transistor radios, a similar search for additional applications was pursued. Early results of this effort were the transistorization of much of the Company's line of tape recording machines, and the introduction of new portable tape recorders for professional use and for the office. The Sumiyoshi line of professional broadcasting equipment, especially microphones, also benefited. Farther afield were experimental applications to analogue and digital computers, data sorting machines, electronic memory units, data recording devices, portable television sets, luminescent lighting, and a heat-transfer device for refrigeration.

By April, 1959, a moderate degree of commercial success had been achieved with the transistorized tape recording units for professional and office use, with microphones, and with the synchronous audiovisual slide projector. None of the other new products were judged to be ready for large scale commercial exploitation.

Total sales of "other products" . . . products other than magnetic tape and tape recorders, transistors and transistor radios . . . for the six months ending in March, 1959, were estimated at 81 million yen.

MANUFACTURING FACILITIES AND PROCESSES

The Company's Osaka plants and offices were located on 2,336 tsubo of land of which 260 tsubo was occupied by a two story office building, 220 tsubo by Plants No. 1, and 350 tsubo by Plant No. 2. Storage buildings, garages, and so forth occupied an additional 800 tsubo of land. Plants No. 1 and No. 2 were of eight story reinforced concrete construction and were designed for light manufacturing. The amount of space allocated to various activities, and the employment in each, is indicated below:

Plant No. 1 had been completed in March, 1954, at a cost of 50 million yen and Plant No. 2 in October, 1957, at a cost of 215 million yen. Adjacent to the plants were company dormitories housing some 200 young girls who were employed in the production of semi-conductors and in various assembly operations. Because of the Company's rapid growth, the provision of adequate space for manufacturing, engineering and research had been a continuing problem. Even now the Company had two construction projects under way—a 350 million yen, 3,820 tsubo addition to Plant No. 1, and a 550 million yen, 5,000 tsubo addition to Plant No. 2. Completion was expected in 1960 and 1962, respectively.

In addition to the Osaka facilities, the Company produced ferrite recording heads and magnetic tape at its 700 tsubo, 100 million yen factory at Nagoya. As noted earlier, this location had been chosen because of its proximity to a local university, with whose research laboratories Sumiyoshi had had a close working arrangement since 1951. About 200 persons were employed at the Nagoya location.

The majority of the production operations conducted by Sumiyoshi consisted of simple manual assembly work. Metal and plastic components, vacuum tubes, condensers, resistors, and so forth were purchased in finished form. These were redistributed (or delivered directly) to subcontractors for the preparation of sub-assemblies for radios and tape recorders. These sub-assemblies were then tested and incorporated into the final products by Sumiyoshi. A major exception to this pattern was the production of semi-conductors which were manufactured from basic materials within Sumiyoshi itself. Approximately 78 per cent of manufactured cost was for purchased parts and materials, 12 per cent for wages, and 10 per cent for other expenses.

All manufacturing operations except those involving the production of semi-conductors were under the direction of Mr. Hosoi, who was also in charge of employee relations and who had been in charge of factory supervision since the founding of the Company. The manufacture of semi-conductors was under the direction of Mr. K. Imai, as was research in the application of semi-conductors and of magnetic tape recording systems.

In commenting upon the Company's extensive use of sub-contractors, Mr. Hosoi estimated that the organizations presently supplying Sumiyoshi had in their employ about 2,000 persons who were wholly engaged in the manufacture of Sumiyoshi components and sub-assemblies. The number of the persons so engaged was approximately three times the size of Sumiyoshi's own factory force employed in transistor radio and tape recorder production. Mr. Hosoi thought that the high cost of land acquisition in Osaka, plus the relatively high wages which Sumiyoshi paid its factory employees, made it likely that the present scale of sub-contracting would continue, i.e., if production were to be expanded 100 per cent, the use of sub-contractors would expand 100 per cent. On the other hand, Mr. Hosoi thought it unlikely that the present proportion of work allocated to subcontractors could be expanded. The operations which Sumiyoshi now performed in its own plants were those which were considered essential to the maintenance of control over the quality of the finished product.

In the long run, Mr. Hosoi desired to increase the proportion of work performed within the Sumiyoshi organizations in order to achieve still better control over quality. At the present time, he observed, the "X" condensers were being made by three different small suppliers and the characteristics of the product of each supplier were sufficiently different to create performed variations in the final product. Yet each supplier was producing an acceptable product according to the Sumiyoshi specifications and acceptance tests.

No one of the suppliers was large enough to produce all of Sumiyoshi's requirements of condenser "X." This was an example, he said, of the additional type of production which the Company should undertake in its own plants.

About 80 per cent of the sub-contractors were located within 10 kilometers of the Sumiyoshi plants in Osaka, and the other 20 per cent were all within 40 kilometers. Delivery schedules were carefully worked out so as to permit uninterrupted production at Sumiyoshi with very low inventories of sub-assemblies and components. Procurement, inventory control, and production control were consolidated in one section, where visual records of Sumiyoshi schedules, subcontractors' schedules, and inventory levels were maintained.

The Company's production schedules were "frozen" three months in advance of final assembly, i.e., on April 1st orders were released for components for radios scheduled for assembly on July 1st. These releases constituted authorization to purchase and to subcontract as well as authorization for drawing materials, allocating personnel, and performing work within the Sumiyoshi organization.

Most of the subcontractors were small . . . the average employment was only 50 . . . and their managements had very limited technical and administrative competence. Sumiyoshi had already assigned several industrial engineers to assist certain of these suppliers with engineering design, manufacturing processes, and quality control. Financial assistance was also provided where necessary. Mr. Hosoi thought that, in the future, even greater technical and administrative assistance would be required. In addition to such temporary measures, Sumiyoshi experts might even be "transferred" to these suppliers on a permanent basis, i.e., they might become permanent employees of the suppliers rather than of Sumiyoshi.

EMPLOYEE RELATIONS

The usual personnel functions of hiring, training, promotion, and transfer; wage and salary administration; health and safety activities; relations with the union; employee recreation and other welfare were grouped in the Employee Relations Department. Mr. Hosoi, vice president for manufacturing, was also in charge of the Department of Employee Relations. Members of the Sumiyoshi top management, and particularly Messrs. Ishikawa, Miyoshi, and Hosoi, were much concerned about the future of the Company's relations with the employees and their union, even though they considered the present state of employee-management affairs to be quite good.

The labor union at Sumiyoshi had been organized in 1956 to replace an informal organization which had been representing employee interests up to that time. The formal organization of a union had been led by a group of Sumiyoshi engineers of comparatively long service with the Company. This group had discussed its organization plans with the management and had indicated that the basis for their action was a desire to "rationalize" employee-management relations, and to affiliate with a national union. Subsequent to its organization, the Sumiyoshi union had affiliated with the National Union of Electrical Workers. The Sumiyoshi management had not opposed the organization drive, and had granted the new union a "union shop" agreement, i.e., all employees of the Company, excepting section chiefs and above, temporary or probationary employees, and employees in "sensitive" positions such as special members of the accounting and personnel departments and secretaries to executives, were obliged to belong to the union as a condition of employment. Union dues were deducted from wages and salaries by the Company and were paid directly to the union.

The first president of the Sumiyoshi union, and the two subsequent presidents, had been graduate engineers. The management considered that the Company had never experienced an acute dispute with the union representatives, and no strikes or work stoppages had occurred.

In particular, Messrs. Ishikawa, Miyoshi, and Hosoi were concerned about three aspects of employee-management relations. The first was the increased difficulty of communication which resulted from the sheer size of the organization. Only a few years earlier, in 1956, the employees had numbered less than 500; now there were over 2,000. The thought of dealing with another increase of similar magnitude within another three years was not very appealing. To maintain effective communication with even the present size of organization was difficult and time consuming. Some measure of the importance which they attached to intra-company communication is given by Exhibit 10 which shows the eight types of regularly scheduled meetings which they or other members of top management attended.

A second problem was the rather flat distribution of ages within the ranks of the Company's nearly 1,000 high school and college graduates. (See Exhibits 11, 12 and 13.) Most of this group would expect that the passage of time would bring increased responsibilities with attendant perquisites of status and income. The college graduates, in particular, would expect to rise from clerk or draftsman or research assistant to assistant section chief, section chief assistant department head, department head, and so forth. In older companies such promotion is facilitated by the existence of a fairly wide age distribution within the ranks. The retirement of a department head, for example, might result in four or five promotions along the management ladder. In Sumiyoshi the average age of the seven top operating executives was only 49 years and the oldest executive was but 59. Moreover, the average age of the men in office positions was 34 years, and that of the men in the plants only 24 years. (See Exhibit 13.) Opportunities for promotion created by retirement were almost nonexistent at Sumiyoshi, either now or in the next five to ten years. Thus far, Mr. Ishikawa observed, the provision of adequate promotional opportunities had not really been a problem at Sumiyoshi because of its rapid and continuous growth. The future might well be a different matter, however, and several members of top management were already aware of some concern among their subordinates in this regard.

A third factor of concern to the President and the other members of top management pertained to the specialized scientific or engineering personnel who had been brought into the Company from time to time to help solve some particularly difficult problem. These men had made key contributions to such

Sumiyoshi Corporation

EXHIBIT 10
SUMIYOSHI CORPORATION (A)
Regular Meetings and Their Attendants

Name of Meeting	Frequency	Chairman, Auditor	President, Managing Director	Three Executive Directors (V.P.s)	Department Heads	Vice-Heads, Sect. Chiefs	Above Sect. Chief Equiv.	Chief Clerks & Their Equiv.	Average Attendants	Notes (Purpose and Character of the Meetings)
(Members as of April 1)		(2)	(2)	(3)	(8)	(38)	(11)	(27)	Total (91)	
Board meeting	once a month	X	X	X	two officers	—	—	—	11	Formal.
Meeting of department heads	about twice a month	—	X	X	X	—	—	—	13	Communication and coordination.
4 men meeting (no. of fincial name)	about twice a month	X	X	—	—	—	—	—	4	Top Management policy discussions and planning.
Luncheon meeting of department heads – above	every day except Monday & Wednesday	—	X	X	X	X	—	—	11	Communication and discussion of special problems including "brainstorming."
Meeting of department heads and Sect. Chiefs	monthly, about 2 hrs from 4:44 p.m.	—	X	X	X	X	X	—	50	Monthly interchange of policies and other information.
Wednesday Luncheon Meeting	every Wednesday	X	X	X	X	Spec. Pers. X	Spec. Pers. X	—	20	Similar to Monday meeting, but participation is optional: free personnel attend.
Luncheon Meeting of Vice-Heads & Sect. Chiefs	every Monday	—	X	X	X	Spec. Pers. X	—	—	20	The purpose of this meeting is to promote horizontal communication among heads and chiefs.
Discussion meeting of Top-Mft. w/ middle mft.	Monday 3 - 4 hrs in the evening	—	X	X	Spec. Pers. X	Spec. Pers. X	Spec. Pers. X	Spec. Pers. X	25	This is held at a hotel outside of the Company. Every chief clerk is invited to participate twice a year.

NOTES: X — Present.
Spec. Pers. — Specified personnel.

EXHIBIT 11
SUMIYOSHI CORPORATION (A)
Personnel Distribution by Amount of Schooling

	Total (%) Jan. 1956	Total (%) Jan. 1957	Total (%) Jan. 1958	Total (%) Jan. 1959
University or college graduate	83 (14.7)	181 (16.2)	292 (21.0)	364 (17.2)
High school graduate	212 (37.6)	339 (30.3)	450 (32.4)	601 (28.3)
Other group	269 (47.7)	597 (53.5)	648 (46.6)	1,158 (54.5)
Total	564	1,117	1,390	2,123

EXHIBIT 12
SUMIYOSHI CORPORATION (A)
Distribution of College and University Graduates by Major Course

As of	Apr. 1956	Apr. 1957	Apr. 1958	Apr. 1959
Electricity & Electronics	42	76	109	131
Physics, Chemistry, Metallurgy & Mechanics	42	83	92	105
Graduates of other courses	26	51	77	104
Total	110	210	278	340

EXHIBIT 13
SUMIYOSHI CORPORATION (A)
Personnel Distribution, April 30, 1958

Classification	Office			Plant			Total		
	Male	Female	Total (Average)	Male	Female	Total (Average)	Male	Female	Total (Average)
Number of employees	157	124	281	612	645	1,257	769	770	1,539
Average pay	¥34,035	¥9,792	¥23,337	¥13,490	¥7,038	¥10,177	¥17,684	¥7,481	¥12,580
Average age	34	25	30	24	18	21	26	19	23
Average duration of service (Year)	3.9	2.1	3.1	2.3	1.5	1.9	2.6	1.6	2.1

Sumiyoshi Corporation

things as magnetic tape production, ferrite development, transistor development, and so forth. In many instances they had been induced to leave companies or universities in which they had "permanent" status.

Since their employment, the Company's needs had shifted to other areas of research and development, and some of these specialists had either been unable to make, or were uninterested in making, a transition to the new fields of inquiry. The problem of how to motivate these men and how to use them effectively was a vexing one. Yet it was felt that they could not simply be dismissed because their usefulness in light of the Company's new interests had diminished.

FINANCIAL MANAGEMENT

Sumiyoshi Corporation's rapid growth had required constant attention to financial planning. Earnings, although excellent, were not sufficient to provide for the expanded working capital requirements or for the necessary additions to plant and facilities.

As already indicated both Mr. J. Momose, chairman of the Board of Directors and Mr. H. Umeda, director and Chief of the Accounting Department had

EXHIBIT 14
SUMIYOSHI CORPORATION (A)
Profit and Loss Statement (unit: thousand yen)

Accounting Period	2	4	6	8	10	12	14	16
	1946 May-Oct.	1947 May-Oct.	1948 May-Oct.	1949 May-Oct.	1950 May-Oct.	1951 May-Oct.	1952 May-Oct	1953 May-Oct.
Sales (net)	722	3,535	11,500	17,759	45,841	102,283	173,664	298,824
Cost of Sales	486	2,745	8,864	11,756	32,104	77,355	129,055	204,215
Profit on Sales	236	790	2,636	6,003	13,737	24,928	44,609	94,609
General Admin. & Selling Expense	247	744	2,229	5,208	9,028	16,455	28,445	43,019
Operating Profit	11	46	337	795	4,709	8,473	16,164	51,590
Non-Operating Revenue	13	10	13	101	99	856	570	846
Total Profit	2	56	350	896	4,808	9,329	16,734	52,436
Non-Operating Expense					38	288	4,287	8,184
Net Profit of this Period	2	56	350	896	4,770	9,041	12,447	44,252

Accounting Period	18	20	22	24	25	26	27
	1954 May-Oct.	1955 May-Oct.	1956 May-Oct.	1957 May-Oct.	1957 Nov.-Apr.	1958 May-Oct.	1958 Nov.-Apr.
Sales (net)	265,376	356,244	667,148	1,773,253	1,672,238	2,527,093	3,353,866
Cost of Sales	179,928	228,283	504,252	1,261,050	1,151,525	1,778,081	2.336.864
Profit on Sales	85,448	127,961	162,896	512,203	521,213	749,012	1,017,002
General Admin. & Selling Expense	57,136	71,423	92,359	267,039	268,476	370,728	544,665
Operating Profit	28,312	56,538	70,537	245,164	252,737	378,284	472,337
Non-Operating Revenue	9,932	2,428	5,170	10,065	8,155	13,442	16,928
Total Profit	38,244	58,966	75,707	255,299	260,892	391,726	489,265
Non-Operating Expense	8,860	13,329	23,154	47,896	62,588	75,247	98,931
Net Profit of this period	29,384	45,637	52,553	207,333	198,304	316,479	390,334

EXHIBIT 15
SUMIYOSHI CORPORATION (A)
Balance Sheet (unit: thousand yen)

Accounting Period	2	4	6	8	10	12	14	16	18	20	22	24	25	26	27
Closing Date	1946 October	1947 October	1948 October	1949 October	1950 October	1951 October	1952 October	1953 October	1954 October	1955 October	1956 October	1957 October	1958 April	1958 October	1959 April
Current Assets	877	2,131	8,769	24,315	31,284	103,674	136,753	228,107	355,858	527,717	705,894	1,575,762	1,665,779	2,582,590	3,280,421
Quick Assets	303	590	4,460	6,305	15,506	38,939	72,861	137,090	149,631	292,264	413,622	1,021,134	995,551	1,805,171	2,485,909
Inventories	574	1,541	4,309	18,010	15,778	64,735	63,892	91,017	206,227	235,453	292,272	554,628	670,228	777,419	794,512
Fixed Assets	168	180	1,373	3,497	9,221	30,776	44,957	74,130	183,648	223,258	380,080	658,867	810,462	932,339	1,194,756
Tangible	168	180	1,373	3,497	9,071	23,596	37,271	71,290	166,811	187,488	343,392	615,259	758,218	872,655	1,029,191
Intangible						120	192	155	3,027	3,875	3,454	1,687	4,514	5,358	6,130
Investments					150	7,050	7,494	2,685	15,189	31,895	33,234	41,911	47,730	54,326	159,435
Deferred accounts									9,336	7,627	3,316	8,079	27,340	26,725	30,126
TOTAL ASSETS	1,045	2,311	10,142	27,812	40,505	134,440	181,710	302,237	550,221	758,602	1,089,290	2,242,708	2,503,581	3,541,564	4,505,303
Current Liabilities	443	1,052	4,643	20,860	18,667	90,395	120,896	185,788	393,275	514,900	730,085	1,495,757	1,583,336	2,417,761	2,862,455
Fixed Liabilities			1,500	2,000	4,000	8,500	13,613	27,879	18,472	23,372	111,103	210,100	336,936	393,589	495,864
TOTAL LIABILITIES	443	1,052	6,143	22,860	22,667	98,895	134,509	213,667	411,747	538,362	841,188	1,705,857	1,920,272	2,811,350	3,358,319
Capital	600	1,200	3,600	3,600	10,000	20,000	20,000	20,000	50,000	100,000	100,000	200,000	200,000	200,000	400,000
Capital Surplus							1,800		3,385	3,394	2,798	2,732	2,625	2,625	2,471
Profit Surplus	2	59	399	1,352	7,838	15,545	25,401	68,570	85,089	116,846	145,304	334,119	380,684	527,679	744,513
(including net profit of this period)	(2)	(56)	(350)	(896)	(4,770)	(9,041)	(12,447)	(44,252)	(29,384)	(45,637)	(52,553)	(207,333)	(198,304)	(316,479)	(390,334)
TOTAL CAPITAL	602	1,259	3,999	4,952	17,838	35,545	47,201	88,570	138,474	220,240	248,102	536,851	583,309	730,304	1,146,984
TOTAL LIA. & CAPITAL	1,045	2,311	10,142	27,812	40,505	134,440	181,710	302,237	550,221	758,602	1,089,290	2,242,708	2,503,581	3,541,654	4,505,303

Sumiyoshi Corporation

had many years of banking experience. Their understanding of financial management and their wide contacts in financial circles proved to be particularly helpful.

The Company followed the practice of obtaining working capital loans from its bank. Long term funds were obtained within the general rule that at least one half the funds should be provided by self-financing (retained earnings and new stock offerings) and the remainder by borrowing from various financial institutions.

To facilitate financial planning and operating control a comprehensive budget was prepared annually. The budget was sub-divided into semi-annual and monthly periods and according to departments and divisions. All department managers and division heads participated in both the budget preparation and the periodic review of operating results for their respective units.

The Board of Directors reviewed budget proposals and acted as the final approving body. The Board received monthly reports of operating results which were compared to the budget and to other measures such as return on sales and return on invested capital.

Profit and loss statements and balance sheets for the fiscal periods 1946–1958 are given in Exhibits 14 and 15, respectively.

MARKETING

Domestic sales of Sumiyoshi's consumer products were made through the Company's wholly owned subsidiary, Sumiyoshi Shoji, Ltd. This organization had its main office at the Company's headquarters in Osaka, and had branch offices in Tokyo, Nagoya, Fukuoka, Sapporo, Hiroshima, and Sendai. Each branch office sold to special agents which, in turn, provided a variety of electrical goods to shops in the vicinity of each branch.

The Sales Department, under the general direction of Vice President Koike, was divided into three sections. "Section One" sold semi-conductors and ferrite products directly to radio makers, communication equipment manufacturers, research laboratories, and others. "Section Two" sold professional models of tape recorders and miscellaneous communication equipment directly to broadcasting companies, motion picture producers, producers of phonograph records, and the Defense Agency. "Section Three" was responsible for export sales which consisted mainly of tape recorders and transistor radios.

Approximately 99 per cent of the Company's exports were being achieved by overseas shipments of Sumiyoshi transistor radios and most of the remainder by exports of home-use type tape recorders.

Mr. Ishikawa also noted that some Japanese manufacturers of transistors and transistor radios had deliberately sought to export parts and components to the United States and to West Europe rather than to export complete products. In this way, he said, they sought to avoid calling public attention to Japanese imports and to avoid restrictive tariffs. Still other Japanese companies exported complete products for distribution by a domestic corporation under its own trade name, "kenmore" for example. Such was not the policy of Sumiyoshi, said Mr. Ishikawa, although it has had many attractive opportunities to export parts, components, and complete products for sale by others.

Instead, he said, the policy of Sumiyoshi was to create a favorable impression of Sumiyoshi as a producer of high quality electronic products for both consumer and industry, and as a leader in electronics applications. It was anticipated that Sumiyoshi would withdraw from a particular field after it had become popularized to the extent that competition had driven profit margins down to a low level. Mr. Ishikawa felt, therefore, that Sumiyoshi would not be adversely affected by tariff legislation. When a Company is "first" in a field, he said, tariffs are not a critical problem.

As a result of these policies, Sumiyoshi had deferred entering the United States market with transistor radios until it was certain that the product would create a favorable impression toward the Sumiyoshi trademark. Moreover, an effort was made to establish a permanent distribution channel for Sumiyoshi products and to establish the Sumiyoshi trademark through skillful advertising and sales promotion. To achieve these objectives, the Board of Directors decided to give exclusive distribution rights in the United States to a single firm. Sumiyoshi was well satisfied with this decision, said Mr. Ishikawa, and similar exclusives had been granted in Canada, Europe, and elsewhere.

RESEARCH AND DEVELOPMENT

In recent fiscal periods approximately 10 per cent of sales had been devoted to product research and development. Of this sum, approximately 35 per cent was devoted to the improvement of products already in commercial production, 20 per cent was allocated to the application of magnetic tape to new uses, 30 per cent to the application of transistors to new uses, and the reminder to entirely new products or techniques.

Classified in another way, 8.8 per cent of the budget was applied to wages and salaries; 81.3 per cent to materials, equipment and space; and 9.9 per cent to administrative overhead.

In an administrative sense, Mr. Hosoi was responsible for research pertaining to recording heads and magnetic recording tape, while Mr. Imai was in charge of all other research activities.

In regard to the general objectives of Sumiyoshi's research and development program, Mr. Ishikawa said that the policy was to emphasize research on new products rather than products already on Japanese market.

On another occasion, President Ishikawa said:

> One of the most important things that I learned during my last visit to the United States was the research policy of the Du Pont Company. Du Pont has a clear-cut policy of always exploiting new products.

For example, when nylon, which the Company had developed through its research, became popular, the Company moved on into new fields, receiving patent fees for nylon manufacture.... Sumiyoshi had advanced by following this policy even before we were aware of its successful application by Du Pont.... From now on we plan to keep this policy and to exploit new technical fields.... We cannot be merely the keeper of a developed industry; we wish to be the pioneer who forever advances. We do not wish to become involved in trivial competition, but plan to move on to new visions.

PATENT POSITION

As a result of Sumiyoshi's research activities, the Company had been granted more than 250 patents and had more than 450 applications for additional patents pending. Even so, Sumiyoshi's expenses for patent licenses and for royalties amounted to several times its income from such sources.

Thus far Sumiyoshi had experienced no difficulty in obtaining access to any patented manufacturing process which it had desired to use or to any patented product which it wished to manufacture. Royalty fees and licensing fees had in no instance posed formidable bars to any action which the Company had wished to take. Sumiyoshi's experience in these respects was probably typical of the radio and electronics industry in Japan and the United States. The patents had been so widely dispersed that the industry had long ago been forced to adopt extensive cross-licensing arrangements and moderate fees in order to progress.

Perhaps the most publicized recent product of Sumiyoshi's research laboratories was a new type of diode which had been invented by the chief of the semi-conductor research section of Sumiyoshi Corporation.

The principal benefit was expected to come from the lead which Sumiyoshi would have in the commercial application of the invention. If the lead were as substantial as that which had been enjoyed in respect to magnetic tape and transistor radios, it was expected that the benefits would be substantial.

PRODUCTION TARGET FOR TRANSISTOR RADIOS

For the past several months, President Ishikawa said, the Sumiyoshi top management had been working on the problem of establishing new production goals for the Company's line of transistor radios. Current output was coming very close to the previously established target, and production would level-off shortly unless a new directive were issued. The tremendous scale of expansion achieved during the past year, from 15,000 per month to nearly 50,000 per month, had brought extensive changes in the composition of the organization, and all of the directors were concerned about the impact of another large scale expansion. Said President Ishikawa:

> A doubling of transistor radio output now means the addition of about 1,000 people together with the necessary space and equipment; a

doubling of output a year ago meant adding only about one fourth this amount of personnel, space and equipment. The business is expanding at a geometric rate.

The Sumiyoshi "image" which most of the directors held was of an engineering research and development organization, and their thinking had been based upon the assumption that the Company would progress and grow by moving from one new development or application to another. The tremendous success of the Sumiyoshi transistor radio had, however, involved the Company in production of a type and a scale which had already altered the character of the organization by adding a large number of "permanent" employees whose skills were suitable only for mass production. Another Company to mass production even more firmly. On the other hand, the sales outlook for transistor radios as reported to the executive committee indicated that two to three times the present Sumiyoshi output could be sold at present prices and profit margins. The "sellers market" in high quality transistor radios was of uncertain duration, however, and aggressive price competition both at home and abroad seemed certain to result within another year or two.

19

Toyokawa Ltd.*†

INTRODUCTION

Toyokawa Ltd., a medium-sized metal fabricating firm with plants located near Fuchu and home offices in Yokohama, produced a line of construction materials (principally items fabricated from sheet metal), appliances for home and industry, and miscellaneous sheet metal products.

In March, 1959, the Company employed about 1960 people and its sales for the six month period just ended had totaled 1250 million yen—50 per cent in construction materials, 41 per cent in appliances, and 9 per cent in miscellaneous other products. Sales data for 1953-1959 and balance sheets and operating statements for the period 1957-1959 are given in Exhibits 1, 2, and 3, respectively.

In March, 1959, the Company's president, Mr. Keizo Nishina was considering a major realignment of the Company's organizational structure—from the present functional arrangement to a divisional arrangement. The proposed realignment had been formulated over a period of nearly two years, and was intended to eliminate friction between the various functional departments as well as difficulty which Mr. Nishina had experienced in planning, coordinating, and controlling the manufacture and sale of the Company's three major product lines. In addition, President Nishina felt that a divisional type of organization would facilitate training of promising top management personnel. In the existing organization only the president and the managing director had responsibility for planning and coordinating the main activities of the business—in the proposed organization each division manager would perform these top management functions guided by the president and his staff. The proposed realignment had not yet been announced although it had been generally known for some time that the company's top management was contemplating a shift to a divisional type of organization.

*Prepared by Frank T. Hartzfeld and Kenneth H. Myers of Northwestern University, Graduate School of Business, assisted by Tadao Miyakawa if Hitotsubashi University, Matsutaro Wadaki of Keio Gijuku University and Takeshi Kikuchi, and in cooperation with the Japan Productivity Center.

†All names have been disguised. This case material had been prepared as a basis for group discussion, and is not intended to present illustrations of either correct or incorrect handling of administrative problems.

EXHIBIT 1
TOYOKAWA, LTD. (A)
Sales Data
September, 1953 - March, 1959

	1953 June 1953 Sep	1953 Oct 1954 Mar	1954 Apr 1954 Sep	1954 Oct 1955 Mar	1955 Apr 1955 Sep	1955 Oct 1956 Mar	1956 Apr 1956 Sep	1956 Oct 1957 Mar	1957 Apr 1957 Sep	1957 Oct 1958 Mar	1958 Apr 1958 Sep	1959 Oct 1959 Mar
A. Operating Revenue												
a. Construction Mat.												
Sales	52,900	205,500	269,400	373,800	249,000	380,700	298,700	698,400	505,100	608,500	465,900	624,000
Cost of Sales	41,600	208,100	248,100	320,700	238,400	417,400	315,200	644,100	411,300	503,700	396,800	564,900
Profit on Sales	11,300	*2,600	21,300	53,100	10,600	*36,700	*16,500	54,300	93,800	104,800	69,100	59,100
b. Appliances												
Sales							185,600	319,800	586,400	833,500	569,200	510,100
Cost of Sales							210,600	318,100	566,400	788,700	525,800	475,600
Profit on Sales							*25,000	1,700	20,000	44,800	43,400	34,500
c. Military Products												
Sales	70,200	11,700	88,700	410,900	488,600	938,600	1,000					
Cost of Sales	45,700	10,000	128,800	473,000	484,900	892,900	4,400					
Profit on Sales	24,500	1,700	*40,100	*62,100	3,700	45,700	*3,400					
d. Others												
Sales	38,200	117,200	98,200	62,000	81,700	79,900	112,800	113,800	174,800	198,100	152,200	114,200
Cost of Sales	47,000	126,800	79,800	47,900	71,200	74,600	111,000	91,100	147,400	159,500	118,900	107,200
Profit on Sales	*8,800	*9,600	18,400	14,100	10,500	5,300	1,800	22,700	27,400	38,600	33,300	7,000
e. Total												
Sales	161,300	334,400	456,300	846,700	819,300	1,399,200	598,100	1,132,000	1,266,500	1,640,100	1,187,300	1,248,300
Cost of Sales	134,300	344,900	456,700	841,600	794,500	1,384,900	641,200	1,053,300	1,125,400	1,451,900	1,041,500	1,147,700
Profit on Sales	27,000	*10,500	*4,000	5,100	24,800	14,300	*43,100	78,700	141,100	188,200	145,800	100,600

*Amounts preceded by an asterisk donate red figures.

Toyokawa

EXHIBIT 2
TOYOKAWA, LTD. (A)
Balance Sheet, September 1957 - March, 1959

DEBIT (in thousand yen)	1957 Sep	1958 Mar	1958 Sep	1959 Mar	CREDIT (in thousand yen)	1957 Sep	1958 Mar	1958 Sep	1959 Mar
Current Assets	1,324,600	1,447,200	1,391,800	1,620,400	Current Liabilities	1,519,000	1,483,900	1,223,800	1,431,500
Cash on Hand	900	2,700	500	3,100	Accounts Payable Trade	376,000	446,800	422,800	510,700
Cash in Bank	47,000	38,800	47,500	38,200	Short-term Debt	420,800	449,000	117,000	199,500
Bills Receivable	149,500	102,000	115,900	193,700	Account Payable Not Trade	700	900	4,200	16,300
Accounts Receivable Trade	473,900	676,000	451,000	460,200	Accrued Expense	140,000	81,100	124,400	69,600
Securities	1,000	1,100	1,400	12,200	Advances Received	99,700	13,000	21,900	13,000
Materials	161,900	98,500	81,100	74,100	Temporary Receipt	6,200	2,900	4,900	3,500
Work in Process*	450,700	462,000	623,300	772,200	Suspended Account Receivable				
Advances	7,800	20,500	11,100	12,800	Suspense Account on Sales	23,100	6,500	5,000	4,100
Prepaid Expenses	9,400	11,000	18,300	23,900	Reserve for Retiring Allowance	430,100	437,500	440,000	521,300
Accounts Receivable Not Trade	19,000	23,000	33,200	18,800	Reserve for Bad Debts	5,900	3,700	18,200	23,400
Suspense Payment	2,900	3,600	4,200	3,100	Reserve for Repairs		5,900	11,800	17,800
Suspended Account Payable	600	4,500	600	4,900	Reserve for Inventory Fluctuations	16,500	23,600	27,600	26,300
Dishonoured Bills		3,500	3,600	3,200					
Fixed Assets	377,900	410,200	425,700	448,600	Fixed Liabilities		13,000	26,000	26,000
Tangible Fixed Assets	371,200	402,500	416,300	435,900	Long-term Debt		13,000	202,500	114,400
Buildings	104,300	123,200	125,100	122,900	Total Liabilities			202,500	114,400
Structures	2,200	2,900	1,800	5,200	Capital 495,600	1,519,000	1,483,900	1,426,300	1,545,900
Machinery & Equipment	221,000	233,600	231,400	237,100	Surplus Profit	495,600	495,600	495,600	495,600
Transportation Equipment	3,100	7,000	10,500	12,000	Net Profit for the Current Term	*300,000†	*119,400	*100,500	31,500
Tools, Furnitures & Fixtures	12,700	14,800	17,500	30,500	Surplus Profit Brought forward from the Last Term	53,500	180,700	18,900	132,000
Land	18,200	18,200	23,900	22,300					
Construction in Process Account	9,700	2,800	6,100	5,900		*353,600	*300,100†	*119,400	*100,500
Intangible Fixed Assets	1,900	2,300	2,000	3,600	Total	1,714,500	1,860,100	1,821,400	2,073,000
Intangible Fixed Assets	1,900	2,300	2,000	3,600					
Investment	4,800	5,400	7,400	9,100					
Securities Caution Money	4,800	5,400	7,400	9,100					
Deferred Accounts	12,000	2,700	3,900	4,000					
Research & Experiment Charges	12,000	2,700	3,900	4,000					
Total	1,714,500	1,860,100	1,821,400	2,073,000					
Footnote - Depreciation	124,900	142,300	156,900	175,600					

*Work in Process a/c – (Suspense Account on Sales - Profit) = Net Work in Process.
"Work in Process" presently includes partial shipments of construction materials, these shipment plus profit are also carried on the credit side of the balance sheet under "Suspense Account on Sales."
†Amounts preceded by an asterisk denote red figures.

EXHIBIT 3
TOYOKAWA, LTD. (A)
Profit and Loss Statement
September, 1957 - March, 1959

(in thousand yen)

		1957 Apr 1957 Sep	1957 Oct 1958 Mar	1958 Apr 1958 Sep	1958 Oct 1959 Mar
A.	Operating Revenue				
	a. Construction Mat.				
	Sales	505,100	608,500	465,900	624,000
	Cost of Sales	411,300	503,700	396,800	564,900
	Profit on Sales	93,800	104,800	69,100	59,100
	b. Appliance				
	Sales	586,400	833,500	569,200	510,100
	Cost of Sales	566,400	788,700	525,800	475,600
	Profit on Sales	20,000	44,800	43,400	34,500
	c. Others				
	Sales	174,800	198,100	152,200	114,200
	Cost of Sales	147,400	159,500	118,900	107,200
	Profit on Sales	27,400	38,600	33,300	7,000
	d. Total				
	Sales	1,266,500	1,640,100	1,187,300	1,248,300
	Cost of Sales	1,125,400	1,451,900	1,041,500	1,147,700
	Profit on Sales	141,100	188,200	145,800	100,600
B.	Non-Operating Expenses Total	92,500	120,300	93,600	61,400
C.	Operating Profit for the Period	48,600	67,900	52,200	39,200
D.	Increase or Decrease of Profit for Previous Terms Modification of Profit			33,300*	
	Profit on Sales of Fixed Assets Sold	4,900	112,800		92,800
E.	Net Profit for the period	53,500	180,700	18,900	132,000

* Tax on gain derived from sale of property in prior years plus allowances and discounts.

COMPANY HISTORY

Toyokawa Ltd. was organized in the early 1920's to manufacture fabricated sheet metal products for the construction industry. A pioneer in its field, Toyokawa prospered moderately during the 1920's, reaching a sales and employment peak of 800,000 yen and 400 men, respectively, in 1925. The world depression which began in 1930 affected Japanese construction adversely, and

Toyokawa's sales and employment declined to 350,000 yen and 200 men, respectively, in 1931. At this point the Akasaka Trading Company acquired 50 per cent of Toyokawa's equity capital and became the sole sales agent for Toyokawa products. An Akasaka representative, Mr. Taro Wada, became the company's auditor. In 1935 the relationship between Toyokawa and the Akasaka Trading Company was further strengthened when the remainder of Toyokawa's equity capital was acquired by various Akasaka interests, and an Akasaka Trading Company representative, Mr. Yukio Muto, became Toyokawa's president.

The Toyokawa product line continued as before until 1937 when war between Japan and China broke out and Toyokawa began the manufacture of airframe sections (aircraft fuselage and wing structures). This line of manufacture expanded rapidly over the next few years and by 1940 the Company's facilities at Fuchu and Osaka were almost fully occupied by military production. At this time the shift in necessary technical and managerial skills which accompanied the transition from construction materials to air frame construction, caused the Toyokawa-Akasaka relationship to be transferred from the Akasaka Trading Company to the Akasaka Machinery Company, and Mr. Masaichiro Kagawa of the Machinery Company replaced the Trading Company representative as Toyokawa's president. During the war years the Company operated plants at Fuchu, Osaka, Nagasaki, and Sapporo, and employment reached a peak of 20,000 persons. Principal activities at Fuchu and Osaka were airframe construction and final assembly of aircraft—at one time the Company produced all major components of a complete aircraft except engine, instruments, and landing gear.

Following World War II, Toyokawa was separated from the Akasaka Group in accordance with GHQ orders and in pursuance of the GHQ objective of reducing the influence of the Zaibatsu in post-war Japan. At the same time Toyokawa was made subject to reparations by GHQ order. No reparations were ever called for, however, and the Company was wholly released from such obligation by 1952.

During the period 1946-1950 the Company resumed the manufacture of construction materials and also developed a considerable volume of business in body repair work on military vehicles and electric street cars. On January 4, 1950 the steps taken to separate the Company from the Akasaka Group were completed and the Company was reestablished as Toyokawa, Ltd.

During the period April, 1950-June, 1953 the Company's operations were generally unprofitable, largely because the Fuchu and Osaka facilities, which were devoted to the repair of military vehicles and street car bodies, were being utilized on an intermittent basis. At times both shops were crowded with work and the combined labor force of some 900 was fully occupied. A few months later the volume of work might be such that only one-third of this force would have been adequate. Since most of the Toyokawa employees had "permanent" status, the Company's labor cost during slack periods was virtually the same as during the periods of peak demand. The Toyokawa management could not seem to develop more satisfactory use of the Company's facilities and personnel and in March, 1953, net losses since April, 1950, totaled some 500 million yen (as compared to total assets of 4,100 million yen and a capitalization of 150 million yen).

Soon after the financial report of March, 1953 became known, the Company's banks urged the Toyokawa directors to consider a change in top management. The banks' request was virtually a command since the Company's current ratio (current assets/current liabilities) on March 31 was about 0.5 and its current liabilities included several hundred million yen in notes to banks.

The reorganization arrangements were consummated in late June, 1953, by which time an additional several hundred million yen in operating losses had been incurred.

At this juncture Mr. Ichiro Ueno was appointed president and the severe losses came to an abrupt halt. Mr. Ueno had first entered Toyokawa as managing Director in 1935, having come from the Akasaka Trading Company. In 1947 he had "retired" (by order of GHQ).

Under Mr. Ueno's direction, Toyokawa's relationship with the Akasaka Group was immediately resumed. Mr. Shigeo Sengoku of the Akasaka Bank was appointed assistant to the president in charge of financial matters, and Mr. Keizo Nishina, chief industrial engineer of the Akasaka Machinery Company, provided continuing guidance as a consultant to Toyokawa on both technical and general managerial matters.

Within a year a profitable and stable contract for military ordinance was negotiated to replace the erratic body repair business. Subcontracts from the various Akasaka Companies helped tide Toyokawa over during the interim period, as did the rising sales of Toyokawa's line of construction materials. Prompt "rationalization" of the labor force and the first steps toward consolidation of manufacturing operations at Fuchu helped to reduce operating losses considerably during the first three months of the new management. Within a year the Company was making a slight operating profit and preparations were being made to sell the now idle plants at Osaka, Nagasaki, and Sapporo. In all, nearly 1,000 "permanent" workers from the latter plants were separated from the Company and another 1,000 were relocated at Fuchu. The total cost to the Company for separation benefits, retirement benefits, and relocation expense was about 260 million yen.

The sale of property, plus the revitalization of the Company's construction materials business and the growth of military production for the U.S. Armed Forces, provided funds with which to reduce the sums owed to banks. The Company's financial position was further strengthened with new equity capital provided by various companies of the Akasaka Group. As a result of these moves, Toyokawa Ltd. emerged in June, 1957 with the Akasaka Group holding slightly more than 50 per cent of its voting stock and with a board composed entirely of Company officers and Akasaka representatives.

With the financial reorganization completed, Mr. Ueno assumed the position of chairman of the board and Mr. Nishina became president.

CHANGES IN PRODUCT LINE, 1953-1959

During the first three years of Mr. Ueno's presidency, the Company's sales volume had expanded tremendously—from about 325 million yen for the six month period ending September, 1953 to nearly 1,400 million yen for the six month period ending March, 1956. About 75 per cent of the expansion had been in arms production, however, and when procurement of this item was terminated in the summer of 1956, drastic measures were again necessary to provide alternate employment for Toyokawa's facilities and personnel.

Fortunately, just at this time sales of the Akasaka Machinery Company's industrial and home applicanes were growing rapidly, and in several instances exceeded the capacity of its plants. Toyokawa began the manufacture of several types of Akasaka appliances in April, 1956.

At first these products were manufactured entirely to the design specifications of the Akasaka Machinery Company but, as Toyokawa's engineers became more familiar with the new products, more and more design responsibility was assumed by Toyokawa. As of March, 1959, Toyokawa's entire output of appliances continued to be sold to the Akasaka Machinery Company's Appliance Division. This Division distributed a broad array of appliances through its 10 branch sales offices and 150 sales agents to nearly every department store in Japan and to many thousands of appliance dealers throughout the country. Akasaka also had an extensive overseas sales organization.

All of these products, including those supplied by Toyokawa, bore the Akasaka brand name. Although sales of appliances similar to those manufactured by Toyokawa were divided between domestic and overseas markets in the proportions of 95 per cent and 5 per cent, respectively, the per cent of export sales had been growing rapidly.

PRODUCTS, MARKETS, AND SALES PROMOTION

Construction Materials

The Toyokawa line of fabricated sheet metal products for building construction was distributed through the Toyokawa home office (Yokohama) two branch sales offices (Osaka and Fukuoka), and two sales agents (Sapporo and Nagoya). Distribution of sales by district and by government and private construction is shown in Exhibit 4. Sales and earnings for the line are shown in Exhibit 1.

The branch sales offices and sales agents paid close attention to major commercial, industrial, and governmental building construction throughout Japan. The first opportunity to make a sale occurred during the design stage

EXHIBIT 4
TOYOKAWA, LTD. (A)
Toyokawa Sales of Construction Materials
1954 - 1958*

By Private Construction vs Government Construction

		1954	1955	1956	1957	1958
Private	%	31.4	59.3	59.2	59.6	65.0
Government	%	68.6	40.7	40.8	40.4	35.0

By District

District		1954	1955	1956	1957	1958
Tokyo	%	47.3	49.7	59.3	53.6	52.7
Osaka	%	22.4	21.3	9.9	16.1	9.8
Nagoya	%	11.9	14.0	8.4	10.0	8.8
Kyushu	%	9.1	9.2	6.5	6.9	10.3
Hokkaido	%	13.8	5.8	15.9	13.4	18.4
Total	%	100	100	100	100	100

*April, 1954 - March, 1959.

when an architectural engineer might specify a standard Toyokawa product "or equivalent."

If the item so specified was one which Toyokawa carried in stock, the Company was likely to enjoy a price and a delivery advantage in relation to a manufacturer which did not stock the item. This advantage diminished as the size of an order increased however, for the manufacturing cost and delivery schedule on a 10 million yen order were likely to be very nearly the same whether the items were "standard" or "special." The particular advantage of standard stock items was, therefore, in the case of small construction projects.

Toyokawa salesmen called upon principal architectural firms and building contractors fairly regularly, partly in order to acquaint them with new technical developments or with additions to the Company's standard products, and partly with the objective of maintaining favorable personal relations with key individuals.

In addition to personal contacts, the use of catalogs and advertising in architectural journals and industry trade papers constituted an important means of promoting Toyokawa products to the building industry.

Price, service, and ability to provide prompt delivery were probably the key factors in making sales of Toyokawa building materials. Although the Company's catalogs listed 40 standard designs (each in a number of dimensions), only a few of these were actually carried in stock. Such standard-stock items accounted for about 1 per cent of Toyokawa's sales of construction materials, and standard (non-stocked) items for 14 per cent. About 85 per cent of sales was derived from non-standard items, i.e. sheet metal products of special design which were "made to order" for a particular building project. All of the special order business was attained on a "bid" basis, as were most large orders for standard and standard-stock items. Bids on all special orders and on large orders for standard items were prepared by the home office. Price lists were not issued to the public, and the branch sales office or sales agent exercised some discretion in quoting prices on even small orders for standard-stock items.

Because of the technical simplicity of the manufacturing process, and the relatively small capital investment required, there were a large number of firms which were considered by the building trade to be competent and reputable manufacturers of the items in Toyokawa's construction materials line. For these reasons, small local producers, whose labor and transportation costs were less than Toyokawa's, were often able to bid successfully on large contracts as well as small ones.

Prices were quoted FOB Fuchu and the average shipping charges for October, 1958 through March, 1959 were 5.0 as a per cent of manufacturing cost and 3.9 as a per cent of invoiced price. Crating and packing costs (which were absorbed in "cost of manufacture") were 2.2 per cent of manufactured cost and 1.7 per cent of invoiced price. Labor rates of small local manufacturers might be as little as 70 per cent of Toyokawa's. Toyokawa's manufacturing costs for a recent period were composed of 18.6 per cent labor, 33.0 per cent material, 21.0 per cent for subcontracted work, 20.4 per cent factory overhead, and 7.0 per cent for field installation expense. General administrative and selling expenses allocated to the construction materials line were 10.7 per cent of shipments for the same period.

To overcome some of the disadvantages suggested by the above figures, the management had set up "service centers" in conjunction with the home sales office, two branch sales offices, and two sales agents. These "service centers" were equipped and staffed to complete the assembly of certain items which were shipped "knocked down" by the Fuchu factory, to provide field repair and alteration service, and to supervise local manufacture of certain items by subcontractors. Exhibit 5 indicates the sales volume forecast for these sales offices and service centers for the six month period ending September, 1959. Subcontracting through the service centers was used extensively during peak periods in order to avoid adding new employees at the Fuchu plant.

The Toyokawa management had observed that the total industry demand for construction materials of the type which the Company manufactured closely paralleled the volume of steel and reinforced concrete construction in Japan (see Exhibit 6). Toyokawa's share of industry sales for the year ended in March, 1959, was estimated at 7 per cent (see Exhibit 7).

It was estimated that Toyokawa was competing with at least 70 companies in its line of construction materials. The five largest competitors (see Exhibit 7) each had a product line comparable to Toyokawa's, and distributed throughout

EXHIBIT 5
TOYOKAWA, LTD. (A)
Selected Data on Sales Offices and Service Centers*
(Estimated monthly averages for 6 months ending September, 1959)

LOCATION

Item	Yokohama (Home Office)	Osaka (Sales Branch)	Nagoya (Sales Agent)	Fukuoka (Sales Branch)	Sapporo (Sales Agent)	Total
Factory sales (000)	¥38,200	¥12,300	¥7,200	¥6,800	¥13,500	¥78,000
Service & subcontract sales (000)	11,600	2,500	300	1,500	2,800	18,700
Freight & packing charges as a per cent of Factory Sales	3.0	8.5	7.2	7.2	9.9	
Office expense as a percent of Factory Sales	8.4	9.5		9.0		

*Factory capacity (one shift, no overtime) estimated at this time was 78,000 yen per month.

EXHIBIT 6
TOYOKAWA, LTD. (A)
Building Construction (commenced)
(unit: billion yen)

| Year | Total | | By Structure | | | | By Use | | | | | |
| | | | Reinforced Concrete | | Steel Frame | | For Public Use | | For Public Utilities | | For Mining & Industry | | For Commerce | |
		Index		Index		Index		Index		Index		Index		Index
1951	170.8	100	49.7	100	7.4	100	31.0	100	4.7	100	25.4	100	37.5	100
52	210.5	123	41.6	84	10.0	135	43.9	141	7.0	149	25.9	102	28.4	76
53	269.9	158	69.0	139	14.1	190	41.5	134	12.4	264	33.9	133	47.0	125
54	294.9	173	83.2	168	14.0	189	54.3	175	13.2	281	30.9	122	49.0	131
55	292.4	171	82.8	167	13.6	184	44.1	142	12.2	260	28.9	114	56.5	151
56	381.9	224	121.1	244	28.2	381	47.0	151	13.8	294	59.6	235	69.9	187
57	456.7	267	157.0	316	39.3	531	52.2	168	16.7	355	89.9	354	76.8	205
58	457.0	267	170.4	344	30.3	409	67.4	217	19.0	404	61.0	240	73.7	196

CONSTRUCTION COST ¥1,000/m^2

| Year | Total | | By Structure | | | |
| | | | Reinforced Concrete | | Steel Frame | |
		Index		Index		Index
1951	5.26	100	18.05	100	7.87	100
52	6.13	117	17.85	99	11.70	149
53	7.68	146	19.65	109	10.54	134
54	8.90	169	20.64	114	12.10	154
55	8.85	168	19.20	106	10.67	136
56	9.33	177	18.60	103	12.65	161
57	10.45	199	20.80	115	15.10	192
58	10.82	206	20.30	113	13.20	168

SOURCE: Ministry of Construction

EXHIBIT 7
TOYOKAWA, LTD. (A)
Market Shares for Construction Materials*
Market Shares of Main Competitors, (1958)

Company	Sales (million)	Shares
A	2,470	15%
B	1,027	6%
C	1,118	7%
D	1,053	6%
E	1,235	8%
Toyokawa	1,092	7%
Others	8,305	51%
Total	16,300	100%

*Estimated by Toyokawa official.

Japan. The remaining companies were much smaller and usually produced a relatively narrow line which they distributed locally.

A trade association official had recently estimated 1959 industry sales for items in the Toyokawa line at 19.5 billion yen (see Exhibit 8). The Toyokawa management observed that the six industry leaders, including themselves, usually accounted for about 50 per cent of total industry sales.

EXHIBIT 8
TOYOKAWA, LTD. (A)
Industry Sales for Construction Materials*

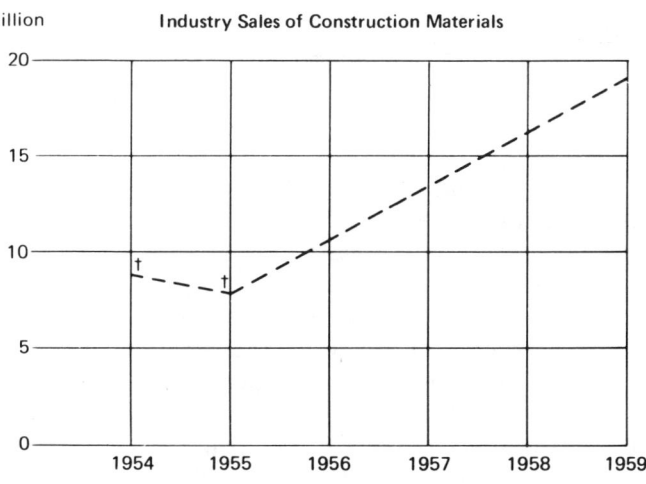

*Items comparable to the line manufactured by Toyokawa, Ltd.
†Ministry of International Trade and Industry
(index discontinued after 1955)
Estimate by Trade Association Official.

Appliances

The circumstances of Toyokawa's entry into appliance manufacture in 1957 has already been noted, as has the ensuing pattern of distribution. Toyokawa was responsible for producing the entire Akasaka line (four models in March, 1959) of appliance "A," and for three models of appliance "B." Approximately 25 per cent of Akasaka's monetary sales volume of "A" and also of "B" was supplied by Toyokawa. In addition, Toyokawa's engineering force had recently designed and tested "B-1," a type of appliance which served the same functional purpose as "B" but which was significantly different in a mechanical sense. The "B-1" design was expected to be quieter and more economical in operation than the "B" design, and to require less maintenance. The manufacturing cost and selling price of B-1 were expected to be about 3 per cent higher than those of a comparable unit of conventional design. No other firm in Japan was manufacturing items of the B-1 type, though they had been manufactured and sold with moderate success in some foreign countries. Exhibit 9 diagrams the relationship between Toyokawa and Akasaka in regard to design, manufacture, shipping, and billing.

EXHIBIT 9
TOYOKAWA, LTD. (A)
Division of Responsibility (appliance line)

Product	Responsibility*†			
	Design	Manufacture	Shipping	Billing
A (4 models)	T & A	T	T	A
B (3 models)	A	T	A	A
B-1	T‡	T‡	T‡	A‡

*T = Toyokawa Ltd.
†A = Akasaka Machinery Company
‡Anticipated relationship

Model changes in both "A" and "B" lines occurred at about six month intervals, at which time new contracts between Toyokawa and the Akasaka Machinery Company were negotiated. The usual sequence of events preceding a production contract was as shown in Exhibit 10. The Toyokawa Management was of the impression that the Akasaka representatives negotiated with the objective of allowing Toyokawa a profit of about three per cent of sales, net after taxes, on the latter's production of appliances. In recent fiscal periods the Akasaka requirements of appliances had varied between 50 per cent and 100 per cent of Toyokawa's "normal" capacity (one shift, no overtime). Recent improvements in the Toyokawa production facilities had increased "normal" capacity in appliances to about 150 million yen per month as of March, 1959. Industry sales of appliances "A" and "B," as well as Toyokawa's sales, are given in Exhibit 11.

Toyokawa

EXHIBIT 10
TOYOKAWA, LTD. (A)
Sequence of Events at Time of Model Change (appliance "A")

Item	Responsibility*†	Action
Design	T & A	Sales and design personnel of both companies meet and decide to test certain modifications
Manufacture models	T	Design and production engineers
Total models	T & A	Sales and design engineers of both companies
Approve design	A	
Estimate sales volume	A	
Estimate manufacturing Cost	T	
Negotiate contract	T & A	Negotiate unit price for a specific number of units, usually to be delivered at a uniform rate over a three month to a six month period. Adjustments are negotiated if A's demand schedule is significantly different from that which was anticipated.

*T refers to Toyokawa, Ltd.
†A refers to Akasaka Machinery Co., Ltd.

Miscellaneous Products

The nine per cent of Toyokawa's sales represented by miscellaneous products was divided among four major categories. Items "one" and "two" were a heating and a ventilating device, respectively, which were sold through the same channels as the Company's other construction materials. Item "three" was a

EXHIBIT 11
TOYOKAWA, LTD. (A)
Appliance Production

Year	Product "A"		Product "B"	
	Industry* (million ¥)	Toyokawa† (per cent)	Industry* (million ¥)	Toyokawa† (per cent)
1954	6,800		2,030	
1955	11,100		2,930	
1956	16,600	1.22	6,490	1.05
1957	19,400	5.06	15,200	2.26
1958	21,600	4.40	24,700	1.43
1959	24,200‡		29,250‡	

*Calendar year.
†Fiscal year (April - March).
‡Estimated by industry association.

filtration device used to purify a wide variety of liquids. It was sold to companies in a number of different industries through manufacturer's agents. The fourth category of "miscellaneous" consisted of subcontracted work received from various Akasaka companies, their affiliates, and some non-affiliated companies. All of the latter involved the fabrication from sheet metal of bodies or housings and the subsequent addition or assembly of purchased items such as hardware, motors, and heating elements.

MANUFACTURING FACILITIES AND PROCESSES

Facilities

The Company's offices and factory buildings at Fuchu contained about 16,000 tsubo of floor space and occupied about 1/5 of a 64,000 tsubo plot. Employee welfare buildings contained about 4,000 tsubo of floor space stood on an additional 12,000 tsubo set aside for welfare purposes. The factory buildings were of light gauge steel frame construction with 40 ft wide bays and a 25 ft clearance for overhead travelling cranes. Originally designed for the manufacture of aircraft wing structures and fuselages, the building provided considerably more height than was needed for the manufacturing processes currently being utilized by Toyokawa. Although the available floor space had been almost completely utilized, it was recognized that the processes and equipment had simply expanded to fill the available space. One member of the factory organization estimated that a 40 per cent decrease in floor space requirements might be accomplished, if necessary, without reducing present production capacity.

Processes

The manufacturing processes and plant layout are indicated in Exhibit 12. Metal cutting and forming operations for all classes of products were performed on general purpose equipment in Building 1 (Area is marked "Shear and Bend, Press and Punch"). The machine shop area in Building 1 serviced all product lines by providing dies, jigs, and fixtures, and by performing machine operations on components. Endless chain conveyors were employed in the painting and baking of appliances A and B. Short 40 ft to 50 ft belt conveyors were employed in the final assembly of A and B.

Other methods of material handling were overhead travelling cranes (2), fork-lift trucks (4), tractor trucks (4), and hand carts (65). Palletization of materials handling was being contemplated. Virtually all production tools and equipment, except for the conveyors would be categorized as "general purpose."

The major components of manufactured cost for the construction materials line has already been noted. For appliances they were approximately 72 per cent for materials, 7 per cent for labor, 15 per cent for sub-contractors, and 6 per cent for factory overhead.

Toyokawa

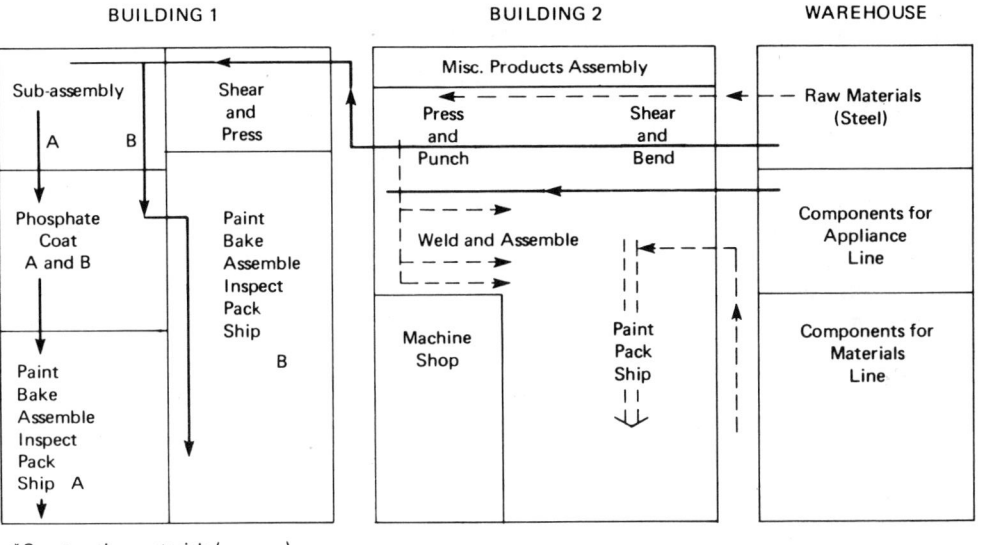

**EXHIBIT 12
TOYOKAWA, LTD. (A)
Fuchu Plant   March 1959
(Schematic Diagram)***

*Construction materials (– – –).
Appliance line   (———).

PROCUREMENT

Of the 989 million yen in materials purchased by the Company during the six month period ending March, 1959, 307 million yen was purchased from Akasaka Companies or their affiliates. In manufacturing the appliances which bore the Akasaka brand name, Toyokawa was expected to purchase Akasaka components where possible. When producing items for distribution under its own name, Toyokawa purchases of parts and components were made from a variety of companies, though it was the practice to buy from Akasaka sources when "other things were equal."

GENERAL ADMINISTRATION

In discussing his activities since becoming president of Toyokawa in June, 1957, President Nishina observed that one of his primary concerns had been to improve employee motivation and attitude. The Company's long record of post war difficulties, culminating in the financial difficulties of 1953 and the drastic actions taken by Mr. Ueno to "rationalize" the Company's operations, had imposed a series of very severe shocks upon Company personnel at all levels.

From the day of his appointment as president, Mr. Nishina said, he had attempted to keep all levels of management and employees informed on matters of Company policy which affected them. He thought it particularly important to keep the management group fully informed—"we have no secrets here" he said with a smile to the case writers at a meeting at which four or five members top and middle management were present, and during which the general objectives of the Company were under discussion.

In accordance with this policy, President Nishina had made arrangements for all levels of management to participate periodically in committee meetings at which matters of policy could be discussed and communicated. President Nishina did not consider committees to be effective decision making bodies, however, nor did he think that they should be expected to act in the sense of an administrator. His organizational objective, he observed, was to clarify areas of responsibility and authority, and to delegate these areas to particular individuals. Except as means of policy formulation, and of communication or coordination, he desired to eliminate conferences and committees from the Toyokawa organization. In March, 1959, five management committees, including the Board of Directors, were active. The membership of these committees is given in Exhibit 13, and the relationship of the committees to the total organization is shown in Exhibit 14.

The Board of Directors met monthly, primarily to give the chairman (Mr. Ueno) and the outside directors (Mr. Nakamura and Mr. Ogawa) an opportunity to review the Company's operating statements and financial reports and to consider major questions of policy. Aside from the monthly financial reports, recent items on the agenda had been the proposal to adopt a "federal" type of decentralized organization at Toyokawa (approved January, 1959), a proposed budget for the development and test of a new construction materials product. The president also reported on the bonus to be offered to the employees at the next union negotiation and on the schedule of annual wage and salary increases. It was customary for the recommendations of the Company's officers to be accepted with relatively little discussion. Financial relationships with the Akasaka Bank and trade relationships with the Akasaka Machinery Company were also regularly discussed at these meetings. Decisions were customarily referred to President Nishina for action.

The Executive Committee, chaired by President Nishina and comprised of all officer-directors, met monthly except for rather rate emergency sessions. It was the most active and influential policy formulating committee of the Company, in addition to which it regularly considered plans for implementing policy decisions. These policy decisions and plans were then communicated to a somewhat larger group, the General Management Committee, with President Nishina again presiding. Following the monthly meetings of the Executive Committee and the General Management Committee, the department managers met at a session chaired by Mr. Ito, assistant to President Nishina. This group had the task

EXHIBIT 13
TOYOKAWA, LTD. (A)
Committee Membership

MEMBERS OF BOARD OF DIRECTORS

    Ichiro Ueno (Chairman)
    Keizo Nishina (President)
    Masao Oki
    Saburo Nakamura*
    Hideo Ogawa†
    Kiyoshi Ito
    Hajime Komori
    Jiro Hori

EXECUTIVE COMMITTEE

    Keizo Nishina (President)
    Masao Oki
    Kiyoshi Ito
    Hajime Komori
    Jiro Hori

GENERAL MANAGEMENT COMMITTEE

    Keizo Nishina (Chairman)
    Masao Oki
    Kiyoshi Ito
    Hajime Komori
    Tetsuo Ishikawa †
    Shoji Yagi
    Kenichi Imai
    Taizo Sugi
    Osamu Sugita
    Isamu Tada †
    Eizo Abe †
    Ken Yamashita†
    Yoshio Hirai †

MEETING OF DEPARTMENT MANAGERS

    Kiyoshi Ito (Chairman)
    Hajime Komori
    Jiro Hori
    Tetsuo Ishikawa †
    Shoji Yagi
    Kenichi Imai
    Taizo Sugi
    Osamu Sugita

MEETING OF HEADS OF DEPARTMENT AND SECTION CHIEFS

    Masao Oki (Chairman)
    Shoji Yagi
    Osamu Sugita
    Taizo Sugi
    Kenichi Imai
    Jiro Hori
    Hajime Komori
    All assistants to department managers
    All section chiefs

*Representative of the Akasaka Bank.

†Representative of the Akasaka Machinery Co.

‡Assistants to department managers.

of further developing any plans of action outlined in the sessions with the President, and of coordinating the activities of the respective departments. The managing director, Mr. Oki, also held regularly scheduled monthly meetings with department heads and section chiefs, primarily to review operating performance and to communicate matters of general company policy.

The membership, purpose, and procedures of each of these committees had been considered carefully by President Nishina and they reflected his concepts of management rather accurately. For example, he participated in the formula-

EXHIBIT 14
TOYOKAWA, LTD. (A)
Personal Data - Directors, Officers and Department Heads
(Ages as of March, 1959)

Ichiro Ueno (62) graduated in economics from X University, Served as Toyokawa's managing director (1935 - 1942), president (1953 - 1957), and as chairman of the board (1957 -   ).

Keizo Nishina (61) graduated in engineering from X University, Entered the Akasaka Machinery Company in 1921. Successively industrial engineer, department manager, factory manager, manager of industrial engineering department (home office) and director. Advisor to Toyokawa 1953 - 1957, president and director 1957 -

Eizo Abe (48) graduated in economics from X University. Entered R Manufacturing Company in 1936 and in 1942 was head of S sales. Entered Toyokawa in 1942 where he has been secretary, head of sales, head of finance, and the assistant manager of the planning department (present position).

Yoshio Hirai (43) graduated from the machinery department of the E Prefectural Engineering School. Entered Toyokawa in 1933 where he has served as a design engineer, process engineer, and industrial engineer and has held various supervisory positions in engineering. He is now assistant manager of the engineering department.

Jiro Hori (51) graduated in Engineering from Z University. Entered Toyokawa in 1937 and has served as engineering designer, chief of inspection, plant manager, chief of design of construction materials, and manager of sales. Elected a director in 1958.

Tetsuo Ishikawa (61) graduated from the electrical department of F Prefectural Technical School. Entered the Akasaka Machinery Company in 1920 where he held a variety of positions in engineering design, process engineering, and production. Entered Toyokawa in 1958 as assistant manager of the manufacturing department.

Kiyoshi Ito (57) graduated in business from X College. Entered the Akasaka Bank 1924 and was a branch manager in 1952. Entered Toyokawa in 1953 as financial advisor and director.

Hajime Komori (54) graduated in economics from X University. Entered Toyokawa in 1931. In charge of general affairs section 1943 - 1958. Became a director in 1958 and is presently head of the planning department.

Saburo Nakamura (64) graduated in economics from X University. Entered Akasaka Bank 1920. Presently a vice president and director of that Bank. Director of Toyokawa since 1957.

Hideo Ogawa (63) graduated in engineering from X University. Entered Akasaka Machinery Company 1920. Presently a vice president and director of that company.

Masao Oki (61) graduated in engineering from X University. Entered Akasaka Machinery Company 1924. Served successively as design engineer, sales engineer, manager of A sales, assistant manager of A manufacturing, manager of B purchasing, manager of C plant. Managing director of Toyokawa 1958 -

Taizo Sugi (47) graduated form the ship building department of E Technical School. Entered Akasaka Machinery Company in 1935. Left the latter to join Toyokawa in 1947 where he has held various managerial positions in the engineering department. Presently chief of the engineering department.

Osamu Sugita (53) graduated from the machinery department of D Prefectural Technical School. Entered Akasaka Machinery Company 1938 where by 1956 he was head of a home office section responsible for manufacturing processes. Entered Toyokawa in 1956 as chief industrial engineer. In 1957 he became chief of manufacturing.

Isamu Tada (50) graduated in business from Z University. Entered Toyokawa in 1934 where he has held several supervisory positions in sales. He is now head of the Company's Osaka branch office.

Shoji Yagi (62) graduated from X Higher Commercial School. Entered Akasaka Machinery Company in 1919 and was head of Q Production office in 1954 when he moved to Toyokawa at head of the Sales Department. He is now Factory Manager.

tion of policy and of general plans of action, and took part in communicating these policies and plans. He did not participate in the detailing of these plans, or in coordinating the actions to be taken by the various departments.

In addition to these steps to insure communication at the management level, the President laid stress on effective communication with officials of the Company's union. He regularly "sat in" on negotiation meetings, and special meetings which were occasionally held to "inform" union officials of recent developments concerning Company policies and plans. The Company had not had a strike or a work stoppage since 1947.

In addition to the monthly operating reports and statements of financial condition, President Nishina received a weekly report, in writing, from the manager of each department—planning, sales, manufacturing, engineering, and administration—as well as from Messrs. Ito, Oki, and Yagi. These reports covered any matter concerning which the writer felt the President should be informed, and any matter on which they desired a decision from him. The President also maintained a series of notebooks in which he jotted down ideas or questions which he desired to refer to members of his management. For example, he had just noted a trade journal's forecast of an increase in industrial construction in a particular area, and he wished to know what special action the sales manager was planning in this regard. This question, and others like it, was written in the notebook almost daily, and the President's secretary was charged with circulating the questions and obtaining prompt replies. All of these procedures reflected President Nishina's stated desire to make clear designations of authority and responsibility, to make specific assignments to individuals, and to follow-up promptly on assignments made.

REORGANIZATION

The successive organizations of the Company from 1955 through March, 1959 are shown on Exhibits 15, 16, and 17. President Nishina "inherited" the second of these organizations (Exhibit 16) when he became president in June, 1957. At this time he succeeded Mr. Ueno, as chief operating executive, while Mr. Ueno became chairman of the Board of Directors. The organization which he acquired did not, in Mr. Nishina's opinion, permit clear-cut assignments of authority and responsibility, nor did it lend itself readily to control through the use of accounting data. Because of the many shocks which the management personnel had already experienced, and because he wished to plan his moves carefully, he deferred making any significant organizational changes until May, 1958. The action taken at that time (Exhibit 17) set up separate sections within each factory department for each major product line. Within the engineering department, for example, were placed sections for appliance "A," appliance "B," construction materials, and miscellaneous products, as well as for research and for scheduling. At the same time adjustments were made in the

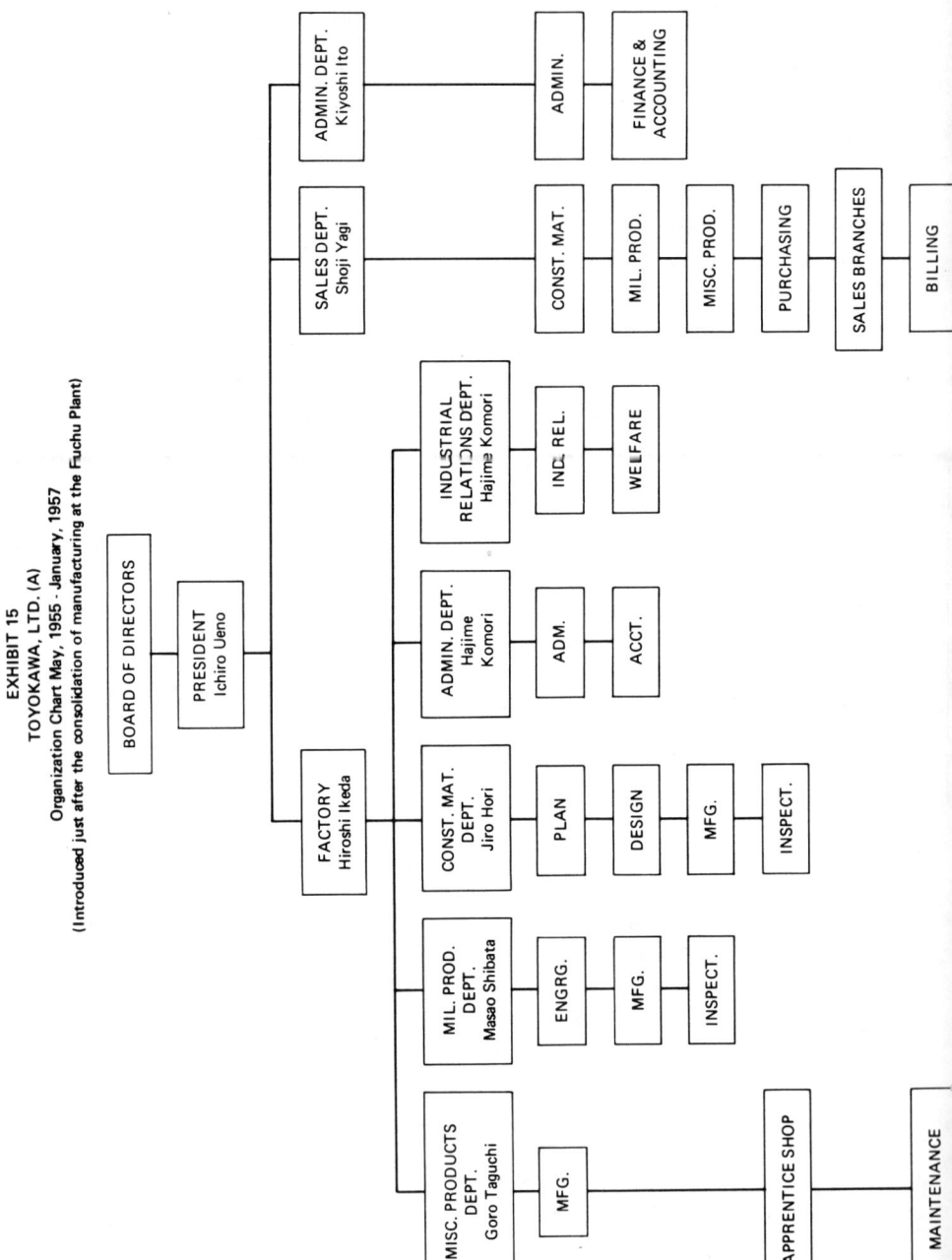

Toyokawa

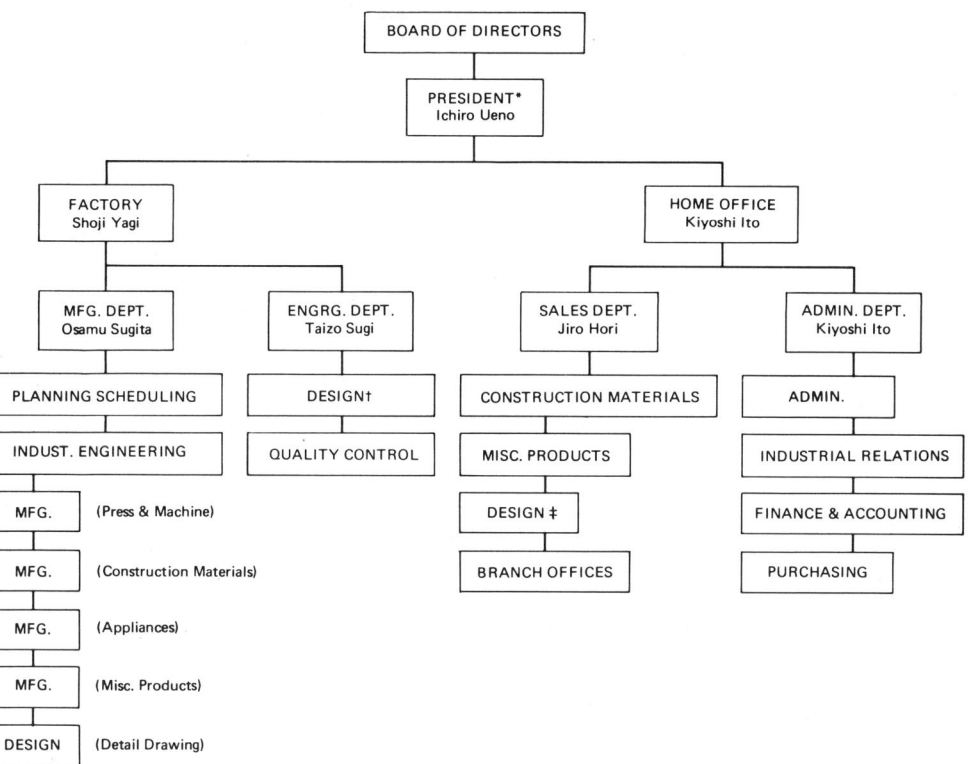

**EXHIBIT 16
TOYOKAWA, LTD. (A)
Organization Chart January, 1957 - May, 1958
(Introduced following cessation of arms production in Jan., 1957)**

*Keizo Nishina became president in June '57.

†Design with other than for construction materials.

‡ Design Proposals for submission to purchasers of construction materials.

Company's accounting procedures to permit cost data to be collected in accordance with the new organizational structure. Increases in salaries were made at the time of the change to ease the shock of reduced responsibility and to help create a favorable atmosphere.

It soon developed that the old problems of coordination were still with the Company, however. On one occasion the sales section for construction materials committed the manufacturing section to deliver 130 million yen of product in a 30 day period whereas "normal" production capacity was only 78 million yen. As a consequence, overtime, subcontracting, and delivery by special truck was necessary to meet the obligations made, all of which increased costs considerably. Even more costly were lengthy stoppages of the production of appliance "A" by order of the Akasaka Machinery Company because of problems in

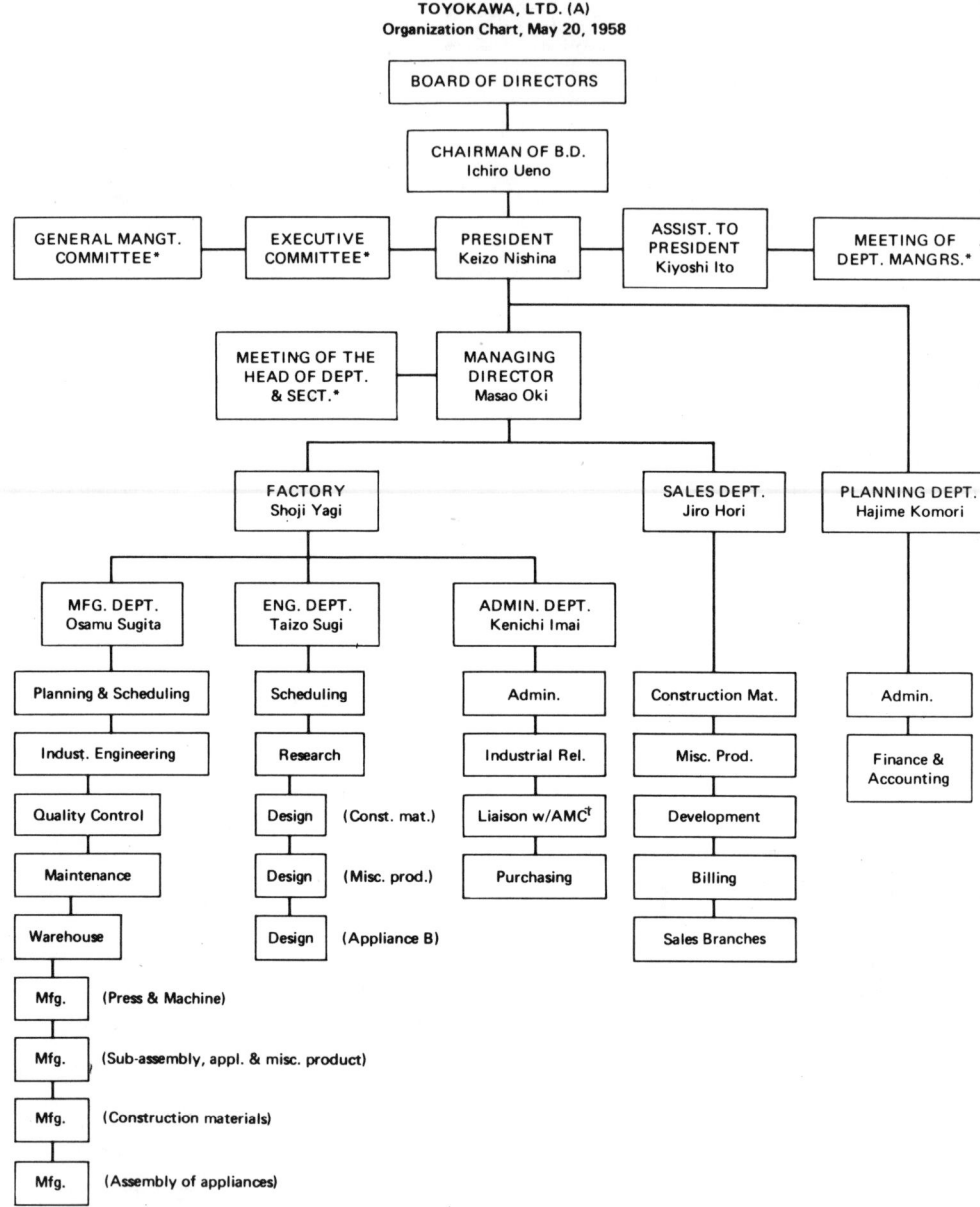

the field. These problems were eventually attributed to Toyokawa's design and inspection sections. A similar problem with appliance "B" also occurred and, to complicate matters, Akasaka reduced its requirements of "A" and "B" so that the lost production volume was not made up.

These events occurred between May and December, 1958, during which time Mr. Komori, Chief of Planning and a director, made a short visit to the United States as one of a team of management specialists. Upon Mr. Komori's return, he and the President discussed at length the possibility of further delineating responsibility and authority through the establishment of product divisions. In addition to providing a cost and profit center for each product line, and simplifying coordination of sales and production, it was thought that the divisional organization would help to develop top level executives. Each division manager would be, in effect, president of a subsidiary company and, as such, would develop skill in coordinating sales, production, and other aspects of a division. After the new organization was introduced, Mr. Nishina expected to devote a major portion of his time to helping the division managers develop the necessary administrative attitudes and skills.

The Board of Directors approved "in principle" the new organizational plan in January, 1959 and by the following March the general framework of the new organization had been decided upon by the Executive Committee. There were to be three product divisions—Construction Materials, Appliances, and Miscellaneous Products. Each division was to include sections for manufacturing, engineering, and sales. In addition to these product divisions, there was to be a Planning Division (industrial relations, finance, and accounting, planning, and administrative), an Engineering Division (industrial engineering, plant engineering and maintenance, research), and a centralized Purchasing Section. The chief of the Planning Division was to report to the President, while the chiefs of the product divisions, the Engineering Department and the Purchasing Section, and all other division chiefs were to report to the Managing Director. Manufacturing facilities were to be physically grouped by divisions.

As of March, 1959, Mr. Nishina and Mr. Komori felt that the following things remained to be accomplished.

> Prepare job descriptions for the new positions beginning with division chiefs.
> Plan the distribution of physical assets (office, factory, and warehouse space, tools and equipment) and personnel.
> Plan new communication vehicles and channels, including committees.
> Plan appropriate changes in accounting procedures and budgets.
> Plan the timing and the announcement of the change.
> Allocate responsibility for these tasks and establish a time schedule for performance.

After outlining these steps, President Nishina observed that he was now thinking about three items in particular. One was the fact that Mr. Osamu Sugita, the Executive Committee's choice for manager of the Appliance Division, though well qualified in manufacturing, was not experienced in product design or in sales.

Mr. Sugita, 53, had graduated from the machinery department of a well-known prefectural technical school, following which he had specialized in manufacturing with the Akasaka Machinery Company. After rising to become head of the latter's manufacturing process section, Mr. Sugita had joined Mr. Nishina at Toyokawa where he again specialized in manufacturing Akasaka Machinery Company. After rising to become head of the latter's process section, Mr. Sugita had joined Mr. Nishina at Toyokawa where he again specialized in manufacturing processes. At present Mr. Sugita was Manager of Manufacturing—a critical position, in Mr. Nishina's opinion.

A second problem concerned the physical distribution of equipment. For a number of reasons—control of costs and of personnel, flow of materials, and so forth—it was desired that each division operate within a particular factory area and that its equipment be concentrated in that area. Because of the similarities in the manufacturing processes, however, much of the present plant equipment located in the factory areas designated "Shear and Bend," "Press and Punch," and "Machine Shop" (see Exhibit 12) was used in the production of two or even three of the proposed divisional products. In cases of such multiple usage, the equipment could either be duplicated or shared. If it was to be shared, there were still some alternatives. In a similar situation at an Akasaka Machinery Company plant, Mr. Nishina recalled, control of certain shared machinery had been given to the division which had previously used it the highest per cent of hours. Intense competition for the use of the shared machinery had then developed, with some divisions complaining of delays and unfair allocation. Finally most of the disputed machinery was transferred to a "neutral" division which operated it on a service basis. Mr. Nishina had suggested a similar neutral division at Toyokawa, but the rest of the Executive Committee favored outright allocation to the major user. "Its their decision," said Mr. Nishina.

A third matter was Mr. Nishina's concern over the reaction of Toyokawa's middle management to the coming reorganization. There were several factors involved—one was the natural resistance to change, especially when it came as frequently as it had recently at Toyokawa. He was conscious of some dissatisfaction on this account, "They say I like to 'play' with the organization," he said. Another was the further diminution of certain positions and the concurrent enhancement of others. Since one effort of the change was to "down grade" some positions by dividing them into three parts, a considerable amount of attention in the management committees was given to advance discussion of the purpose of the change and its anticipated benefits.

Finally, Mr. Nishina wondered whether it was really advisable to prepare position descriptions in advance of the actual organizational change. He thought that the new incumbents might benefit from writing their own position descriptions after they had begun their duties. Also Mr. Nishina was certain that the position descriptions for activities below the level of division manager should be written after the organizational change had occurred so that their preparation could be supervised by the respective division managers. The preparation of position descriptions would be a new experience for the Toyokawa management —no such descriptions for managerial posts were now in use nor had they been in use previously. Presently the only activity or responsibility descriptions within management pertained to the functions of sub-divisions within sections ("units").

COMPANY OBJECTIVES

When President Nishina reflected on the future of Toyokawa, Ltd., one of his first concerns was that of assuring the Company's independence. He recalled that when he had first come to the Company the Toyokawa employees had been worried about the possibility that Toyokawa would lose its independent identity, that it would become merely a sub-contractor for the Akasaka Machinery Company. Mr. Nishina had felt that the employees' fears were unwarranted, that it was quite possible for the Company to enjoy an independent existence, and he explained that he had made a great effort to dispel the feeling that Toyokawa was dominated by Akasaka.

The basis of all of the Company's policies, he said, was service—service to customers, service to employees, service to stockholders, service to the community. In respect to customers, the rendering of service could be accomplished by establishing control over quality, control over costs, and control over delivery (by means of production control). In regard to employees and the community he said,

> We want our employees to have a feeling of satisfaction, of well being and security in their work. Our organizational changes are not merely to improve our operations, but also to provide opportunities for employees to develop. We want to develop all levels of employees by appropriate means—from study in specific fields such as motion study and plant layout to personal coaching at the general administrative levels. In all of our activities we want, of course, to contribute to the welfare of the nation.

In the application of these principles, President Nishina stated that he had three immediate objectives:

1. to reduce the cost level of the construction material line through increased use of "service centers"
2. to reduce the cost of appliance production through concentration on purchasing activities and to improve appliance deliveries by the provision

of a five-day inventory level for all components of products "A" and "B"

3. to expand sales of "miscellaneous" products by applying more aggressive sales effort to the products which Toyokawa had already developed.

In thinking about product development, President Nishina was particularly desired that Toyokawa manufacture appliances and other products for distribution under the Toyokawa brand name. In respect to consumer products he said,

> We do not have direct contact with the public now, and I am thinking about how this might be arranged without disrupting our relationship with Akasaka. Perhaps by a lower priced line of products "A" and "B," or perhaps we might produce new products which, after market testing could be transferred to Akasaka if that was desired.

In selecting new products for development, the President noted that the first requisite was that the Company possess the necessary engineering "know-how." Next in importance to the development of the product from a design standpoint, he considered the existing sales organization to be the most probable limiting factor.

As soon as he felt that the immediate problems connected with the coming reorganization were under control, President Nishina planned to turn his attention to a long range program of "managerial development." This would include the training of the division managers and the preparation of position descriptions as first steps, followed by the installation of a "standard cost system" in 1960 and increased emphasis on the application of industrial engineering techniques to the manufacturing process. These items, he said, would be part of a step by step program for increasing the effectives of the Toyokawa management. President Nishina was having some difficulty, however, in deciding which items in this step by step program warranted the highest priority and the most emphasis.

The Philippines

20

Interview with Earl Carroll*†

Mr. David B. Zenoff:	There's a statement which goes, "What's good for business is good for the economy." Would you say that's true in the Philippines?
Mr. Earl Carroll:	Good business is good for the government, especially business that is geared to and has its sights on the common good of the masses of the people. Conceivably there could be businesses which would not be good for the government, depending on management and management's outlook with reference to its contribution to the over-all good. I fully feel and believe that as between private enterprise and what might be called government socialism, private enterprise represented by alert, wide-awake, and dedicated business would be much better for the economy of any country.
Mr. Zenoff:	From your viewpoint, at what stage in industrialization is the Philippines now in?
Mr. Carroll:	We are inclined to think that the Philippines is now in what is referred to by some economists as the "take-off" stage. I believe that this is true. The base or the runway has been prepared, and, I feel that to carry the analogy further, the airplane is basically sound and is ready for the take-off.
	I feel that here in the Philippines there has been an overemphasis on so-called industrialization, and so far the concern with developing industry has lost sight of the basic necessity for agriculture. Our company is now engaged in the development of a large-scale, agricultural project in the northwestern part of Luzon, primarily for the purpose of bringing to the attention of the people as well as business leaders and government officials the importance of agriculture as the base for the further development of industry, and partly to demonstrate how private enterprise can help solve the "land for the landless" problem. We propose to

*This case *Interview with Earl Carroll,* PC30, was prepared by Mr. David B. Zenoff under the direction of Professor Harry L. Hansen of the Harvard University Graduate School of Business Administration as the basis for class discussion rather than to illustrate either effective or ineffective handling of an administrative situation.

†Copyright © 1966 by the President and Fellows of Harvard College.

provide small farms for qualified, trained graduates from the various agricultural schools and to build the individually-owned farm project around a central farm and community owned by the company. While there was in our mind the idea of demonstrating how land could be provided at very nominal cost to prospective, good, young farmers, we did want to demonstrate in what might be called a "glamorous" way, the necessity for providing the agricultural base for an industrial development.

There is management personnel in the Philippines thoroughly capable of managing their own projects or cooperating with foreign groups which may enter the country on a joint basis. There is considerable latent or hidden capital in the nation which needs to be mobilized and which, if mobilized, can be used for industrial purposes and for agricultural development projects. Added together, these factors seem to me to indicate that the Philippines is in what was referred to at the outset as the take-off stage on its development flight.

Mr. Zenoff: Following up on what you were just saying, as far as its investment portfolio is concerned, do you feel that your company has a definite responsibility to the country to undertake such projects as this large agricultural experiment?

Mr. Carroll: The original decision to incorporate ... the original concept for the incorporation of the Phillipine American Life was primarily to mobilize the savings of the people and to retain those savings in the country and invest them for the good of the nation. We have followed this policy rather strictly and consistently, and the cooperation of thousands of persons who have become policyholders has enabled us to accumulate assets of approximately 150 million within a period of 14 years. Excepting for reinsurance premiums and very nominal dividends, this money has been plowed back into the economy of the nation and programs, such as the agricultural project, housing project, industrial projects, etc. We sincerely feel that as a private financial institution we should make investments of this nature and contribute as best we can to over-all economic development of the nation. We feel also that other American and foreign-owned institutions operating in the country should do likewise and that, if they should, the need for government-to-government or government-to private-enterprise aid, commonly known as AID, would become less and less necessary and would demonstrate the basic American principle of development through private enterprise.

Interview with Earl Carroll

Mr. Zenoff: Would you say in addition that a foreign company investing in the Philippines has an extra-special duty to this country to invest its capital in ways which will necessarily help in the over-all economic development of the country? Or, conversely, do you feel that a foreign company has no more responsibility to industrialization of the Philippines than does a 60%-or 100%-owned Filipino company?

Mr. Carroll: I am not sure that too many would agree; but I feel that any company, completely foreign or partly foreign-owned, has a definite responsibility under the present world-wide concept of developing underdeveloped countries to invest their capital and some of their profits on that capital in the nation for the development of the country. This may be considered an altruistic attitude, but the United States Government is spending roughly $4 billion annually for aid to so-called underdeveloped countries, using taxpayers' money for such purposes. It seems to me that private enterprise operating abroad and seeking to make profits abroad should feel some responsibility for improving the countries where they operate, not only from an altruistic or idealistic viewpoint but from the viewpoint of increasing their own potential for business. We feel in Philamlife that to the extent we contribute to the development of the over-all economy and the prosperity of the individual family, we create prospects for improved and increased business for our company. I feel that this present situation in Cuba would not have developed had the foreign companies operating there been more concerned with the situation of the peasants; and had the lot of the peasant been better, the success of Castro might not have been possible. I have observed here in the Philippines that the people as a whole look with great favor upon American—especially American—and other foreign concerns that take an interest in the development of the country and demonstrate that interest through practical investments. And it seems to me that even the United States Government should encourage private enterprise to do more of this type of thing.

Mr. Zenoff: Do you think that under this present system of decontrol, where capital flowing into and from this country has fairly free rein, the Philippine government would be wise to legislate the kinds of feelings that you have expressed about the responsibility of a foreign firm doing business here, so that it will be ensured that the foreign firm will indeed be helping in the growth process of this nation?

Mr. Carroll: Personally I would prefer that this type of thing not need nor require legislation. We have not sought in this country any legislation other than an amendment to the insurance laws which were lightly antiquated to enable the investment of the funds available to us for projects such as we felt were good for the country. Conceivably there are other business and industrial establishments which would prefer or want or require guarantees through legislation of continuing government policies favorable to their interests. But our feeling and experience have been that if we demonstrate good will, sincerity, and an earnest desire to help build the nation, we do not need any legislative guarantees. However, I realize that there is much capital or funds for investment abroad which might be called timid due to the lack of long-term experience in dealing with so-called underdeveloped countries and their economies. For this type of investor legislated guarantees would be most attractive and would be good for the country passing such legislation.

Mr. Zenoff: What is your attitude about the existing Filipino First legislation?

Mr. Carroll: I sincerely doubt that the nation can legislate its people into priority business positions, and emphasis should be placed more on helping the nationals to compete with so-called foreign-controlled groups rather than to seek to force them out of certain types of business by legislation. There is no doubt that the nationals of the country should adequately participate in the economics, in the business of the nation, retail and otherwise, and that in the long-range viewpoint they should dominate, if they do not dominate at the present time. Personally I would prefer to see this type of control or domination by the nationals come about through normal, competitive, free enterprise methods than to be forced through legislative processes. And I think here in the Philippines it remains to be seen as to whether or not some of the so-called Filipino First legislation will prove to be entirely beneficial.

Mr. Zenoff: Looking ahead to the further growth of the Philippines, what are the kinds of present shortages in this country's factors of production and resources which will be important in determining the rate and the direction of whatever growth that does take place in the future?

Mr. Carroll: I feel that compared to some of the other countries of Southeast Asia, the Philippines is in a favorable position. I recall several years ago when Caltex contemplated the construction of an oil refinery and their officials were discussing with us a housing project for foreign technicians and managers, the project was abandoned because they found many more qualified technicians in the Philippines than they had expected to find based on their experiences in other countries. While the Philippines is fortunate in having qualified technicians and a fairly reasonable source of management personnel, there is still an inadequate number of such qualified technicians and managers for the big development which this country should have and to which it is entitled. There is also a definite lack of capital even though there is much latent or hidden capital in the nation which could be used if properly mobilized. As for the export market, there are many things in this country which would be acceptable abroad, but one of the problems has been the lack of understanding of the potential and the necessity for large-scale production to meet requirements of a large selling organization, such as Macy's of New York for illustration. There is also an understandable lack of knowledge of the requirements of the foreign market for uniform quality, uniform size, and other uniform standards. To maintain a constant market abroad, the product shipped during the second year should be equally as good and as uniform in size and quality as the original product.

Mr. Zenoff: One of the aspects of doing business in this country that has been a source of surprise to me is the concept of a very high rate of return on invested capital by most companies here. Would you say that the concept that a business isn't worth getting into unless you could make 20% or more rate of return on equity, and I would say that's quite a minimum figure from what I have heard, is damaging to this country's economy?

Mr. Carroll: I believe that too much emphasis has been placed by both foreigners and Filipinos on how much they can get instead of how much they can contribute. I recall a board of directors meeting of a Philippine corporation (American-owned) several years ago when, during a discussion about a certain investment, one of the more discerning, more mature Filipinos present impatiently banged at the desk or director's table and asked the same question I have previously asked; namely, how long must we think in terms of what we can get rather than in terms of what we can give? To the extent that each business, financial, or industrial organization seeks to squeeze out the greatest possible profit, to that extent the economy of the country on an over-all basis is handicapped because the products which should flow to the common man throughout the nation cost more than he is able to pay, and consequently distribution or sales is correspondingly limited. Cement, for illustration, can be delivered in this country at U.S. Armed Forces bases at a lower price than the local cement companies can produce cement and deliver it to the bases, thereby handicapping the cement industry in this country. The same situation prevails with reference to sugar because the cost of production of sugar in this country at the present time is such that, or to state it differently, the profits which the sugar barons have become accustomed to are such that when the tariffs are applied by the United States in an increasing degree, the sugar industry will be adversely affected. I feel that unless and until investors in the Philippines are willing to take less of the income from their businesses, or until they are satisfied with a smaller return than is now expected, the continued development of the country agriculturally, economically, and industrially will be retarded.

Mr. Zenoff: Now if we could ask a few questions about what we might term as your "management philosophy," about the way that you feel is best to manage the affairs of the Philamlife company. Could you talk about your concept of delegation of authority in the company? Has it changed over the time that the company has been in existence and, if so, why? Do you find any especially great difficulties along this line which you might attribute to being in a new, emerging country as compared with, let's say, the United States or Europe? And, if so, how in any way are you trying to erase such problems for the future benefit of the company and its personnel?

Mr. Carroll: From the very outset we have insisted on a policy of recruiting and using to the fullest extent the best Filipino personnel we could obtain locally, and I feel that our efforts along this line have been most successful. Presently I am the only American actively engaged in the management of Philamlife and with few exceptions have been the only American involved in direct company management. At the very outset our first president was a Filipino, and we have sought out what we considered to be some of the best brains of the country to serve as vice presidents. As they have been recruited, they have been given authority and responsibility commensurate with their titles and abilities.

Our junior personnel policy has been the same, i.e., with reference to junior executives, we have quickly and gladly taken on young men who have returned from the United States and Europe who have shown ability for our type of work and who have educational backgrounds which qualify them for our type of operation. At the present time we have approximately twenty assistant vice presidents, all of whom are very capable, comparatively young Filipinos who have the background of education and experience which make them capable of accepting and carrying out responsibilities assigned to them. We have delegated responsibility and authority to vice presidents and assistant vice presidents and department managers as rapidly as these responsibilities and this authority could be absorbed. On many occasions our executives have visited my office to get what they refer to as a policy decision. Having obtained such a policy decision, they have gone out to implement this so-called decision on the basis that they felt was most appropriate. We have followed a policy of allowing these men to work out their own solutions to problems and their own methods of implementation.

I have found that in the delegation of authority and responsibility, my associates have accepted and reacted in a manner which could be expected in the Orient. Sometimes most of us from the Occident are too overconcerned with having things done our way and usually wrongly feel that it must be done the occidental way rather than in the so-called oriental way. This poses a problem for many foreigners who come to the Orient and who are too impatient to get going on their basis rather than on the ways of the Orient. I have had occasion to observe persons who have been exceedingly successful in the United States in certain types of business, who upon coming to the Orient have not been successful because they have not been able to orient their thinking and their method of acting to the pattern of operations and thinking in this part of the world. The so-called high-pressure, hard-hitting tactics used in American selling, American management, and American methods of doing business are not always acceptable in this part of the world and must be modified to conform with established customs, the thinking of the people, and the habits of the people. I feel that the most successful foreign businessman in the Orient is the one who, while sticking to his basic and fundamental principles, still seeks to adjust himself to his surroundings and to mellow his basic tactics with the sometimes superior method of doing things in the Orient. I have found in my own organization that when my associates have worked out their own solutions in accordance with basic policy decisions, the results have been better than if I had personally attempted to seek the solution or implement the decision. In other words, there are many fine, capable, young and older men who in their own ways and in accordance with their own understanding of other people

	can do a fine job and sometimes and most frequently a better job than an imported outsider who may or may not have a much broader and much keener technical ability.
Mr. Zenoff:	From the few weeks that I have spent in and around your company writing cases, I have heard it said by a number of people that in their own case, or in cases of other men whom they know working in Philamlife, if they were given offers of higher pay or slightly higher positions in other companies in the Philippines, probably the greatest deterrent to their leaving Philamlife would be their respect and loyalty to you. Without embarrassing you by asking for too much comment on this, I wonder if it would be possible for you to explain how you, the man, deal with both men within your company and outside and why your behavior has elicited such great loyalty from your employees?
Mr. Carroll:	I have been told about this type of loyalty by many persons and some of the persons directly involved, and of course I deeply appreciate it. I suppose that it is based partly on a sincere feeling of respect for all persons with whom I am associated, from the janitors and elevator boys on up to the executive vice president. I have been told also by many persons that they can always expect a sympathetic hearing and a fair decision and a consistency in dealing with the various people in our organization. I feel that Filipinos respect fairness, sincerity, and straightforwardness, and they will accept a decision adverse to their own interest if they feel it has been made in good faith. I recall some years ago making a decision against one of our men which cost him several hundred pesos; but once the decision had been made, he asked me to join him for a cup of coffee along with his opponent. In the coffee shop he said he wanted to sit down for coffee because he respected my decision even though it was costly to him because he felt it had been absolutely fair, and that all of the factors impinging on the problem had been clearly and fully discussed. This person died only recently, but until his dying day he remained one of my very good friends.

Only a few days ago, I received a letter from one of our top sales managers in which he reported having received a picture taken of me in my office sitting in the little rock garden. I was not aware that the picture had been sent to him or I had forgotten about it. Meanwhile I had sent him a more formal picture in response to his request for a picture for his office. He replied that he was discarding the businessman picture and taking the other picture which he fondly referred to as the "father" picture. He went ahead to say that even if we had 80,000 agents, one |

billion of assets, and 100 billion of insurance in force, and 10,000 employees, and 10 or 15,000 other miscellaneous persons involved in our organization, I would still be the father to all of them. The foregoing may seem impertinent or bragging, but nevertheless it actually happened and probably is a partial answer to the question you have asked.

21

Eduardo Mendoza, Inc.*†

Eduardo Mendoza was a ₱3,000 a month account executive for the Motta Advertising Agency, one of the Philippines' largest agencies. His responsibilities included planning advertising strategy, layout, and campaigns for three large accounts: Fresh-Up, a leading selling carbonated beverage, Lapu milk products, and Ram's Bars, the largest selling Filipino candy bar.[1]

As a result of his 11 years of advertising and promotional experience, Eduardo had come to occupy the key account executive's role with MAA and was informally considered to be the "number two man" in the firm's operation. The manager, Abelardo Victoria, was the same age as Mendoza, 41, and had occupied his position for two years. He, too, had over 10 years of advertising experience and was considered by MAA owners, employees, and Philippine advertisers to be competent, hard working, and "a leader in promoting the role of advertising agencies in the Philippine economy."

At this time, Eduardo was considering the merits of leaving MAA and beginning his own agency. He stated the situation:

> The volume of advertising in this country has been greatly increasing since the war (see Exhibit 1 for a review of Philippine advertising). I feel that I have the background and ability to share directly in this growth; yet, as I set here with MAA I ask myself, where am I going? No place! Abe (the manager) is my age, does a good job, and is probably here to stay for years to come; so what can I expect in the way of advancement? I now have, and have had for four years, the three largest accounts this company handles, but apparently this is as far up the management ladder Ed Mendoza can go; they haven't even seen fit to create an assistant manager's title for me.
>
> What I'd like is to be my own boss and to improve myself financially. I've always figured that it takes three ingredients to go on my own and be a success: guts, self-confidence (from experience), and capital. Before, I might have had one or two of them but never all three. Now I have them all.

*Copyright ©1966 by the President and Fellows of Harvard College.

†This case, Eduardo Mendoza, Inc., PC30, was made possible by the cooperation of a business firm which remains anonymous. It was prepared by David B. Zenoff under the direction of Prof. Harry L. Hansen of the Harvard University Graduate School of Business Administration as the basis for class discussion rather than to illustrate either effective or ineffective handling of an administrative situation.

[1] These three accounts comprised one of the largest advertising budgets in the country covering all media of advertising.

Eduardo Mendoza, Inc.

EXHIBIT 1
EDUARDO MENDOZA, INC.
A Prewar History of Advertising in the Philippines*

Before the Battle of Manila Bay, firms in the Philippines were not advertising-conscious. The local retail store doing business on a corner location depended for its volume of business on actual contact with consumers. The science of advertising was practically unknown except for announcements in the local publications available at the time.

With the advent of the American regime, which closely followed the Spanish-American War, Filipinos were introduced to the American way of doing business. Soon merchants found out that by spending a little more in advertising they could expand their operations not only within their immediate locality but also within a bigger area embracing the surrounding provinces. Hand bills were one of the few advertising media introduced by the new group of American entrepreneurs. Bigger and better sign boards at places of business appeared. However, it was not until the advent of modern newspapers and publications that advertising forged ahead.

During those days most of the advertisements did not carry any illustrations to enhance the messages. The use of bigger types and poster-style ads were in effect. The advertiser usually left the appearance of his ad to the advertising solicitor who was not an experienced or trained ad writer himself. However, with the organization of the trading firm, Pacific Commercial Company, advertising layouts began to look more attractive. One of the most important departments in the new organization was the advertising and sales promotion department. Leaflets, over-all brochures, and metal signs were distributed by the firm to complement their newspaper advertising.

The University of the Philippines and several other private colleges existing at the time did not have any subject on advertising in their curriculums. The training of advertising men was left in the hands of the advertising managers of the newspapers.

Before the war there was only one advertising agency, the Advertising Bureau, which was operated without any conformity to the standard practices of United States advertising agencies. Because of the big demand for advertising work, the firm handled not only the advertising of firms but also the solicitation of advertisements for their own publications.

Shortly thereafter, another agency went into the field, and this was followed by a third agency specializing in screen processing. Because of the limited number of agencies and the type of service that they were giving to their clients, almost all of the big firms had their own advertising departments complete even to artist and messengers.

With the advent of World War II, advertising became an extinct profession during the Japanese regime. Most of the big advertising men refused to work for the Japanese information bureau. Some of them eked out a living by farming and selling real estate while others went underground.

After the war, there was a great demand for all kinds of American products, and with the volume of advertising demanded it was only natural that advertising agencies began to develop.

The Philippine Advertising Industry

(from *Insurance and Finance*, August 1958)

The postwar development of modern advertising in the Philippines is characterized with phenomenal strides stimulated by the growth of new industries manufacturing consumers goods and of new media for advertising.

What is today's status of advertising in the Philippines?

Art Domingo, President of Art Domingo and Associates and of the Association of Philippine Advertising Agencies, observed that the Philippine advertising industry is on a par with that of other countries. He said that most of the advertising agencies in the country are either branches of large advertising companies or affiliates of international advertising networks. Their work has to pass rigid standards acceptable everywhere.

William J. Dunn, general manager of the Philippine branch of J. Walter Thompson, said: "If business here was so backward and poor, we would be the first to go out. The performance of the agency here has equalled that of the other branches and even that of the home office."

In the art and copy work, advertising factors in the Philippines report excellent performance. Local copies in many instances are original and can compare well with American ad copies. "Many of the original ad copies created in town are mistaken for copies done in the United States," Mr. Dunn disclosed. To emphasize his point, Dunn pointed out that the ad copies of the Philippine Manufacturing Company, a subsidiary of the Procter and Gamble Company of the United States, are all processed here in Manila.

EXHIBIT 1 (continued)

The advertising agencies are expanding their services. They are going into marketing and management research.

According to Francisco T. Lopez, President of the Philippine Advertising Research Association, research budgets are improving. Lopez revealed that there have been researches on both the quantitative and qualitative values of advertising.

Moving forward thus, the Philippine advertising industry is on a par with that of other countries, and in the East, the Philippine advertising industry is believed to be ahead. However, the industry plans more improvements in its techniques and methods.

Views of Advertising Executives
By J. C. Brambles

(from *Insurance and Finance*, August 1958)

FORDHAM J. JOHNSON
Goodrich International Rubber Company

I'd say the local advertising industry is comparable with that in most of the areas of the world I have worked in before, much better than most of the European countries.

Everything we use here originates in the country. Whatever originates from the States, our agency gives it the local flavor. All of the radio jingles we use for our radio programs have been created in the country.

I'd say there are not really many problems. We have everything, papers, magazines, radio, TV, and they're just as good as those anywhere else. But as far as we are concerned, it is impossible to follow an advertising budget. There are so many supplements that come up. And in this case advertising budgets cannot be realistic.

I cannot give the figure in our budget. The largest item goes to print, then radio, TV, and billboards come next. We have all sorts of advertising gimmicks like give-aways and displays, but we are not using direct mail. I don't think it would be effective for our purpose.

JAMES BRAMBLES
Goodyear Tire and Rubber Company of the Philippines, Ltd.

I think there is a growing consciousness here of the value of advertising.

Problems? Let's put it this way. We have an advertising budget and have to follow it right to the penny. There are so many Sunday magazine supplements that come up in the major publications, and it is difficult for us to turn them down. These things disrupt our advertising budget. But in this event we take it from our reserves or take the money from the smaller items or smaller magazines.

I think there is a tremendous amount invested in advertising. I cannot reveal the amount my company is setting aside for advertising. But I'd say that 50% of the budget goes to print, 30% for radio-TV, and the rest is divided among the other media.

I always believe that advertising is doing its job, but to what degree, I can't say. I mean there is no way of telling as yet how effective advertising is. Well, in the United States the home company has done that, but we have not done it here. I would not be able to say how much sale is generated by advertising. We may measure the effectiveness of our advertising, but that will be in the future. And I can't say when.

ERNESTO PERALTA
Standard Vacuum Oil Company

There is a growing consciousness here of advertising as a sales tool. The foremost problem of advertisers now is the budget. This has been brought about by controls. Major advertisers are being faced with a decreasing budget, forcing them to make a rigid selection of media.

With a limited advertising budget our hands are tied. Figures in our advertising budget I cannot release to you. In our case, a petroleum company, we have a wide gamut of advertising activities. We have prints, radio-TV, trade magazine displays, show window displays, give-aways, and other sales and promotion gimmicks. The largest portion of our budget goes to print. Radio-TV comes next. The rest is spread over the other media.

At the moment there is no way to gauge the effectiveness of advertising campaigns. We are trying to find means how to gauge it. But this would take a large sum of money to do effectively. One thing sure, we are convinced that advertising is effective. Just in what degree of effectiveness each of the media is, we have not figured it out yet.

Eduardo Mendoza, Inc.

EXHIBIT 1 (continued)

The New Role for Advertising-Marketing Management
By Antonio R. de Joya
Executive Vice President, Advertising and Marketing Associates

In considering the new role for advertising-marketing management, there is observed the subtle but nonetheless positive change in the longstanding partnership between sales and advertising, as more and more concerns gear and reorganize for consumer-oriented marketing. So far, advertising has played a predominantly minor role. Advertising practitioners have been hired in the manner of an expert who is expected to provide mechanical or technical skill while planning and supervision have been reserved to the "senior partner," who, in many cases, has been the sales executive. To illustrate, it is a fact that many concerns assign the advertising executive immediately under the oversight of the sales executives; a condition, indeed, that confirms the subordinate role of advertising in the business enterprise. Yet, it is heartening to perceive that a definitive and substantive change in this relationship is in the making. Concerns reorganizing under the integrated marketing concept have come to an awareness of this fault and have tried to rectify this by elevating the status of advertising alongside sales, market research, and product planning. In some others, the functions of market planning are left for advertising to handle. But, undeniably, advertising is assuming newer and more responsible roles as the production-minded concern gives way to the modern consumer-oriented organization. We can anticipate therefore that in the very immediate future (and we are already working towards this ideal) marketing management will have under it several departments, sections, or divisions which possess a certain degree of automony but which are responsible to the marketing director. Such automonous entities will assume, coordinate, and co-equal roles. In my own personal conception, these units will likely be sales, advertising, sales promotion, market research, product planning, product development, brand management, public relations, and marketing finance. All of these will work together to accomplish integrated marketing operations.

Certain indications are present that promise a greater role in the planning and development areas for the advertising manager. Take the case of the advertising manager. The difficulty, it seems, with the present job of advertising manager is that he acts as an account executive in reverse. A lot of times, advertising managers do not think or act as advertising managers. They act as account executives. Consequently, they take over the job that properly belongs to the advertising account executive. And this is a trend which we must try to avoid.

The former role of "account executives in reverse" is evolving into one of staff assistant to the vice president or manager in charge of marketing, on the level equivalent to the sales manager, director of marketing research, product planning manager, and other related positions. In the spirit of all these developments, it is perhaps justifiable to expect the full assumption into the top marketing team of the communications executive. The mechanical services within the concern formerly rendered by advertising will be turned over with increasing frequency to the service departments of advertising agencies and other similar service organizations. And, too, the advertising director will have become a planner rather than a doer.

These developments may have engendered animosity between sales and advertising as a result of the loosening of the strong bonds of union that once were there. However, as the time lapses, this animosity is tending to disappear and be minimized due to the mutual recognition of the importance of coordinated effort for better sales performance. Under the modern marketing concept, there is the necessity of interdependence of the participants in the selling, advertising, and sales promotion processes. And naturally so since their objectives are singular and indivisible.

It is evident that the principal objective of advertising is not to create advertisements that will win awards or programs that will entertain. Advertising management must evaluate all its operations from the pragmatic, practical viewpoint of profit-creation. Advertising may only be considered an art from the viewpoint of the pure artist. From the standpoint of marketing management, however, it must be considered mainly as a marketing function capable of realizing defined corporate and marketing goals. If necessary, advertising must be forced out of its traditional role of information bearer to the consuming public. It must serve as a vital and dynamic force influencing the total demand sectors of the economy. All these changes need to come when we take on the new economic frontier, and while our time is a transition period bound to bridge the gap, we are to acknowledge the fact that the significance of the communications mix in general and of advertising in particular is fated to increase. This, of course, comes out of our realization that as the times become more complex and competitive, the total marketing function, the demand side of the economic coin, will yield more demands.

EXHIBIT 1 (continued)

An Advertisement Promoting Advertising
Manila Chronicle · July 14, 1961

MORE

to

SHARE . . .

Today, more people enjoy fine food, good clothes, better furnished homes at lower cost than ever before possible . . . because of advertising.

Mass selling, through advertising, has provided the impetus for continuous mass production which brings about, through competition, better quality goods at lower cost.

And other benefits show that there is greater employment all around and, therefore, increased purchasing power for more and more Filipino families. It is an endless cycle that generates better standards of living for everyone.

Doesn't it stand to reason we all should patronize advertised goods and services?

ASSOCIATION OF PHILIPPINE ADVERTISING AGENCIES

*SOURCE: PHILPROM, Inc.

Eduardo's past activities, position, and accomplishments included a college education, promotional activities for a liquor distiller in the Provinces, industrial partner and manager of an officers' club after the war, promotional work for a number of United States movie producers, and managing partner of an outdoor advertising company. In his opinion, these activities had given him wide experience in promotion, selling, merchandising, and advertising and had led to his becoming well known and respected in the marketing and media field.

As for acquiring the capital necessary to start his own firm, Eduardo thought that his reputation in the advertising field would attract lucrative clients. Furthermore, two of his close friends had shown interest in investing in his proposed agency.

Eduardo estimated that an initial ₱100,000 paid-in capitalization would suffice to get the new firm established. Exhibit 2 presents the estimated initial expenses and monthly working capital requirements. Although the usual practice among Philippine advertising agencies had been to obtain 100% paid-in subscription before commencing operations, Eduardo planned to deviate from this

EXHIBIT 2
EDUARDO MENDOZA, INC.
Total Estimated Advertising Volume in Philippines

1. Media	1960	Percent	1961	Percent	Percent Increase
Press	4,689,000	27	5,044,000	25	7.6
Radio	3,820,000	22	4,641,000	23	21.5
TV	1,563,000	9	2,220,000	11	42.0
Other*	7,293,00	42	8,273,000	41	13.4
TOTAL†	17,365,000	100	20,178,000	100	

†SOURCE: Survey of Members of Philippine Association of National Advertisers (30 of 48 answered).
*Others: Sound trucks, cinema, billboards, printed brochures.

2. Projections:

   (a) 100% of PANA members would bill ₱32,285,000

   (b) Historically, PANA's gross billings = 20% of gross billings in the country; therefore, total estimated advertising expenditures for 1961: ₱150,000,000.

3. NOTE: PANA is an association of 48 manufacturers and service-oriented businesses in the Philippines each having at least a minimum annual advertising budget of ₱50,000

"rule" for two reasons: (1) He decided to require that an investor in his agency must bring in one or two accounts in addition to ownership of capital. In this way, at the outset, the proposed firm would be the recipient of both pesos and business. (2) He desired to "keep the top open" on the ownership, so that in the future it would be possible to attract additional investors who also had sizeable business to bring in. Eduardo was convinced that this "capital plus business" policy for potential investors would enable his agency to circumvent a new agency's usual expectation of a 12 to 18 months' period of financial losses.

Obtaining trained personnel presented a greater problem in opening a new agency: the advertising agency business in the Philippines suffered from a lack of sufficiently trained personnel. Local colleges offered only one or two semesters of advertising courses, and the majority of established agencies either could not afford or had not yet begun training programs for young men in the field. Thus, Eduardo had the problem of trying to obtain capable and versatile personnel" who *knew* what advertising and marketing were all about," yet whose present salary demands were within the realm of the new firm's financial resources. As an example, Eduardo estimated that his art director and account executive at the outset would have to be satisfied with ₱500 a month salaries. Such compensation was only one-half to one-third of what experienced young advertising men were earning elsewhere.

EXHIBIT 2 (continued)

Selected Radio and TV Industry Figures*

1. Source of advertising billings:

   80% agencies
   20% direct from advertisers

2.
	1960	1961 (est.)	1966 (est.)
Total TV billings:	₱ 850,000	₱ 1,400,000	₱ 2,900,000
Total radio billings:	₱11,150,000	₱14,600,000	₱26,000,000

3. Total airtime billings by geographical sources

	1960	1966 (est.)
Manila	50%	30%
Provinces	50%	70%

4. Number of Radio Homes†

   a. In established radio centers: 20% of number of families

   b. In new radio centers: 10% of number of families

   c. In Manila and suburbs: 66% of number of families

   d. Total radio homes: 945,000

   e. Total TV homes: 32,000

   f. Average annual increase in number of radio homes since 1946: 20%

5. Number of Commercial Radio Stations (1961):

   a. 19 in Manila

   b. 51 in Provinces

6. Number of Commercial TV Stations (1961):

   a. Manila: 4

*SOURCE: ABS-CBN Network (Alto Broadcasting System-Chronicle Broadcasting Network)
†Estimated. Source: Ace Advertising Agency, Inc.

  The dearth of trained personnel and the limited payroll budget with which he contemplated commencing operations raised a further question: Would it be possible and, even if possible, advisable to start with a "skeleton" crew which might be hard pushed to handle the initial volume of business; or, alternatively, should he employ a "full" staff which would both impress the prospective clients with its size and have the necessary reservoir of personnel to actually handle the business? Exhibit 2 is based on the "skeleton" staff Eduardo had in

Eduardo Mendoza, Inc.

EXHIBIT 2 (continued)

Sample Print Media Costs (1961)

		Column Inch Rate*
1.	**Magazine Supplements**	
	Saturday Mirror Magazine	₱ 4.00
	Chinese Weekly	6.00
2.	**Newspapers**	
	Manila Chronicle	₱ 8.00
	Manila Times	10.00
	Philippine Herald	5.00
	Daily Mirror	3.00
3.	**Periodicals**	
	Weekly Graphic	₱ 8.00
	Philippine Free Press	18.00
	Woman's World	9.00
4.	**Movie Magazine**	
	Kislap-Movie	₱ 8.00
	Movie World	6.00
5.	**Rural Publications**	
	Baguio Midland Courier	₱ 2.50
	Mindanao Cross	2.50
	Zamboanga Times	3.00
6.	**Miscellaneous**	Full Page Rate
	Newsweek (Pacific Edition)	$515.00
	Orient Tours	₱250.00
	Phil. Inst. of Nursing	120.00
	American Chamber of Commerce	400.00

*One peso = one-third of a dollar.

mind. Exhibit 3 presents the additional expenses associated with a minimum sized "full" staff.

In assessing the growth and profit prospects for a new agency Eduardo noted that the experience of many United States and Filipino advertising agencies making a 15% commission on the gross billings they handled was a 1% to 3% profit on commissions.[2] Furthermore, it generally took one to two years for an agency to develop sufficient billings to become profitable. Eduardo's goal was to break even by the end of the first year.

[2] Appendix A gives some evidence on costs and profits of United States advertising agencies.

EXHIBIT 2 (continued)

Prewar and Postwar Publications and Their Estimated Circulations

Prewar Publications

Dailies		Estimated Circulation
The Tribune	(English)	25,000
La Vanguardia	(Spanish)	12,000
Taliba	(Tagalog)	20,000
Philippine Herald	(English)	22,000
El Debate	(Spanish)	12,000
Mabuhay	(Tagalog)	18,000
Manila Daily Bulletin	(English)	10,000
Fookien Times	(Chinese)	5,000
Chinese Com. News	(Chinese)	3,000
Kong Li Po	(Chinese)	3,000
La Opinion	(Spanish)	4,000

Weeklies | |
---|---|---
Liwayway | (Tagalog) | 110,000
Bannawag | (Ilocano) | 28,000
Bisaya | (Cebuano) | 32,000
Hiliggaynon | (Ilonggo) | 30,000
Ilang-Ilang | (Tagalog) | 5,000
Sunday Tribune | (English) | 78,000
Monday Mail | (English) | 105,000
Midweek Herald | (English) | 50,000
Philippines Free Press | (English and Spanish) | 30,000
Graphic | (English) | 65,000

Postwar Publications

Dailies | |
---|---|---
Manila Times | (English) | 129,000
Daily Mirror | (English) | 15,178
Manila Daily Bulletin | (English) | 23,000
Manila Chronicle | (English) | 44,655
Evening News | (English) | 31,000
Taliba | (Tagalog) | 20,206
Mabuhay | (Tagalog) | 20,371
El Debate | (Spanish) | 5,705
Philippine Herald | (English) | 44,837
Chinese Com. News | (Chinese) | 10,693
Fookien Times | (Chinese) | 12,765
Kong Li Po | (Chinese) | 8,858
Great China Press | (Chinese) | 7,817

Weeklies | |
---|---|---
Sunday Times Mag. | (English) | 181,713
This Week Mag. | (English) | 54,840
Weekly Women's | (English) | 53,221
Philippines Free Press | (English) | 87,400
Kislap-Graphic | (English) | 62,159
Liwayway | (Tagalog) | 161,776
Bulaklak | (Tagalog) | 110,274
Bisaya | (Cebuano) | 57,049
Hiliggaynon | (Ilonggo) | 44,176
Bannawag (Ilocano) | (Ilocano) | 45,956
Woman and the Home | (English) | 47,694
Saturday Herald Mag. | (English) | 46,284
Aliwan | (Tagalog) | 30,327
Alimyon | (Cebuano) | 29,250

Eduardo Mendoza, Inc.

EXHIBIT 2 (continued)

Volume of Print Advertising in the Philippines

Year	Print Ads*	% Change	Noncommercial Ads	Theater Ads	Shipping Ads
1955	₱16,640,442	—	—	—	—
1956	15,320,018	(7.94)	—	—	—
1957	17,173,795	12.09	—	—	—
1958	18,562,696	8.08	₱1,938,515	₱2,035,742	₱958,995
1959	21,708,193	16.94	2,771,057	1,996,267	993,061
1960	22,112,343	1.86	2,286,382	2,246,499	1,153,394
1961 (Jan-July)	12,084,475	—	1,221,538	1,437,988	777,744

SOURCE: Robot Statistics

*The above totals are a measure of print advertisements appearing in 60-70 leading Philippine publications. The peso values of the advertisements are based on rate cards and do not take into account volume discounts and combination rates.

PROSPECTUS

1. It is planned to incorporate "Eduardo Mendoza, Inc.," an advertising agency to conduct the business of servicing advertisers. The firm will act as advertising counselors to plan and execute advertising programs to include: press, radio, television, outdoor, print, point of sale, tec., promotions, merchandising, and press relations.

2. Capitalization: (Common Shares of ₱10.00 par)
   Authorized - ₱200,000.00
   Planned initial subscription - ₱100,000.00
   Present investors pledged are:
        Eduardo Mendoza - ₱20,000.00

   Additional subscriptions, whenever required, will be offered on first priority to the original incorporators or to new investors if the additional investors do not cover the required amount, provided original investors on a majority vote accept the new investors.

3. Income

   The corporation will derive its income from the 15% legitimate commission derived from client billing placed by the advertising agency with media, i.e., publications, radio-TV stations, outdoor manufacturers, printers, etc. Extra income over the normal 15% commission is derived from the art department billing and special promotions requiring special production fees.

4. Organization

   The following departments are required in the function of an agency:

        Administration
        Account executives
        Media department
        Production department
        Art department
        Radio-TV department
        Accounting department
        Copy chief - press relations department

EXHIBIT 2 (continued)

Of course, the number of personnel in each department will depend on the volume of business handled by the agency from its origin through its growth. However, for purposes of establishing a pilot force initially, the proposed agency will operate with personnel immediately necessary for its proper function and build up according to schedule.

To this end, the following personnel and salaries are proposed:

General manager	₱2,500.00	(plus 10% of
Secretary	250.00	profits as
Account executive (1)	500.00	originator)
Media director	275.00	
Media assistant	150.00	
Art director	500.00	
Artist A	250.00	
Artist B	250.00	
Artist C	180.00	
Production man	200.00	
Production assistant	120.00	
Bookkeeper	275.00	
Clerk-typist	175.00	
Messengers-janitors	240.00	

15-men staff   ₱5,865.00 Total monthly payroll

The above does not include: copy writer, radio-TV directors, full-fledged accountant. However, for the present these can be dispensed with and considered when actual billing permits same.

5. Operation overhead:

Payroll (see item 4)	₱5,865.00
Social Security	120.00
Rent	750.00
Office expenses (transportation, repairs, mail, etc.)	100.00
Light and water (approx.)	50.00
Telephones (2 with 4 extensions)	200.00
Art supplies (approx.)	100.00
Legal expenses	75.00
Audit fees	75.00
Licenses	60.00
Depreciation	120.00
	₱7,665.00
	₱8,000.00

6. Operation supplies and equipment

Furniture and fixtures, office and production equipment for the pilot staff is estimated at approximately ₱10,000 to ₱11,000.

Initial stationery, office and art supplies for a period of six months would cost approximately ₱1,500 to ₱2,000.

Roughly, as soon as the agency is ready for business (October 1, 1961) there would be an approximate operating capital of ₱85,000 left.

Eduardo Mendoza, Inc.

**EXHIBIT 3
EDUARDO MENDOZA, INC.
Additional Expenses with a "Full" Staff**

1. Payroll

Copywriter	₱ 400.00
Radio-TV director	600.00
Accountant	200.00
Account executives (2)	1,000.00
Total extra monthly payroll	₱2,200.00

2. Operational overhead

Payroll	₱2,200.00
Social Security	35.00
Rent	250.00
Others	150.00
	₱2,635.00

Eduardo did not think this expectation completely unrealistic as the volume of advertising in the Philippines had grown significantly since 1946 along with the number of agencies and their gross billings (Exhibit 1). Eduardo (and others) expected this growth to continue because:

1. The circulation and number of newspapers in the Philippines would increase with more widespread literacy and higher per capita income.
2. More and more companies were being educated to both the advantages of advertising expenditures and the use of advertising agencies.
3. The number of radio stations in the country would grow in response to the availability of power sources and the popularity and cheapness of transistor radios.
4. The increase in corporate profitability would allow businesses to spend more on advertising and promotional expenses.

Eduardo figured that the operations of his proposed firm would certainly reflect this growth in the industry. Two possible limits to his proposed agency's volume existed, however. First, he had decided on ethical grounds not to solicit business from any of the existing MAA clients. These represented many of the largest advertisers in the Philippines. Second, his firm would have to compete with the 15 to 20 established firms for existing and new accounts.

Assuming from others' experience that his proposed 15-member skeleton staff could handle up to ₱850,000 annual billings that he could expect to obtain the normal 15% agency commission on all billings handled, and approximately ₱8,000 a month operational overhead expenses (Exhibit 2), Eduardo estimated the agency would need to bill ₱55,000 a month or ₱660,000 a year to break even. At the time of his planning, Eduardo thought he could count on a minimum monthly billing of ₱25,000 from prospective clients already contacted. Furthermore, two additional companies were considering committing their business to him if he would begin operations within two months.

Some considerations of ethics and policy also circumscribed Eduardo's freedom of action. As already mentioned, Eduardo had decided not to solicit business from existing MAA accounts; he would accept their business, however, if they openly came to him.

A second ethical consideration was the "house agency." As generally described by United States and Philippine advertising men, the house agency is "controlled by one or several substantial advertisers or by one or several media or whose owners own a controlling share of the capital of any major medium of advertising." Exhibit 4 contains a more complete discussion of the house agency. While Eduardo knew that the line between being a house agency and one that was not was often a fine one, the ethics of the advertising business as well as his own cautioned against such ownership of his own firm. Yet one of his potential investors was the owner of a large company whose advertising volume readily could be solicited by Eduardo's firm if Eduardo were inclined to desire it. Furthermore, despite the ethical proclamation of advertising agencies and professional associations, Eduardo was aware that a number of successful Philippine competitors could be truthfully classed as house agencies.

In order to protect his present position with MAA, Eduardo thought that he must keep his plans completely secret from his boss, Abelardo Victoria, the owners of MAA, and probably most of his associates. Yet, before he could possibly open the doors of a new business, Eduardo had to secure capital, line up a staff, and attract at least a minimum of "sure-bet" clients.

Eduardo did not fear any "information leaks" from his actively solicited capital subscribers, because most of them were personal friends who realized his position, but, as he said:

> The dangerous thing is going to be in lining up a staff and new accounts. There are a couple of good boys right in this office that I'd like to take with me, but once I ask one, then probably the whole office will know of my intentions. It's almost the same with potential clients. Advertising managers and agency men here are a closely knit group. Once a couple of them know, it might end up all over town.

Eduardo was not sure how to proceed.

The Philippine Media Association (PMA) was an organization which existed to judge the competence, capitalization, and structure of new advertising agencies and was composed of leading publications in the country. It "recognized" those agencies which it felt qualified under their statutes and kept a watchful eye on those that could become house agencies. The PMA had economic powers to "approve" or "disapprove" a new agency, thereby constituting one of the biggest obstacles to overcome should the PMA classify Eduardo's

Eduardo Mendoza, Inc. 307

EXHIBIT 4
EDUARDO MENDOZA, INC.
A Discussion of the "House Agency"*

1. House agencies are advertising agencies controlled by one or several substantial advertisers or by one or several publications, radio broadcasting stations, or any other major medium, or whose owners own a controlling share of the capital of any major medium of advertising.

2. What would be the effects if house agencies take the upper hand in the advertising business? In self-defense, independent agencies, for fear of losing ground, might resort to the same tactics inviting big clients to put in money in the agency business. Such an independent agency will not need fresh and big capital, and as it must seek an investment outlet, it might as well go all the way in establishing or controlling forms of media such as newspapers, magazines, radio stations, etc. Is this good for everybody? Will it not hurt the independent publications which exist today? Is this fair to them? In resorting to something unethical, all the industry becomes unethical, something of which the Philippines would subsequently be ashamed.

3. It naturally follows that when one or more substantial advertisers put up an agency, since they are protecting their own interests first and the interest of the agency is only secondary, they often use this agency to pressure or intimidate mass media like newspapers and radio stations on editorial matters. In the case of an independent agency, when it does this, publishers and radio station owners may call the advertisers or clients of such an independent agency and appeal to them to prevent an independent agency from strangling press freedom. How can an aggrieved medium of the press resort to such a remedy when the agency itself is owned by its own clients?

4. When a house agency is established, it is not primarily interested in servicing the whole community and in making other small businesses grow; it is primarily interested in serving a few big interests of its owners. Naturally it cannot contribute much to our national economy, and it cannot contribute much to the development of the advertising industry as a whole. It will comply merely with requirements to be recognized at the beginning by mass media and by the community in which it thrives. In its immediate need, it usually pirates the trained men of independent agencies by offering salaries beyond the reach of an ordinary business. It will certainly not take the trouble to train new graduates because its experience and technical know-how in advertising and public relations are limited. But in automatically trying to eliminate the independent agencies, it also eliminates the opportunities open today for young graduates of journalism, commerce, and other lines who emerge from the right seeds in developing an independent advertising agency.

5. The house agency is in itself an unfair practice. The mere fact that house agencies usually try to represent themselves as independent agencies is positive proof that even the organizers themselves know that they are doing something wrong. Unethical practices are always camouflaged, and those independent agencies that observe strict ethics are at an unfair disadvantage.

6. When a house agency owns a medium of advertising, this is not only contrary to the standard of ethics but it is also unfair to the businesses which it handles and unfair to agencies which follow the straight and narrow path. The advertisers' money is channeled to the publications, radio stations, and other major medium that such an agency owns. If it owns a magazine or a newspaper, it becomes unfair to the other media of advertising. The advertising appropriation becomes a patronage fund to be given to the owned medium, even if this medium is not the right kind to be used in promoting certain products.

*Source: PHILPROM, Inc.

agency as a house agency. Yet, many of the presently successful firms that commenced operations after 1946 had a capital structure similar to that of a house agency and these firms had succeeded in obtaining PMA approval.

The sanctions PMA could impose on a disapproved firm were "considerable," in the words of Mendoza.

The PMA can withhold approval and with their decision goes the

15% agency commission to be gained from billings in most of the country's print media. Without their approval, agencies can't possibly get their due from a number of publications of the PMA which are the publications most widely used in the newspaper medium.

According to PMA procedures, Eduardo would have to submit an application for agency approval and await approval for 60 days. Along with the applications, Eduardo would have to show the capitalization structure of his proposed firm and evidence of at least five clients.

As he reviewed his position and plans on July 1, 1961, Eduardo saw four possible courses of action:

1. To open his own agency
2. To stay with MAA
3. To accept an offer from Mike Elsy, 100% owner of the eighth largest Philippine agency, on the following terms:
    (a) Purchase 45% of the business (3000 shares) at the current book value of ₱19.57 per share (par value ₱15.00). The company showed a ₱147,000 profit in 1960.
    (b) Position: Executive vice president
    (c) Salary ₱3,750 a month plus year-end bonus of ₱3,000 and a share in the company's profits commensurate with ownership.
4. To accept the offer from a smaller agency, which had a 1959 profit of ₱90,000, of becoming the general manager and 10% owner without any investment in the business. The salary would be ₱3,000 a month plus ₱1,100 transportation and representation allowance.

Both of the last two alternatives offered Eduardo a better income and position of responsibility than did his present job with MAA. If he chose to go ahead with his own agency, Eduardo would have to act quickly: He needed the PMA approval, which took 60 days of waiting; he needed to line up capital, clients and a staff before applying to the PMA; and some of his prospective clients wanted immediate confirmation of his decision to start the new agency. All of these actions would have to be done under the cloak of maximum secrecy so as to protect his present position with MAA should all other opportunities fail.

Four days after the casewriter had concluded his conversation with Mendoza, a note was received from the latter.

Dear Dave:

This morning I received a memo from our manager, Abe, saying that he had heard rumors to the effect that I was going on my own. He demanded to know what the truth was and wants my answer by tomorrow noon.

Sincerely,
Eduardo

Eduardo Mendoza, Inc.

QUESTIONS

1. What are the critical factors facing Eduardo in his decision?
2. Do you agree with his tentative policy decisions regarding (a) requirements for investors, (b) not becoming a house agency, (c) skeleton staff, (d) low capitalization, etc.?
3. What are the breakeven points under the two alternative personnel plans?
4. How would the new agency compare to Eduardo's other opportunities?
5. Do you agree with the nonhouse agency "ethic" described in Exhibit 4?
6. What should Eduardo Mendoza do now?

APPENDIX A

Agency Costs and Profits—1955

(General Averages—211 Agencies of all Sizes)

	Percent of Gross Income (i.e., Agency Commissions and Charges)
Payroll	64.64
Rent, maintenance and repairs	4.75
Travel	2.58
Entertainment	1.91
Payments into pension or profit sharing plans	1.62
Supplies, stationery and petty equipment	1.80
Telephone and telegraph	1.66
Taxes other than U.S. income	1.53
Memberships, dues and subscriptions	1.35
Depreciation	1.26
Unbillable client expense	1.15
Agency's own advertising	0.84
Doubtful account expense	0.46
Insurance—employee benefit	0.40
C.P.A. fees	0.40
Postage and express	0.52
Insurance—operating	0.32
Light	0.29
Legal fees	0.24
Donations	0.24
Interest, bank discount and exchange	0.12
All other expense	1.93
Total expense	90.01
Profit before U.S. income taxes	9.99
U.S. income tax	3.08
Net profit after taxes	6.91

SOURCE: American Association of Advertising Agencies. Reproduced from Albert W. Frey and Kenneth R. Davis, *The Advertising Industry* (New York: Association of National Advertisers, Inc., 1958), p. 55.

22

Peter Paul, Inc., in the Philippines*†

Senior officers and staff of the Peter Paul Philippine Corporation, a wholly owned subsidiary of Peter Paul, Inc., had developed machines capable of replacing much of the hand labor then employed by the company for the processing of desiccated coconut. The company calculated that if plant conversion were begun January 1, 1959, it could be completed by June of that year. To date 110,000 pesos ($55,000 at the official exchange rate of 2 to 1) had been invested in development of the machinery and an estimated additional investment of 200,000 pesos would be required. The conversion was expected to produce an annual reduction in costs at current production rates of 700,000 pesos or $350,000 and to provide certain other advantages.

The reduction in costs would arise chiefly from a reduction in the work force at the coconut plant from 960 persons to about 490. The relatively small Philippine community in which the plant was located offered limited alternative employment.

Peter Paul, Inc., the parent company, maker of the widely advertised "Mounds," "Almond Joy," and other candies using coconut, had been organized in 1919 as a Connecticut corporation by six men, five of whom were relatives of Armenian extraction. At the start the company produced a general line of confections, but in the early 1920's it decided to specialize in coconut candy products. At that time, coconut candies were not common. In 1929, the company became a Delaware corporation.

Up through the early 1930's, most desiccated coconut came from Ceylon, though only a very small percentage of the total coconut crop went into desiccated production. Even in 1958, 90% to 95% of world coconut production went into the copra trade. During the 1930's, the desiccated coconut percentage was even smaller, and most of what was produced was marketed in Europe. During this period, Peter Paul purchased its coconut requirements through independent importers buying from Ceylon.

*This case, Peter Paul, Inc., in the Philippines, BSI42, was prepared by Mr. M. T. Gragg under the direction of Professor G. A. Smith, of the Harvard University Graduate School of Business Administration, as a basis for classroom discussion rather than to illustrate either effective or ineffective handling of administrative situations.

†Copyright © 1962 by the President and Fellows of Harvard College.

310

Peter Paul, Inc., in the Philippines

During the early 1930's various business interests began to explore the possibility of developing a Philippine coconut industry. As a result of the political pressure they applied, the United States erected a tariff against Ceylon desiccated coconut, the upshot being that Ceylon coconut could no longer be imported profitably to the United States, although it still was sold in Europe. Almost immediately, the Philippine coconut industry became important; by 1941 the Philippines were exporting approximately 100 million pounds of desiccated coconut a year to the United States. At that time, desiccated coconut was selling at between 5 and 10 United States cents a pound. The United States duty on Ceylon imports then was 3 1/2 cents a pound.

By 1941 Peter Paul had become the largest single user of desiccated coconut, buying its requirements directly from three large Philippine producers. In 1939, with general unrest throughout the world, the company had begun to stockpile coconut, so that at the start of the war in the Pacific it was able to continue operations. Later during the war the company obtained some supplies from the West Indies and Central America and had even operated small processing plants in Florida and Puerto Rico.

As the end of the war neared, the company approached its former suppliers of Philippine coconut. They said they intended to get back into production but at the same time indicated this involved many problems. Virtually all the desiccated coconut plants in the Philippines had been wiped out. As Mr. Kazanjian, executive vice president of Peter Paul, stated: "We felt that we could get into the business faster than our former suppliers." The company needed a larger and cheaper source of supply than that provided by its Puerto Rican plant, and it needed it quickly. Hence, it decided to move directly into production in the Philippines.

After conversations with Philippine government representatives in Washington and various United States government officials, Mr. Louis Zeun, chief engineer, was sent to the Philippines to investigate in April 1946. After some three weeks, Mr. Zeun recommended that the company build a plant in Candelaria, Luzon Province, about 90 miles from Manila. This was the town nearest the densest growth of coconut trees on Luzon.

The company accepted the recommendation and employed a Chinese contractor to build the plant. Because of his local connections and ingenuity the plant got on very quickly. Excavation started in June 1946 and the plant went into partial operation on October 7. The Philippine venture was incorporated in the Philippines on June 29, 1946, as the Peter Paul Philippine Corporation. On July 4 of the same year Philippine independence had been proclaimed.

Although the Philippine Corporation was wholly owned by the United States parent company, it had its own board of directors. Mr. Tatigian and Mr. Kazanjian, president and executive vice president of Peter Paul, Inc., were members of the board, but all other board members were Philippine residents though not necessarily Philippine citizens.

Mr. Kazanjian thought it was essential to have an American component in the top management of the Philippine Corporation, so as to shield it from political influence and possible conflicts of interest. However, the American group had been limited to four. The idea was to make the company as Philippine as possible. Mr. Kazanjian believed that if the American component were too large the company might look unduly "foreign" and thus be vulnerable to politically inspired attack and charges of exploitation. There were 16 Filipinos on the senior staff of the corporation.

Mr. Kazanjian observed that the four American families had been instructed to remember at all times that they were in the Philippines and not in the United States and should respect local customs. He felt very strongly that there should be no discrimination between the "white" and "yellow" men, that such discrimination had been an important reason why the communist appeal had been so successful in large areas of the Orient.

The president of Peter Paul Philippine Corporation was Howard R. Hick, an American with many years of experience in the Orient. Before the war, he had been with Franklin Baker, Division of General Foods, in the Far East. During the war, he had been captured by the Japanese, and for over three years was in the Santo Tomas prison camp in the Philippines. The other American members of the management of the corporation were the vice president, the purchasing officer, and a man who acted as an assistant to his three associates. The vice president was, in late 1958, on the verge of returning home to become assistant general manager of a new Peter Paul plant in New Frankfort, Indiana; the other two men would be moved up in the organization. One reason the vice president was being returned to the states was to enable him to place his children in high school. The company employed tutors for children of its American employees in the Philippines but such instruction was believed satisfactory only through grammar school.

In a case study of Peter Paul Philippine Corporation prepared by Albert Ravenholt of the American Universities Field Staff in 1958, the following comments appeared with respect to the labor situation and the effects a conversion to mechanization might have:

> Among the 950 workers employed in three shifts, 60 per cent are men and 40 per cent are women. Perhaps 6,000 persons depend directly upon the Corporation for their livelihood. Indirectly, the entire municipality of Candelaria with a population of about 45,000 is affected by operations at this plant. The lowest wage paid is ₱4.64 daily; the 70 per cent of the labor force engaged in shelling and paring coconuts on a contract basis averages ₱6.20 for an eight-hour day.
>
> For the workers and the community of Candelaria such mechanization would create critical problems. Although this is a coconut-growing region where rural privation is far less in evidence than in the rice-growing sections of Central Luzon and many ordinary citizens have a family interest in small plantations, the Peter Paul workers have no desire to return to farming. Their relatives and friends who crack coco-

nuts with a bolo or machete to make copra or burn the shells in old 53-gallon gasoline drums to make charcoal earn at most two or three pesos daily and the work is irregular. Also, an employee at Peter Paul has a status that can be matched in the community only by owning income-producing land, a considerable business, or holding a government job. The ₱700,000 savings in production costs at Peter Paul will come from the annual payroll of the community and will mean a good part of that amount out of the till of local merchants.

By Philippine standards the Corporation has taken a better than average interest in the welfare of employees. Just as there is a swimming pool and play area for the foreign management staff near their residences, so is a larger swimming pool provided for the Filipino personnel beside the plant. The recreation area for Filipino employees and their families also includes an open air theatre where films are shown regularly, a large play field for sports events that are part of the life that centers around the plant and a scouting activities building for the children of workers.

Peter Paul Philippine Corporation, however, has had its labor troubles. Two unions are active within the factory: *Lakasing Pagkakaisa*, which is affiliated with the Philippine Trade Union Council but is on the inactive list because of failure to pay dues; and *Peter Paul Banahaw*, which inclines toward another federation, the National Labor Union. In 1952-1953 these two unions became involved in an ugly jurisdictional struggle. Operations were halted for one month. Mrs. Hick was roughed up when she helped visiting Rainbow Girls through the picket line into the Corporation compound. On another occasion, Howard Hick was stabbed with a bamboo spear while moving through picketing workers at the gate. There are 17 security guards at the plant, but the policy has been not to use force against the strikers even when they resort to extra-legal means. This reliance upon good sense eventually prevailing is dictated in part by the fact that the local municipal police and the Philippine Constabulary (which forms the national police force) have been reluctant to take any action to insure that only legal methods are used by the strikers.

The Corporation in time secured an injunction against the strikers after Howard Hick showed the court movies of the tactics used by the two unions. The injunction, however, did not prevent a ten-day strike in 1955 after the unions had charged that a one-month shutdown of the factory was a lock-out. Then some union members pressured others to remain out by such methods as visiting them in their homes to explain the hazards of trying to go to work. A former mayor of the municipality stopped this intimidation by packing a "forty-five" when he called on the strike leaders. His successor has yet to indicate a stand under similarly difficult circumstances. Huk guerrillas led by communists have operated in the Candelaria region, particularly on the slopes of Mt. Banahaw, the extinct volcano that towers 7,400 feet above the community. They have never taken concerted action against Peter Paul Philippine Corporation but it has not been uncommon for these guerrillas to stop company trucks, and they might try to capitalize upon unrest in the Candelaria community.

So far the workers in the plant have evinced some pride in the experiments and pioneering with new machines which they consider make them more progressive than the neighboring desiccated coconut factories some 15 miles away. There has been no sabotage of the machines, although there is general knowledge of their labor-saving potentialities. Management hopes that, if a strike should materialize, it could be settled in one or two months, thereby avoiding serious curtailment of supplies of desiccated coconut for the parent company. The great danger is that the laying off of so many workers combined with a strike could lead to mobilization of the community against the Corporation. National politicians, some of whom delight in an opportunity to vent antiforeign sentiments, could then penalize Peter Paul in its innumerable and necessary dealings with the Central Bank and other government regulatory agencies.[1]

The Candelaria plant was designed to handle three million pounds of desiccated coconut monthly. Actual production was between 16 million and 18 million pounds annually, all taken by the parent corporation.

The pricing of desiccated coconut as between the Philippine subsidiary and the parent American firm depended upon the market price for copra and fluctuated with the change in the price of copra. The price charged to the parent concern was adjusted occasionally so as to enable the Philippine subsidiary to make a "reasonable profit" during the year. At the current level of business, the Philippine company was realizing an annual profit of something like $5,000, which was admittedly very little for a firm capitalized at $230,000, but competitors reportedly showed about the same return. The company's costs of production were about average for the islands.

Of 2,000 shares of authorized stock, the Philippine Corporation had issued only 1,000. Total assets came to about $1.9 million as of June 1958. Peter Paul, Inc., showed in its balance statement for June 30, 1958, an investment in and advances to the Peter Paul Philippine Corporation of $1,338,611, which was slightly higher than the 1957 figure of $1,282,796.

At the start, the parent corporation provided a $500,000 loan to its Philippine subsidiary and took in return a first lien on its property. It was understood that if all went well with the venture, the Philippine Corporation would either capitalize this loan or repay it. In fact, the parent company had asked for repayment and some installment payments had been made. But in 1951, the Philippine Government introduced monetary exchange controls that prevented further payment. The books of the parent company still showed, as of 1958, a loan outstanding of $280,000.

There was some Philippine participation in the ownership of the parent corporation in that it had somewhere between 10 to 20 Filipino stockholders, individuals who had had some association with the company either as employees or suppliers. Peter Paul stock was not listed on any United States exchange (over

---

[1] Albert Ravenholt, American Universities Field Staff, 366 Madison Avenue, New York 17, New York, Peter Paul Philippine Corporation, "A Case Study in United States Foreign Business Policy," September 23, 1958.

the counter), but there were some 9,000 shareholders. Control of the company was held by members of the founder group and their heirs. Management had told the Filipinos associated with the Philippine company that Filipino stockholders were welcomed. Most of the Philippine-held stock had been purchased prior to 1951 and was not really a significant portion of the total outstanding. The dollar exchange control exercised by the Philippine Government since 1951 made it very difficult for individual Filipinos to purchase stock in an American corporation.

In 1958 there were various pressures on the Philippine Corporation to lower costs. Both raw material and labor costs had been rising. Tariff protection on United States imports of desiccated coconut from the Philippines had been reduced from the 3 1/2 cents a pound in effect in 1941 to 1 3/4 cents in 1958, and by agreement between the Philippines and the United States Government all protection would cease by 1974.

If costs could be sufficiently reduced the company might be able to sell production above that needed by the parent company to the European market, then supplied chiefly from Ceylon. Reportedly about 50 small factories in Ceylon were making an inferior and cheaper coconut product. The other main competition came from Indonesia, where a good grade of coconut was produced in a modern government-owned plant.

The company's officers did not think it would be possible to compete in the United States, except for sales to the parent company. Four of the nine Philippine producers who resumed operations after World War II had closed down because of inability to compete in the United States and European markets.

If Peter Paul Philippine Corporation mechanized its operation, various possibilities were open to minimize adverse effects on the local labor force. Mr. Ravenholt, in the case study quoted earlier, discussed some of these.

> Peter Paul Philippine Corporation is exploring the possibility of meliorating the consequences for the community of its mechanization by fuller utilization and industrialization that would also provide added employment. Throughout the past two decades, use of coconut by-products has been an often discussed possibility by scientists, engineers and inventive lay folk. Numerous abortive attempts to accomplish this have foundered, not only for lack of adequate capital and an organized market, but also such industrial use of the coconut requires a considerable change in the social organization affecting harvesting, transport, etc. As a starter in this direction, management of the corporation is investigating installation of an oil-pressing plant. The former purchaser of dried parings and discards has sold out his business and a once happy commercial relationship has become a less satisfactory one. An investment of ₱100,000 in cookers, expellers and related equipment promises to pay itself out in three years, while making an annual profit of 15 percent. It could offer employment to about 50 workers. Equally important would be the opportunity it would afford for the testing in operation of another Hick invention, a mechanized process for making copra of superior quality and extracting a fresh edible oil, as contrasted

to present copra oil which must be processed. There are many ramifications to this development, including the possible production of a coconut flour with about 12 per cent protein, instead of the present copra meal that is used for animal feed or fertilizer. The market for these new products has not yet been examined in detail.

The husk of the coconut now is generally left on the plantation for fertilizer or burned. It contains a coir that has numerous industrial possibilities. The Japanese and others make small machines for decorticating this fiber but none of them have thoroughly satisfied the folks at Candelaria who are experimenting with their own models. Already a machine has been developed here for mechanically husking the nuts. With an investment of about ₱60,000, it is estimated that they could begin making coir for mattress fiber, bristle and brush fiber, material for carpets, mats and other purposes. This again could be paid off in three years with a 15 per cent profit and employ about 50 workers ... Here at Candelaria, management sees a possibility that an additional investment of ₱250,000 in equipment could provide, within two years,

EXHIBIT 1

PETER PAUL, INC.
Balance Sheets, June 30, 1957, 1958

	June 30, 1957	June 30, 1958
Current Assets	$ 8,692,864	$ 8,252,889
Plant expansion fund (Frankfort, Indiana plant)	2,990,223	565,038
Plant assets (at cost less accumulated depreciation)	2,527,318	2,690,395
Construction in process (Frankfort plant)	544,331	3,355,631
Land and improvements	112,322	111,922
Investment in the Peter Paul Philippine Corporation	1,282,796	1,338,611
Patents and trademarks (amortized value)	8,042	7,472
Deferred charges	169,693	182,012
Total Assets	$16,327,589	$16,503,970
Current Liabilities	$ 2,263,660	$ 2,329,628
Reserve for contingencies	69,791	73,344
Capital	13,994,138	14,100,998
Total	$16,327,589	$16,503,970

SOURCE: Peter Paul, Inc., Annual Report, June 30, 1958.
NOTE: There was no long-term debt outstanding. The corporation had guaranteed payment of bank commitments of Peter Paul Philippine Corporation not to exceed at any one time the aggregate sum of $360,000 and payment of temporary bank advances in an amount not to exceed $150,000.

employment for another 400 workers in the utilization of this by-product presently indicated.

If unhusked nuts are to be brought in, the transportation cost will be doubled unless the Corporation installs its own modern trailer system, which would effect savings sufficient to warrant carrying the husks. This will require an investment of perhaps ₱50,000 in transportation units already tested here. Once the planters learn that there is value in the husks they now throw away, however, a price may also be demanded. The Corporation will then also be crowding the contractor, who today buys nuts on the tree, harvests, piles, husks and transports them in *carabao* carts to the roadside where commercial truckers pick them up for Peter Paul. The Corporation has found that the surest method of insuring a dependable supply of nuts with the husks on may be to enter the plantation management business and mechanize culti-

EXHIBIT 2

PETER PAUL, INC.
Statement of Earnings - Year Ended June 30, 1958

Balance, July 1, 1957..		$10,347,054
Net income (after provision for depreciation of plant assets of $235,972)............................	$1,810,368	
Dividends paid - $2.50 per share..........................	1,703,508	
Net Addition to Earnings Retained for Business Needs.......................		106,860
Earnings Retained for Business Needs, June 30, 1958..................................		$10,453,914

The 1958 "President's Report" read in part as follows:

To Our Stockholder Family:

I am pleased to submit this annual report of your company's operations for the fiscal year ended June 30, 1958. It was a satisfactory year considering the serious adverse economic conditions experienced throughout the country.

Earnings for the year were lower because of the increased cost of materials and supplies, particularly chocolate, one of the most important components of our quality confections. Higher costs of transportation, labor and warehousing were other contributing factors. It has been through the over-all efficiency of our operations and constant attention to cost reduction that we have been able to offset in some part these increased costs.

Earnings before taxes were $5.54 per share compared to $6.13 the previous year. Our net earnings after taxes were $1,810,368 or $2.66 per share compared to the previous year when they were $2,014,242 or $2.96 per share. Estimated federal and state taxes were $2.89 compared to $3.18 per share for the corresponding period of last year.

Cash dividends of $2.50 per share amounting to $1,703,508, being 94% of earnings, were paid. This represented a yield of 6% on the market value per share at the end of the fiscal year. The regular quarterly dividend of 50¢ per share was paid, together with extras of 10¢ and 40¢, during the year. Dividend payments were therefore at the same rate as for the previous year and continued our uninterrupted dividend payments for the thirty-sixth consecutive year.

Since our last annual meeting 866 new members joined the stockholder family, bringing it to an all time record high of 8,900. The family includes members residing in forty-two states and seven foreign countries.

vation and harvesting. While it promises to be profitable, this again would add a new dimension to operations.

These developments which within about five years could enable Peter Paul Philippine Corporation to restore to the community of Candelaria the employment that otherwise will be lost through mechanization will lead the company far afield from production of the desiccated coconut for candy manufacture.

Mr. Kazanjian also had in mind the possibility of making capital available to others for commercial enterprises to create additional employment in Luzon in the event it was decided to mechanize the present plant.

It was known, in 1958, that some of the company's competitors in the desiccated coconut field also were developing mechanized processes. Mr. Hick had pointed out to the parent company officials on his last visit to the United States that even if Peter Paul refrained from using these new machines, its competitors would not. The Philippine subsidiary would thus be placed at a serious competitive disadvantage. Mr. Kazanjian had replied: "Let them go ahead. If we don't have the machines for a year, we won't go broke. Also, if the others go ahead and put in the machines first, it will place us in a better position in respect to the labor situation."

Financial data and other information from Peter Paul, Inc., *Annual Report* as of June 30, 1958, are shown in Exhibits 1 and 2.

23

Coproducts Corporation*

LOCATING CAPITAL SOURCES TO FINANCE AN
OVERSEAS PROCESSING OPERATION

In 1962 the Coproducts Corporation of San Francisco was seeking funds for the establishment of the first commercial Hiller coconut processing plant in the Philippines. The plant would convert fresh coconut meat into an edible oil and meal by a new process. Local currency and ownership/management participation, a factory site, and adequate raw material were assured. The major remaining problem for the company was to locate an American investor, or group of investors, prepared to advance about $140,000 of risk capital. This sum was required to purchase some of the machinery for the factory and for other American dollar expenditures. If the first plant was as successful as management anticipated, a sizeable market for other plants should develop.

Prior to the development of the new Hiller Process, coconut oil has been the primary product of the coconut. It has been made from copra, the dried meat of the coconut. Copra making is a tedious and time consuming operation requiring approximately 30 days and spoils the coconut meat for human consumption. The oil from copra, however, can be refined, bleached, deodorized and made edible. The residue meal can be used only for animal feed. Most of the copra is not processed in the country of origin but is shipped to other countries for the extraction of oil. This requires another 30 to 60 days before the copra is manufactured into finished products.

The Hiller Process takes the specially developed machinery to the source of the coconuts and processes the nut as it is picked from the tree into edible oil and flour in one half hour.

This has taken some seven years of research and development and the process has become available at a time when there is increasing pressure to relocate the process plants in the country of origin rather than the country of use. This process will increase the value of the products, and improve the economy of newly emerging nations, into which category most coconut countries fall, and eliminate or reduce nationalistic resentment of foreign exploitation of natural resources. Since the Hiller Process is designed to handle fresh coconuts and is therefore capable of producing higher quality and more valuable products,

*Copyright © 1963 by the Board of Trustees of the Leland Stanford Junior University.

the entire coconut industry can benefit from adoption of the Hiller Process, the company officials believed.

1. The Coconut Industry[1]

Coconuts are an important source of income in many tropical areas. Major growing countries in terms of production volume are the Philippines, Indonesia, India, Pakistan, Ceylon, Malaya, and Mexico.

Copra is the single most valuable coconut product. This is the dried meat, made by removing the husk, cracking the shell, extracting, and finally drying, the meat, in the sun, over charcoal fires or in kilns to stop decay. In 1961, 3,390,000 metric tons of copra were produced, with a value of approximately $500,000,000. Copra is converted into a crude oil and a meal cake by passing copra through expellers or by the use of solvent extraction. The oil is further processed and refined for the manufacture of soaps and detergents, margarine, shortening, and other products. The cake or meal is used for cattle feed.

Other coconut products are relatively minor in significance. Next most important is desiccated coconut of which, in 1961, 100,000 metric tons, worth about $16,000,000 were exported to all parts of the world from Ceylon and the Philippines. These two countries produce most of the desiccated coconut and export the major share of production. Desiccated coconut, the familiar coconut used in confectionery and bakery products, is meat which has been dried, and ground or shredded under controlled factory conditions without oil removal.

Some coconuts are taken directly from the tree for local consumption or for sale abroad as whole nuts. Their number accounts for a small percentage of total coconut production.

Two major by-products are secured after removal of the coconut meat. The husk or outer fibrous protective coating is used for coir, woven into mats, rugs, brushes, and similar items. The hard protective shell inside the husk and around the meat is burned to produce charcoal or to fire the boilers of process plants or copra kilns.

2. History and Development of the Hiller Process

In 1956, at the invitation of President Magsaysay, Stanley Hiller, a California inventor with many patents in various forms of food processing, shipped to and set up in the Philippines a plant to make fresh coconuts into edible oil and meal. The plant operated successfully and produced edible oil and meal, but the equipment had two defects. Coconut meat lodged in the dryer and enzyme action raised the free fatty acid content of the oil to a value higher than desirable. The mechanical energy of the oil press was imparted into the press cake

---

[1] Food and Agricultural Organization of the United Nations, "Coconut Situation" June 1962. Quantitive data in this section is based on derivations from statistical charts and tabulations recorded in subject publication. In some cases it has been necessary to combine data from several charts to arrive at the values stated herein.

Coproducts Corporation

and scorched it slightly, giving the meal a light brown color instead of pure white.

Hiller returned to the United States to redesign the plant to overcome these difficulties. Just before the second plant was completed, President Magsaysay was killed in an airplane accident in March, 1957, and progress on the process was delayed indefinitely in the Philippines.

However, the inventor continued to work in the United States. To remove the trouble of spoilage in the drying process, he conceived the idea of drying coconut meat while suspended in hot coconut oil.

The oil press was altered to remove the scorching effect on the press cake. Mr. Hiller was not able to run a full scale coconut test because of the difficulty of supplying it with large quantities of dried fresh coconut meat. However, he performed tests with materials that approximate the consistency of coconut meat (a mixture of animal meal scraps and chicken and turkey parts) until he was convinced the scorching problem was overcome.

In October 1959, Herbert Rogers, a San Francisco consulting engineer, heard of Hiller's work and saw possibilities of developing the process into a profitable machinery sales and engineering business. A laboratory scale plant was constructed and the feasibility of drying the coconut meats in oil was proved. Large or small batches of meat could be dried down to 5% moisture in less than one half hour.

Having proved the feasibility of the process to his own satisfaction, Rogers formed the Coproducts Corporation, to take over all of Hiller's American and foreign patents applicable to the process and to sell complete plants throughout the world. Hiller joined the company as vice president and technical advisor. The process was called the Hiller Process in honor of the inventor.

3. Description of the Process

Ripe coconuts are brought to the processing plant usually with husks removed by the grower. In most countries the nuts are opened and meat removed by hand labor, paid on a per 1,000 nuts basis. In countries where labor costs are high, in excess of $2 per day, machine nut opening and meat extraction would be more economical. Coproducts had techniques for machine cracking and meat extraction.

Meat is first passed over an inspection belt where small bits of shell or husk fibers are removed by inspectors. The meat is then ground in coconut oil and the mixture, or slurry, pumped into a storage tank to be heated in preparation for drying.

To keep the process simple, drying is done in batches taking about 30 minutes per batch. Batches are pumped out of the storage tank into the batch dryer, where drying takes place under a vacuum.

Each batch of oil and dried meat is pumped into a tank, from which a conveyor feeds the meat at a uniform rate into the continuous oil press. The oil from the dried coconut meat and discharges the press cake. The cake is cooled, ground to a fine meal, and conveyed to a bin for storage and eventual bagging.

The oil produced by the continuous oil press, together with excess oil drained from each batch, is pumped to a crude coconut oil tank. Small amounts of meat in suspension, known as "foots" are there removed by filtration. The filtered oil is run to a filtered oil tank and the foots returned to the press.

Coconut oil produced from fresh coconut has a very low free fatty acid content, less than 0.5% compared to 5% or more in oil made from copra. The free fatty acid of copra oil is removed by caustic treatment and the oil requires further treating to produce an edible product free of coconut flavor and satisfactory in color. Oil from fresh coconuts, in contrast, requires only deodorizing. After deodorizing, the oil is pumped to a finished oil tank and then to tank trucks or other containers for shipment.

The plant is designed for an input capacity of about 100,000 pounds of raw coconut meat in a 24-hour day (or 100,000 coconuts if the meat averages 1 pound per coconut.) The output would be about 30,000 pounds of oil and 20,000 pounds of meal a day. The company believed that, after a few plants had been built and operated, it could determine the size of smaller capacity plants which could be economically produced.

4. Products Obtained from Processing

(a) *Coconut Oil*

Refined oil produced by the Hiller Process is suitable immediately for human consumption. This high quality edible oil is produced simply by taking advantage of the natural purity of the fresh nut. Mr. Hiller had conducted tests which indicate that the oil that comes directly from a fresh coconut is completely asterile or neutral. By taking oil from fresh coconuts this advantage is retained. Fresh coconut oil can be used for cooking oil, for the production of margarine, shortening, and candy. Other uses of coconut oil include the manufacture of cosmetics, soaps, detergents, synthetic resins, insecticides, germicides, and special lubricants.

(b) *Coconut Meal*

In the opinion of the Coproducts Corporation management, production of edible meal was the most significant factor in the process. The meal had a high protein content of approximately 18% to 20% and should have value in underdeveloped countries to increase nutrition standards. Since it was somewhat fibrous, its use in bread would appear to be in mixture with wheat flour, in proportions of approximately 25% meal to 75% flour, which would produce a palatable and nutritious flour. In addition, since the coconut countries do not ordinarily grow wheat, some savings of exchange on purchase of this seemed to be possible. The meal could also be micronized for use as a fortifier with the protein content raised to possibly 35% or 40%.

Coproducts Corporation

(c) *Other Coconut Products*

The company believed that some plants might purchase whole nuts, so that husks and shells would be available for sale. One Hiller plant would make available nearly 6,000,000 pounds of fiber annually and a considerable world market for fiber existed. Management felt that a coconut fiber processing plant might be operated in conjunction with each Hiller plant, depending on the economies of the processing area.

Each plant would have approximately 14,000,000 pounds of waste shell also available for sale each year. The company had determined that plants exist to take such shell and process it into acetic acid, tar, and high-grade charcoal. As with fiber, there appeared to be some basis for operating a shell processing plant in conjunction with the coconut processing plant, again dependent upon circumstances.

5. Market for Coproducts Process Plants

The Philippines for which the Coproducts Corporation sought funds in 1962 was, the company hoped, merely to be the first of many. If this plant was as successful as management anticipated, Mr. Rogers and his associates believed that demand for similar plants, larger or smaller dependent upon local conditions, would be considerable. The basic need was to get one full-scale plant into production so that those who had expressed interest would have some tangible basis on which to proceed. The company and Mr. Hiller had received numerous inquiries since news of the process was first made public.

In order to develop some idea of the market for the Coproducts Process, the company used statistics of copra production which were obtained from published sources. It was apparent that the competitive impact of the new process would be felt mainly in the copra industry.

In 1961 world copra production was reported to be approximately 3,390,000 metric tons. This gross figure, company investigation showed, required adjustment to take into account the following factors:

(a) The basic 4,000 pounds/per hour Hiller machine required about 30 million pounds of fresh coconut meat per year. Many growing areas could not produce the required quantity of coconuts and it was uneconomical to ship whole fresh coconuts over very great distances.

(b) Many countries would continue to demand copra for existing processing equipment.

(c) Custom and market preference would retard acceptance of the new process in some areas; traditional methods were deeply implanted and agricultural operations are usually slow to change.

(d) While Coproducts possessed effective American and foreign patent protection, some competition might develop other fresh coconut processes.

For those reasons, it was estimated that only about 15% of the world copra production would be replaced by the Hiller Process within 10 years. Based on

1961 copra production statistics, the market potential for plant sales would be 80 plants located throughout the coconut growing countries.

6. The Philippines Operation

Since 40% of the world's coconut production was in the Philippines, Coproducts Corporation preferred to establish the initial plant in that country. A very active interest existed among members of Government and industry in improving both coconut product quality and processing techniques which would provide maximum benefits to the local coconut industry.

In addition, the company had an associate who owned a large plantation and was a recognized leader in the industry. He had agreed to participate with Coproducts in a joint venture to establish the first Hiller coconut processing plant on his plantation. He stood ready to provide 50% of the $350,000 capital required to establish the first increment of the first plant. The Coproducts Corporation participation in the first plant required that an additional $140,000 cash be available to the Coproducts Corporation.

Under the agreement between the Corporation and the Philippine partner, a plant with a capacity of 4,000 pounds of fresh coconut meat per hour was to be built in two stages so that initial requirements would be minimized; the first stage would provide a plant of 50% capacity. After successful operation at 2000 #/hr capacity the second stage would be constructed to increase the plant to its full 4,000 pounds per hour capacity. The Philippine associate undertook to provide fresh coconuts and the company was to retain full management of plant operations under a management contract.

Estimates of contribution and participation by Coproducts and their associate in the Philippine plant were as follows for the half capacity plant:

	Coproducts Corp. Contribution	Philippines Contribution	Total Project
1) Equipment and facilities presently available (Estimated Value)	$ 40,000.00	$ 40,000.00	$ 80,000.00
2) Equipment, facilities and erection costs	135,000.00	85,000.00	220,000.00
3) Working capital	5,000.00	45,000.00	50,000.00
TOTAL	$180,000.00	$170,000.00	$350,000.00

Coproducts Corporation would receive approximately 50% ownership of the Philippines venture. Item No. 1 in the table represented estimated value of equipment, buildings, and facilities which had been constructed and were available for use. The Coproducts contribution of $40,000 represented process equipment on hand. The Philippines contribution of $40,000 represented existing buildings, roads, facilities, and utilities which had been constructed on the plantation.

Coproducts Corporation

Construction of the Philippines plant was to be undertaken under a joint venture agreement between the two parties. Upon completion, the plant was to be transferred to a Philippine corporation and parties in the joint venture would be issued stock in this corporation on the basis of actual contributions as established at the time the plant was placed in operation. It was planned that the new company would also act as agent for the sale of subsequent Hiller process plants in the Philippines.

Coproducts Corporation had prepared a cash flow projection for the benefit of proposed investors. (See Exhibit 1.) During the initial year, Philippine oper-

EXHIBIT 1
PHILIPPINES COPRODUCTS PLANT
Projected Cash Flow
10-Year Period

Description	1	2	3	4	5	6	7
RECEIPTS							
1 Oil Revenue (11¼¢/lb)	$526,500	$972,000	$972,000	$972,000	$972,000	$972,000	$972,000
2 Meal Revenue (5¢/lb)	132,000	288,000	288,000	288,000	288,000	288,000	288,000
3 Loan - 6%-5 years (Expansion)	200,000						
4 Working Capital Contribution	50,000						
5 Total Receipts	$908,500	$1,260,000	$1,260,000	$1,260,000	$1,260,000	$1,260,000	$1,260,000
EXPENDITURES							
6 Raw Materials	406,000	811,000	811,000	811,000	811,000	811,000	811,000
7 Plant Labor	37,700	55,800	55,800	55,800	55,800	55,800	55,800
8 Operating Overhead (Less Depr.)	17,600	24,300	24,300	24,300	24,300	24,300	24,300
9 Selling & Distribution Expense	36,300	57,200	57,200	57,200	57,200	57,200	57,200
10 Administration & Clerical	19,200	19,500	19,500	19,500	19,500	19,500	19,500
11 Management Services	24,000	17,000	10,000	10,000	10,000	10,000	10,000
12 Subtotal	$540,800	$984,000	$977,800	$977,800	$977,800	$977,800	$977,800
13 Expansion to 4,000 lb/hr	200,000						
14 Amortization & Interest 6% Loan		26,000	24,800	23,600	22,400	21,200	
15 Amortization & Interest (Raw Mtl. Loan) (1st year) Initial 3 months period)		7,200	47,200	44,800	42,400		
16 Total Expenditures Before Taxes	$740,800	$1,018,000	$1,049,800	$1,046,200	$1,042,600	$999,000	$977,800
17 Taxes (30% Taxable Income)	25,000	63,000	53,000	54,000	55,000	68,000	75,000
18 Total Expenditures	$765,800	$1,081,000	$1,102,800	$1,100,200	$1,097,600	$1,067,000	$1,052,800
19 Net Cash Available (Receipts - Expend.)	$142,700	$179,000	$159,200	$159,800	$162,400	$193,000	$207,200
20 Dividends (60% after 1st year)	$50,000	$108,000	$96,000	$96,000	$98,000	$116,000	$124,000

ations were estimated at about two-thirds capacity to allow for startup period adjustments. After the first year the plant was scheduled to operate 300 days annually. Operating cost including labor and supplies in the projection were based on industry experience.

Revenue projections from oil and meal shown in the projection were based on market estimates for sales in the Philippines. Coproducts estimated that payments for oil sales would be made within 30 to 40 days of production and that, therefore, the Philippines plant would be essentially a cash operation.

Coconut costs would be related to current copra prices which were subject to some fluctuations. Such fluctuations, however, would be reflected in corresponding increases or decreases in the prices of coconut products.

As a 50% owner of the Philippine plant Coproducts Corporation was to receive approximately 50% of any dividends declared by the Philippines operation. The projection assumed that 60% of the cash available annually would be distributed to stockholders after the first year.

7. Product Sales

(a) *Oil*

To keep distribution and inventory costs to a minimum, Coproducts planned to sell the edible oil produced from the initial plant to oil processor-distributors in Manila, using a figure of 11¼¢ per pound which industry sources regard as reasonable. Preliminary investigation indicated the possibility of contracting with processors to take the total output at a premium of approximatelly ½¢ per pound above copra oil prices and this premium was included in the company's income projections. Sales for oil from future plants would be dictated by local conditions. However, the company believed that its refining cost savings over copra oil would have the effect of a premium over such oil equal to or greater than that envisaged for the Philippines.

(b) *Meal*

Since an edible meal free of significant discoloration was a new product, no established market price existed for this product. The company calculated that a price of 5¢ per pound might be obtained, based upon discussions with potential users and the market price for related commodities. Some indication of demand is contained in the following examples:

1. A food broker operating in the U.S. and Europe had a client who had been seeking a supply of edible coconut meal for use in specialty bakery products. The initial requirement was for an estimated million pounds annually at a price in the range of 7¢ to 8¢ in Manila.
2. The management of a large bakery chain in the U.S. had stated a desire to market a bread containing coconut meal when a guaranteed supply of the meal was available. Coconut meal in this case would replace up to approximately 20% wheat flour, at current costs of about 7¢ per pound.
3. Desiccated coconut prices were in the range of 13¢ to 15¢ in Manila, and about 110,000 metric tons of desiccated coconut was produced in 1961. Coproducts meal appeared to have some possibility of sale as a replacement in part for desiccated coconut. A meal made from corn was being promoted for use as an extender of the coconut content in confectionery products at a price of 8¢ to 10¢ per pound.

Other possibilities included use as an extender in meat products, as a replacement for wheat thus saving foreign exchange, particularly important in coconut-producing areas, as a breakfast food, and if necessary to prevent inventory buildups during early marketing stages at a premium over copra cake, as cattle food. Copra cake is rancid and burnt during pressing and Coproducts meal was believed to be sufficiently more desirable to be able to secure at least 10% premium over the Manila price for copra cake of about 2.9¢ per pound.

8. Plant Sales After Philippines Plant Operation

Coproducts Corporation anticipated that expansion of plant sales after demonstration of the success of the initial Philippines operation would be rapid and profitable; a ten year corporate income projection is shown as Appendix 3. The company's optimism was based on potential client contacts in a number of countries and investigations of sites in the Philippines, in Mexico, Malaya, Pakistan, India, Thailand, Guam, South Vietnam, and British Honduras. As a result of a few articles by Mr. Hiller, 45 potential clients actively engaged in the coconut business had indicated considerable interest in the potential of the Hiller Process. It felt that in many cases the interest would lead to negotiations and sale once the initial plant was a demonstrated economic and technical success.

Sales of plants following that in the Philippines were expected to be made on a participation basis. The company felt that, after proof of the Hiller Process, considerable financial aid would be available for investment in coconut-producing countries from international government lending agencies. Considerable private capital in the countries might be expected also to become available for investment in local industries which have a demonstrated operating capability and attractive profit potential. Finally, after the 5th or 6th year of Coproducts operation, the company anticipated that earnings available to Coproducts Corporation would be substantial enough to permit the Corporation itself to help customer-clients in financing new plants.

QUESTIONS

1. How would you classify the investment potential offered by Coproducts Corporation?
2. How should the company go about securing the necessary investment?
3. If you were to invest in this proposal, what safeguards would you seek to establish? What changes in operations or other aspects of the undertaking would you try to have made?
4. Do you consider the Philippines the best choice for an initial plant, if a local associate were available in other coconut-producing countries?

APPENDIXES

1. Financial statements, Coproducts Corporation, as of Sept. 30, 1962.
2. Patent Data.
3. Income Projection, Coproducts Corporation, 10 year period.
4. Coproducts Capitalization after new investment.

APPENDIX 1
COPRODUCTS CORPORATION
Balance Sheet, September 30, 1962

ASSETS

Current Assets - Cash in Bank...................................		$ 189.38
Equipment & Patents		
Equipment & Patents	$69,812.00	
Equipment Engineering - (Incurred Costs)	54,411.84	
Patents - (Incurred Costs)	7,600.16	
Total Equipment & Patents		131,824.00
Organization Expenses - (less amortization)		872.24
Deferred Equipment & Patent Payments (Payable to S. Hiller - payments based on a percentage of future plants' sales)..		40,000.00
Total		$172,885.62

LIABILITIES

Current Liabilities		
Advances Payable to Rogers Engineering Co., Inc.	$ 40,008.72	
Total Current Liabilities		$ 40,008.72
Deferred Equipment & Patent Payments (Payable to S. Hiller - payments based on a percentage of future plant sales)...		40,000.00
Total		$ 80,008.72
Capital & Surplus (Deficit)		
Common Stock, Par Value $10/share:		
Authorized 50,000 shares; reserved for promotional services 5,000 shares; issued and outstanding 15,286 shares (H. Rogers, Jr. 7,786 shares; Stanley Hiller 7,500 shares)	152,860.00	
Preferred Stock, Par Value $10/share:		
Authorized 20,000; issued and outstanding	none	
Surplus (Deficit)	(59,983.10)	
Stockholders Equity		92,876.90
Total		$172,885.62

Coproducts Corporation

APPENDIX 2
COPRODUCTS CORPORATION
Revenues and Expenses

Total to-date, Revenue & Expenses for the period
Beginning May 1, 1960 and Ending September 30, 1962

Revenue		$12,000.00
Expenses		
Business Promotion	$ 1,857.64	
Car Expense	23.98	
Insurance	547.40	
Office Rent & Utilities	3,826.22	
Office Supplies	2,912.98	
Office Services	10,249.27	
Printing & Reproductions	145.96	
Services - General Manager	18,205.22	
Services - Engineer	11,933.67	
Travel Expense	2,731.49	
Transportation	4,370.32	
Legal Expenses	783.79	
Telephone & Cable	962.75	
Miscellaneous Technical Services	11,412.92	
Amortization & Organization Expenses	436.16	
Taxes - Payroll	881.18	
Taxes - Other	702.15	
Total Expense		71,983.10
Deficit		$59,983.10

APPENDIX 3
COPRODUCTS CORPORATION
Projected Income
10-Year Period

Description	Development Period 5/60-8/62	Initial Plant Constr. Period	1	2	3	4	5	6	7	8	9	10
1 Number of Plants Sold	0	0	1	2	6	7	10	10	11	11	11	11
2 Cumulative Plants Sold	0	0	1	3	9	16	26	36	47	58	69	80
3 Income (Sales Margin and Plant Operations Participation)		0	$25,000	$270,000	$728,000	$932,000	$1,369,000	$1,538,000	$1,810,000	$1,986,000	$2,162,000	$2,338,000
4 Expenses (Net Operating)		$12,000	31,000	123,000	233,000	262,000	283,000	283,000	290,000	290,000	290,000	290,000
5 Net Profit (Before Tax)		(12,000)	(6,000)	147,000	495,000	670,000	1,086,000	1,255,000	1,520,000	1,696,000	1,872,000	2,048,000
6 Taxes (50% Estimated)				35,000	248,000	335,000	543,000	628,000	760,000	848,000	936,000	1,024,000
7 Net Profit After Tax	($60,000)	(12,000)	(6,000)	112,000	247,000	335,000	543,000	627,000	760,000	848,000	936,000	1,024,000
8 Annual Return Earned on Original Investment (Note 1)				32%	70%	96%	155%	180%	217%	242%	267%	292%
9 Earnings Per Share (Note 2)				$3.20	$7.00	$9.60	$15.50	$18.00	$21.70	$24.20	$26.70	$29.20

NOTES:
1. Coproducts Capitalization at End of Initial Plant Construction Period - $350,000 (Rounded)
2. Shares Issued at End of Initial Plant Construction Period - 35,000 (Rounded)
3. Year One is Same as First Year of Initial Plant Operations

Coproducts Corporation

APPENDIX 4
COPRODUCTS CORPORATION
Coproducts Capitalization (after new investment)

Possible Forms of Capitalization

At the time of completion of the Basilan Coproducts Plant, the total capitalization of Coproducts would be as follows if common stock were issued for the new capital required.

Stock Issued as of 8/31/62	15,286 Shares	$152,860	45%
Promotional Shares Authorized............... (Assigned to H. Rogers on completion of investment)	5,000 Shares	50,000	15%
New Investment - Basilan	14,000 Shares	140,000	40%
TOTAL CAPITAL	34,286 Shares	342,860	100%

The preceding distribution of capital stock has been presented for illustrative purposes to give an indication of the approximate equity ownership in Coproducts Corporation for an investment up to $140,000.

The final form of capital structure would depend on the method agreeable to the Corporation and the subscribers. Depending on the investors requirements, possible altervatives to the above are many, such as: issuance of preferred stock; corporate notes with common stock shares attached; serial notes given to the manufacturers for process equipment, or stock issued for equipment, materials, or services in kind.

Brazil

24

Credibook S.A.*†

In Table 1 are the records of sales and collections of Credibook S.A. for the period from September 1958 through April of the current year. (All currency figures are expressed in "Cruzeiros.")

TABLE 1

Months	Gross Sales	Net Sales	Collections	Invoices
September	2,160,336	1,916,376	1,287,771	272
October	1,962,963	1,739,348	1,283,360	229
November	2,538,690	2,228,145	1,305,169	334
December	2,196,453	1,864,715	1,583,102	256
January	1,509,486	1,132,241	1,203,814	236
February	2,539,170	2,009,171	1,759,604	307
March	2,862,249	2,362,770	1,156,649	388
April	3,499,434	2,869,967	1,472,511	442

Credibook S.A. is a firm specializing in selling books on credit. It was founded in 1957 by a group of directors of Bublibook S.A., a traditional publishing company in São Paulo, Brazil, who realized this would be a means of increasing the sales of some of its best selections. Thanks to an efficient group of salesmen and the good acceptance of the works selected, sales increased rapidly till they reached the present level. The firm has no retail store.

The selections are generally sold in 16 equal installments and their prices vary from Cr$3,200 to $10,500. The sales force is composed of 18 men who work chiefly with schools, offices, clubs, etc., and whose remuneration is exclusively based on commission. The mark-up is 80% distributed as follows:

    22% Salesman commission
    13% Collector commission
    25% Operating expenses
    20% Net profit

The income tax is paid on the basis of 30% of the net profit. The excess profit tax for publishing and book distributing companies is paid only when the

---

*Case written by Prof. Alfonso C.A. Arantes with data collected by the author. This material has been developed at the School of Business Administration of São Paulo, Brazil.
†Distributed by the Intercollegiate Case Clearing House, Soldiers Field, Boston, Mass. 02163. All rights reserved to the contributors. Printed in USA.

net profit at the end of the fiscal year represents more than 40% of the registered capital.

In the middle of May 1959, Mr. Joaquim Pires, director of Credibook, while examining the trial balance of April, became worried about the small amount of cash balance shown. He then asked his accountant to give him the records of these balances for the last months of 1958 and all the months of 1959 up to the nearest date. (See Exhibits 1 and 2.)

EXHIBIT 1
CREDIBOOK S.A.

Income Statement for the Period from Jan. 1, 1958 to Dec. 31, 1959

Debits

To General Expense	$3,022,448.20
To Taxes	90,937,20
To Insurance	6,372.50
To Interests	71,110.00
To Depreciation Expense	92,757.60
To Legal Reserve	59,340.00
To Allowance for Bad Debts	1,584,120.00
To Net Income for Stockholders	1,523,833.40
	$6,450,918.90

Credits

From 1958 Balance	$ 396,393.10
From Gross Profit of Social Operations	4,504,547.00
From Reversion of Provision for Bad Debts	1,097,668.80
From Other Income	452,310.00
	$6,450,918.90

The record presented by the accountant with the cash balances at the 10th of each month since September 1958 is shown below:

September	$511,203	January	$387,642
October	257,414	February	347,452
November	565,213	March	307,227
December	834,086	April	258,664
		May	256,803

From the figures presented Mr. Pires came to the conclusion that if the trend kept on in the same direction the firm would soon face a difficult financial situation. The sales had been increasing continuously since the beginning of the year, and salesmen's forecasts for the next months were as good as possible.

In a meeting of Credibook's directors, held on May 19, it was decided that maximum sales quotas should be established for each salesman—in an amount equal to half of the monthly average obtained in the first four months of the year—and that some of the weaker ones should be dismissed. Other alternative

# Credibook S.A.

EXHIBIT 2
CREDIBOOK S.A.
Balance Sheet as of December 31, 1958

ASSETS

Fixed Assets
Furniture, etc.	$ 414,897.70	
Vehicles	256,338.00	$ 671,235.70

Current Assets
Cash	89,635.20	
Banks	907,081.20	
Inventory	1,215,726.00	
Unpaid subscribed stocks	570,000.00	
Compulsory deposits	17,460.00	
Notes receivable	231,728.30	
Accounts receivable	84,582.00	
Accounts receivable (credit department)	15,889,488.90	19,005,701.60
		$19,676,937.30

LIABILITIES AND NET WORTH

Net Worth
Capital stock	$ 6,000,000.00	
Legal reserve	150,733.70	
Reserve for depreciation	167,114.30	
Allowance for bad debts	1,584,120.00	
Profit and loss	1,523,833.40	$ 9,425,801.40

Current Liabilities
Accounts payable (miscellaneous)	1,012,509.70	
Notes payable	542,005.70	
Accounts payable suppliers	67,813.20	
Other accounts payable	92,677.30	1,715,005.90

Long-Term Debt
Accounts payable (miscellaneous)	5,447,380.00	
Accounts payable suppliers	417,656.10	
Notes payable	2,671,093.90	8,536,130.00
		$19,676,937.30

solutions examined at that meeting were:
1. Increase the capital of the firm.
2. Bank financing. The firm could give as a collateral its promissory notes on accounts receivable in the city of São Paulo (approximately 30% of the total) and obtain renewable loans for a maximum period of 150 days each, with an interest rate of 1% a month plus expenses of 3% to 5% of the amount received.
3. Financing through participation of an acceptance company on the basis of approximately 2.5% a month of the amount represented by the promissory notes given as collateral.

25
The Liomar Printing Co. Ltd.*

This firm was organized around 1933 mainly to put into use the business contacts that its founding partners had with large companies which in their everyday activities, needed very much the service of a print shop.

Its original proprietors and founders were Mr. Almeida, Mr. Leme, Mr. Junqueira, Mr. Dias, Mr. Camargo, and Mr. Silveira.

Of these, only the first three, Almeida, Leme and Junqueira possessed the necessary qualifications to lead the company through its development. The others merely contributed sums of money as investments, but did not enter actively into its affairs either because of advanced age or through lack of interest in this particular field.

Mr. Almeida and Mr. Leme, the more interested ones, involved themselves primarily in the general decisions, which gave them an opportunity in retaining a big portion of their time for other business activities.

Thus it was that Mr. Junqueira, the partner who, as manager, gave all his time to the Liomar Printing Co. Ltd. He was helped by two subordinates; Mr. Lombardi who was in charge of the office and its daily routine, and Mr. Moacir, who was in charge of accounting and who enjoyed a very high confidence from Mr. Leme and Mr. Almeida by virtue of having long worked in another of their enterprises.

We could distinguish two well-defined periods in the development process of the print shop.

The first period, which extended from its start to the year 1960, was characterized by a conservative attitude of the management and a sense of self-preservation. Many innovations have been introduced since then, but let us proceed to enumerate first the original principles and the adopted methods as this will aid in understanding the subsequent development that followed. All right then, the basic idea was to deal only with those companies in which the partners had an interest also. From which arose the following situation:

Sales: These limited themselves almost entirely to filling the existing clients' orders. As the latter did not require estimates, these were not made which eliminated the necessity of reviewing the current prices asked on the graphic market in general to see how competitive were the work estimates that were given. There was only one salesman who actually acted just as an inter-

*School of Business Administration of The Getulio Vargas Foundation.

The Liomar Printing Co. Ltd.

mediary in the transactions, simply recording the orders and bringing them to the firm for execution. It should be observed that this procedure really created an artificial climate within the firm not in step with the actual situation existing on the graphic market, that of an unyielding competition.

Production: Yet as the result of the mentioned business relationships, free from competition and attuned to the normal work schedule of the client companies, the same kind of accomodation was felt also in this sector. The clients' work orders themselves served as basis for daily work programming. On the other hand, the constant repetition of the same formats and styles that never were altered helped to reduce production problems, as their solution became repetitive and automatic.

Around 1959 the company possessed two manual printing presses and four automatic ones.

At that time it had six pressmen, one typographer, one cutter and three workers in the finishing section.

Finances: The Liomar Printing Co. had no serious problems in this sector. Due to the solid credit rating of their clients and the other business interests of its co-owners, there was no difficulty of cashing commercial notes or even getting a long-term loan.

Office: Until the end of 1959, Mr. Junqueira held the post of manager assisted by Mr. Lombardi, who assumed the post after the former's death.

After the passing of Mr. Junqueira, there have been made some changes in the firm's structure. It was changed from a limited company to a corporation, having Mr. Leme as its major shareholder. Some new persons were admitted mostly to fulfill the exigency of the legal "quorum."

This is how the company's new organization chart looked:

President: Mr. Leme
Vice-President: Mrs. Leme
Managers: Mr. Lombardi and Mr. Leme, Jr.

Mr. Lombardi and Mr. Leme, Jr. were elected to managerial posts. The latter was the eldest son of Mr. Leme. He brought a good deal of dynamism, so typical to his age which contrasted with the old spirit in the company. Under his active leadership many changes and even enlargements were effected. This characterized a transitory phase that led to the second stage in the development of the firm.

Some presses were changed and new ones were acquired. The breakdown then became: 5 automatic machines; 3 manual machines; 1 paper cutter.

Besides Mr. Lombardi, Mr. Leme, Jr. and Mr. Moacir three other persons began working in the office. One was in charge of sales and the emission of fiscal notes; the second was responsible for the emission of work orders and the third prepared the pay sheet and kept the account books.

A work order is prepared before the start of each order and is intended principally to furnish information used in establishing prices and controlling the cost of each service. After updating the machinery, Mr. Leme, Jr. managed to increase substantially their sales, even getting orders which were not possible to fill before.

In 1959 the firm had a volume of sales of about 700,000,000 cruzeiros.

In 1961, after the updating which opened new sales opportunities, this sales volume increased to approximately 3,000,000,00 cruzeiros.

At the end of 1960 the firm suffered yet one more loss through death. Mr. Lombardi passed away from a stroke. Because of this, Mr. Leme, Jr. became the only manager for about a year, helped by Mr. Moacir who assumed a wider authority.

In view of the rapid growth of the Liomar Printing Co. and in spite of Mr. Moacir's efficient assistance, Mr. Leme, Jr. felt the need of another person who could help him with decisions. Thus in 1962, Mr. Carlos Medeiros, 23 years of age, a newly-graduated economist and brother-in-law of Mr. Leme, Jr. was invited to fill the post of manager vacated by the death of Mr. Lombardi. Mr. Medeiros has already had some previous print-shop experience, as he had been at one time, owner of a magazine with a small circulation when he was in charge of composition or, in other words, of setting type and of paging the magazine thus necessarily maintaining a very close contact with several printing firms.

Mr. Carlos Medeiros occupied himself initially with working out a system of controls and criteria for work schedules and stock inventory. This was non-existent until then. He found this necessary because he envisaged gaining a big slice of the graphic market with the modern and high-output machines they acquired. This would rid the firm of its dangerous dependence on a few select companies for their subsistence.

Both Mr. Leme and Mr. Moacir did not accept this reasoning. They thought that the firm was in good condition and new problems should not be sought as work did come in normally, although, they admitted not in great quantity, but everything should be left "well alone." However, the system of output programming increased the machine's efficiency which began producing all that was required and yet stood idle for long periods. This showed that their output capacity was greater than the company's work load.

From this point the whole management saw the necessity of increasing the firm's clientele even if it meant catering to customers outside the old group.

With the advent of new customers, Mr. Carlos Medeiros was obliged to take charge of production exclusively as the necessities of giving detailed estimates and stringent delivery dates topped with the appearance of new printing formats and types, brought about a rash of production errors and delivery delays. Due to these circumstances, Mr. Moacir, with Mr. Leme's full backing began reiterating that these problems were the result of their sales expansion beyond the original group of customers. And, besides the above mentioned problems there appeared another vexation: their high prices were responsible for losing about 90% of the potential orders, provoking frustration and dissatisfaction among the salesmen.

The Liomar Printing Co. Ltd.

Nevertheless, Mr. Medeiros, strongly backed by the shop superintendent, Mr. Alberto Mendes, insisted upon adjusting the production to conform with the new production demands. The fruit of their labor began appearing gradually when the average waiting period for delivery went from 30 days to between 20 and 15 days, depending upon the case.

At this time the company had a monthly sales volume of about 8,000,000,00 cruzeiros.

Due to the stable financial position enjoyed by the firm and also to the interest of its president, Mr. Leme, in investments an English "offset" press was acquired in 1963 which opened the possibility of producing high-quality prints, in great numbers. With this, the need to expand their sales to fully use the new potentialities became more urgent.

Simultaneously another event came to complicate matters at the firm. Mr. Leme, Jr. at his father's invitation began working exclusively for another company of which his father was president.

Managerial responsibility became practically divided between Mr. Moacir and Mr. Carlos Medeiros. This was because the latter was already so named and the former enjoyed the aforementioned confidence and also possessed the company's power-of-attorney which required his assent to all the daily administrative functions. The corporation's statutes stipulated that all administrative or commercial documents would be valid only if signed by two directors or by a director and the proxy.

Nearly simultaneously, there opened an opportunity for Mr. Carlos Medeiros to take post-graduate courses at E.A.E.S.P. In virtue of this it became impossible for Mr. Medeiros to give all his time to the corporation, only half a day. These circumstances obliged Mr. Moacir to intervene personally in the solution of occasional production problems when Mr. Medeiros was not available.

In March 1964, Mr. Moacir went to visit Mr. Leme and Mr. Leme, Jr., reporting to them some complaints from the salesmen to the effect that it was very hard for them to compete with rival establishments because of the high prices they had to quote. At their vehement dissent, he sided with the salesmen. "Low prices are reached only through low production costs which, in turn, can only be maintained by a rigid production control," he pointed out, adding "I cannot always be interfering with Mr. Medeiros' department unless I have his express authorization."

Mr. Leme and his son, recognizing that the facts presented to them needed their special attention resolved to call a meeting at which both Mr. Carlos Medeiros and Mr. Moacir would be presented, for such a state of affairs could not be left unattended.

At the meeting, with all the four directors on hand, after all the facts and figures had been presented, Mr. Moacir suggested to Mr. Carlos Medeiros that he recognize the situation and relinquish his administrative authority for the time being so that he, Mr. Moacir, would be in full charge until Mr. Medeiros could again devote all his attention to the corporation. This change could be effected very easily by simply notifying personally all the shop foremen.

Still a little surprised, Mr. Medeiros observed: "Gentlemen, although I am taken aback by the intent of this meeting, I find it a good opportunity to make some points clear to all! I would like for Mr. Moacir to answer some questions if all of you don't mind." As all agreed to this, the following dialogue developed:

Medeiros: Now that we have touched upon the question of prices, could Mr. Moacir explain to us why our final price always consists of the cost of materials directly used for the job, plus three times the cost of labor.

Moacir: Well, considering the record of our labor cost of last year as 100% it is easy to verify that our expenditures, the materials used indirectly, the social welfare payments, in short our overhead, is equal to an index of 300. Thus, it suffices to multiply the labor cost by three to get, along with the cost of the direct raw material and the labor cost of the job, the rest of the total charged.

Medeiros: But, in this case, if the total indirect charges equal three times the labor cost would it not be right to multiply by four instead? And there is something else I would like to know. How much of this total actually constitutes costs and how much is a margin?

Moacir: Well, I did not include in this total index of 300 a sum for workers' indemnization, which was not really extracted from our books but which would be in the event that we had to fire all our workers. As this is not a current fact, it is obvious that it constitutes a certain margin.

Medeiros: If I understood correctly, we would have "a certain margin" but would not be able to define exactly its amount, is this it?

Moacir: This is more or less so, but the truth is that at the end of the year I have shown how we profited by this, and no one can deny it!

Medeiros: My reason for asking was not to cast any doubt about our year-end's profit, but I got the answer I needed. Apparently we do not know exactly our margin of profit on each job we do. In fact our general expenses include numerous items that have nothing to do with direct production expenditures, but may be spent on our public relations activities and contacts with other firms and yet these also figure in your "production overhead."

Moacir: Certainly! Aren't we obliged to pay these expenses too?

Medeiros: I would like to bring your attention, gentlemen, to a comparison of the relationship between production potentiality and our sales volume. Do they compare favorably, and how does this relationship reflect upon our costs.

The Liomar Printing Co. Ltd.

Moacir. I respect your theories, but I think that if we have a greater output capacity than our sales warrant, battling as they are, against a stiff competition, it would be better to reduce our equipment and to close our sales department. Thus we shall lower our costs and still continue to sell to our original customer companies as before. For this we shall not need salesmen as our sales will be assured.

Medeiros: I believe that all of you, my fellow directors, will be able to form your own opinion as to the situation, if you just examine our sales records and the final balance as well as our profit and debit statements. (See Exhibits 1 through 4.) As for me, I accept Mr. Moacir's first suggestion but I shall defer to any final decision arrived at by this board, with the request that it should be made only after a full examination of the situation and of the contentions and facts brought to this meeting.

EXHIBIT 1
LIOMAR PRINTERS, INC.
Balance Sheet, December 31, 1962

ACTIVE

Frozen Assets		
Buildings	23.798.972	
Machines and accessories	24.431.285	
Printing materials	1.114.962	
Furniture and utensils	509.148	
Installation costs	757.483	
Motor vehicles	2.510.950	53.122.801
Realizable		
Bonds belong to us	109.700.000	
Compulsory loan	692.114	
Notes to collect	3.990.303	
Stock of raw material	2.368.002	116.750.419
Available		
Cash	4.610	
		169.877.830

PASSIVE

Not Required		
Capital	90.000.000	
Reserve fund	17.387.239	
Depreciations	3.660.000	111.047.239
Required		
Bank deposits	14.119.215	
Current obligations	26.064.372	
Notes to pay (payable)	9.150.000	
Supplied Securities	612.575	
Bills payable	560.000	
Contractual obligations	8.324.428	58.830.591
		169.877.830

EXHIBIT 2
LIOMAR PRINTERS, INC.
Balance Sheet, December 31, 1963

ACTIVE

Frozen Assets
Buildings	33.584.172	
Machines and accessories	28.270.198	
Printing material	1.114.962	
Furniture and utensils	1.074.170	
Installation costs	3.630.083	
Motor vehicles	4.292.470	71.966.055

Available
Cash and Bank Balance	161.477	

Realizable
Bonds owned	201.009.262	
Compulsory loan	1.149.459	
Notes to receive	77.422	
Notes being collected	205.888	
Stock of raw material	7.806.594	210.248.625
		282.376.157

PASSIVE

Not Required
Capital	90.000.000	
Reserve fund	17.387.239	
Fund for increasing the capital	23.863.869	
Depreciations	7.357.600	138.608.708

Required
Bank deposits	2.515.488	
Current obligations	12.959.233	
Notes payable	14.001.373	
Supplied securities	225.379	
Contractual obligations	114.065.976	143.767.449
		282.376.157

EXHIBIT 3
LIOMAR PRINTERS, INC.
Statement of Profit, and Debits, December 31, 1963

DEBITS

Depreciations	3.697.600	
Commercial expenses	20.560.979	
Sales expenses	11.079.543	
Financial expenditures	12.855.815	
Uncollectable notes	16.975	
Net profit for credit to "fund for increasing the capital"	3.526.869	51.737.781

CREDITS

Production sales	42.442.565	
Interest and discounts	224.435	
Rent revenues	680.000	
Other revenues	1.861.581	
Dividents on bearer stock certificates	6.529.200	51.737.781

The Liomar Printing Co. Ltd. 345

EXHIBIT 4
LIOMAR PRINTERS, INC.
Statement of Profits and Debits, December 31, 1962

DEBITS

Depreciations	812.291	
Commercial expenses	8.273.055	
Sales expenses	3.719.430	
Financial expenditures	5.495.812	
Uncollectable notes	74.916	
Resultant profit transferred to "Reserve fund"	7.268.575	25.644.079

CREDITS

Production sales	23.604.874	
Interest and discounts	178.005	
Rent revenues	480.000	
Dividends from shares	1.311.200	25.644.079

Mr. Leme and Mr. Leme, Jr., who had followed closely the foregoing conversation, found the proposition reasonable. It was agreed to meet again in two days at which time a final decision would be reached as to what guidelines to follow.

ELUCIDATION OF THE MANUFACTURING PROCESS

Generally the manufacturing process can be divided into four distinct phases:

1. *Cutting*: The paper comes in sheets of 66 × 96 cm. These have to be cut to the size required by the specifications. This has to be done most efficiently, bringing paper waste to the minimum.
2. *Composing*: The text is set into type in the composing section. Here are also stored such cliches of figures or signs that are not found in the existing type faces. These are usually ordered from an outside source especially for a particular job. Printing plates are then made and sent to the printing section.
3. *Printing*: The cut sheets and the assembled plates are then sent to the printing presses. Here inks are mixed to obtain the needed tonalities. The plates have to be mounted in a correct position relative to the paper upon which they will print, and then secured with bolts. The type and the cliches have to be aligned so that they are all at the same height. This will result in a firm contact on the whole page, avoiding having some parts of the page come out too dark and others too light. This preparation can take from five or ten minutes to three or four hours, depending upon the kind of job and only when it is finished can the printing proper begin. Besides, if there are multicolored prints to be made or if the printing is

done on both sides of the page, the above preparation will have to be repeated as many times as it is necessary.

It can be observed, in effect, that the costs of the printing section and the costs of the press preparations are fixed, irrespective of quantity ordered. From this comes the logic of the fact the cost of a single copy is inversely proportional to the total number of copies produced. That is, the larger the total quantity made, the cheaper each copy will cost and vice versa.

4. *Finishing*: At this phase the printed sheets are trimmed, counted, sorted, intercollated (when there are several different pages to assemble), stacked, glued, perforated or folded, folded etc.... Here the work is manual and repetitive. At this point the order is ready to be dispatched.

VARIABLES TO BE CONSIDERED FOR PRODUCTION PLANNING

The manual machines are distinguished from the automatic ones by their feed system. In the former, paper is fed by hand as fast as the attendant cares to do it. The average output of these machines is 700 copies an hour; the latter place each sheet where it receives the print and then, similarly, stack them after printing. Their average output is between 2,000 and 2,500 copies an hour.

On the other hand the operating cost is smaller for the manual machines. Thus, it is more advisable to use the manual machines for orders of less than 5,000 copies, as the low cost of the adjustments and preparations will not raise the unit price excessively.

Besides, the printing speed, such factors as the size of the print, how it compares with the maximum size of the machine is designed for and the paper's weight will have to be considered.

TABLE 1
List Showing Sales Distribution in 1964 Quoted in Cruzeiros, According to the Customers Type

Month	Group	Diverse	Percent of Diverse	Total
January	19.589.500	11.288.740	36,00%	30.878.000
February	24.028.000	7.370.000	23,47%	31.398.000
March	19.416.000	9.230.000	32,22%	28.646.000
April	15.600.000	11.278.000	41,95%	26.878.000
May	24.708.000	6.500.000	20,82%	31.208.000
June	22.936.000	7.642.000	25,00%	30.578.000
July	32.454.000	12.402.000	27,64%	44.856.000
August	30.464.000	9.788.000	24,31%	40.252.000
September	21.646.000	14.336.000	39,84%	35.982.000
October	26.000.000	16.000.000	38,09%	42.000.000

OBSERVATIONS: Until 1961 all the firm's clients were exclusively of the group. In 1962, 5% of sales were made to diverse buyers. In 1963, the percentage of sales to outside buyers was 15%.

The Liomar Printing Co. Ltd.

Among the automatic machines, the firm possesses one "OFF-SET" press whose average production is about 6,000 copies per hour. Its characteristics differ from those of the other presses in that its plates are not set locally and it cannot take the cliches. Its zinc plates are made outside by skilled professionals who first photograph the text or the figure to be printed then reproduce it on the plate by a chemical-photographic process called etching.

It would not be practical to set-up such a processing laboratory within the company unless it operated at least five such presses. Obviously their operating expenses are high, running to about three times the costs of the other automatic presses.

In view of its characteristics, its use is most indicated for high quality orders, possible in colors (it's capable of giving different gradations of one color at each pass through the rollers) or where the quantity of copies required is greater than 40,000 or 50,000.

It is important to note that these variables are the basic restrictions to be taken into account when trying to set-up any production schedule.

26

Peter Werner S.A.*

The industrial and commercial firm of "Peter Werner S.A. Industria e Comércio" was founded in 1935. It is based in Curitiba and today is one of the country's biggest manufacturer of fine containers which are made of wood covered with paper, leather-like cloth or just leather. This process gives the container a much greater resistance than if it were made of cardboard. Manufacturers of high quality fountain pens and jewellers in general, who need boxes for their products are its biggest customers.

The firm was founded by Peter Werner, a German businessman whose family had lived many years in Brazil. After its beginning the firm went through good and bad phases, through periods of prosperity and stagnation. World War II helped the firm's business, but during the following post-war period that brought a great influx of imported goods, there was somewhat of a recession. The most recent market tendency (around 1962) is favorable to the firm. Its sales have climbed and the market seemed to be expanding enough to absorb more than Peter Werner S.A. entire production.

Around 1958 Mr. Werner, little by little, began to disassociate himself from the business. The firm's Production Department was not under his supervision. He had given it, from the start, to Mr. Rudolfo Heuser, who was a small shareholder of the firm. Mr. Heuser was a competent man in his field, although he did not keep in touch with the latest developments in the methods of organizing and controlling production.

He was acquainted, however, with all the secrets of container manufacturing. He was a good technician who knew how to control his workers and keep them happy without too much friction or inefficiency.

Mr. Werner supervised all the other departments of the firm. In the past few years, however, he began losing interest in the firm's affairs. He was more than 50 years old and thought that he had achieved enough during his life to give him and his family a secure future. He fully owned some high priced real estate. Thus it looked to him that the time had come to enjoy his life, to travel, to hunt and to relax a little.

In 1961, his son-in-law Walter Schmidt, recently married who had finished a post-graduate course at the School of Business Administration of São Paulo, returned to Curitiba and was invited to take over the direction of the firm at Mr. Werner's side. He had a country house in Bariloche and some relatives in

*School of Business Administration of the Getulio Vargas Foundation in São Paulo.

Peter Werner S.A.

Europe. In any case, he took special pleasure in travelling. Thus, nearly the whole administration of the firm went into the hands of Walter Schmidt, who divided his time between the firm and the Bank of Regional Development of the Extreme South at its branch in Curitiba where he was the consultant in economics. This latter post, although not too well-paid, gave him a certain prestige and self-independence. Besides the work was pleasant and in which he was interested, so he did not plan to leave it.

Walter Schmidt noticed immediately that a series of steps had to be taken. Before this, however, he made a review of the general state of the company. (See Exhibits 1 through 6.) The conclusions he arrived at were the following:

1. The sales revenues had been mounting steadily in cruzeiros, but only because of inflation, whereas the actual production volume has been steady for some years.
2. The firm depended for about 40% of its sales upon just five salesmen, which eased in a way its selling effort.
3. The company's work force was composed of (a) 80 workers of which 75 were women and of these 30% were minors. (This was because there were many simple manual tasks to be performed like assembling and stacking the containers.) (b) 4 employees who did the accounting, prepared the pay sheets and did other general office work, and (c) the three directors.
4. The factory was located in an old two-story building which gave rise to a very inefficient system of internal movement of materials and products. The management had a long-standing plan to move the factory to a building next door, which was more suitable. This building was built especially to house a factory, but, when there appeared an opportunity to open a general warehousing business, the first plan was abandoned. The warehousing business was started by Mr. Werner and its direction was given to another son-in-law of his, who was thoroughly acquainted with this type of business. Because a series of changes in the market recently this business had become less interesting. The old plan of moving the factory was again revived, but nothing has been decided as yet. It was estimated that the cost of moving would be high and there was hesitation to take any final action in this matter.
5. The factory machines were reasonably modern. The majority have been acquired from São Paulo industrialists who first imported them but subsequently did not find an easy market for their products. They were specially-made machines. Some cut the thin panels of wood, others glued the boxes together.
6. The company's products enjoyed a good reputation on the market because of their high quality, which was greatly superior to that of their competitors. On the other hand, their prices were generally considered high.

EXHIBIT 1
PETER WERNER S.A.
General Account as of June 30, 1961

ACTIVE

	CR$	CR$
Available		
Cash and Deposits		2.613.706,30
Realizable in Short Term		
General Merchandise (Warehouse)	2.033.000,00	
Various Creditors	8.306.040,60	10.341.040,60
Realizable in Long Term		
Compulsory Loan for Income Tax	472.577,40	
Peter Werner, with Realizable Capital	292.687,50	
Peter Werner, with Private Funds	807.396,10	
Wilheim Heinrich Kohlman with Private Funds	767.734,60	2.340.395,60
Frozen Assets		
Machines and Equipment	2.719.334,80	
Furniture and Utensils	242.672,10	
Tools	5.535,60	
Motor Vehicles	2.036.786,00	
Shares (All Types)	191.250,00	
Revaluation of the Active Funds (Law 2862/56)	1.000.000,00	
Trade Names and Patents	70.000,00	
Bonds	1.700,00	6.267.278,50
Balance (Offset)		
Suspended Dividends		11.764,00
		21.574.185,00

PASSIVE

	CR$	CR$
Realizable in Short Term		
Creditors	2.013.296,20	
Sum Outstanding to the "Agricola Mercantil S.A. Bank"	239.268,60	
Income Tax payment	994.700,00	
Additional Income Tax Payment	136.600,00	
Contributions to be Paid to I.A.P.I.	163.506,70	
Contributions to be Paid to I.A.P.E.T.C.	1.594,50	
Various Taxes to be Paid	121.306,30	3.670.292,30
Realizable in Long Term		
Brunhilde Werner-JACONO-Private Funds	590.608,20	
Astrid Werner - Private Funds	451.253,20	
Werner and Co. Ltd.	11.429,50	1.053.290,90
Unrequirable		
Capital	5.000.000,00	
Social Laws Fund	1.980.654,70	
Special Reserve Fund	6.000.000,00	
Depreciation Fund	3.027.579,10	
Recalcitrant Debtors Fund	830.604,00	16.838.837,80
Balance (Offset)		
Dividends to be received		11.764,00
		21.574.185,00

Peter Werner S.A.

EXHIBIT 2
PETER WERNER S.A.
Account of Profits and Liabilities

General Account as of June 30, 1961

	CR$	CR$
Credits		
Sales for the Period of July, 1960, to June '61		38.268.161,20
Stock of Raw Material as of June, 1960	1.460.983,10	
Raw Material Bought	11.944.570,70	13.405.533,80
Balance on 6/30/61		24.862.607,40
Inventory of Raw Material Stock Made on 6/30/61		2.035.000,00
Inventory Total		26.897.607,40
Recalcitrant Debtors Fund		
Last Balance Brought Forward		348.220,00
Share Dividends		
Dividends Received from Various Shares		2.866,80
Interest and Discounts		
Balance of Account		10.405,00
Gross Profit		27.259.099,20
Liabilities		
Rents	119.000,00	
Taxes and Duties	5.224.785,50	
Various Securities	360.961,30	
Salaries	7.465.469,70	
Renumerations	1.658.118,80	
Overhead for Personnel	959.790,00	
Work Charges	316.175,00	
Payments into Social Funds (I.A.P.I & I.A.P.E.T.C.)	971.985,70	
Gasoline and Lubricants	199.279,60	
Maintenance and Cleaning	119.703,90	
Office Supplies	61.092,30	
Electric Power	120.695,20	
Contract for Technical Assistance	536.290,00	
Deliveries, Telegrams and Telephones	62.028,70	
Freight and Haulage	847.356,20	
Transportation	2.209,00	
Sales Commissions	108.476,20	
Monthly Subscriptions, Newspaper & Magazine	7.220,00	
Banking Charges and Commissions	313.024,10	
Travel Expenses	187.312,90	
Advertisement and Publicity	55.421,80	
Costs of Agencies	117.580,00	
Machine Repairs and Installations	165.418,70	
Accessories for Machines and Installations	252.329,80	
Various Expenses	689.360,00	
Repair of Vehicles	106.932,00	
Interest on Profits	530.000,00	
Various Debtors		
Invoices Considered Unpayable	98.891,40	
Administrator's Salaries	1.252.800,00	
Depreciation Fund		
10% on Machines and Equipment	271.933,50	
10% on Furniture and Utensils	24.267,20	
10% on Tools	553,60	
10% on Vehicles	407.357,20	704.111,50
Fund Against Recalcitrant Debtors		
10% on Various Debtors		830.604,00

Gross Profit Brought Forward	27.259.099,20	
Liabilities Brought Forward	24.444.413,50	
Net Profit Brought Forward	2.814.685,70	

	CR$	CR$
Transferred into the following		
Special Reserve Fund	2.200.000,00	
Reserve for Social Funds	614.685,70	2.814.685,70

EXHIBIT 3
PETER WERNER S.A.
General Account as of December 31, 1961

ACTIVE

		CR$	CR$
Available			
101 - Cash		263.415,20	
111 - The "Agricola Mercantil S.A. Bank"	23.298,50		
114 - The "Expansao Economica S.A. Bank"	1.433,40		
115 - The "Banko do Brasil S.A."	808,30		
116 - The "R.G. do Sul S.A. Bank"	1.000,00	26.540,20	289.955,40
Realizable in Short Term			
110 - Various Debtors Already Billed		12.544.225,40	
303 - General Merchandise (In Stock)		2.374.560,00	
125 - Advanced Payments to Employees		8.750,00	14.927.535,40
Realizable in Long Term			
126 - Compulsory Loan (Income Tax)		472.577,40	
221 - Peter Werner - Private Funds	1.100.083,60		
222 - W. Heinrich Kohlmann	847.734,60	1.947.818,20	2.420.395,60
Frozen Assets			
120 - Machines and Equipment		4.356.288,40	
121 - Furniture and Utensils		1.106.229,50	
122 - Tools		5.675,60	
123 - Motor Vehicles		2.373.836,00	
109 - Shares		191.250,00	
108 - Revaluation of the Active Fund		4.000.000,00	
119 - Trade Marks and Patents		70.000,00	
118 - Bonds		1.700,00	
133 - Installations (stock room)		76.877,70	12.181.857,20
Transients			
129 - Various Debtors of the Warehouse		1.479.704,80	
128 - Peter Werner & Co. - Capital		9.766,00	1.489.470,80
Balance (Offset)			
132 - Suspended Dividends			11.764,00
			31.320.978,40

PASSIVE

		CR$	CR$
Realizable in Short Term			
Creditors		1.731.466,60	
Contributions to I.A.P.I.		316.325,60	
Contributions to I.A.P.E.T.C.		3.960,00	
312 - Duties and Taxes (Sales Tax)		91.644,30	
112 - The "Frances e Brasileiro" Bank		793.633,40	
213 - Bonuses to be Paid		356.200,00	4.293.299,90
Realizable in Long Term			
223 - Brunhilde Werner - Jaconi		250.688,20	
224 - Astrid Werner - Schimidt		203.013,20	453.701,40
Unrequirable			
201 - Capital		11.700.000,00	
202 - Fund for Payment under Social Laws		1.980.654,70	
203 - Special Reserve Fund		8.088.833,50	
204 - Depreciation Fund		3.538.372,40	
205 - Fund Against Recalcitrant Debtors		1.254.422,50	26.562.283,10
Balance (Offset)			
232 - Dividends to be Received			11.764,00
			31.320.978,40

Peter Werner S.A. 353

EXHIBIT 4
PETER WERNER S.A.
Account of Profit and Liabilities

General Account as of December 31, 1961

Credits

301 - Sales for the Period of July to December 1961			25.805.736,00
303 - Raw Material as of 6/30/61	2.035.000,00		
303 - Raw Material Paid Till 12/31/61	4.615.660,90		
303 - Raw Material on Credit as of 12/31/61	2.731.466,60	9.382.127,50	
Balance on 12/31/61		16.423.608,50	
303 - Raw Material on Inventory as of 12/31/61		2.374.560,00	
Grand total		18.798.168,50	

Recalcitrant Debtors Fund

Last Balance Brought Forward	830.604,00

Shares Dividends

Various Shares - Dividends Received	3.600,00

402 -	Interests and Discounts	
	Balance of Account	5.044,30

410 -	Profits and Debits		
	Proceeds from Sale of the "vacuum forming" machine		49.994,00
	Gross Profit		19.687.410,80

Debts

311 - Rents	474.000,00	
312 - Duties and Taxes	3.063.718,40	
313 - Various Insurance Policies	362.811,00	
314 - Administration Salaries	1.026.080,00	
315 - General Salaries	5.153.940,40	
316 - Wages	873.131,00	
317 - Overhead for Personnel	415.120,00	
318 - Work Charges	24.400,00	
319 - Fund for Payment to I.A.P.I. & I.A.P.E.T.C.	881.811,00	
320 - Secondary Material	4.928,00	
321 - Gasoline and Lubricants	183.942,10	
322 - Maintenance and cleaning	276.321,70	
323 - Office Supplies	76.933,20	
324 - Electric Power	119.503,50	
325 - Contract for Technical Assistance	199.750,00	
326 - Deliveries, Telegrams and Telephones	42.192,50	
327 - Freight and Haulage	446.047,70	
328 - Transportation	1.951,00	
329 - Sales Commissions	94.044,00	
330 - Subscriptions to Newspapers and Magazines	5.880,00	
331 - Banking Charges and Commissions	209.572,40	
332 - Travel and Lodging Expenses	116.599,90	
333 - Advertisement and Publicity	450,00	
334 - Other Costs of Agencies	610.653,90	
335 - Repairs and Installation of Machines	160.261,50	
336 - Machine Accessories & their Installations	110.312,20	
337 - General Expenses	54.996,20	
338 - Repairs of Motor Vehicles	35.970,00	15.025.321,50

Depreciation Fund

From June 30 to December 31, 1961

120 - 5% on Machines and Equipment	217.814,40	
121 - 5% on Furniture and Utensils	55.311,50	
122 - 5% on Tools	283,80	
123 - 10% on Motor Vehicles	237.383,60	510.793,30

Recalcitrant Debtors' Fund

110 - 10% on Unpaid Invoices	1.254.442,50	16.790.537,30
Net Profit		2.896.873,50

Transferred to
Special Reserve Fund 2.896.873,50

EXHIBIT 5
PETER WERNER S.A.
General Balance Closed on December 31, 1962

ACTIVE

Available

Cash	2.976.881,10	
The "Banco Agr. Mercantil S.A."	190.072,80	
The "Banco Fr. Brasileiro S.A."	1.807.799,60	
The "Rio Gr. Exp. Econ. S.A."	1.433,40	
The "Banco do Brasil S.A."	204.808,30	
The "Banco Est. R.G. do Sul S.A."	1.000,00	
The "Banco Ind. e Com. do Sul"	714.526,70	
The "Banco Merc. S. Paulo"	2.605.837,90	
The "Banco do Brasil (Farrapos)	1.557,90	8.503.917,70

Realizable in Short Term

Various Debtors	29.043.573,40	
Stock	3.236.640,00	32.280.213,40

Realizable in Long Term

Compulsory Loan to Internal Revenue Service	560.577,40	
Peter Werner - Private Capital	785.658,70	
Wilhelm H. Kohlmann - Priv. Capital	645.221,60	1.991.457,70

Frozen Assets

Machines and Equipment	4.649.306,40	
Furniture and Utensils	1.952.237,50	
Tools	15.902,20	
Motor Vehicles	2.088.354,00	
Shares	191.250,00	
Revaluation of the Active Fund	4.000.000,00	
Trade-Marks and Patents	70.000,00	
Bonds	1.700,00	12.968.750,10

Transients

Various Debtors of the Warehouse	91.806,50	
Goods kept in Warehouse	76.877,70	168.684,20

Balance (Offset)

Suspended Dividends		29.164,00
		55.942.187,10

PASSIVE

Requirable on Short Term

Creditors	6.510.021,20	
Sales Commissions	180.374,00	
Bonuses to be Paid	21.842,40	
Advance Payments to Employees	5.315,00	
Active Bonds	2.904.971,00	
Invoices to be Paid	1.066.400,50	10.688.924,10

Requirable on Long Term

Werner, S.A. Funds	1.162.649,90	
Brunhilde W. Jaconi - Private Funds	260.813,90	
Astrid W. Schmidt - Private Funds	213.138,90	
Claudio L. Jaconi - Private Funds	1.265,70	
Walter Schmidt - Private Funds	1.265,70	1.639.134,10

Unrequirable

Capital	15.200.000,00	
Fund for Payments under Social Laws	1.980.654,70	
Special Reserve Fund	8.088.833,50	
Legal Reserve Fund	184.829,10	
Depreciation Fund	4.607.776,60	
Recalcitrant Debtors Fund	2.904.357,30	32.966.451,20

Transients

Fund for Bonuses	800.000,00	
Investment Fund (Law No. 3470)	550.000,00	1.350.000,00

Balance (Offset)

Dividends to Receive		29.164,00

Pending Results

Results Incomplete (gains)		9.268.513,70
		55.942.187,10

Peter Werner S.A.

EXHIBIT 6
PETER WERNER S.A.
Statement of Profits and Debits

Credits

Sales for the Period of July to December 1962		56.453.827,00
Existing Raw Material in Stock on 6/30/62	2.850.350,00	
Raw Material Bought	19.747.937,80	22.598.287,80
Balance on 12/31/62		33.855.539,20
Warehouse No. 302		
Raw Material on Inventory as of 12/31/62		3.236.640,00
Merchandise in Stock		37.092.179,20
Recalcitrant Debtors Fund		
Last Balance Brought Forward		1.673.626,50
Results of Shares Owned - 401		
Various Shares Received Dividends		7.800,00
Interest and Discounts - 402 Balance of Account		217.605,10
Credits and Debits - 410 Proceeds from the sale		
of the Scraper		191.000,00
		39.182.210,80

Debits

311 - Rents	474.000,00	
312 - Dues and Taxes	5.351.106,80	
313 - Various Insurance Premiums	220.032,30	
314 - Administration Stipends	725.760,00	
315 - Salaries	9.035.470,00	
316 - Wages	1.964.114,60	
317 - Overhead for Personnel	1.649.607,50	
318 - Work Charges	213.600,00	
319 - Fund for Payment under Social Laws	954.494,10	
320 - Secondary Materials	56.990,00	
321 - Gasoline and Lubricants	214.720,50	
322 - Maintenance and Cleaning	325.058,30	
323 - Office Supplies	120.832,70	
324 - Electric Power	252.463,20	
325 - Contract for Technical Assistance	61.000,00	
326 - Deliveries, Telegrams and Telephones	121.362,80	
327 - Freight and Haulage	1.185.904,80	
328 - Transportation	8.502,00	
329 - Sales Commissions	2.372.044,50	
330 - Monthly subscriptions for Newspaper & Magazines	25.464,00	
331 - Banking Expenses and Commissions	251.456,70	
332 - Travel and Living Expenses	137.641,60	
333 - Advertisement and Publicity	15.000,00	
334 - Other Costs of Agencies	195.945,00	
335 - Maintenance of Machines & Installations	128.765,20	
336 - Accessories for Machines & Installations	149.346,00	
337 - Various Expenses	105.534,70	
338 - Repair of Motor Vehicles	153.414,80	
	26.469.632,10	

Depreciation Fund

120 - 5% on Machines and Equipment	232.465,30	
121 - 5% on Furniture and Utensils	97.611,90	
122 - 5% on Tools	975,10	
123 - 10% on Motor Vehicles	208.835,40	
	539.707,70	

Recalcitrant Debtors Fund

205 - 10% on Various Debtors	2.904.357,30	

Pending Results

411 - Results Incomplete (gains)	9.268.513,70	
Total	39.182.210,80	39.182.210,80

7. As the buyers themselves came to the firm and as there were but some 50 industries in all that did the buying, the company did not have salesmen. In São Paulo they have made a local company their representative.
8. The company's earnings were comfortable although not exceptional. To avoid paying higher taxes because of the company's growth a third firm was established to control the other two. The earnings of the two subsidiary companies were absorbed by the controlling firm, that later reinvested them.
9. The company's financial state was very solid. It seldom went to banks for loans. Walter Schmidt had calculated its index of solid-to-liquid assets; it varied between 3 and 4.
10. Cost accounting was done informally by Mr. Werner and, more recently, by Mr. Rudolfo Heuser. Both were very experienced in this work and knew how to calculate very precisely the cost of any product. In recent times, however, Mr. Heuser found it somewhat difficult because of inflation.

The first problem he tackled was that of cost estimate. He evolved an elaborate system of controls based on "cost centers" geographically disposed throughout the factory. With these "cost centers" a relationship between the firm's general expenses other than labor costs and the cost of labor alone, could be established and monitored. It was relatively easy to calculate the labor costs for the majority of the operations performed by the workers (an incentive system per linear part produced was widely used). Also, it was possible to determine precisely what operations went into manufacturing a container, and the latter's weight. Thus it was enough to add the cost of the raw materials to the cost of labor of each operation and to this add an overhead cost of each operation derived by comparing the general overhead gotten from all the "cost centers" to the labor cost of a particular center. This gave the total cost of a product. The biggest problem was to determine correctly the costs of the production centers. For example, because of inflation, all the machinery was revalued quarterly and over the total revaluation, 1% was deducted as a monthly depreciation. This method, however, made the product too expensive, pricing it out of the market.

One of the first results of these costs calculations was to show that 20% of their sales accounted for 80% of their profits. These were the sales of luxurious boxes for jewelry. However, Mr. W. Schmidt could not find any solution for this problem except, perhaps, through increasing their production of the Jewel boxes, as the buyers for the 80% of their production were old-time customers who paid promptly and, finally, accounted for the biggest part of the factory's output. The factory's modernization program was Walter Schmidt's concern. He had imported an automatic machine and installed it on the ground floor although there were two similar machines already on the first floor. This was because he was looking into the future when the whole factory would be moved

Peter Werner S.A.

to the adjacent building. He was thinking now of buying another automatic machine complementary to the one bought previously. He judged that it will cost 10 million cruzeiros, this price including all importation costs and that it will replace 10 factory girls.

After a year under his administration sales climbed so much that it was necessary to start a second work shift and to expand, in two steps, the numbers of workers to 120. Office personnel, however, was not altered.

Walter Schmidt thought that the moment had arrived to expand the factory. Not all the profits have been reinvested but there existed the possibility of obtaining the extra funds within the family. Mr. Werner, however, did not favor the idea. It seemed to him that the country's political and social situation was unstable. He preferred to be more cautious. Walter Schmidt disagreed: "The more cautious we are, the worse for us. Neither the government nor the politicians determine what the situations will be. It is us the directors of companies. It is us who can invest, increase our production and the scope of our factories, we who can influence directly the economic development of the country. This is not the time in my opinion to act as an ostrich hiding its head in the sand at the approach of danger. The best way we have to contribute to our country's progress is to attack boldly our company problems and to expand our factories as much as it is feasible. But this is not the only reason why we should try to enlarge Peter Werner S.A. Today, we have a real opportunity to obtain better profits. Why waste it?"

Walter Schmidt's plan for expansion included, besides buying new equipment, to start a publicity campaign among their customers of the jewel boxes, which were mostly in São Paulo. He also thought of diversifying their production line, possibly by bringing out also cardboard and fiber containers.

27

Arco Industrial S.A.*

For the past several years the Directors of "Arco Industrial S.A." have faced a series of administrative problems which were finally analyzed in September 1959 by its President, with a view of taking steps towards solving all of them as a whole. The various isolated measures taken in the past did not bring the needed results, making it necessary to make out an inventory of existing administrative practices and of the material potentialities and the labor pool so as to trace directives aimed at bettering the situation. This was, at least, the President's wish.

After a detailed analysis, the directors present at the last meeting, called together for this purpose, agreed to an elaboration of six resolutions whose purpose will be to establish norms of conduct, the distribution of assignments and authority so that the company could function better.

The company "Arco Industrial S.A." has currently two industrial sites in the township of São Caetano do Sul, S. P. employing approximately 300 workers in such sectors as smelting, tooling, assembly metallurgical factory and related services, these located at rua Josi Bonifácio. The factory that produced cold-rolled metal sheets had approximately 100 workers and was located at rua Antônio Lopes.

The firm was started in 1925 as a private enterprise. In 1953 it was bought by an industrial group and changed into a corporation. Its corporate capital is 100 million cruzeiros, after revaluation of the active fund. The President of "Arco" is the corporation's representative. He was employed under contract to function as an administrator.

1ST RESOLUTION: REDISTRIBUTION OF THE ADMINISTRATIVE FUNCTIONS

Problems That Present Themselves

The biggest part of the administrative work of the company has been nearly from the start, the exclusive responsibility of the senior Director, Mr. Rudolfo Mazzini, in spite of the fact that the firm has had a big growth in general during this period.

The scope of this Director's work has progressively become wider and by the same token, more vulnerable.

*School of Business Administration of the Getulio Vargas Foundation in São Paulo.

Arco Industrial S.A.

In view that the volume of administrative work tended to grow gradually and in parallel with the social contracts, it became necessary to limit partly Mr. R. Mazzini's duties, transfering them to other persons just as competent as he in these matters, who were already on "Arco's" staff.

After discussing the matter in all its aspects the following was approved:

Division of Administrative Functions

I. The following responsibilities are ascribed to the senior Director, Mr. Rudolfo Mazzini. These are besides those prescribed by law and by our statutes.
- (a) To direct, orient and control sales promotion
- (b) To direct, orient and control the rolling mill, which belongs to the Corporation, situated on Rua Antônio Lopes
- (c) Give to the manager of the factory located on Rua José Bonifácio, technical assistance when requested.
- (d) Reorganize, economically, the sales services.
- (e) Make up price lists for wholesalers and consumers.
- (f) Guide and control all the activities of the local and travelling salesmen and of the representatives.
- (g) Make up catalogs or rewrite the existing ones, with a view to making the company's product better known thus alleviating even more the difficulties experienced by the salesmen and the representatives in promoting their wares.
- (h) Construct a permanent display of samples of hardware made by the factory at the main office.
- (i) Keep in touch with other departments under control of other persons, through regular reports.
- (j) Conduct the financial affairs of the company.
- (k) Take part in weekly meetings at which Mr. Lucas Cordeiro, Mr. Alberto Vieira de Mattos and Mr. José Sanches will be obliged to appear also. These are, respectively, the Factory Manager, the Main Office Manager and the Factory Chief Foreman;
- (l) Finally, to act in any situation not exactly defined in the present list but which, however, still pertains to his general responsibilities.

II. The duties of Mr. Lucas Cordeiro, the factory manager, will be:
- (a) To buy the merchandise and the materials necessary for the financial and industrial activities of the Corporation.
- (b) What concerns the merchandise destined for resale and the materials needed for the rolling mill the factory manager will buy it by means of a purchase order detailing all items and signed by the senior Director;
- (c) To direct and control all the factory's work, but always with the technical guidance of Carlos Costa de Souza, the Engineer;
- (d) Schedule the factory's production with the help of Mr. Carlos Costa de Souza and, when necessary, that of the senior Director, Mr. Rudolfo

Mazzini, who will know whether a particular product is commercially acceptable.
- (e) To have under control the stock of raw materials intermediate materials, half-manufactured products, finished products and merchandise bought from third parties and destined for resale.
- (f) To direct, orient and supervise the work of contracting out the finishing of the products, as much work has to be done outside the factory on some items;
- (g) To select the personnel that will work at the factory, giving each a test before hiring him;
- (h) To control the quality and the quantity of the factory's output;
- (i) To make a time-study of all the manufacturing operations that lend themselves to being executed as tasks;
- (j) To have a tab kept on the price and especially the quality of all the production materials and those for internal consumption that enter the premises.
- (k) To keep tab on all the products of the factory and the items of internal consumption taken out of stock, never allowing anything to leave without the proper documentation;
- (l) To control the consumption during the various phases of production and in different sectors of the corporation;
- (m) To control the labor costs estimates, section by section, within the factory;
- (n) To tabulate daily and monthly each section's production
- (o) To regulate the trips made by the truck working out practical itineraries to be followed when making deliveries giving special notice to gasoline consumption and to the work done by the men.
- (p) To direct and supervise the factory's office routine.
- (q) To send daily to the main office, all the documents needed by the Accounting Department.
- (r) To send periodically to the main office the attendance records of the factory's employees along with their respective time cards;
- (s) Finally, to act in any situation not exactly defined in the present list but which, however, still pertains to his general responsibilities.

III. To Mr. Alberto Vieira de Mattos, the Head Office Chief, is given:
- (a) To direct, orient and supervise all the activities at the Head Office, except those in connection with the Sales Department;
- (b) Supervise the activities of the factory office;
- (c) To supervise all the transactions of funds and materials of the corporation.
- (d) To maintain the Accounting Department's work up-to-date.
- (e) To organize a cost accounting section.
- (f) To take care of the managerial and financial problems.

Arco Industrial S.A.

(g) To be responsible for the Personnel Department except where it concerns analizing the technical qualifications of applicants for positions at the factory. This will be the personal responsibility of the factory manager.
(h) To be responsible for the guards, the files, all the documents and company property.
(i) To list and tag all company property
(j) Look after the proper use of the office machine
(k) Direct and supervise bill collection
(l) Direct and supervise the financial activities
(m) Finally, to act in any situation not exactly defined in the present list but which, however, still pertains to his general responsibilities.

2ND RESOLUTION: DEFINITION OF THE LINE OF PRODUCTS MADE

Problems That Present Themselves

The diversity of the factory's products is too extensive. Due to the lack of cost accounting it is not known, at present, which of these products are being manufactured economically and which are not.

No one has any idea, either, as to the future sale feasibility of the products made by the company.

It is quite possible that, at this moment, there exists an over supply of some products which are not easily marketable and a need for other products which have ready buyers.

Evident Solutions

1st) To establish a new line of production after a joint study by Mr. Lucas Cordeiro and Mr. Rudolfo Mazzini;
2nd) To manufacture such articles as would return a good margin of profits;
3rd) Not to manufacture articles that cannot find a ready market or that will not return a good margin of profit.
4th) To buy from third parties, at best price possible, articles that cannot find a ready market or that will not return a good margin of profit if manufactured by the factory.
5th) To incentivate and expand, by all possible means, the production of articles that are readily sold and afford a good margin of profit.

3RD RESOLUTION: UPGRADING THE QUALITY OF THE PRODUCTS

Problems That Present Themselves

One of the biggest impediments to an effective sales promotion lies in the fact that products manufactured by "Arco Industrial" are of poor quality and bad appearance.

The name of "Arco" not only as a producer but even as a mere supplier, has a bad reputation on the São Paulo market.

Evident Solutions

1. To supervise the manufacturing process, stage by stage, and especially at the time the article enters the finished product stock-room. All the defective or badly finished pieces will be systematically rejected.
2. To extend the same quality control to merchandise bought outside from third parties at the time that it enters our warehouses.
3. To inspect and test immediately all the articles already in stock, whether they are of our manufacture or were bought outside.
4. To inspect and test all the unfinished articles as yet on the production lines to avoid the extra loss of having them rejected later at the final inspection.

4TH RESOLUTION: NEW FACTORY EQUIPMENT

Problems That Present Themselves

Generally speaking, the machinery at "Arco" is old, giving rise to a low production rate.

This is responsible for high labor costs of the production and thus, obviously weak possibilities to meet and overcome competition on the market.

Evident Solutions

1. To begin a progressive change of the equipment, as the financial situation will allow, so that a better quality and a cheaper production can be eventually achieved.
2. A gradual reconditioning and repair of such machines that are not working at their full capacity, for whatever reasons.

5TH RESOLUTION: SELECTION OF PERSONNEL

Problems That Present Themselves

"Arco's" labor costs can be characterized by the following:
    (a) There is too much of it.
    (b) It is expensive.
    (c) It is deficient in quality.
This results in having an abnormal percentage of labor costs in the total price of the finished articles.

Evident Solutions

1. Eliminate the socially undesirable and the slow workers.
2. From now on, carefully select the right person for each job among the applicants that present themselves.

Arco Industrial S.A.

3. Training and specialization for those workers that are initially acceptable.
4. Change in the pay structure. All the operations whose cost can be mathematically estimated should be performed on the basis of piecework, eliminating for these operations any hourly, weekly or monthly wages. Such operations will go through a reasonably lengthy time study period to establish an adequate basis for piecework renumeration.

6TH RESOLUTION: INCREASE IN SALES

Problems That Present Themselves

Certain serious difficulties have presented themselves in sales promotions which have not been solved yet.

Friction and disharmony are noticeably present between sales and production. Out-of-stock items are being sold and orders cannot be filled, whereas the factory produces, usually items that are not readily marketable.

The order on books is not dispatched within the stipulated time because the factory is busy with other problems. This results in getting the customers very dissatisfied and undermines excessively the firm's status.

Delivery dates are quoted off the cuff without any basis in fact and with the knowledge that they will not be honored; then, when the delivery is finally made, the customer already upset by the delay, verifies that the quality is unacceptable.

If the order is for some equipment that "Arco" itself has to install, the customer passes through another series of crises.

This is the general outlook as presented to the salesmen each time they pay a call to the company office.

Evident Solution

1. Not to accept any delivery orders for quantities beyond the factory's production capacity.
2. Not to promise anyone that which cannot be fulfilled to the letter. The customer should not and cannot be deceived.
3. To regain the clients' confidence by delivering on time exactly what was ordered.
4. Reorganize the Sales Department with the view of increasing its activities immediately.
5. Make a study of the market tendencies and requirements so as to define better what to produce.
6. Make up a list of prices charged for similar products by rival companies to both the wholesalers and the consumers.
7. Especially to increase the sale of the rolling mill's line of products.
8. Push the sale of stock and unfinished items without taking any loss from it.
9. Prepare price lists both for wholesalers and consumers. These lists will be

periodically revised and the prices readjusted accordingly to existing market conditions.
10. Rewrite the catalogs listing the company's products.
11. To set up a showcase of product samples at the main office.
12. To choose and hire new salesmen, preferably with previous experience. If it will be impossible to find experienced salesmen, those who will be ultimately chosen will have to spend a training period at the factory where they will receive detailed instructions before beginning their work as salesmen.
13. To direct and instruct systematically all the travelling salesmen with the object of increasing continually the volume of sales within the State of São Paulo.
14. To advertise directly and continually all the products of "Arco".
15. Organize register of customer's standing, showing the allowable credit line for each one.

QUESTIONS

1. Give your opinion as to the distribution of responsibilities within the administrative and the permanent functions mentioned in the first Resolution.
2. What would be the relationship between these persons' qualifications and the detailed responsibilities?
3. What results in the analysis of the problems said to exist in the definition of the industrial products line?
4. How would it be possible to set up quality inspection?
5. How would the selection proposed for labor cost be achieved?
6. Would the steps proposed for bettering sales result in the improvement of the Corresponding Department?
7. Would all the measures in general do what they were intended to do by the President of "Arco Industrial S. A."? What other measures, in your opinion, would be necessary for a full implementation of the resolutions listed herein? How long, in your judgment, would it take before any positive results appear?

28

Caldaço S.A.*†

Caldaço S.A. is a big metallurgical firm, specialized in manufacturing custom-made boilers and steel tanks of great variety. Each product requires individual specifications, so that each one is first designed by the Engineering Department, and only then manufactured.

Caldaço is controlled by Flavio Claro. He is 45 years old, active and strong-minded. Aside from heading Caldaço, he has had several high-ranking posts in the public service.

Besides Flavio Claro, the Board of Directors includes Fernando Setti and Renato Gonçalves. The former is 40 years old, a mechanical engineer trained in the U.S. He is the firm's Director of Production. He was Flavio Claro's childhood friend, and till now they are good friends. Many of their points of view are similar. For example, frequently they would contend that no workman is worthy of confidence. "They are all unprincipled" they would say to Renato Gonçalves, the Personnel and Finance Director, who, they know, does not share their beliefs. "We are more experienced than you. Workmen are lazy and cunning by nature. The right attitude is to resist them, or they will ride you."

Renato Gonçalves is not yet 30 years old. He has graduated from the School of Business Administration of São Paulo, where he was a brilliant student. He is the only member of the Board who does not own any company shares (Fernando Setti is a small shareholder). His fellow directors consider him as a sort of workmen's champion. Two years ago as the Head of the Personnel Department and Assistant to the Board of Directors, he maintained himself in constant touch with the workmen. After getting on the Board, he took over the management of a subsidiary firm, and these contacts were interrupted. Recently, he dropped the managerial post to become the Director of Personnel and Finance. The past contacts were reestablished. As he is young, very active, and always ready to debate, the workmen feel a certain sympathy towards him. They have given him a nickname "The Golden Rooster."

Fernando Setti became the Director of Production just a little less than two years ago. Before this, he was the production manager of a big textile mill. One of the first things he noticed when he took up his new post was that there was a great number of small groups of five to six workmen under the direction of a foreman. Each group worked at one or two projects simultaneously. When for

*S.A. = Sociedade Anônima—Co. Inc.
†School of Business Administration of the Getulio Vargas Foundation in São Paulo.

any reason like the lack of material the work stopped on one project, the group turned to the other one. The foreman had such a small number of subordinates that he could also work in the actual production himself. Everybody had non-repetitive assignments.

Fernando Setti did not approve this system. It impeded production planning. Besides, every small group did not contain the specialists required to complete the work. Also, all the groups were too autonomous in work execution, which resulted in inefficiencies. His coming to the Board coincided with a great increase in production, as much of boilers and tanks, as of other lines (various types of custom-made industrial equipment). In one year the number of workmen increased from about 300 to over 600. Fernando Setti used this increase to enlarge the groups. This way the foreman did not need to work directly in the production and production planning, with detailed specifications as to "who would do what" became the responsibility of the office. This system worked very well in the textile mill where Fernando Setti had been the production manager. However in certain not too well articulated manifestations the senior workman of Caldaço showed they considered the old production system better.

We mention the "senior workmen" because with the great increase of the company's work force there have been formed a group of "seniors" and a group of "juniors." The majority of the "seniors" has been employed for more then 10 years. Many of them were not pleased to see so many new workmen hired (those "baianos"[1] they would say) in just one year. On a certain occasion a "senior" told Renato Gonçalves "I don't know why so many "baianos" have to be hired. We could do all the work better." The director answered: "This means that you could work more. Why don't you work then? There is plenty of work. What is missing is the will to work."

Fernando Setti is considered by all the employees of Caldaço as a "hard" administrator, although he rarely fired or suspended anyone. He keeps his distance from the workmen. Being a mechanical engineer, he devotes a great part of his time to solving technical problems in production. He talks to the workmen only about subjects pertaining to their work. Once or twice a workmen's delegation tried to talk with him about some of their claims, but they found it very hard to get an appointment with him, so they gave up.

Relations between the administration of Caldaço and its employees were always considered relatively good, although there were always ups and downs.

A recent fact, though, has been brought to the attention of the administration. The local of the workmen's union had issued a document in which it denounced in violent terms a series of mistakes and injustices committed at Caldaço, affirming that the salaries were low, that work conditions were awful, etc.... This document was printed and distributed in great numbers in São Caetano. This worried us, said Renato Gonçalves: "This was never the case. If the workmen have anything to complain about, why not come to us? Most of

[1] Baianos are natives of the State of Bahia, meaning here, "outsiders."

Caldaço S.A.

the statements in that document are lies. Our salaries, for example, are very good, and we also do something that very few concerns do—we give various raises before receiving the union's claims, thus in 1962 to reach the 60% raise in salaries determined by the Regional Labor Court, we had to add only 4% to our pay voucher. In any case, the document was made. I answered as I should to the Union. Such things are not done."

LIBRARY OF DAVIDSON COLLEGE